The True Accoun
Little

DARK
SECRET

THE COMPLETE STORY

Child Search Al

Alexan
Chriss
Sull

DOE
Har
Eye
Weigh
Heigh

Stranger Abducted

Last Seen: In Radcliff, KY
on October 26, 1989

Call Child Search with an
about this child at 281-350-6

Child Search Ministries P.O. Box 7375

NYSSA REBECCA CORBIN

ASIN: B07GL8WN4M

Front cover by Judith San Nicolas at Judith S. Design.

Editing and ebook design by Cortni Merritt at SRD Editing Services.

Printed by Nyssa Rebecca Corbin, in the United States of America.

Second edition 2020.

Nyssa Rebecca Corbin
nyssacorbin@gmail.com
www.facebook.com/darksecretbook

This is a work of creative non-fiction. All events in this memoir are true to the best of the author's memory. Some names and identifying features have been changed to protect identities. The author in no way represents any company, corporation, or brand, mentioned herein. The views expressed in this memoir are solely those of the author.

DARK SECRET

THE COMPLETE STORY

NYSSA REBECCA CORBIN

TABLE OF CONTENTS

PURPOSE

Alexandria Christine Suleski seemed like a typical little girl. From the outside, her homelife seemed also, quite typical. Yet, there were signs of extreme dysfunction and gross neglect and abuse, if someone had taken the time to see them. That is the purpose for this book: The children living in abusive homes rarely understand that the circumstances they live with every day, are in fact 'abuse.' Because they have grown up in this type of environment, they don't understand that it is abnormal, unacceptable, or that a different way of life even exists. This means that it is the responsibility of those around them to protect them.

People need to know that this type of evil exists.

The signs need to be seen and reported, as soon as possible. Children must not be subjected to violence in their homes, because those around them choose to turn a blind eye. We cannot allow another child like Alex to suffer, when we have the tools needed to save them.

JUST THE BEGINNING

I was born on February 3, 1977, in ritzy, snobby and exclusive Beverly Hills, California. I was not born to some wealthy yuppie couple. I was born to a young couple who were pushed into getting married by their parents, when it was apparent that my teenage mom was pregnant. My father, Benny Bruno, was twenty-one, and my mother, Roxanne 'Mica' Najera, was only seventeen.

They had been convinced by my grandparents that it would be the honorable thing to do. Get married, that is. As for me being born in Beverly Hills .... my mother always told me that she wanted the place on my birth certificate to be a place I could be proud of later in my life. She had my father drive an extra twenty minutes to the Beverly Hills hospital, instead of going to a much closer (but not as well known) hospital, just so I could be proud of my birth certificate.

She brought this up to me several times in my life, as if to show not only did she want the best for me while I was alive, but even before I was born. For sixteen years of my life, I based my reality on this notion. My mother always had my best interest at heart. Always.

No matter what.

I have very few memories of my parents being together.

They separated when I was very young. I guess it was better that way. It had been so long since they had been together, that it seemed natural to me that they were apart. People would say to me, "Oh, I'm so sorry to hear that. It must be so hard not having your parents together like that." I really didn't understand what they meant. Of course my parents weren't together. I only had one or two vague memories of them actually living together, and I was so young that the memories were fuzzy and confusing. Maybe they weren't real memories at all, but just wishful thinking. I assumed that most parents became separated at some point, until I grew a little older and realized that a lot of couples stayed married.

My mom and dad both dated a lot of people after they separated from each other. My mother's boyfriends seemed to change more frequently than my father's girlfriends did. Maybe I just noticed it more with my mom, because I lived with her longer than my dad. It seemed like men were always interested in my mom, and she seemed to enjoy the attention she got from them. I knew my mom was very attractive—even before I had a clear understanding of what "attractive" meant. Grown men acted goofy around her, and people were always giving her compliments. With a petite build, porcelain white skin and shiny auburn hair, she turned heads without even trying. She enjoyed the attention so much, and I began to want that attention as well. I wanted to be like her; her looks, her attitude, her confidence, and even her intelligence. Yes, she was very smart, as well. She had keen street smarts and noticed small things about people and the environment around us. She was constantly reading books about anything she could get her hands on, and so was extremely book smart, as well. Whenever a subject got her attention, she would research it, as if she was going to write a term paper on it. She would say, "Don't do a half-ass job. Do it right, or don't do it all." She defined that motto.

My father, on the other hand, was the most easygoing person I had ever known in my life. He had a way of making people comfortable around him, like he was an old friend to everyone he met. I could be very open and honest around my dad. No matter what, I felt like my dad accepted me for who I was. His sense of humor and ability to make people open up were qualities I wanted to learn from him. That is, until my mother pointed out that these were not respectable qualities, rather they were traits my father hid behind to disguise his weak and ignorant nature. For everything good I had to say about my father, my mother had something negative to combat it. She said these things as if they were quite apparent to everyone else but me. She taught me not to look up to my dad, but to tolerate him. I believed everything my mom told me. I learned at a young age that the alternative to not agreeing with her could be traumatic.

The first incident that instilled in me the lesson of doing what my mother asked without question and listening to her without comment happened when I was about five years old. At least, it's the first memory I have of an occurrence like this.

My mom and I had gone over to meet her boyfriend (of the week) and his two children at their house for dinner. I wasn't accustomed to being around other children, since I was an only child. I remember I was feeling very nervous to be eating in front of this stranger and his stranger children. I was also concerned about the dish that was set before me as "food." It was something very foreign to me, and I had no desire to put it in my mouth. I began to feel homesick and wanted to leave this overtly strange place. I was too scared to say anything to my mom, because I could tell she really liked this man. She had spent so long getting her makeup and hair ready for this dinner, and she was wearing her nicest dress. So, I sat there, staring at the plate of mushy green stuff and stringy brown things—not eating at all.

Eventually, my mom noticed my lack of appetite and explained I had eaten a snack before we arrived. This was not true but saved us both from an embarrassing situation. Then, it was time to move into the living room for a board game. His two daughters were thrilled to be playing a family favorite, which I had never heard of before. I lay on the couch and was soon closing my eyes. I vaguely heard the man say, "She can sleep in Tina's room, if you want," before I drifted off to sleep.

I woke up to my mom moving my arms through my coat and trying to get us out the door. I realized that they had not played the game, since it was not even completely set up. Although my mom made it sound like it was no big deal that I hadn't eaten dinner and I had fallen asleep, ("It's not her fault, poor thing isn't feeling well."), I knew that she was upset about leaving early. I crawled into the back of the truck and fell asleep.

When I awoke, we were parked in front of our house. My nose was bleeding, and it took me a second or two to realize that it really hurt. I was in shock and trying to figure out what had happened, when my mom's fist slammed into my face again. I began to cry hysterically. She hit me again. She screamed at me to get out of the truck and into the house. As I was climbing out of the truck, she yelled at me to stop crying. She then raised her fist again, silently telling me that she would hit me again if I didn't do as she said.

Once inside the house, I saw the blood on my shirt where it had dripped down, and on the back of my hand where I had wiped the blood away. I could taste the blood dripping down the back of my throat. I was terrified to be bleeding and to be covered in my own blood. I was also terrified that my mom would continue to hit me. I apologized to her, although I had no idea what I was apologizing for. I begged her not to hit me anymore. I pleaded with her, "Momma, stop the blood! Please, Momma. Make it stop!"

Instead of appealing to her, I must have enraged her further, because she raised her hand to hit me again. That's when I ran. I ran into our bedroom and tried to hide under the bed, but I couldn't fit.

The space under our bed was less than a few inches tall. I had seen people hide under their beds on TV and couldn't understand why this wasn't working for me. So, I continued to try to wedge myself in the sliver of space that was available. This is where my mom found me. The anger on her face seemed to melt into amusement, and then laughter. She doubled over with laughter and had to sit on the bed, so she didn't fall on the floor. She thought it was so funny to see me attempt something so ridiculous. She was obviously not mad at me anymore.

She told me to come to her. I hesitated, but she smiled. "I'm not mad at you. You're so silly. Come here." I felt I had no choice but to go to her.

She led me to the bathroom and cleaned me off. She changed my clothes and took me back to the bedroom. She held me and told me, "Don't ever embarrass Momma again." I was angry at her for hitting me, and worried that she was tricking me, so she could hit me again. But I eventually became comfortable and comforted by her holding me. I fell asleep in her arms. I was so content that she wasn't angry with me anymore, and so at peace in her arms.

Whatever had happened earlier, she made me feel safe and loved again. That was how I wanted my mom to be. I always wanted that warm and caring side, not the side I had seen earlier.

That was my first small taste of what my mom was capable of. As the years went by, she became even more ruthless and forceful in engraining her "lessons" into me, and later my stepsisters. Eventually this resulted in her losing the one thing she prized over everything else. The one thing she spent most of her life trying to take from others: Control. Control of herself, control over others, control over any situation she was put into, and control of her own mind.

It took me a long time to see how out of touch with reality she had really become over the years, because as her child —her reality was also mine. However she said the world and its people were, I perceived to be true. When I was finally able to see beyond the façade she created for our family, it was too late for one of us. Now, I must live with everything my mother has done.

She has to live with it all, too. But that doesn't bring much consolation for me, because I know she has justified everything she has ever done—justified it all to herself. And in the end, that's who she really cared about anyway.

Nyssa Rebecca Corbin

THE TURNING POINT

Until I was about seven years old, I spent my life being shuffled back and forth between my mom and dad. I would spend a few years with my mom, followed by a few years with my dad.

Sometimes I would spend only a couple of months with my mom and a couple of months with my dad (depending on what each of them had going on in their own lives). From one extreme (disciplined and controlling) to another (entirely too relaxed about everything). If anything, I learned to adapt to completely separate and opposite environments at an early age.

Now, my mom wasn't so bad when I was younger ... or maybe it was that I had learned to deal with her temper and appease her before she could lash out at me. My whole purpose with my mom was to keep her happy. When she was happy, I loved being around her. She was the prettiest, coolest, and the most fun to be with. My friends would come over and think my mom was the best, because they never saw her temperamental side. If I was careful, I didn't see it that much either. Then, all that started to change when I was seven.

Like I mentioned earlier, my father had his fair share of different girlfriends when I was younger. I have to admit that the aspect I liked best about his numerous girlfriends was that they were always trying to impress me. They would bring me gifts or praise me for, "being such a good girl ... such a cutie ... so smart for her age." I definitely received more attention from them than I ever did from my mom's boyfriends. It helped me not to feel jealous when my dad brought home another new date for me to meet. He was obviously making it clear to them that I was important to him, and that is why they went out of their way to impress me.

Then, when I was seven, everything changed dramatically.

My dad and I were living with my grandma (his mom) and one of my aunts (his youngest sister). My grandma wasn't around too much, and it seemed like she was always working. When she was around, she was like a surrogate mother to me. I liked watching her do things around the house, and I felt comforted by her female presence while I lived with my dad. My aunt who lived in the house mostly stayed in her back bedroom, and I don't remember her coming out very often. Her bedroom was strictly off-limits to me (which made me want to explore it even more), and I had a strong feeling that she felt I was very spoiled. I felt like she tolerated me for my dad's sake, but mostly thought I was a brat. I, however, thought she was super secretive and super cool.

My dad had two younger brothers and three sisters, and I thought about how neat it seemed to have such a balance in the genders of your children. Three boys to hang out together, and three girls to take care of each other. It did seem like he was close to all his siblings, and they all tried to make an effort to collect with their various children at my grandmother's house for special holidays or birthdays. I had overheard bits and pieces of my father's childhood during some of these gatherings. Things he never talked to me about.

Like, how hard it was on him and his siblings when my grandparents divorced. Or, how much they all had to help my grandmother, while she was trying to raise them by herself. It seemed these were some of the events that fostered their strong sibling friendships.

Then one day, I remember my dad getting sick with the flu or something that made him feel very tired. He told me that a lady he recently started dating was coming over to visit him. I guessed it was to take care of him, because he wasn't feeling well. I was expecting a woman to show up and not only take care of my dad, but maybe spend some time with me. My dad wasn't in the mood to play any games with me, and I was feeling very restless. I was looking forward to a new person to talk to.

When my dad's new girlfriend showed up, my dad was attempting to get up and clean the dishes. This new lady seemed appalled at his attempt and told him to lie back down and relax. She smiled at me and introduced herself. Her name was Jay. Then, she turned to my dad and asked, "Why doesn't she do the dishes?"

My dad explained to her that I had never cleaned the dishes before. Jay scoffed, "My boys were washing dishes when they were a few years younger than her. There's no reason for her not to do the dishes."

She walked over to the kitchen sink and began to fill it up with soapy water. At first, I didn't think doing dishes would be so bad. Then, I looked into the sink. I couldn't see what was beneath the sudsy water. I tried to remember what had been in the sink.

Weren't there knives in there? Maybe some other sharp objects that would hurt me? I started to think of all the scary things lurking in the dirty, soapy water. I must have been standing in front of the sink for a little while, because Jay had already walked back over to my dad in the living room.

She asked my dad, "Why is she just standing there?"

Then she called over to me, "The water is ready now. You can start washing."

My dad explained to her that I had never washed the dishes before and probably needed to be shown how. Jay thought that was absurd. "What are you talking about? I'm sure she's seen you do it before. She just doesn't want to wash them. You have to be more forceful, Ben."

Jay walked over to me. I was peering into the sink, unsure of what I should be doing. I was too scared to stick my hand into water that I could not see into. She put one hand on her hip and said, "Look, your dad is not feeling well. You will have to do the dishes, whether you like it or not. It's not even that many dishes. Okay?"

I opened my mouth to answer her, but she had already turned around and was walking back to the living room. She ridiculed my dad for not having me do the dishes. She was talking to him about me, as if I wasn't there at all. I felt awful when my dad answered her, also like I wasn't there. They had a whole conversation about my inadequacy as a dishwasher. I felt like I had failed to do something that should have been like second nature. I was used to feeling that way when I was with my mom, but this was the first time I had felt like a failure to my dad.

I didn't care for this girlfriend named Jay. I didn't like the way she made me feel. I didn't like the way my dad didn't stick up for me with her. My father's house was the only place I never felt judged. I always felt like I could act like myself, until that day.

However, after that day, most of the time I spent with my dad and Jay became more and more like time I spent with my mom. Appease or be intensely ridiculed and made to feel like a moron. She looked to my dad only when she got too tired or distracted by something else to properly enforce an issue with me or her two sons.

Life changed dramatically after that.

My once-close relationship with my dad grew more and more distant. He became someone new and different to me. There were times when he said or did things that my dad of the previous year would have never said or done. This angered me more than the discipline that arrived with Jay. I felt like she had taken from me the only place I had felt completely free to be myself. It had turned into a place just like my mom's. The difference was I expected my mom to be like she was. I had always experienced that controlling and claustrophobic atmosphere at her house. It was very hard to see this being imposed onto my dad, by someone I hadn't known for very long.

Instead of this being one of my dad's many short-term relationships, Jay and her boys became a permanent presence in our lives. It was a hard transition for me to make, and an even harder one for my mom. Jay was not received well by my mom.

THE BELT

I had always known that there was not much love lost between my parents after they separated. They never asked me about each other's love lives or who they were dating. They each seemed like they had moved on, and the only tie between them was me. It was nice that they had been, for the most part, cordial with each other—until my dad met Jay.

The first time my mom began to question me about Jay was when I told her about some of Jay's new rules that were being enforced around the house. It was one of the weekend visits I had with her, since I was living with my dad. She asked me, "How serious is your dad about this woman?"

I wasn't sure what she meant by that question, so I just began to describe the relationship that was growing between my dad and his new girlfriend. I told her that they were looking for a house to rent together. My dad and I were preparing to move in with Jay and her two boys. As I continued to explain the situation, my mom became more and more irritated. It seemed like the thing that bothered her the most was Jay expecting me to follow her rules and accept her punishments for breaking those rules. Jay was moving in on my mom's "control turf." How dare some other woman tell me what to do!

She knew my dad would never try to control me. If anything, he gave me too much freedom, which was probably why my aunt thought I was a brat. That was something she could trust about my dad, but not this new woman. Another underlying annoyance was the feeling that my mom always shared with me; she believed my dad would always have only one true love—herself. Now, too many things were changing, and she did not like change being imposed upon her.

My mom had not been a big part of my life for a couple of years, and I actually enjoyed my current living arrangement. Living with my dad had been less stressful, and the short bursts of time spent with my mom had never been long enough to cause any problems between us. But suddenly, I began to think that living with my mom would be the better choice. I knew how to appease my mom, but Jay didn't seem to work the same way, and I resented her bossing me around. Somehow, I didn't feel like she should have that right.

"Momma, I want to come and stay with you again," I said as sweetly as I could.

"Oh, baby ... it's not really a good time for that right now. I've got a lot of things going on right now." She saw the tears in my eyes and continued, "But, I promise to come and visit you more often. Okay?"

She continued to make excuses all the way back to my dad's house as to why I couldn't live with her. She had moved into a really small apartment with her new boyfriend. She was working so many hours as a dance instructor and wouldn't have much time for me. I hugged her and told her that I understood, even though I didn't.

Several days after that visit, my father and I moved into a house with Jay and her boys, Charlie and Tony. I had my own room (being the only girl), the boys shared the next bedroom, and my dad and Jay had the master bedroom. While we were moving in, it became apparent that Charlie and Tony both wanted to have their own room, and they didn't understand why I got to have it.

"Mom—I'm the oldest, so I should get it," Charlie said.

"That's not right," Tony complained, "Just cause I'm not a girl or the oldest, I don't get my own room?"

They complained until Jay began to yell at them. It wasn't the yelling that was the scary part; it was what she had yelled. She had said something about "getting the belt." Now, all the times my mom had punished me, she had never used an object other than her hands to do so. My heart raced as I struggled to imagine what "getting the belt" would look like.

It wasn't long before I got a glimpse into Jay's uncontrollable temper. She seemed to have absolutely no reason for her sudden outbursts. She could be happy one minute, then extremely angry the next. Something the boys and I did one day might not bother her at all—but if we did it the next day, she would become enraged. If we talked back to her, we might get sentences to write, or we might get the "the belt." It seemed completely dependent upon Jay's mood at the time. When I tried the same tactics for survival that I always used with my mom, Jay saw right through me. "Don't try to kiss my butt. Nice try," she would say with a smirk.

True to her word, my mom did visit me more often, and when she was not able to come, she would send my grandma (her mother) to pick me up for a while. I really enjoyed the visits with my grandma and grandpa the most. I especially enjoyed time with my grandpa. Everyone called him "Tata," because when I was a baby, my first word had been that sound directed at him. My first utterance became his new nickname.

He was the strongest male role model I had for most of my life. He encouraged me but didn't sugar coat things. He praised me but stressed staying grounded and not becoming prideful. Tata was tall and strong. He had broad shoulders and strong hands, and I always felt so protected when I was with him. His back story was very interesting, and he always had great stories to share about his life experiences. He was American Indian (some small tribe in Arizona), and had worked hard his whole life to achieve a class status that was not common in 1950s Torrance, California. He had retired as a foreman for a Mobile gas plant, which some would say helped to establish the city of Torrance many years ago. He had a decent retirement that afforded my grandparents a very nice upper-middle class lifestyle. However, having both lived through incredibly difficult times during the Great Depression, they were not ones to be frivolous with what they had.

They had a deep appreciation for all that they had and told me so quite often.

My grandmother was a bit more "in the clouds" than my grandpa. She fiercely nurtured my creative side. She was a piano teacher, and loved to play while I sang. She was also great at making up fantastic stories or using her imagination with me. I remember when my mom painted the ceiling of one of our rented homes to look like outer space and the solar system. She even used special paint to make the stars shine at night. When my grandma came over to watch me, we would act like we were camping and sleep on the floor, looking up at "stars and planets" in the ceiling sky. She was so much fun to be around.

If my grandparents weren't fun enough, their house was like a dream come true. There were always yummy treats or delicious meals being prepared. They had a swimming pool, tons of plants with fruits that they let me pick, musical instruments that they let me play, and a sewing room full of fabrics that I could use for whatever crafts I felt like creating.

I never got tired of exploring their house or spending time with them. But, of course, it would eventually come to an end. I would have to go back to my dad and Jay. It was back to our house in Hawthorne, where we had to be careful about playing outside because gang members cruised our streets frequently. It was back to our dark and dusty house, where my exploring was limited to my own room. I know Jay was always cleaning the house (sometimes in the middle of the night, strangely), but it never seemed really clean to me. There seemed to be a permanent mustiness in the house.

Maybe that was just the way that I felt when I was there.
It wasn't too long after living together as a blended family that I began to adjust to Jay's style of discipline. In many ways, she was actually a lot like my mom. She expected us to do as we were told, and back-talk was not tolerated. Same as my mom. Jay was quick to administer punishment for rules that she felt had been broken, also like my mom. The main difference between them was how they acted when they were not angry. My mom was loving and supportive. She talked to me and listened to what I had to say, as if I were a close friend whose ideas were of value. It made her unpredictable temper worth living with.

Jay, however, made me feel like I was "just a kid," and could not possibly have a view on the world worth listening to. She would make fun of me in front of her two sons, and worse, in front of my dad. She thought it was especially funny when I tried to act "like a grown up" or talk about something that she felt was out of my league as a child. I began to feel like I was stupid. It wasn't worth putting up with her temper, just to have her make fun of me.

Soon, I was asking my grandparents if I could live with them.

It seemed like it had been forever since my mom had made her excuses for me not living with her. I couldn't wait for her to change her mind anymore. I was crying in my room at night. The only time I really enjoyed was when I was in my room alone, or when the boys and I were playing without Jay yelling at us. Then, I began to beg my grandma not to return me to my dad's house. She immediately became concerned, "What's wrong? Are they mistreating you there?"

I didn't understand what "mistreated" meant. I said, "No, I don't think so." After all, I had food to eat and a place to sleep. I guessed there was nothing that could be done about my living situation. I would just have to wait until I saw my mom again and see if her circumstances allowed for me to live with her again. Then, something happened that changed my living arrangements, my parents tolerating nature towards each other, and my relationship with my dad.

I had seen Jay use "the belt" on her sons. She had threatened to use it on me a couple of times, but I was sure my dad would not let her do something so obviously barbaric to me. I was wrong.

It was a typical mild and sunny day in Southern California, and I was eager to join Charlie and Tony outside and play. As I ran for the front door, Jay shouted, "Get some socks on! Your feet are disgusting when you play outside with no socks."

I explained to her that I didn't have any clean socks to wear and turned to run outside.

"Nyssa, I just did laundry a couple of days ago. There is no way you wore all your socks in a few days." She narrowed her eyes at me, "Go put some socks on."

She was actually in a good mood that day, and I didn't want to be the one to put her in a bad one, but the fact remained that I didn't have any clean socks in my room. So, I repeated that fact.

"You never look hard enough," she huffed, "I'll bet all you have to do is move something out of the way and you would find some socks. But that would be too hard for you, right? To actually move something? Wouldn't it?"

Sarcasm was her favorite weapon. She made me feel like a lazy brat. But, since I knew that I didn't have any socks in my drawer when I got ready that morning before school, I thought that I had nothing to worry about. "Jay, you could even go and look in my drawer. I really don't have any socks," I said confidently.

"Okay, Nyssa. Let's go look. But, if you're lying to me, I have no choice but to get the belt. That's what the boys get for lying to me, and you're no different than them. So, you'll get the same punishment." It seemed like she had already made up her mind that I was about to get spanked with her belt. How was she so sure that I was not telling the truth?

We went into my bedroom and stood in front of my chest of drawers. I paused. I was nervous about opening the drawer. Could there be a pair of socks that I missed earlier? Did I not look hard enough? All it would take was one pair of missed socks for me to get hit with Jay's infamous belt. I was seriously doubting myself and didn't want to open the drawer.

"Well, what are you waiting for?" Jay teased me. "You are so sure that there are no socks in there, so just show me." She seemed so confident. Did she know something that I didn't? Had she put socks in the drawer while I was at school? Why was she acting like she knew there were socks in there? I was definitely stalling. I was just standing in front of the drawer, wishing that any socks that might be in there would just go and hide in the very corner of the drawer.

I opened the drawer. There were a couple of pairs of clean socks sitting right on top. Jay was right. I would get the belt.

What had gone wrong? My thoughts raced to figure out how I had missed those socks or where they had come from, when I suddenly realized that I had more important things to worry about.

"You know what this means, Nyssa. I have to punish you."

Jay left the room to get her spanking belt. When she returned, I got my first up close look at the belt she used to hit her sons with. This was the belt she was about to use on me. It wasn't exactly what I had pictured it, from the quick glances I had got of it in the past. It wasn't as thick as I thought it would be. It was more wide and flat.

Was it shaped like that to maximize its stinging capability? Maybe she was looking for a short-term shocking burn to our butts, instead of a long-term aching. I could only imagine her reasons for choosing this particular belt.

"Lay down on the bed. I won't make you take your pants down this time. It will be quick." She seemed to be all business, but somewhat compassionate about how I felt. I guessed I was lucky. I had heard Charlie and Tony scream from their room, after being smacked on the bare butt, even from the other side of the house. I just wanted to get this over with, so I did as she said. I began to cry even before she hit me. I was so scared.

She hit me three times. The first time was mostly a shock to me. I let out a yelp of fright, when the belt made its smacking sound across my behind. The second and third times were the ones that really hurt. I knew the blows were coming and could concentrate on the pain, instead of worrying with anticipation.

When she finished, I was crying loudly. Jay looked at me for a second, and then sat on the bed next to me. She put her arm around my shoulder. "I'm sorry I had to do that. I just can't let you think that you can lie to me." Ironically, I felt closer to her at that moment than I ever had been. She sighed, "You might not want to sit down for too long. Walk around or something. Or maybe you could just lay on your stomach for a little while." She had obviously been through this a few times. Maybe even had it done to her?

Suddenly, I remembered something. When I had come home from school, I had been in a hurry to do my homework and get outside to play. When I first got home, Jay had asked me to put my clothes away before I did anything else. I hurriedly stuffed some clean clothes that were left on my bed into my drawers, and then grabbed my homework to do at the kitchen table. In my rush, I had not really noticed what articles of clothing I was putting away. I was about to tell Jay this conclusion, when I realized that she would not care. Plus, I didn't want ruin this somewhat strangely bonding moment that we were having. It was the first time she had partially hugged me for that long.

We sat on the bed for a little while, then she said something about having to go and take care of something. She said, "I want you to stay here until dinner time and think about what you did and why I had to hit you. Okay?" Then she left.

I did sit in my room and think about what she had done. I wondered if she really thought I was lying to her, or if she knew I might have just made an absent-minded mistake. Didn't she think it was strange that I would try to lie to her about something that she was sure to find out about? Why would I risk getting hit with the belt? I sat in my room and grew more resentful towards her. I became more and more convinced that she had deliberately set up this whole situation, just so she could finally hit me with her almighty, powerful instrument of control.

I knew that the next time I saw my mom, I had to appeal to her somehow. I needed to get out of that house. I was sure that since Jay had hit me with her belt, she would now feel freer to use it on me whenever she wanted. I had to make my mom understand. This was surprisingly easier than I had anticipated.

"She did what?!" My mom's face held such rage, that she seemed to shake slightly. She immediately got on the phone with my grandma and they talked for a very long time. When my mom finally got off the phone, she seemed calm and determined. She seemed to have a plan. "I am not taking you back to that place," she told me.

A wave of relief came over me. All my problems seemed to melt away. My mom was saving me from my dad's crazy girlfriend, and I was filled with such love and gratitude toward her. Instantly, I could see this plan of hers was not going to be an easy one. She was sitting at her desk with a notebook and a pencil. "We have to get a lawyer and tell them what Jay did to you. Then, we will have to go to court, and you'll have to talk to the judge. So, we need to get all our facts straight. Okay?" She was writing as she talked to me.

"Okay, Momma." I wasn't really sure what she was talking about, but I knew that when she was this determined, it was best to agree with whatever she was saying. I was right; she turned and smiled at me. Once again, I could rely on her predictable nature.
Appease her, and I would be in a happy environment.

We began to go over the types of punishments that Jay would use on the boys and me. Then we went over how frequently she used those punishments. She wanted to know how I felt when I was with my dad and Jay. How did they treat Tony and Charlie? After a while, I began to feel tired and hungry. I was getting confused on my facts and forgetting some of the things that we were going over. It seemed like it was way past my bedtime. I finally asked my mom if I could go to sleep and we could finish talking about this in the morning.

She was not happy with that idea.

"Do you want to live with me or not? We need to finish this, so when I talk to your father tomorrow, I'll have some ammunition. Understand?" She turned back toward her notes. I had no idea what she meant by ammunition. But I felt the right response was to agree.

So, I did. But I still couldn't concentrate on what we were talking about. She was asking me to recall exact times and dates of certain punishments I received. She wanted me to remember time frames of when I was living with her and when I was living with my dad. I was getting too tired to think straight, and she was becoming irritated.

"Do you want me to take you back there right now? If you don't want this bad enough to stay up and work on these questions, then I will take you back there right now. Hey, I'll even tell them that you don't want to live with them. How's that?" She made me feel so ungrateful. Here she was trying to save me from a bad environment, and I couldn't even stay up a little passed my bedtime. I apologized. She made us both some coffee and we continued.

We talked the entire night. I saw the sun coming up as we finished "getting our facts straight." I was so tired; I desperately wanted to fall asleep. But something was bothering me. During the course of the night, it seemed like we had changed some of the facts around. We had turned Jay's hitting me with the belt once, to her hitting me with the belt once a week. We had also said that I had been living with my dad for a couple of months instead of a couple of years. My mom told me that these changes weren't a big deal, and it would just help to speed up the process of moving in with her.

Otherwise, as she explained, I might have to stay with them longer and Jay would be mad at me for not wanting to live with them. It all made sense when my mom explained it like that. She always had a way of explaining her rational thinking to me. I was able to fall asleep, content that my mom would take care of everything.

TESTING MY LOYALTY

The next day, when I awoke from what seemed like an eternity of sleep, my mom and her boyfriend were discussing the news that I was going to be moving in with them. He was surprised but supportive. He had always been very nice to me and was kind of like a big kid himself. He liked to play board games, and when he got excited about something, his whole face would light up like a kid on Christmas. I had to admit, one of the reasons I enjoyed visiting with my mom in the last year was so I could also visit with her boyfriend.

Her boyfriend was a well-built Chinese guy named Andy. He was also her dance partner at the dance studio where they both taught, called Fred Astaire Dance Studio. He was about the same height as my mom. But at 5'2", he was incredibly strong. He could lift my mom during their dance routines like she was as light as a feather.

Sometimes, he would lift me over his head, and I felt like I was flying. As strong as he was, even he couldn't compare to the domineering personality of my mom. When she wanted things her way, Andy had no choice. He might half-heartedly try to convince otherwise, but in the end, I think he knew it was inevitable that she would get what she wanted. I gave him a little credit for at least trying. Most people who knew my mom wouldn't clash opinions with her if you paid them. I felt especially close to him when he tried to protect me from my mom's temper. There were times when he actually veered her anger toward himself, so I would be spared from her sharp temper.

Andy was extremely angry when my mom told him that Jay beat me. While she was talking to him, I couldn't help but notice that she had added a few additional "facts" to the story that we already embellished upon. She was now saying that my dad and Jay didn't feed me enough, and they didn't allow me to get enough sleep.

"Didn't you notice how much she slept today? She practically slept the whole day! And doesn't that explain her incredible appetite when she visits us?" My mom was looking at Andy to verify her findings.

Andy saw something wrong with her conclusions. "Um, weren't you guys up kind of late last night? And I know it seems like she eats a lot to you, but that might be because you hardly eat at all. I mean, she's a growing girl, so..."

Andy stopped what he was saying when he saw he had opened the floodgates of Mom's anger. He didn't backpedal or apologize. Maybe he knew that it was too late to shut off the flow of hatred that was about to be spewed at him.

My mom glared at him for a second or two. I imagined she was trying to think of the best way to belittle and embarrass Andy. I wanted to run away and spare him from having an audience to this unfortunate situation.

"Do you even care what she goes through with her father and that bitch?" she sneered at him.

This was an avenue I don't think Andy nor I could have imagined she would go down. Maybe she couldn't argue with what he said, so she had to think of another way to make him feel like dirt. She knew Andy cared for me, as if I was his own daughter.

What better way to hurt him, than to accuse him of being insensitive towards my sorrowful predicament?

"I didn't mean..." Andy began, but then stopped. He could see that arguing with her was clearly not the approach to take with her at that moment.

My mom turned toward me, "See what we're going to be up against? Even Andy doubts what we're saying. It's hard to believe that people could treat their kids like your dad and Jay treat you. That's why we have to be sure of our facts and stick to what we believe in. We can't let anyone tell us different." She put each of her hands on my shoulders and pulled me in front of her. "It's me and you. Okay?" She stared at me, her eyes keeping eerily still.

When she finally turned and walked out of the room, she shot Andy one last look of piercing hatred before exiting. She had made her point and left Andy before he could make his. This was her way of making sure she had the last word and that her point overshadowed any others. I had the feeling that Andy wouldn't be around too much longer.

I also had the feeling that I needed to go along with whatever my mom said. It was going to be just me and her, and she needed me to assist her in our battles. This was made evident to me from her last comments, and the look she shared with me before leaving the room. As much as I cared for Andy, my mother needed me, and I desperately needed her.

Andy and I shared a few moments of awkward silence. His eyes were pleading with me. He seemed to want to explain what my mom said wasn't true. Possibly, he wanted to talk about the whole situation with my dad and Jay. But my mom had walked out of the room and was no doubt expecting me to follow her. After all, it was just me and her. Did I really understand that? I did. As I slowly got up and began my journey across the room, Andy also started to get up. Then our eyes met, and he sat back down. He would not try to follow me or talk to me about it anymore. I'm sure he knew that I didn't believe what my mom said about him not caring about me. But, I'm also sure he knew I had to follow her.

I needed to be saved from my dad and Jay. I never doubted that he understood why I made the choices I did that day. I felt an incredible sadness at knowing that our father/daughter-like relationship was coming to an end, and I wondered if it had been hard for him to accept, as well.

Andy was left alone in that room to wonder where he had gone wrong with my mom. The saddest part was that he hadn't done anything. My mom had just decided to move on, and taking me from my dad was a start on a new and different path for her.

As my mom and I worked on our strategy to make my dad and Jay look like the worst parents ever (with guidance from my grandma), Andy slowly faded from our lives. It seemed like he kind of just stood in the background for a while, until he was less and less of a presence. Then, it was like he had never been there at all. My mom didn't mention him again, so I never did either. Although I missed him, greatly.

Life with my mom was all about moving on, so that's what we did. We focused on our goal of defeating my dad and Jay. My mom seemed to have such a foolproof plan. We had established an abusive home (although we had tweaked the number of outbursts that occurred) and my grandma knew a really good attorney who guaranteed success. Everything seemed so easy. I briefly wondered why my mom hadn't saved me sooner.

Then, my mom informed me, "You know you'll have to inform your dad that you don't want to live with him anymore. He's expecting for me to drop you off around that time, and you need to let him know that you won't be there. Oh, you should also tell him why you don't want to go back. Tell him how Jay makes you feel and how scary she is. Um, you should also mention how it makes you feel when he doesn't protect you. Here," she handed me an index card with her perfect handwriting on it, "I made you some notes."

Suddenly, I didn't want to go through with this. I still had a soft spot in my heart for my dad. We had so many good times together, even after he met Jay. I never really felt threatened by him. It was more what he didn't do, than what he did, that really hurt me. Wasn't there a way to pin this all on Jay?

I must have had an unsure look on my face, because my mom asked me, "Got it?" The look on her face told me I should say "Yes," so I did. She returned to writing dates and information down in her notes. She had spent the last hour trying to figure out how to fit the instances of claimed abuse into a time frame that didn't make it look like she had been neglectful and turned a blind eye to my suffering.

It was clear she had a lot on her mind.

The time passed too quickly, and before long, it was time for me to make the phone call to my dad. My mom wanted me to talk to him first, then she was going to get on the phone and give him the phone number of our attorney. Any questions my dad had would be directed to our lawyer.

When I called my dad, he seemed surprised to hear from me. He was expecting me to be returning to the house any minute.

"What's going on?" he asked. "Where's your mom?"

I knew that the only way I was going to get through this was to just blurt out everything I had to say and quickly hand the phone to my mom. "Daddy, I want to live with Mom. I don't like the way Jay treats me and..."

"What do you mean? What is 'the way' Jay treats you? Look, you have school tomorrow, and you need to get home now. Let me talk to your mom." He had no way of knowing that my mom had already decided my fate, and I would not be returning.

"Um, Daddy ... See, I'm not coming home. I'm living with Mom now." As I was reiterating the first part of what I needed to say to him, my mom hurriedly scribbled something down on a piece of paper and shoved it at me. It said, "Hurry. About Jay." I really just wanted this conversation with my dad to be over already. He didn't want to listen to what I was saying and continued to interrupt me.

Even at the age of nine, I understood that he was having a lot thrown at him.

"Look, Nyssa. We can talk about this when you get home. You have to get up early in the morning for school, and I need for your mom to bring you home. Put her on the phone."

I couldn't argue with him anymore. I tried to hand the phone to my mom. She looked at it in confusion. Then, she slowly looked at me, and I could see that she was working up a rage inside of her. I was changing our plan, and she was not happy about it. She snatched the phone away from me, huffing in disgust. As she began to talk to my dad, she continued to glare at me. Her look said, "You screwed up, and now I have to fix this."

"So, Ben. Would you like to talk to me about how Jay has been treating Nyssa?" She was quiet for a moment, as my dad said something I couldn't hear. She seemed to get bored with his explanation and suddenly decided that she wanted to end the conversation. "Look, you can talk to our lawyer about this. Nyssa is not coming home tonight. She will be staying with me from now on."

She listened to him for another minute, then said, "Goodbye, Ben. I'm hanging up now."

Then she hung up on him. I heard him talking while she placed the receiver back into the cradle. She smirked and seemed very pleased with herself. She looked up and saw me, and she seemed to remember how I messed up. Her smirk turned into a glare. "Next time, you had better stick to our plan. Got it?"

"Yes, Momma. I'm sorry. Daddy wouldn't let me..." I tried to explain to her what had happened. Maybe if she knew that he wouldn't listen to me and just kept talking over me, then she would understand.

"First, let me repeat. Next time you better stick to the plan. Also, be aware that I am doing all of this for you. Don't ever forget that. Lastly, your father is no longer your 'Daddy'. That is how you need to refer to him, from this point on. I don't want to hear any endearing names for that man who didn't care enough for you to protect you from that woman."

She wasn't yelling at me, only speaking very firmly. Then as an afterthought, she added, "He obviously loves Jay more than he loves you." She went back to her writing and that was the end of the conversation. She didn't want to hear what I had to say.

I thought about what she said. It made sense. The reason my dad never stuck up for me was because he loved Jay more. My mom was right. She was the only one who was willing to go through all of this, for my benefit. Next time, I wouldn't disappoint her. No matter what, I had to back my mom up and do as she said. She was the only person who really cared about me and wanted what was best for me. She told me not to forget that, and I wouldn't. Even after I stopped believing it, I have not forgotten.

Dark Secret

TEACHING DECEPTION

Our lawyer was a distinguished man in my grandparents' community. He had an excellent record of case wins and had studied at some university that seemed to impress both my mom and grandma. Plus, my grandma said, "He's such a nice young man. When I told him about the case, he said not to worry. He said he would take care of everything. Isn't that great?" She seemed to be reassuring my mom, who was having some doubts about the ease of this process.

"Are you sure that Ben won't be able to drag this whole thing out? I don't want to be stuck in some long court battle. And what about Jay? I don't want her to be allowed anywhere near Nyssa. Can he do that?" She sounded like a little girl, asking her mother for guidance. I wasn't used to hearing my mom sound like that. Normally, she would have everything under control, and never had any doubts about what she could get accomplished. But, sometimes, when she was around my grandma, she relapsed into a more childish tone.

"Of course, he can take care of that. He told me not to worry about anything." My grandma seemed too trusting sometimes. She evidently believed everything this lawyer told her. I wondered how he knew he could win if he hadn't even talked to me or my mom yet.

When we entered the lawyer's office, I was taken aback at its size. It seemed too large to be an office for one person.

Everything inside the office gave off an expensive aura. I sat softly on the sofa in the waiting room, unsure if I should even be sitting on it in the first place. It was a Victorian style sofa, like the one my great aunt had. She never wanted anyone to sit on that sofa. But, since my mom sat on this one, I followed her lead. The table looked like something out of a modern art book. It had a glass top, with legs that looked like giant leaves. The giant pictures on the wall were of geometric shapes, all contrasting colors. The secretary was young and pretty. Even she looked expensive, with her hair perfectly piled on top of her head. Her nails were long and shiny, and her makeup was so flawless I thought she looked like a porcelain doll.

"Mr. Van Cleave will be with you shortly. Can I get you something to drink?" The secretary spoke so sweetly, yet in a monotone voice, that made me wonder if she was actually a very expensive secretary robot of some kind.

The three of us politely declined and continued to wait for the great Mr. Van Cleave to make his appearance. I was staring at the double doors that led to his office. They were enormous and made of the most beautiful dark wood I had ever seen. I was wandering what this lawyer was going to look like. Maybe he would be like Mr. Pennybags from that Monopoly game that I had played with Charlie and Tony.

Maybe he looked like the rich character from the game Clue. What was his name? Mr. Green? Something Mustard? I pictured an older man, wearing an expensive suit, with maybe a mustache that was neatly trimmed and smoothed onto his happy face. Like a handlebar mustache or something.

"Are you listening to me? You better quit zoning out and concentrate on what I'm telling you." My mom had been talking to me. I turned to listen to her but kept the double doors in view. I just couldn't wait to see the man who could afford to have his office look nicer than any home I had ever been in.

"Remember what I said about sticking to the plan, Nyssa. When this lawyer asks you a question, you answer him clearly. You tell him everything we talked about. Don't forget anything. Got it? And mind your manners. Understand?" My mom had unyielding severity in her voice.

"Yes, Momma. I'll remember. I understand." This time I would not disappoint her. I would be strong and polite and whatever else my mom wanted me to be. I would make her proud, and then she would feel like I was worth all the trouble we were going through.

"I know you'll do well, Nyssa." My grandma put her hand around my shoulders. She squeezed me slightly and said, "Don't be too nervous. Okay? You'll be fine." I smiled at her but still kept the doors in my peripheral vision. "Good girl." Grandma kissed me on the cheek.

Then, the doors opened. Rather, one of the doors opened. A short, balding man wearing a dingy suit came out and extended his hand toward my mom. "Ms. Najera, it's so nice to meet you. Would you step into my office and we can talk?" We began to follow him into his office, and he noticed me. "Oh, you must be Nyssa. It's very nice to meet you. How are you?" He smiled warmly at me, but instead of seeming nice and friendly, he seemed awkward and greasy. I looked at his hand, which was waiting for me to shake it, and after some hesitation, I shook it.

"I'm not doing so well." I answered, thinking that would be the safest answer to give. My mom had made sure to stress how important it was for me to express how miserable I was living with my father. I figured that letting him know from the get-go would be a good idea.

"I'm sorry to hear that. Let's talk about what's going on." He gestured to the seats in front of his desk, and we sat in them. His office wasn't as nice as his waiting room. It was plainer looking, like he was. I was beginning to feel a little disappointed at that point. Not only did the great Mr. Van Cleave not make a grand entrance, but his office actually looked like it was in need of a good cleaning.

We were all sitting around his desk, which was cluttered with files, Post-its, and loose papers. I wondered how he kept track of all his important cases. I could see my mom was a bit uneasy about this guy, as well. She was also eyeing the great mound of papers that littered his desk. My grandma was the only one who didn't seem to notice the clutter.

"So, you already know the gist of this case, from what I told you on the phone. My daughter and granddaughter can tell you more of the details." My grandma wanted to get this ball rolling and didn't want to waste time with small talk. For the first time, I realized that my grandma was actually the one in control of the situation.

"Um, yes. Of course, we should start right away." Mr. Van Cleave was obviously taken aback by my grandma's commanding comment. He recovered quickly and shuffled some papers together on his desk. He turned toward me, "Well, Nyssa. If you don't mind, I would like to talk to you about some things that would help me to help you. Okay?"

I nodded. When I noticed my mom glaring at me, I spoke clearly to him, "Yes, sir. I understand." Then, there was a small awkward silence, as we all waited for his questions to start.

The attorney looked up from his papers, confused, and said, "I think it would be better if Nyssa and I could talk alone for a few minutes." He looked at my mom and grandma for approval. "If that's alright with you, ladies." He flashed a clumsy smile at them.

My mom stood up and started for the door. My grandma squeezed my shoulder with one hand and said, "If you need anything, we will be right outside that door. Okay?"

"Yes, Grandma." I smiled at her. I felt a renewed desire to please my mom and grandma. I would not let them down. Once the door shut behind my grandma, I looked over at this man. As he continued to gather some papers together, I wondered if he was really some kind of fraud. I guess I felt so duped by his extravagant lobby and pretty secretary; I wasn't as impressed by him anymore.

The good news was: this made me less nervous about talking to him.

"First, let me say that you seem like a very mature young lady. I'm sure that your mother and grandmother are very proud of the way you hold yourself." His smile was friendly, but something about his demeanor felt very phony to me.

"Okay, so let's start with how your father treats you and why you want to live with your mother, instead. Just tell me anything you think is important for me to know. Anything that you think might be important to the case. Alright?" He sat back in his chair, with is big yellow pad of paper and a pen. He was ready to hear all I had to say.

I started off by explaining that the main problem in the house was Jay. I wanted him to understand that she was the one who scared me, not my dad. I wanted Jay to get the blame I felt she deserved for wrecking the relationship between my dad and me. Mr. Van Cleave was taking quick notes as I talked. I felt a little better that he seemed more organized than I first thought.

As I began to explain in more detail how mean Jay was, my eyes began to wander around his office. He had an entire wall of books on one side of the office. I had never seen so many books outside a library. I was still talking to the attorney, but at the same time, I was noticing more details about his office. His books needed to be dusted, badly. I was responding to his questions about how many times a week Jay hit me. (Gee, his lamps looked really old.) I was telling him how many times she would hit her boys. (I really wished he would open the blinds in the office, because it seemed so dreary.) Oh, we were done with the questions, and my mom and grandma were coming back into his office and sitting down.

"How did everything go?" My mom looked directly at me but meant for the question to be answered by the attorney.

"Would it be alright if I talked to you two alone? Nyssa could read some magazines out front, and Tina will watch her for us." He didn't look up much from his notebook as he talked. He seemed to be reviewing the information from our interview.

I waited in the lobby, glad to be out of that cluttered office. I had no problem keeping myself busy. I watched his secretary answer the phone and flirt with someone on the other end. I studied his furniture and paintings. I tried to figure out what the sculptures in the corner of the room were supposed to be. Melting men? Deformed tree trunks? Whatever they were, I really liked them.

Eventually, my mom, grandma, and Mr. Van Cleave came out of the office. They all seemed like they were having a good time, laughing and smiling as they walked together. The three of them shook hands and said it had been nice to meet one another. Then, we headed out of the lobby and outside to the parking lot. I noticed that he hadn't said anything to me as we were leaving. I thought something strange had happened, but I couldn't figure out what it was.

Then, I noticed my grandma wasn't holding my hand or praising me for a job well done. I started to feel my stomach sinking into my feet. I really didn't want to, but I knew the time would come where I would have to look at my mom. I had to get it over with and find out what had gone wrong. I slowly turned to look at my mom and instantly regretted my decision. She was ferociously staring at me. Her eyes were so piercing; they seemed to be looking straight through me. My stomach felt like it was being sucked into the center of the earth. My only hope was that we would spend enough time with my grandma for my mom to calm down a little.

We quietly got into my grandma's car and drove a few blocks before my grandma finally asked me, "So, what happened in there?" She was calm and sounded a little concerned. I felt like such a failure, without even knowing why I felt that way.

"I just told him that Jay hit me. I told him that I wanted to live my mom." I thought that was the right answer, but somehow it was not what they wanted to hear.

My mom mimicked me, "I just told him that Jay hit me," she repeated in a whiny voice. "That's just great! What about your father, Nyssa? Did you forget about how he let her hit you?" She didn't look at me in the backseat but continued to face the passenger door. I thought she was afraid to face me, because she didn't want to end up hitting me in front of my grandma.

"Now, Mica. That is not going to help the situation." My grandma began to explain what the lawyer had told her. "Nyssa, Mr. Van Cleave told your mom and I that you couldn't remember dates of very memorable incidents of abuse by Jay. He also said that you defended your father and gave conflicting numbers for how many times Jay hit you. He was concerned that you didn't have your facts straight and that would make our case too weak to win. Do you understand?" I told her that I did.

"If you weren't such a space cadet, maybe you would have done a halfway decent job. Jesus, Nyssa, I can't believe you f***** this up!" My mom was losing control of herself.

"Mica! There is no need for that!" My grandma despised cursing and was quick to reprimand my mom. "What your mom means, Nyssa, is that we have to go over a few things a little more carefully. We need to make a strong case. Mr. Van Cleave is not sure he wants to take our case. We need to show him that we have a winning case. Can we do that?"

I felt awful. I squeaked out an apology. I couldn't believe that I had messed up so badly. Even though there were many "facts" I had to remember, I had spent a lot of time practicing with my mom. Although we had changed so many things, and I knew I had jumbled some of the information around, there was no excuse for letting them down. My mom was right. I totally spaced out in his office and ruined everything. I couldn't contain it any longer and began to weep. I felt like my mom would be better off leaving me on the side of the road. I was an ungrateful, irresponsible little brat. I deserved whatever I had coming from her.

I sobbed the whole way to my grandparents' house. When we got inside, my grandma held me and stroked my hair. She talked low and softly, reassuring me that everything would be alright. I fell asleep with my head on her chest. When I woke up, my mom was gone. She had gone back to her house and left me to spend the night with my grandparents. I wasn't sure if she had done that for my benefit, or she was too disgusted with me to even be around me that night. Either way, my grandma turned it into a fun "girly sleepover."

We played games and painted our toenails. We ate way too much ice cream and stayed up really late. It was a much- needed break from all the drilling I had been through over the last few days.

"Tomorrow, you will need to go over some things with your mom again. I know you'll do better this time. Okay?" My grandma tucked me into one side of her bed, and then crawled into the other side. As I felt her queen size feather bed envelope me like a cloud, she said, "We'll show your dad that he can't mess with the Najera women."

My last thought for the night was "I have a lot to learn about being a Najera woman."

Dark Secret

TATA'S HIDDEN LESSONS

"How could this have happened?" My mom was both angry and confused. "I just don't understand." She looked at my grandma for answers. "You said this attorney would take care of everything. How could he let this happen?" Now she seemed concerned.

We were leaving the courthouse after waiting for weeks to see a judge and present our case. Things hadn't gone as smoothly as I thought it would. The judge felt that Jay was not so much of a threat that I couldn't be around her when I visited my dad. He also felt that my dad should get a lot of visitation with me. He gave him every other weekend and extra days when there was holiday or when I was off school. My dad had hugged me in the hallway of the courthouse and kissed me on the cheek when the hearing was over.

He told me that he would be seeing me soon. It seemed he was pleased with the judge's ruling.

"That lazy attorney didn't even argue with the judge! He didn't fight for us at all! What exactly are we paying him for?" My mom was pacing in front of the courthouse, ranting to no one in particular. Someone needed to say something to her, before our attorney walked out and got blasted by her.

"Momma?" I was taking a big chance by trying to talk to her at the moment. If I could say something that made her feel better, I would be her pet for the rest of the day. If I made things worse, then I better hope she would take it out on the lawyer and not me.

"The judge wants us to come back later. Maybe it will be better for us next time," I spoke softly to her and smiled as sweetly as I thought I could.

She stopped pacing and stood still, briefly contemplating what I said. "Let's see—the judge wants us to come back in six months. I'm supposed to work out my schedule for your father's convenience for the next six months and hope that the judge grows some brain cells by then?"

It didn't take a genius to figure out that she was using her sarcasm to vent off some anger. I wasn't going to say anything else and push my luck with her. Besides, maybe Mr. Van Cleave had it coming. He had been responsible for presenting our side of the case. Hadn't he?

"I know what you mean, Mica. That lousy lawyer isn't getting a penny out of me." My grandma was also upset but didn't react to anything like my mom did. She sat on the bench in front of the main entrance and looked off into the main road. She seemed to be thinking of the next plan of action.

I continued to watch my grandma, deep in thought. I turned and watched my mom, still pacing and cursing under her breath. I looked at the main entrance to the courthouse, waiting for our doomed lawyer to show his face.

Soon, Mr. Van Cleave came out of the courthouse, talking and smiling with another man in a suit. He seemed entirely too happy for having just lost our case. He was getting closer to us, and I began to think that he had better wipe that smile off his face, before my mom did it forcibly.

"You call yourself a lawyer? What the hell was that?" My mom pointed to the courthouse, to show him where he screwed up.

"Mica, please." My grandma spoke softly, but sternly. In response, my mom backed away. She was still mumbling to herself and clenching her fists, but she walked away to let my grandma handle things. Maybe she was planning how she would kick his butt. If this guy knew my mom like I did, he would have jumped in his fancy car and driven away.

My grandma and the lawyer walked away from my mom and me as they talked. I couldn't hear what they were saying, so I watched their faces. My grandma looked concerned, while the lawyer looked sympathetic. Then, my grandma smiled and waved across her chest, as if to say, "That's it, and we are done now." She walked back over to us, leaving the attorney looking dumbfounded. His eyebrows scrunched together, as he struggled to understand what my grandma told him.

"Why are we leaving? What did you say to him? I want to go and give him a piece of my mind!" My mom was still ranting. She was letting my grandma usher us to the car, but never taking her eyes off the attorney. She was like a child who had too much energy; asking constant questions, but not giving my grandma enough time to answer before cutting her off with another question or irate declaration. "Did he tell you why he screwed up? Did he even apologize? Is he going to fix things? Oh, he will after I get ahold of him."

We were at the car, and it was clear that my mom was not getting into the car without an explanation for why she wasn't able to "pound" the attorney. I, however, was tired from standing around the courthouse all day and started to climb into the backseat of the car. My mom grabbed me by the arm, "Do you even realize what happened?"

She seemed amazed that I was not ranting like she was. Honestly, I really didn't understand what had gone so wrong that day. At least I didn't have to go back and live with my dad. But I wasn't about to admit that to my mom. I tried to think of something to say to her, but I was tired and hungry, and nothing came to me.

"Mica." My grandma came to my rescue again. "I told that ridiculous excuse for a lawyer that since he had not done what he had promised, he would no longer be representing us. I also told him that I would not be paying him the rest of the money he requested, and if he sent the bill to a collection agency or in any way tried to force the issue, I would take legal action against him with a "real" lawyer. Then," My grandma finished, "I told him to have a good day."

My mom contemplated what my grandma said. During the silence, I held my breath. Was my mom going to be angry because it was not what she would have done?

"So, we're not going to continue paying him?" Mom asked in the softest voice she had used all day.

"Of course not. I told you he wouldn't be getting one penny from me." Grandma turned toward my mom. We were all in the car, and Grandma started it. "Honestly, you really need to have a little faith in your mother. I know how to handle things, Mica." We were rolling out of the parking lot, and I was feeling more assured that there would be no attorney begging for his life at the hands of my mom.

There was more silence in the car. Finally, my mom asked what was going to happen next. As they talked in the front seat, I began to see that my grandma really was running the show. I was seeing my mom in a role I had never seen her in before. She was being a follower, and my dear old grandmother was leading her around. It didn't matter too much to me, as long as I didn't have to go back to my father's house. Although it was interesting and a little confusing to see my mom act like a child.

"Are you listening back there?" Lately, my mom had been catching me off guard. I had to be more careful. Day dreaming was something that my mom said flaky people did. I wasn't sure what a flaky person looked like, but they must have been pretty bad.

"Yes, Momma," I said. I prayed that would be sufficient.

"Please don't drill me," I thought. I really hadn't been listening at all.

The last thing I wanted was to have the built-up anger that was not released onto Mr. Van Cleave to be released on me.

"Oh, Mica. Really, now." Grandma was my savior once again. "You know what the big problem is? You're expecting Nyssa to remember everything. She's a child. If you fill her head with too many insignificant facts, then it will be harder for her to remember the things that are really important." We had already arrived at my grandparents' driveway, since the courthouse was up the street.

My grandma turned off the ignition and turned around to face me.

"Don't worry too much about what your mom and I talk about. We'll let you know what's important for you to remember. Okay?"

"Yes, Grandma." I smiled warmly at her. I felt so much love and admiration for her. She was strong, yet gentle. I marveled at how she accomplished balancing the two.

Once we were inside the house, my mom and grandma separated themselves from me. They went into the kitchen to make some tea and discuss the new "plan." I sat on the porch, next to my grandpa, Tata. I just wanted to relax after such a drawn-out day.

My grandfather spent a lot of time sitting on the sofa that had been placed on the porch a few years ago. It had been placed there around the time he had his first stroke. It allowed him a place to sit and watch the world, without too much effort. His first stroke left him paralyzed on the entire right side of his body. He used his cane for support and would slowly take a step with his left leg, and then drag up his right leg. His second stroke happened a year later. It was then that he began to talk slower and have times where he became "removed" from the world. When I did it, my mom called it "spacing out," but my grandpa would not have allowed himself to do such a thing on purpose. Even in his disabled state, he was determined to do everything for himself and without help from anyone. It was hard for me to see how frustrated he would get when he was unable to do something he had done so easily before, but I tried not to intervene. I didn't want to hurt his pride.

"Hey there." Tata's face lit up when he saw me sitting next to him. He rarely had company to talk to. "How's my baby girl?"

"Oh, Tata." I acted like I was getting too old for him to be calling me that pet name, but really I loved it. I would always be his baby girl.

I looked out at the traffic passing the house and enjoyed the relaxing moment I had with my grandpa. Tata leaned back and looked through the front window. "What kind of scheme are those two cooking up? Something about your dad?" Tata always knew more about what was happening than my grandma and mom gave him credit for.

"Baby girl, did I ever tell you the story of the mean old sheriff in my hometown and my best friend, Sam?" Tata was about to start one of his stories that seemed to take place in ancient history to me. I loved hearing his life stories. He was so good at giving details and making the story sound like a movie. I could picture what he was telling me, and I could easily get sucked right into one of his tales, until the rest of the world just melted away.

I shook my head, "No." So, he began. "Jeez, I musta been about your age." He took a slow breath that whistled through his teeth as he drew it in, and I knew he was embarking on a journey down memory lane. "Sam was my best friend. He was loyal, smart, and the only one in the world who meant anything to me. When my daddy would come home drunk, I would camp outside with Sam. We would hide all night, until I thought it was safe to go home again. Yes, he was the only one who would stand up for me against my dad. Boy, he was a brave one."

My grandpa had told me stories of his father before. I got scared listening to them. He had been a mean alcoholic who abused his family frequently. He had been large and strong and quick to get physical with anyone. I couldn't imagine anyone going up against such a man.

"Did I mention that Sam was also my dog?" Tata grinned mischievously. He knew full well that I would not have guessed that Sam was a dog. "Yeah, he was my dog. Best dog I ever had. I swear, most times that dog thought he was people." Tata looked off into the sky, remembering. "Most times, I thought he was better than people. I would take him everywhere with me. He walked me to school and would wait for me while I was in my class. Can you believe that dog waited for me the whole class? There he would be, just waiting for me and ready to walk home. Such a good dog.

"Well, in our town, we had this sheriff; he was a mean man who really didn't care for Indians at all. He would say the meanest things to the little Indian children and harass the adults something awful. He really looked down on anyone who wasn't white. Mental problems, I guess." Tata always attributed odd behavior to some kind of mental deficiency. "Anyways, his daughter was in my class, and we had become somewhat of friends. She would walk with me and Sam after school sometimes. Nice girl. Really liked Sam. I think that's why she wanted to walk with us ... to play with Sam.

"I guess her daddy didn't like his little girl walking with an Indian, 'cus he came to my house one day and talked to my dad. Of course, my dad didn't want to take responsibility for nothing I was doin', so he directed the sheriff to the backyard where me and Sam were playing."

Tata grew more serious, as he said, "That sheriff told me that if I walked with his daughter again, he would shoot me and my dad." I gasped and Tata continued, "Now, I tried to explain to him that his little girl really didn't like me, but my dog, and I thought that I'd be outta trouble. Do you know that just made him even more mad? He was so mad that I dared to talk to him, he drew his gun. He pulled his gun out of his holster and pointed it straight at my face." Tata took another whistling inhale of air as he reached this climactic point. "Then, that evil man swung his pistol around and pointed it square at Sam." Tata paused again. He looked up at the sky, blinking back tears and struggling to regain his composure. "He shot my dog." Tata was finally able to blurt out.

I leaned slightly up against him, careful not to put too much weight on his disabled arm. He held my hand, with his un- paralyzed one, and we were both quiet for a few minutes. Then, when he was capable of continuing his story, he picked up where he had left off.

"Baby girl, I never felt so bad in my life. When that sheriff shot my dog, I had to go and look for him. Sam had run off into the hills. I guess the loud noise from the gun scared him. Boy, I spent all night looking for him. When I finally found him, he wasn't dead yet.

"He had been shot in the jaw and was bleeding all over the place. I carried him back home and tried to take care of him ... but he eventually died of starvation. Poor Sam couldn't eat anything with a broken jaw. I had to watch my best friend slowly die." Tata looked away from me, and I knew he was trying not to lose it. My heart ached for him. It was like I was listening to my grandpa as a child, telling about this great loss. I had never seen him look and sound vulnerable before.

Tata took a deep breath and pulled himself up straight.

"Alright, this is why I told you this story. That same sheriff was involved in a shooting about one year later at an attempted robbery near my house. I heard that he had been responding to a call about some noises from a house that was supposed to be empty, on account of the homeowners being on vacation. When the sheriff arrived on the scene, he ran into the robber as he was leaving the house. Well, the robber drew his weapon first and fired it. Do you know that he hit the sheriff right in the jaw?"

Tata's face was full of amazement. "Right smack in the jawbone!" Now, Tata was enjoying himself. "And..." He paused for a second or two, then finished, "he didn't die right away. Oh no, he lived for a couple of weeks. Until he starved to death, almost one year to the day that Sam died." Tata leaned back on the sofa, satisfied he had made his point.

Besides feeling astounded at the quality of his story, I was surprised at how his point was so fable-like. His story painted a perfect picture to me of "what goes around comes around." But the point of him telling me that story, at that particular time, was lost on me. I now regret that I didn't reason more deeply into his intention for telling me that specific story at that specific time. As I look back, I feel that he was trying to warn me of the chain of events I was involving myself in. He wanted me to take responsibility for my actions, instead of blindly following my mom and grandma. But I couldn't see his underlying message, and now it is too late.

My grandpa and I sat on the couch and watched the traffic go by. We sat closely and enjoyed each other's company, silently.

When my grandma came outside to fetch me for some "going over facts" lessons, I went with her. My grandpa sat on the porch for what seemed like a long time after I had left. Possibly, he was wondering if I had truly seen the significance of his story. I'm sorry to say that I didn't.

Tata, I'm sorry.

Dark Secret

SEPARATE WORLDS

So, how long does it take for two adults to get back at each other for a relationship gone bad? Eighteen years. When their child can no longer be legally used as a pawn. I lost many years of my childhood helping my parents play their revenge game. The object of this game was to see who could hurt the other worse. I'm sure they both thought they were doing what was in my best interest, but their sick game was not really for my benefit. The strangest part was how they were both able to draw me in. At times, I was on my mom's side. At fewer times, I was on my dad's.

"What did your father say to you?" My mom would always grill me when I got home from my court-ordered visits with my dad. "You tell me everything he said about me."

She would then stare at me, so demanding, and wait for my reply. I knew that I would not be allowed to leave her presence until I told her what she wanted to hear. I briefly thought about lying to her and telling her that my dad hadn't said anything at all. But I was always too scared to be caught by her. I was better off telling her what had been said and letting her focus her anger on someone else. Besides, my father should not have been talking about my mom to me in the first place.

That was all I needed to convince myself to come clean.

"Daddy said you were lying in court about how mean he is to me. He also said you were getting me to lie about Jay and that was wrong. He said I should tell the truth." I blurted everything out quickly. Then, I took a deep breath and awaited the inevitable explosion.

My mom got up from my grandma's sofa and walked into the kitchen. I could see her pour a glass of water and slowly sip it. Her body was slightly turned, so that I could not see the emotions on her face. Was she mad at me? Was she mad at my father?

What had I said wrong? Should I run and hide while she still had her back turned to me? At that moment, she whirled around and glared at me. I felt my stomach turn, and for a moment I thought she had read my mind somehow. She knew I wanted to run away, and now I would be punished!

I came back to my senses, and she began to talk, "First, you better stick up for me when your father calls me a liar or says anything else that is unflattering or derogatory. That is the least you can do, considering what I go through to protect you.

"Second, if you want to 'tell the truth', you go ahead and go live with your father and Jay and tell the truth over there. We'll see how much they appreciate the hell you've put them through so far. And last..." she walked over and grabbed the front of my shirt.

Her hand tightened the fabric into a ball in her fist. She pulled up on my shirt, and I had no choice but to rise to my feet. She then pulled me close to her face, and I had to turn my head slightly, so we didn't collide. "Don't you ever call your father 'Daddy' again. You got that?" Her breath felt hot against my cheek.

"Yes, Momma," I answered. Then, quickly added, "I understand."

She let me go, slowly. Then, she took a couple of steps back, slowly. All the time, she didn't lose eye contact with me. Finally, she turned around and walked toward the stairs. Still, she turned and glared at me. Even as she was walking up the stairs, her eyes were like fire burning into me, until she entered the part of the stairway covered by the ceiling. It was then that I gasped and let out a breath of air I had been holding. I greedily inhaled and collapsed on the sofa.

That's when I saw I was crying and shaking uncontrollably. I realized I didn't know my mom's moods as well as I thought I did. But there was nothing I could do now. I couldn't go back to my dad. I was sure my mom was right about them hating me for exaggerating. I thought life with them had been hard before, I couldn't imagine what it would be like if I crawled back after all the drama of the last few months. I had dug myself into an abysmal pit. I had no choice but to try and make the best of the situation I put myself in.

During the next two years, I learned to adjust to my self-inflicted circumstances. When I was with my father, I tried not to talk too much about what was on my mind. I kept my distance from Jay and avoided talking about any of our custody hearings or court matters. Eventually, my dad caught on, and for the most part, our visits were quiet and uneventful.

Every once in a while, Jay would rant about something that we said about her in a court paper from the year before. I wasn't scared of her (our new lawyer made it very clear that she couldn't touch me), instead, I thought she was strange and child-like. Her temper was like that of a toddler. Sadly, her sons and I were not able to go back to the bond we once had. As much as they told me that they didn't like many things about their mom, they resented me for saying those things in court about her. I felt like they endured my company, because my father asked them to. Besides the occasional moments of time alone with my father, I really saw no reason behind our visits.

As for my mom and I, I felt like our relationship was getting stronger every day. The longer I lived with her, the fewer violent outbreaks she would have. We became more and more like "friends," and she seemed to enjoy my company. As long as she felt I was in complete agreement with her on whatever she said, our life together was pretty fun. I would make her laugh by imitating Jay when she got mad or acting like my father being Jay's servant ("Yes, Dear. Yes, Dear").

My mom and I would go camping, horse-back riding, take singing lessons and even dance lessons. I was also going to a private school, thanks to the financial support of my grandma. I was so enchanted by my new surroundings. I felt lucky to be learning about so many things that fascinated me before, but I knew were out of reach for most kids my age. My mom and grandma always made sure that I was aware how lucky I was. All my new extracurricular activities and all the time I had to spend doing homework and studying (I had to catch up to what my private school peers were learning) left me with little extra time and made my father very uneasy. "Why does her mother have to keep Nyssa so busy? Every other time I call to set up a visit with Nyssa, it seems like she has a singing lesson or a dance lesson or she's studying. What is going on? I don't have any say in what Nyssa does anymore."

My father was complaining to Jay and acting like I wasn't in the room. I hated when they did that. Maybe it was a way for them to let me know how they felt, without getting in trouble for saying it to my face. It really just made me feel like I wasn't valuable as a person. I was just a child.

"Babe, I just don't know what to do." My dad was still complaining. "I can't fight them." The 'them' my father always referred to, was my mom and grandma. He always assumed that anything that happened was a result of collaboration between the two of them. "The courts think that the child is always better off with the mom." My dad finished.

Since I had been living with my mom and grandma, I was used to them talking to me like I was a coherent being. So, this made it more and more difficult for me to sit through my father and Jay discussing me, as if I was unable to understand their "grown up" talk.

I really wanted to say something and imagined what I would say, if I ever had the nerve to interrupt them. Maybe I would say something that would show them how stupid and selfish they were being.

Maybe I could say something so intelligent that it would instill instant respect for me in them. Or ... I would just march up to them and tell them off. I could let out all the built-up frustration and resentment I had toward them. Yeah, I could tell Jay how mean and childish I thought she was. Then, my father would see her as she truly was and leave her. My dad and I could live together like before, and I would still be able to take all the great lessons I took at my mom's and ...

"Can you believe this? There she is, spacing out again. Helllloooo! Are you awake?" Jay had been trying to get my attention. For how long, I wasn't sure. I was sure, however, that my face was bright red. I felt hot all over. In my daydream, I had been so cool and confident. Now, in reality, Jay had made me feel dumb and flustered.

"Uh, I didn't know you were talking to me. I thought you two were still talking to each other." I hoped that they would understand what I was trying to say. But I knew they didn't realize how confusing it was to have them talk about me and then suddenly switch to talking to me. I had seen Tony and Charlie get yelled at for the same thing, so I knew I wasn't the only one who experienced this from my father and Jay. It was hard to know if they were talking about you or directing the conversation at you.

"Uh, duh." Jay had no idea where I was coming from. Now she would make me feel even more dumb. "My name is Nyssa, and I am a moron." Jay mocked me and then turned to my father, "I think Mica is telling her to ignore us. They already have her turned against us, now all they have to do is have her screw up our home. She can get away with almost anything now." Jay paused and turned to direct the last sentence toward me. "And she knows that the court says we can't lay a finger on her." Then, she smiled at me sarcastically, "Aren't you the lucky one, Nyssa?"

I despised Jay like I never despised her before. My mom was right about everything she said about her. It was then that I understood what my mom had been trying to explain about "us vs. them." Jay was trying to turn my father against me, my father didn't care enough to see through her mind games, and the boys were too young to stand up to anything that happened in that house. Fine. If Jay wanted to play games, then I could play them too.

Since I had my grandma and mom on my side, I felt Jay wouldn't stand a chance. I felt a renewed connection with my mom and grandma. I couldn't wait to go home with them and tell them how I felt. For so long, my mom had been trying to convince me I needed to be more ruthless with Jay, but I always felt that it would be wrong of me to question an adult (any adult), much less try to play mind games with them. But now, I felt Jay had given me no choice. I would not let her play my father against me and try to poke holes in my newfound confidence.

"So, what exactly are you saying?" My mom was trying to understand my befuddled effort to explain my newfound sense of purpose. I wanted to engage my revenge on Jay.

"Momma, she is telling my dad that I'm a brat. She's trying to make everyone think I'm a mean person, and she makes me feel like I'm stupid." I knew that my mom would take personal offense to my last comment. She was always telling people how smart I was and loved to see me interact with other adults. She took full credit for my ability to communicate maturely with people twice or even three times my age. "I want to make her feel that way. You know, the way she's trying to make me feel." I hoped I had conveyed my intentions clearly enough to her.

"Well, I see. Hmmm." She looked like she was carefully considering what I told her. Then, she looked at me with a sly grin slowly growing on her face. She suddenly wrapped her arms around me. "You really are a smart one! You know that? I thought it was going to take you years to figure out how the world works. But look at you. Barely ten years old, and you have more of an understanding about life than most people my age!" She was hugging me tightly. I had only seen her this happy a few times in my life. "We have to tell your grandma. She's going to love this. Now, we can start teaching you things that will help you be strong inside." She put her hand on her chest, slightly over her heart. I took that to mean that my dad and Jay wouldn't be able to hurt me emotionally anymore. "Come on, let's go find Grandma."

My mom held my hand, and we walked up the stairs together. I felt so close to her. I was feeling a friendship and an equality that I never felt with an adult before. No, wait. I had felt that way with my dad, but now that time was over.

My grandma was in her sewing room when my mom and I practically came skipping in to talk to her. My mom explained to her what I said. When she was done, we both stood in front of her and waited for her to join in our jubilance. Instead, my grandma stared at us blankly, seeming a little confused. Finally, she put down her fabric on her sewing table and swiveled her chair around to fully face us.

"Mica, I thought I made it clear to you that I don't think Nyssa should be involved with our mind battles against that woman." My grandma had stopped using Jay's name a while ago and only referred to her as "that woman."

"The only involvement Nyssa should have is in her testimony at the court proceedings. We need to wait until she is a little older and has a better understanding of life, in general." She lowered her eyes and peered at my mom over her glasses. "Building her psyche is no joke."

I had no idea what a psyche was, but it sounded very important. I wanted mine to be strong, if it meant I could defeat Jay.

"Grandma, I'm ready. I really am. I understand how the world is. Mom already showed me." I had to convince her. I felt like I was close to having so much power, and I desperately wanted to know the secrets that my mom and grandma knew.

"I'm sure you think you're ready, Nyssa. But, you just need a little more time. You should enjoy your childhood while you still can. You will have plenty of time to worry about other things when you get older. Okay?" She was speaking to me like she was the great, old, and wise woman of the world.

I was frustrated but humbled by her worldly way of speaking. I thought she must know what was best for me. Although I was upset that I would have to wait, I accepted her decision. "Okay, Grandma," I said, reluctantly.

"No way." My mom spoke up. I had assumed that the decision had been made. I completely forgot that my mom already set her mind on my readiness. "I say she is ready, now. The longer we wait, the harder it will be for her. By the time you think she's ready, she won't need to defend herself against Jay. The damage to her self-esteem will already have been done. We have to start teaching her now."

My mom was adamant. My grandma was equally sure of her decision. Who would win? I didn't want to know, and I definitely didn't want to be in the room any longer. I slowly backed up a bit. I moved to the side of the room and opened one of my grandma's books of clothing patterns. I didn't want to be included in this exchange, in any way.

My grandma made another attempt to reason with my mom.

"Mica, what are a few years? We don't have to wait until she's a grown up, but we should wait until she's at least a teenager."

My mom looked at the floor, pondering what my grandma said. Then she seemed to realize something and looked at me. A small smile spread on her face, and I knew that she had made her decision. She quickly turned her head toward my grandma and nodded.

"Okay, I see. If you don't have the energy to help me, or you don't have the faith in your granddaughter, then I'll do it myself." Before my grandma could respond, my mom walked over to me and grabbed my shoulder. She led me downstairs and we took our coats out from the hall closet. Silently, we put on our coats and walked outside. I had no idea what was happening or where we were going.

"Let's go for a walk," my mom spoke sullenly. She was upset, and I wanted to ask her what was wrong, but I didn't know if she was in the mood to talk. So, without saying a word, we walked through the neighborhood. We walked for what seemed like a very long time without talking. Eventually, we came to a park, and we both sat on the short brick wall that bordered the playground. It wasn't until I heard her sniffle that I realized she was crying. I didn't know what to do. I had only seen her cry one or two times in my whole life.

"I have spent my whole life trying to make that woman happy." She choked back sobs as she spoke. "Your grandmother is someone you will never really know, Nyssa. Not like I know her." I was surprised that my mom was opening up to me in this way. I felt like this was a counseling session, and I was the counselor. My mom was sharing a part of herself that I knew she didn't share with many people. I put my arm around her shoulder, hoping to encourage her to talk more.

"Ever since I was a little girl, I can remember the frustration I felt just trying to make her proud of me. The aching I felt, because I knew that she never really cared for me.

I felt like such a bastard child." Her face turned bitter. I slowly slid my hand off her shoulder and back to my lap.

My mom looked at me, contemplating. "You know, maybe it was because she was jealous of the attention that Tata gave me. I was, after all, the only girl." She thought about her statement and smiled. "You understand what I mean, don't you?" She sighed with some relief, then spoke again, before I could answer her.

"Of course, you understand. You are way ahead of most kids your age. You know that, Nyssa? I must have done something right, to raise such a smart girl." This time, she put her arm around my shoulder. "It's just you and me, now. We can count on Grandma for some things, but most things should be kept between you and me. I can help you deal with Jay, but you can't tell your grandma. From now on, you won't be able to talk to her about anything that's on your mind. Understand? It's just you and me."

I felt like she was initiating me into some secret club. If it meant that my mom would open up to me and I could feel this closeness to her, then I would agree to almost anything. She was really the only person in the world that I felt really understood me.

"Yes, Momma. I really do understand."

"Good." She took a deep breath. "Wow. I feel really good right now. Don't you?" She glowed with energy and her eyes sparkled, like a child. "Let's go play. Want to?"

I giggled and nodded my head. She jumped down from the brick wall and put her hand out for me to balance on. I took her hand and also jumped from the wall. We stood facing each other, smiling and laughing. I was so happy. It was a wonderful feeling to know where I belonged in the world. I belonged with my mom.

She pulled back from me slowly and looked towards the playground. "I bet," she paused, then continued, "that I could beat you to the swings!" She bolted from me, as soon as she finished her sentence. I ran after her, feeling like I was flying. No one in the world felt like that. I had to be the happiest I had ever been in my life. It was just my mom and me, running through the park together. It was the two of us, swinging so high that we almost touched the clouds. It would be just the two of us—until she met Tom.

Dark Secret

MOM'S NEW PROJECT

Thomas Suleski. He was a tall man, at six feet and two inches tall. He especially looked like a tree when standing next to my mom, who was only five foot two inches tall (or short, depending on how you look at it). He was one of the instructors at the technical school my mom was attending, called ITT Tech. I had seen the commercials for the school during my afterschool cartoons and thought it was very cool that my mom's school was on TV. This guy, Tom, was supposedly some kind of math wizard and very into new age things, like my mom. This was how he was explained to me, right before I met him the first time.

Because I was used to the many different types of men my mom would date, I was never really surprised by the wide array of personalities she brought home. She would date cowboys to businessmen, and some in between. However, Tom was definitely a new character for my mom. When he showed up to have dinner with me and my grandparents, we were shocked by his appearance. He looked like a dirty hippie. He had long hair that was pulled back into a ponytail. He was wearing a headband around his head. His jeans were old and dingy and his t-shirt had stains on it. His tennis shoes looked like he had owned them since he was a kid. I could not believe that my mom actually wanted us to hang out with this person.

Tom and I sat down in the TV room after dinner and I knew what he was going to say to me. Most of the guys my mom brought home approached me with this speech; I'm not stealing your mom from you, I really care about your mom. I hope we can be friends, etc. I was curious about how this hippie would word his speech, though.

"First of all, let me just tell you, I am so amazed at how mature you are for your age." So far, his speech was okay. I was kind of flattered. "When I was watching you and your mom talk to each other—it was like you were friends or something. Whoa, it was really blowing my mind."

Now, I was beginning to feel a little awkward. "Cause, like I have two daughters, and one of them is almost the same age as you. But like, I would never be able to converse with her like you guys did. That was so cool." I was squirming in my seat and wondering if my mom knew just how weird this guy really was. "But, like I wanted you to know that I really care about your mom, and I can see how much you mean to her, and vice versa. So, like I have no intention of trying to come between the really cool relationship you have. Your mom and I are just on the same wavelength. Ya know?" He paused for a moment, and then finalized the conversation with, "Yeah."

For some reason, I almost lost control of myself and laughed right in his face. But instead, I took a deep breath and answered,

"Okay." I just wanted the conversation to be over, so I could let out this huge bundle of giggles I was containing inside my body.

This guy was too weird.

"Cool." Tom sighed. "Well, I guess I better get going. It was really cool meeting you. Next time, we should all go and hang out together. Sound cool?"

"Sure." Was he ever going to leave? I felt like I was going to explode. I was really trying not to laugh right in his face. "It was nice meeting you, too." I added politely.

Tom walked through the dining room to say goodbye to my grandparents, on his way to the door. Then, he and my mom went out to the porch to say goodbye to each other. I waited until my mom returned, and then burst out laughing. I lay down on the couch and laughed so hard, my stomach hurt. My mom came over and joined me on the couch, laughing a little as well.

"He's a character. Huh?" She giggled. "So, what exactly did he say to you?" she asked.

I breathed deeply to calm myself and then told her everything he had said. I imitated him completely, even down to all the "likes" and "cools" that he said. When I got to his last comment about their common wavelength, my mom burst out laughing. We both continued to laugh, until we had tears in our eyes. When we both stopped, we were laying on the couch, exhausted.

"Well, I thought he was a very nice man." My grandma had silently watched our little laughing fit. Now, she apparently wanted to put in her own opinion. "He was a little on the scruffy side, but that can easily be fixed. He just needs a woman to clean him up a bit. He definitely has potential." I thought that my grandma could not have been talking about the same person. My mom and I began laughing hysterically again, and my grandmother left in a huff. We had offended her by laughing at her serious opinion. Grandma quietly turned and walked upstairs to her room for the night.

Once my mom caught her breath again, a more serious look came over her face. "You know, your grandma is right. I hate to say that—you really know I do—but, she's right." I didn't understand what my mom was getting at. Was she seriously going to date this man who was stuck in some kind of demented time warp?
My mom sat down close to me. I could see that she was preparing for a "serious talk." I didn't really mind, because lately we had been getting along really well. Every time we had a serious discussion, I felt like I was walking away a stronger, smarter, and more mature person. More like my mom.

"Now, I know that Tom may seem kind of dorky or something. But the truth is, I think I want to give him more of a chance to prove himself to me. He's got a really good job, and he makes pretty good money. Also, believe it or not, he's actually really smart. You just have to get to know him to see that side of him." She smiled at me, and it seemed like she was thinking about my first impression of this man. "Trust me, he's not really as much of a nerd as he seems. Okay?" She stared at me, awaiting my approval.

"If he makes you happy, Momma." I really did just want her to be happy. I also really didn't think that this guy would be around for very long. Once my mom got over whatever weird 60s phase she was going through, he would be gone, and my mom and I would move on together.

My mom hugged me tight, "Tomorrow, we're going out to dinner with him. Oh, and next week we're going to be helping him move into his apartment. It's practically around the corner from here." I nodded and smiled. Yeah, okay— whatever. At least this guy would be a good laugh, for a little while.

The next week, we ended up eating pizza at Tom's new apartment, while my mom told him where he should put his few pieces of furniture. Apparently, his first wife had taken most of their furniture and other belongings after they divorced. His two daughters also lived with her. When he began to tell me about his first wife, I began to feel sorry for him and a little ashamed that I had made fun of him so badly.

"My ex-wife is Korean. I met her while I was stationed in Korea. Did your mom tell you that I was in the army?" I wondered if his odd behavior could be attributed to his time served in the military. Didn't the government test medicine on them or something? In any case, my opinion of Tom got significantly better once he told me this bit of information about himself. I had relatives who served in the military and had great respect for them. I guessed Tom should be included, as well.

"Tom, tell her how you met Kang, or Kim, or whatever her name is." My mom shouted from down the hall, where she was rummaging through some of his boxes in his bedroom. I knew she was trying to give Tom and me some time to get to know each other and had purposely left us in the kitchen to eat pizza and talk.

Tom smirked at her request. "That's my ex's name, it's Kim." Tom took a deep breath and sat back in his chair. He looked like he was getting ready to tell me a very long story. I wasn't sure if I had the patience to listen to him, when I thought about our last bizarre conversation at my grandma's house.

"So, I met my ex-wife while I was stationed in Korea. We got married pretty quickly after we met." He stopped talking and began eating pizza again. I was partially appreciative that it hadn't been a long story, but disappointed at how boring his explanation had been.

My mom walked into the kitchen, "Tom, you have to tell her how you actually met." She pulled up a chair and took a slice of pizza to eat next to us. She looked at me with wide eyes, "You are not going to believe this," she said. Then, because Tom was stalling and looking very uncomfortable, she reassured him, "I know she's only ten, but she's very mature for her age. Go ahead—tell her."

Tom still hesitated for a moment, and then added to his story,

"I pretty much ordered her out of a magazine. You see, they have these magazines out in some countries, where you can pick girls to come and be your girlfriend. Most of the time, these women want to get married to an American so they can become U.S. citizens. That's what my ex-wife wanted. She got her citizenship, then decided that she could do better than me." He shrugged his shoulders, as if to say "that's the way life goes," but I knew that last comment had to hurt.

My mom interrupted again. "Tell her what she put you through, before she finally left." My mom faced me again, "You just won't believe what this witch did." I turned to look at Tom and hear what he was going to tell me. I couldn't help but notice that he looked a little embarrassed about sharing this bit of information with me. I couldn't imagine what could be more embarrassing than ordering your wife out of a catalogue. I was fully drawn into his story and wanted to hear more.

"Well, she always threatened to leave me, after we were married and had our first daughter. She got worse every year, threatening to leave if I didn't earn more money and buy her fancy things. After she had our second daughter, she said she would take the girls and leave me, if I didn't earn more money. So, the only way I could provide the type of life she demanded was to work two, sometimes three jobs. The last few years that we were together, I was like a zombie— always tired and not really there, ya know? Everything was about money to her. Finally, she decided that I could not give her the lavish life that she deserved, so she did leave me."

Tom looked off and seemed like he was in another world for a moment. So, my mom jumped in and finished for him, "She still gets almost half of what Tom earns. She gets child support and spousal support. Can you believe that? She made his life hell and now she gets paid for it! Isn't that just great?" I could understand my mom's anger toward this woman. She sounded terrible. I felt sympathy for Tom and realized that he must actually be a pretty nice guy. He had tried so hard to make his first wife happy. His weirdness didn't seem like so much of an issue to me, at that moment.

My mom got up from the table and started walking back down the hall. "Well, I better finish up in here. Jeez, Tom— you don't have much stuff." She left that last comment in the kitchen with us, as she tried to work magic in Tom's bedroom with a few of his meager possessions.

Tom glanced around his new apartment, "Yeah, she's right. I really don't have much. Kim took almost everything after the divorce, even some of the things that I know she didn't like or want. She just didn't want me to have anything." I thought I saw tears forming in his eyes. But he blinked, and I wasn't sure if I had actually seen them. Tom looked at me with a real seriousness. "You know, I really am lucky I met your mom. I think she can really help me get my life back together."

I nodded. I wasn't sure what to think of this guy. He was nice, but he lacked a backbone. This made me think of how my dad was with Jay. Tom also seemed like a very confused person. My mom and I were just getting to a point in our relationship where we understood each other, and things were going smoothly. I didn't think a "confused" person would help our growth in any way. However, I knew there was nothing I could do with my concerns. I was just hitching a ride with my mom, and if she decided to take a ride from this guy, then I would have to follow.

After our first evening in Tom's new apartment, the relationship between Tom and my mom moved along quickly. It wasn't long before we had moved in with him. Since it was a small two-bedroom apartment, it was decided that, for a while, I would have one bedroom and Tom's girls would have the other bedroom when they visited. Eventually, all three of us "kids" would move into one bedroom, and Tom and my mom would occupy the second.

During this transition period, the adults would sleep on the futon that was used as a couch during the day in the living room. Although I was not comfortable with suddenly forming a new family, I wanted to please my mom. After all, she had made so many sacrifices for me. This was no time for ungrateful thoughts or actions. I made sure to present myself as being thoroughly excited about this new way of life. Always smiling and always happy. This is what would please my mom ... I thought.

Things were fairly awkward between Tom and me, as we tried to get to know each other and still include my mom in everything we did. I usually ended up feeling like a third wheel, while my mom poured much of her attention into Tom, and he continued to work to impress my mom. They tried to do activities with me, to secure a bond among the three of us. On the weekends, my mom would let me stay up very late with them and watch movies. Tom had a huge collection of old movies that were all on some kind of weird tape called a "beta" or something. This added to my feeling that he actually stepped into a time machine. It explained his appearance and the way he talked. Maybe he grabbed his collection of movies before closing the door and entering our time period.

I was not really enjoying my time "bonding" with my mom's giant hippie boyfriend, but I put on a happy face for her. I really didn't have much respect for him, as I continued to see more of his weirdness and lack of masculine traits. My mom had found a man to be her lump of clay. I wondered how she would form him and for what purpose. I didn't have to wait long to see her more intense methods.

Late one Saturday night, my mom had gotten a sweet tooth and also needed more cigarettes. We spent most of the day and night watching Tom's old movies. Although I was very tired, I thought it would be fun to go out so late at night. The nearest place that was open at the time of night was the 7- 11 up the street. So, the three of us piled into my grandpa's old van (that he had recently given to my mom) and headed to the store for a late-night snack.

When we pulled up to the store, there were a few cars already parked in the lot. I could see inside the store, there were about a dozen teenage to college-age people buying various items.

We pulled alongside a VW Beetle with two girls sitting inside. As the three of us got out of the van, I noticed the sunroof of the Beetle was open. I glanced down into the car, as I was climbing out of the side of the van. The two girls looked like older high schoolers or possibly young college girls. They were both heavily made up and wearing brightly colored little dresses.
My mom was finishing a cigarette and told Tom and I to wait while she smoked the rest of it. She stood by the passenger door of the van and took her last few drags. One of the girls in the Beetle either sneezed or coughed, which upset my mom. I wasn't sure if the girl had done that to intentionally make reference to my mom smoking, but my mom obviously thought she had done it for that purpose. Mom walked passed the open roof of the little VW and flicked her cigarette into the car, while it was still lit.

There was shrieking and screaming in the car, as the three of us headed toward the store. My mom was laughing, while Tom and I exchanged nervous smiles.

"You bitch!" someone yelled from behind us. We all spun around to see the two girls glaring at my mom from inside their car. "Are you f***ing crazy?" one of them yelled out her window.

Before I had time to process what was happening, my mom had run over to the car and reached down into the sunroof. She was pulling on both girls' hair and dresses and just about anything else she could get her hands on. While she was pulling and punching, she was also screaming, "What did you call me? Huh! You wanna say that to my face?"

Tom and I ran over near the car, but unsure of what to do and still in shock, we just stood there. One of the girls was somehow able to get out of my mom's grasp and exit the car. Once she stepped out of the car, I could see that she was taller and a little thicker than my mom. She pushed my mom and they began to claw at each other.

The second girl got out of the car a little slower and seemed like she was still in shock. After a moment, she regained her senses and began yelling her friends name and telling her to "Kick that lady's ass."

By this time, the small group of people who had been shopping inside the store was now standing in the parking lot. Some seemed unsure of what to do, while some seemed entertained by the fighting. One guy came out of the store and announced, "Hey, the manager just called the cops." Then, he hurriedly walked to his car. The parking lot seemed to clear out quickly after that.

The shock of the situation was wearing off, and I was getting scared. I noticed that the bigger girl was getting more slaps and punches on my mom. But my mom wouldn't back down. I frantically asked Tom, "Can't you do something?" I thought we should probably leave before the cops showed up, as well. My mom was the one who started this fight, and I didn't want her to get into trouble.

Tom looked at me, puzzled. Then, he turned toward my mom and her fighting partner and said, "Now, you girls stop that." He wagged his finger at them, like a mother scolding her children. "I said, you better stop right now," he half- heartedly told them.

My mom and the other girl were in their own little world and didn't hear a thing Tom said. They didn't even notice the patrol car pull into the lot, until it briefly sounded its siren. Finally, the two women broke apart. They must have realized that they had more important things to worry about than pounding each other. My mom walked over to Tom and me, and the three of us stood by the front of the store.

Two cops came out of the police car. One was a woman and the other was a man. The woman walked over to the two teenagers, while the man came over to us. We could hear the girl that was fighting my mom yelling at the police officer. She was hysterically explaining that my mom was crazy and had jumped on her for no reason. Her friend was eagerly nodding her head to support her friend's story. I heard the female officer tell the girls to "stay put" and she began to walk over to us. The male officer had been waiting for my mom to catch her breath and calm down before asking her side of things. With both officers standing in front of us, I suddenly became very scared that my mom would be arrested and began to cry. The woman cop was instantly at my side.

"Everything is going to be alright." She put her hand on my shoulder. "We're just here to find out what happened and help. Okay?" She glanced around and asked my mom, "Did you drive here?" My mom pointed at the van. The cop asked, "Would it be alright if she sat in the vehicle, while we figure out what happened?"

My mom nodded. The lady led me over to the van and shooed the two teenagers to the other side, so they wouldn't be right next to me.

She smiled and said, "I'll be right back. I just want to check on your mom. Okay?" I nodded and wiped my tears. She gave me one last concerned look, and then walked back over to my mom and Tom.

I glanced over at the two girls, just to make sure they weren't too close to the van. They were leaning on the other side of their car and talking animatedly. I couldn't hear what they were saying, but I could hear voices coming from somewhere. I turned around and saw that the window on the side of the van was slightly cracked open. It was the side of the van that was closest to where my mom and Tom were being questioned by the two officers. I could hear everything that was being said. I strained to hear what my mom was telling the cops about the event that had taken place.

My mom's voice was shaking as she spoke, "I don't know what happened. I was just walking past their car and one of them said something about not liking the way I looked. Then one of them attacked me." My mom sniffled as she spoke. "There were a bunch of their friends all around us, but they left when they heard you guys were coming." I was amazed at how scared she sounded and how quickly she had come up with this phony story. I heard Tom agree with her. Then, I heard the lady cop ask if it was okay that she came back to check on me and ask me some questions. My mom agreed, but told her, "I don't know if she saw much. She was running into the store when it all happened." The cop said, "Okay," and walked around the van to where I was sitting.

"Hey, how are you feeling?" she asked, as she sat on the footstep on the van. I smiled and nodded my head to indicate that I was feeling better. She then leaned closer to me and asked, "Did you see anything that happened between your mom and that girl over there?" She pointed to the bigger girl. I nodded. She asked, "I mean, before they were fighting," she clarified. I nodded. Then, I told her exactly what I had heard my mom tell her minutes before.

When I was done, she said, "Thank you so much. You have been very helpful." She looked around the van to her partner and motioned toward the two girls. She said to me, "I'm going to let your parents come over and sit with you, while we talk to those girls. Okay?" I nodded, again. She motioned for my mom and Tom to come over and then met her partner over by the two girls.

As soon as my mom could, she asked, "What did you say?"

I explained (quietly, so the officers wouldn't hear) about the window being cracked open and how I heard everything they said. Then, I explained that I just repeated the same story. My mom hugged me and kissed me. She whispered, "You're the best, Nyssa," in my ear. We sat hugging each other for a while, until the sound of arguing and raised voices caused us to pull apart and look toward the girls and the cops. Both the girls were yelling and seemed very agitated.

"This is bull****!" the heavier girl yelled. Then she pointed at my mom and screamed, "She's the one you should arrest! She's f***ing crazy!" She looked like she had come to the end of her rope and was about to lose it. The male officer said something to her that calmed her down a little. I thought it might have been a warning or a threat. The woman cop walked back over to us. She explained that since we all had corroborating statements, they had concluded the two girls were at fault. They were ready to arrest the girls, if my mom wanted to press charges.

"Oh, I am so tired from everything. I don't want to ruin their lives; I just want them to learn their lesson. Do they seem scared about getting into trouble?" The female officer said it seemed like they were. Mom sighed, "Well, I guess that's good enough. I just want to go home now." The officer remarked at how nice my mom was and how brave she thought I had been. Then, the police detained the two girls, until we had left the parking lot. It was over.

All the way home, mom was laughing and smirking about the whole incident. She praised me for being so resourceful and not caving under pressure. She told me that she loved me very much. She laughed at the "stupid" teenage girls and how lucky they were that she didn't press charges. Although I didn't understand how they would have gone to jail, when they hadn't started the fight. It was all still confusing to me.

Once we were in the apartment, Mom suddenly turned to Tom and asked, "Hey, why didn't you help me out?" She looked puzzled. Then her eyes squinted, and she began to look angry. "Why didn't you pull that huge tramp off of me?" she asked him, with some ferocity in her voice. She stood in front of him, with her hands on her hips, awaiting his answer. Instead of an answer, he looked at the ground and shuffled his feet. He looked incredibly nervous. I felt bad for him, so I offered the first thing I could think of on his behalf, "Well, Momma. Tom did say something when you two were fighting," I told her.

Mom turned towards me, "Oh, really? What did he say?" she asked.

I started, "Well, he said..." I thought carefully about what I was going to say. I wanted to show her exactly what he had said. I wagged a pointed finger at my mom and said, "Now you girls stop that." Then I realized what I had done. In trying to help him, I had sealed his fate.

My mom turned and glared at Tom. She took a couple of steps forward, so she was toe to toe with him. She had to tilt her head upwards, so she could look at him. She spoke slowly, "Tom, I want you to take your glasses off." She spoke as if she was concentrating on her keeping her voice low and calm.

When Tom tried to speak, my mom cut him off by repeating her order louder. "Damn it, Tom! I said take your glasses off, now!" she screamed at him. Tom instantly flung his glasses off. He was undoubtedly shaken up by my mom's behavior that night. He had not seen that side of her, and it apparently scared the crap out of him.

"Now you better hold real still, Tom. I want you to feel what I was feeling when you were standing there like a little wuss, instead of helping me." As my mom was speaking, her hands were balling up into fists by her side. Tom tried to say something again, but it was too late. My mom shut him up by punching him in the face. It made a loud smacking sound, and I thought it had landed somewhere by his eye. He stumbled a little. Before he could react, my mom landed another blow. The second time was harder, and I definitely saw it land near his left eye. He put his hand up in a defensive position. He was going to block the third strike. But there was none. Mom had made her point and wasn't about to expend too much energy. It had been a tiring night for her.

Mom smiled scornfully, "The next time you see me in need of help, you better stop acting like a little girl and help me." She thought about what she said, then added, "Wait, that's an insult to Nyssa. She handled herself perfectly well for a little girl. I mean, you better not act like a wuss around me anymore. Got it?" she asked. He nodded, sheepishly. She sent him to the other bedroom, and she and I hung out in the living room until I wanted to go to sleep.

My mom tucked me in with hugs, kisses, and praises for how I had handled the night's events. Once she was gone, I reflected on those events. What happened? Did I really see my mom fist fighting with some teenagers? Why didn't those police officers know that we were lying? Weren't they supposed to know things like that? Was my mom actually able to beat up a grown man? Did any of that really happen? The whole situation seemed so surreal. I reasoned I may have imagined some of it or possibly all of it. I was, after all, extremely tired.

I yawned and rolled over in my bed, too exhausted to think anymore. Yet, one last thing still bothered me. That thing was – Cops could be tricked. That was unsettling to me. It was also something that would come into play many more times in the next few years.

Dark Secret

MOM'S LESSONS ARE HARD TO LEARN

The Suleski-Najera family was not off to an easy start. Tom's girls seemed to be carrying a lot of emotional baggage or something from the sudden change of their home life and separation from their mother. Although I couldn't imagine why they would miss the dysfunction of their previous home, I figured they didn't know any better. Eventually, I was sure they would see that my mom was much better. Eventually ...

My hope began to diminish as the events of the first morning repeated itself, again and again. Every single morning Alex would be sitting on the toilet, and Dawn would be crying. We had to wake up extra early, just to make it to our different locations on time. My mom tried to talk to Alex about why she wanted to sit on the toilet so much, but Alex wouldn't talk. My mom also tried to talk to Dawn about why she was crying, but this would only be answered by more crying. It was about a week and half into this ordeal when my mom began to crack. She was pulling Alex off the toilet and pushing her where she wanted her to go. Mom pushed her into the bedroom, when she wanted her to get dressed. She pushed Alex into the living room, when she wanted the bathroom to be free for others in the apartment. Her pushing seemed to work, although Alex cried sometimes. Alex hadn't really had a problem with crying, until then.

As for Dawn, my mom had resorted to standing her on a chair, facing the bathroom mirror and making her stare at herself as she cried. She would tell Dawn to look at her reflection and say, "Look at the ugly faces you make when you're crying. Do you think it's fair that the rest of us have to look at you when you're crying and crying?" At first, Dawn would cry harder, then she would eventually stop. When she quieted down, my mom would let her come down from the chair and rejoin us.

I thought my mom was tough, but fair. The girls just needed a little extra discipline that I knew my mom was capable of. Soon, I felt they would be at the level I was at and not need my mom breathing down their necks. They just needed a little time to adjust.

After a few weeks, Tom showed up to pick me up from school. This was unusual, because he was always working too late to pick me up. I was used to seeing my mom after school but said nothing as I quickly climbed into his car. I was still embarrassed to be seen with a hippie-looking man and glanced around quickly as I slumped into my seat. I saw that Dawn was the only other person in the car and was even more confused. When my mom came to pick me up, she usually had Alex and Dawn in the car with her, since Dawn got out of school earlier than me, and Alex's daycare was practically next door to Dawn's school.

As I looked around the car, trying to guess the circumstances of this new schedule, Tom explained, "Um, your mom and Alex are at the apartment. I guess the daycare isn't going to take Alex anymore, because she has a problem wetting herself or staying in the bathroom or something like that. Anyways, the daycare called your mom, and she had to leave school to go and pick her up." Tom sighed and turned to look at me in the back seat. "I guess I should warn you that your mom isn't in a very good mood. She missed a very important test, because she had to leave in the beginning of her class."

I knew what that warning meant. I would need to be extra careful about how I acted and what I said to my mom. Anything could set her off. I couldn't help but be a little upset with Alex. I kept thinking about how happy my mom was before the girls came. I was grateful that Dawn seemed to get with "Mom's program" fairly quickly, but what was Alex's problem? I felt a little closer with Dawn, also, because we had been spending a little time together. I had actually taken her for a walk around the neighborhood, and she had been able to talk more normally with my mom and me, in the last week. I just wished Alex would stop being difficult and do as my mom said. How hard could that be?

When we got back to the apartment, everything was dark. At first, I thought my mom and Alex weren't home. But then I heard a voice say, "Tom, you better do something about your daughter." I recognized my mom's voice and struggled to quickly adjust my eyes to the dark. "I will not have her ruining my schooling," she continued to talk, and I squinted to see where she was. "I can't miss another class, or I'll be too far behind." Finally, I saw the silhouette of my mom laying on the futon against the living room wall. She was lying on her back, staring up at the ceiling. She did this sometimes when she was trying to calm herself. She meditated or did some kind of deep breathing technique that helped her not to explode. She called it "centering herself."

"Okay," Tom answered. "I'll go take care of it right now.

Where is she?" he asked.

My mom continued to stare at the ceiling. "She's in the kitchen. I made her stand in the corner, to think about what she did."

Mom took a deep breath and said, "You know Tom, we can't help her unless she stops being so stubborn. She knows when she has to pee, but she would rather just sit on the toilet all day or use the bathroom on herself than tell someone she has to go." She took another deep breath. She called them her "cleansing" breaths.

Tom was walking to the kitchen and answered her on his way, "Yes, I know. Her mom always babied her too much, and now she doesn't want to do anything." He turned into the kitchen, and we couldn't see him anymore. Dawn and I stood by the front door, neither of us knowing what to do. We were still standing by the door, when Tom pulled Alex over to the kitchen table, and we could see them both. Mom was still in her own world, with her deep breathing and meditating. Dawn and I stood and watched Tom address Alex. He did the same finger wag that I had seen him use with my mom that night at 7-11.

"Young lady, you can't pee on yourself anymore. You can only pee in the toilet. Okay?" Tom asked.

Alex didn't respond. She stared at him, with her huge and quiet eyes. I really didn't think she understood what Tom said to her. I wondered how much English she actually knew.

From the living room futon came a slow chuckle that grew and grew. My mom slowly sat up and laughed with her head in her hands. "Oh, Tom," she paused to laugh some more. "What the hell was that?" She stood up and walked over to the kitchen table. "You can't pee-pee on yourself." She bent over with one hand on her hip and the other hand wagging a limp pointed finger. "You go pee-pee in the toilet." She was mocking him terribly and laughing at him, as well. "Oh, please Tom. She's not going to take you seriously. I mean, look at her. She's trying not to laugh at you." She pointed at Alex. To me, it seemed like Alex was trying not to cry, but maybe I couldn't see what my mom was seeing from up close.

Tom nodded, and tried again, "Young lady, this is not a joke. The next time you have to pee, and you don't tell someone..." Tom seemed at a loss to finish his sentence.

By this time, I could see that my mom was fed up.

She huffed and sat in one of the chairs. Then, she turned to Alex and said, "Look, if you pull your peeing on yourself routine one more time, then you will get spanked. If you do it again, then you'll get spanked two times and then three. Got it?" Mom bent close to Alex, "You are not a baby. Your mom may have treated you like one, but you are not one. Understand?" My mom put her face very close to Alex's face, and the little girl nodded slightly. Mom sat back in her chair and continued, "Maybe next time you piss on yourself, you'll get hit with a belt. That's what happened to Nyssa, where she used to live." She pointed over at me, still standing by the door. "You should be grateful that you never had to live with Nyssa's dad's girlfriend. Doesn't that sound terrible? To get hit with a belt?" Alex nodded, very slightly again.

Mom nodded back, "Good. Go on," she shooed at Alex, "Get out of my sight." Mom turned around and rested her elbows on the table. Alex still stood there, looking at the floor. She seemed unsure what she was supposed to do.

Tom spoke to her, "Alex, go to your room." Alex turned and walked to her room.

"Jesus, Tom," Mom was angry, but was too tired to raise hell. "You can't just tell her what she's supposed to do all the time. That's why she's so stubborn. She always has someone telling her what to do, and she never has to think for herself. She's not a baby or some little robot." Mom put her head down on the table. "Tom, make yourself useful and make me some tea." Tom got up immediately and started some water heating in the kettle. Mom looked over at Dawn and me, "Come over here, you two."

Dawn and I hesitated, then slowly made our way over to the table. Mom made a gesture for us to sit, so we did. She looked so tired. "Look," she spoke softly, "I know it's not your fault all this happening. You two are the good children. Don't forget that, okay?" She smiled at us, and then nodded for us to agree.

We did. "Yeah," Mom seemed happier and more at ease, "we should order some pizza tonight. Maybe Hawaiian?" She smiled at Dawn and me nodding so strongly. She knew that Hawaiian pizza was our favorite. Then, Mom added, "But, we won't let Alex have any. She can sit and watch us." Mom's eyes seemed kind of dazed. She looked like she was imagining Alex's unhappiness at not being able to eat pizza with us. She smiled mischievously, "Yeah, that'll teach her. If she wants to be a part of this family, she had better start acting like a normal kid." Satisfied with her plan, she sat back and sipped her tea.

That night, Alex had a peanut butter sandwich while we ate pizza. The next few days, my mom reminded her constantly about peeing in the toilet and getting spanked if she didn't. I lost track of how her progress was going, as Dawn and I spent any extra time that we were not in school playing outside together.

But, a few days later, Tom showed up again to pick me up from school. As soon as I got into his old and enormous car, (the kids at my school called it the big banana boat), Tom turned around to look at me. Next to me, Dawn was quiet and nervous.

"I'll make this brief," Tom sighed and began, "Your mom had to leave school and go pick up Alex from daycare again, because she wet herself. We think that your mom has been kicked out of school, because she has used up all her allowed absences. And..." Tom sighed again, "Your mom is not very happy, to say the least."

Tom looked at me, pleadingly, "Maybe you can calm her down. You know your mom so well." He smiled at me, hopeful.

"I'll try," I answered, although I didn't think there was anything I could do. I had seen my mom's anger towards Alex growing steadily since she arrived. She was oblivious to my mom's rules and what was expected from her. Either that or she didn't seem to care. I wasn't sure, but I knew that Alex was going to ruin things for all of us if she didn't start fixing herself. I felt sick as we drove home. I wasn't sure if I would even be able to save myself from the overflow of my mom's anger.

Even as I wished for time to slow down and for the car ride to last forever, it did end, and we did arrive at the dreaded apartment.

The three of us slowly walked up the stairs. Tom entered first, then me, then Dawn. I think I saw Alex before Dawn even entered the apartment. I stood in shock at the front door. I heard Dawn gasp behind me, as she finally entered our home. The three of us stood at the entrance and gaped at what we saw.

Alex's skinny and extremely frail-looking body was naked.

She was standing at the entrance to the kitchen, but she was facing the wall. The disturbing scene of her standing naked was mild compared to what could be seen after our eyes adjusted to the dimness of the room. Her back had long red stripes running all over it. Some of the streaks were an angry red and moist looking. I couldn't understand what my mom had been doing to her.

It seemed like an eternity before my mom came out from behind the back of the kitchen. She looked tired and a bit crazed. It reminded me of a movie I had seen where a lady was coming down from some incredible drug high or an extreme excitement that was just wearing off. After she saw us, she seemed to become excited again, "Close that door!" she screamed at us. Tom swung around immediately and flung the door shut. The three of us had been in such shock, we had completely forgotten about the door being wide open behind us.

"What the hell are you staring at?" my mom screamed at us.

She stood in a stance that suggested that she was ready to fight one of us. Her feet were firmly planted on the floor, and her arms hung strongly by her side. Her fists were clenched so tightly that I thought she would make herself bleed.

I mumbled, "Nothing, Momma," and walked straight back to my room. Soon after that I heard Dawn's door close, and I knew that she had made it out safely. That just left Tom still in my mom's grasp. I found that I wasn't really concerned about him. I didn't think anyone really deserved what my mom was capable of dishing out that day, but part of me blamed him for my mom's actions.

Before we met Tom, my mom had stopped having meltdowns like the one she was apparently having in the kitchen with Alex. My mom and I had been getting along better than we had my entire life. All that began to change once we met Tom. As far as I was concerned, he could deal with whatever my mom wanted to do to him.

I stayed in my room and listened to my radio (I made sure that it was barely audible, so I didn't disturb my mom) and worked on my homework. After a few hours, I began to feel hungry and knew that it had to be close to dinnertime. I sat on my bed and listened to my stomach growl. I thought to myself, "It doesn't matter how hungry

I get, starving to death had to be better than having to face my mom right now." So, I read some more of my schoolbook. I changed the dial on my radio and listened to all the different stations that I would have normally never cared about. I opened the window in my room and watched cars pass on our street. I did everything to make the time pass, and not think about my hunger.

Just when I had convinced myself that we were not going to be eating dinner that night, there was a soft knock on my door. Since the knock did not have much force behind it, I guessed it was probably Dawn. I couldn't believe that she would risk being seen by my mom, just to come and talk to me. "Come in," I whispered, just loud enough to be heard outside the door.

My mom's head slowly poked itself around my door. She had a small smile on her face and asked, "Aren't you hungry?" She opened the door and walked over to my bed. She sat down next to me and motioned for Dawn to come inside and sit down with us. I guessed that my mom had retrieved Dawn from her room, while on the way to mine. Neither of us knew what my mom would say or do next.

I answered my mom's question in the most neutral and polite way I could think of, "I'm a little hungry, Momma. But I could skip dinner, if you don't feel like cooking." My mom looked at Dawn and me, as Dawn nodded her head in agreement.

Mom put her arm around me and leaned over to hold Dawn's hand. "You two know that I'm not mad at you. Right? You girls have really done your best to behave." She smiled warmly at us. Then, she looked off to the kitchen and her smiled disappeared.

"Alex is the only one with a problem." She glared down the hall for a minute and seemed unaware of her surroundings, as she thought of Alex. Then, she snapped back to her current place and smiled once more. "Would you two like to learn how to cook?" she asked Dawn and me.

We both nodded and smiled, neither one of us wanting to ruin this moment of relief we both felt. We would have agreed to anything to make my mom happy. As we followed her down the hall to the kitchen, we could see Alex still standing with her back toward us. Only now, she had her underwear on. Her back still looked a bright red and as we passed her, I realized why her back had looked wet or moist to me from across the room.

I could see now that she had been bleeding and in some place on her back, the blood was slowly dripping down. The red stripes I had noticed earlier actually seemed to rise up from the skin on her back. In one area, the blood was actually streaked, like someone had tried to wipe her once, but gave up and let her bleed instead. She stood facing the wall and her tiny body shivered. I wasn't sure if she was cold, scared or so exhausted from her day's events that she could barely stand without shaking.

I walked past her and struggled to keep my composure. My heart was racing, and I fought to keep my breathing under control. I did not want my mom to wonder if I disagreed with her method of punishment. As Dawn and I entered the kitchen and faced the stove (awaiting our instructions), I saw Dawn for the first time since Alex had come into view. I could see that she was struggling greatly with what she had seen of her sister. I looked intently at her and silently tried to get her attention before my mom finished getting the pans and ingredients for dinner. I waved my hands and desperately tried to get her to stop staring at her suffering little sister, but Dawn's eyes wouldn't budge. She seemed in a trance and unable to peel her eyes away from a scene that she had, no doubt, never witnessed in her life.

At one point, my mom completely turned her back on us and bent into a lower cabinet. I took a silent step to Dawn. It was just enough to reach out and touch her. I tugged on her shoulder and pointed toward my mom. Then, I put my fingers to my lips, begging her to keep quiet and regain her composure. Dawn looked at my mom standing up and seemed to realize where she was, once again.

She quickly wiped the tears from her eyes and stood up and straight as she could. As we watched my mom assemble some of the ingredients around the stove, I could see Dawn having some kind of internal struggle. Her eyes squinted, as she fought back tears and her mouth pursed tightly, as she tried not to let her sobs out. I really thought that she was about to lose it, when my mom spun around and asked, "Are you two ready?"

Luckily, one of my mom's passions was cooking and she didn't seem to notice Dawn's awkward behavior. She was completely immersed in watching what she was cooking and telling us, step by step, how to make hamburgers. She positioned herself so that we could see what she was doing and periodically glanced back at us, to make sure that we were watching. When she turned around to pour her "secret" teriyaki flavor to the hamburger meat, I sidestepped over. In my new position, I could no longer see Alex. I motioned for Dawn to move closer to where I was, and she did.

Soon, the two of us were able to be more involved in my mom's cooking lesson, without Alex's terrible distraction. Mom asked us to toast the buns and showed us how to clean the lettuce. Dawn's internal war seemed to be calmed, for the moment. Then, dinner was ready. But this meant that we would have to sit at the table to eat together. This would place us all right next to where Alex was standing.

"Tom! Get your ass in here!" Mom yelled down the hall.

Tom had been working on something in Dawn's room. I assumed it was grading papers for his class or something like that. Tom walked down the hall and sat down at the table, as Dawn and I finished setting the plates and silverware.

Mom spoke to Dawn and me, "You two can grab your plates and serve yourselves." Dawn and I did just what she said. When we walked back to the table, I quickly took the seat that was in the position where Alex could easily be seen. The only other chair was the one that would place Dawn's back to her sister. I wished I could say that I did that just for Dawn's benefit, but I was covering my own butt as well. I knew that if either one of us upset mom, we could both be punished. I had to make sure that she didn't have to stare at her sister and lose control of herself. It seemed like the rules for survival.

Dawn and I silently began to eat, while my mom poured us each a glass of milk. She then served herself and sat down in her seat to eat. Tom stood up, and my mom shot a penetrating glare at him, "Just where do you think you're going? She asked menacingly.

Tom slowly sat back down in his seat and softly answered, "I was going to serve myself some dinner."

My mom smiled mischievously at him and said, "Oh, no you don't." Then, she took another bite of her hamburger.

Tom sat silently for a moment, trying to decipher what my mom meant by her comment. "Why not?" he finally asked.

Mom put down her hamburger and wiped her mouth. She finished chewing and then swallowed, finally looking at Tom, "Look at your daughter," she ordered. She pointed over at Alex, although we all knew what daughter she was referring to. "It's because of her that I can no longer go to school. It's because you don't have the balls to stand up to her and be a strong father figure, I have to be both a mother and father figure to her."

Mom was completely calm during her little speech. She picked up her hamburger and before taking another bite, added, "You can eat a shit sandwich for all I care. You just won't be eating any of our good cooking. Huh, girls?" she smiled over at us and took another bite of her burger.

Dawn and I smiled back at her, but neither us answered her.

She didn't seem to mind that we hadn't said anything. She was enjoying her food and seemed very satisfied with the discipline she had administered to Tom. The three of us finished our dinner, with Alex less than three feet away and Tom sitting at the table, neither of them eating.

When we were finished, Dawn and I both walked quietly to our rooms and got ready for bed. Once we had both turned in for the night, I sat awake in my bed and wondered where Alex would be sleeping. Would my mom feed her anything before she went to sleep? I knew that in her own room, Dawn was probably wondering the same things. Maybe she was even crying, like she did when she first came to live with us. Only this time, I knew what she would be crying about.

Dark Secret

WHEN DISCIPLINE ENDS AND TORTURE BEGINS

When I awoke the next morning, I saw that the sun was already up. Startled, I jumped out of bed and grabbed my alarm clock. Had we all overslept? Would Dawn and I be late for school? I saw that it was almost nine o'clock in the morning and sat baffled on the edge of my bed. That clock couldn't be right. My mom would have never let us sleep so late and miss school. After a few more seconds, I was fully awake and realized that it was actually Saturday.

Then, dread sunk in. I must have let wishful thinking overcome my usual amazing talent for keeping track of the weekends. I normally looked forward to days off from school. Dawn and I had made friends with some kids in the neighborhood and had fun playing outside with them. However, that morning all I could think about was having to face my mom and her unpredictable temper. I shuddered at thinking about having to see Alex again. Where had she slept? Had my mom given her more "discipline"? Did I really want to know? No, I didn't. And I didn't want to leave my room, either.

I sat in my room for almost an hour. I got up periodically to listen at my door. All I could hear was the sound of the TV in the living room. I wondered what Dawn was doing. I knew that she had to be even more terrified about leaving her room and facing my mom than even I was.

Eventually, having to use the restroom after sleeping through the night without a bathroom break was too much for me. I slowly cracked open the door, so I could peek down the hall. I could see half the TV lit up with Saturday morning cartoons. My mom liked to watch them, so I reasoned that she was sitting on the futon and facing the TV. This was good, because I could walk down the hall to the bathroom, without her seeing me. I just needed to be careful and quiet.

Slowly, I inched my bedroom door opened, hoping that it would not squeak and ruin my mission. I could hear the soft sound of the door moving over the carpet, so I slowed opening it even more. I could feel my heart pounding and little beads of sweat forming on my forehead. Finally, it was cracked wide enough for me to squeeze through and slide out of my bedroom. By then, my bladder felt like it was about to explode, so I decided to leave my door open instead of trying to close it. The opening was so small that I didn't think my mom would notice it from down the hall, anyways.

I looked down the hall and thought that the bathroom door looked much farther away than it had ever been before. I felt like I was about to lose control of my bladder and quickly, but quietly, stepped lightly across the hall and slid into the bathroom.

Luckily, the door was already open and all I had to do was close it. It closed quietly and I was finally able to use the bathroom.

When I was finished, I stood with my hand on the door handle of the bathroom. I contemplated my return trip to my bedroom. I had already felt exhausted from the secret operation to get to the toilet and was not looking forward to having to do it all again in reverse. I knew I shouldn't be wasting time thinking too much about it, because I needed to get back my room before my mom got up for anything.

I slowly turned the bathroom door handle and opened the door, with the same slow-motion technique I used on my bedroom door. Again, I felt like my heart was about to beat out of my chest. I briefly glanced down the hall and saw that everything looked as it had before I had entered the bathroom. I took several large and quiet steps to my bedroom and entered the same way I left. I slid my body through the crack, while keeping my face looking down the hall. I wanted to make sure that my mom wasn't going to stand up from the couch and see me (although I couldn't really see the futon from where I was). At least I would see her if she got up to change the channel or go to the kitchen.

As soon as I was completely in my room, I quietly closed the door. I rested my forehead against the door frame and took several deep breaths. I couldn't believe I had made it! I was so exhausted, but I also had the most amazing adrenaline rush. I had outsmarted my mom and I couldn't believe it! Maybe, I was getting to the point where I knew her better than she knew me. I felt like I had conquered a fear or an obstacle that allowed me to reach some new level.

"What are you doing?" a voice asked from behind me.

I spun around and came face to face with my mom. She was standing in front of my bed and had the most perplexed look on her face. "Are you okay?" she asked, with concern.

It took me a few seconds to realize that I was sweating, and I felt like I was having some kind of heart attack. My mom had scared the crap out of me. I couldn't believe that she had seen me enter the room like I did. What was she thinking and how could I explain my odd behavior? I had to come up with something quick. "Um," I paused, "I'm not feeling well," I finished. I thought that would explain my appearance and odd behavior better than anything else I could think of.

"Did you throw up or something?" Mom asked, looking a little worried.

"Yeah," I answered. So, she had heard me use the restroom. My secret mission was a failure. I should have known better than to try and outsmart my mom. Now, I would have to make sure she didn't suspect anything, and she continued to believe I was sick.

I knew she would be really upset if she knew that I had tried to hide anything from her. Even if it was just that I had to pee really bad.

Mom stepped toward me and felt my forehead. "Wow. You're sweating pretty bad. Come lay down on the couch. I'll get you some stuff to help you feel better." She walked into the bathroom, while I went to the living room and lay on the futon. I could see Alex out of the corner of my eye but focused my attention on the TV. I stared at the cartoons and struggled not to look in the direction of the kitchen where I would be forced to see Alex standing and suffering.

When my mom returned from the bathroom, she handed me a couple of antacids and a cold, wet rag for my head. "I hope it wasn't anything you ate," she wondered aloud, before she sat next to me and leaned back into her sleeping pillow that was still on the folded-up futon. I reasoned that she had put most of the sleeping blankets and other pillows away, when Tom had woken up to go into work that morning. She often woke up once he did, and I knew that sometimes he had to go in for a few hours on Saturday to input grades or something like that. Since I hadn't seen him that morning, it seemed like that was the logical conclusion. Either that or my mom had thrown him out. With Alex still standing in the same corner she had been the night before, I knew my mom was capable of throwing Tom out on his butt in the middle of the night.

While I sat on the futon with my mom, pondering the whereabouts of Tom, I continued to fix my eyes on the TV to act like I was watching cartoons with her. I was hungry, but too scared to say anything. I needed to keep up the story that I was sick that morning. I began to wonder what Dawn was doing in her room, to amuse herself for so long—when my mom said, "I am so hungry. Are you able to eat, yet?"

I took a deep breath to say something, but she cut me off, "I guess I better wake Dawn up. I can't believe she's still sleeping."
Mom stood up and was gone down the hall to Dawn's room. Soon, Dawn was sitting on the futon next to me. Mom was in the kitchen making breakfast for the three of us (minus Alex). I leaned over towards Dawn, once my mom had disappeared into the back of the kitchen. "So, what were you doing in your room for so long?" I asked her. "I just laid in my bed, most of the time," she whispered, "I also looked out the window and saw Nicole and Mickey playing outside." These were two of our new friends from the neighborhood.

I was betting that they were wondering where Dawn and I were. I worried that they would come to the apartment looking for us. Mom was just too unpredictable, and Alex could be easily seen from the door. I prayed they wouldn't come looking for us. I was going to ask Dawn what Nicole and Mickey had been doing, when I noticed the expression on her face. She was staring at her sister in a daze.

She looked like she was trying to understand what was happening to her little sister. A look of confusion, fear, and heartache enveloped her face. I had to make sure that she wouldn't start crying. I looked around quickly, searching for something to give me a plan of action.

I was still faking an illness. Mom was still in the kitchen. Dawn couldn't tear her eyes away from her sister. What was I supposed to do? Dawn was getting closer and closer to losing it. I had to do something.

"Dawn, let's go help my mom cook. Okay? We had fun helping her last night. Remember?" I asked her. Then, I pleaded, "Please ... remember?" I watched her closely, until eyes slowly peeled away from Alex, and she focused on me.

Quietly, she answered, "Yeah. That was pretty neat." She slowly nodded, and I could see that she really was remembering.

"Okay," she smiled a little, and we both got up to go to the kitchen.

We both walked past Alex and neither of us looked at her. We couldn't have kept our wits if we had looked at her up close like that.

And if she had turned and looked at us, well, who knows what would have happened. I know Dawn would have broken down for sure, and I probably wouldn't have been able to handle that either. I was grateful that I had not met her eyes since this episode had started the day before.

Dawn and I walked into the kitchen, and my mom seemed surprised to see me up and about. "Feeling better?" she asked.

"Yes, Momma. I am feeling a little better. Dawn and I just wanted to know if you needed any help. You know, like you did yesterday?" I wanted to turn the topic away from my fake illness. It wasn't safe to lie any more than was necessary to save myself. The longer I tried to stretch out this "sickness," the more chance I had that she would find out I made it up. That thought made me look back at Alex for a moment. There was no way I wanted to upset my mom at that point.

Mom's face brightened, and she overenthusiastically remarked, "Well, isn't that nice? Of course, you can help me." Then, she leaned over, so she could see Alex and said more loudly, "What nice young ladies the two of you are. You make me so proud. Not like some little brats I know." Her last sentence had a nasty sting to it. She seemed to shoot those words straight at Alex. At that point, Alex had turned her face slightly to look at my mom. She seemed unsure about who my mom had been talking to. Then, it seemed she was really trying to make sense of what my mom said.

Finally, I saw that she really just looked dazed and exhausted. The more I looked at her face, the more it became obvious that she hadn't slept very much the night before. She was slightly weaving as she stood. I wondered if she actually stood there the whole night.

Suddenly, my mom bolted from the back of the kitchen and ran over to where Alex was standing. She grabbed Alex by her hair and threw her to the ground. I felt like my heart was about to come out of my throat! I was so scared and sick feeling. I hadn't even noticed that Dawn was clutching my arm with both of her hands. She was pale white and shaking with fear. I hoped I didn't look as shaken up as Dawn did. If mom saw our fear, there was no telling what her reaction would be. In her current state, I doubted that she would be very compassionate.

Dawn and I could no longer see my mom or Alex, but we could hear them. Mom was screaming, and Alex was crying. Mom would yell, and Alex would yelp. Then, there was a thump sound on the floor of the living room. Finally, I heard my mom say something that would forever change my view of her.

She walked into the kitchen and grabbed something that was hanging on the wall. I hadn't seen it, and I doubted Dawn had, either. But we both heard my mom say, "You wanna act like an animal, Alex? Then, I'll treat you like one. You'll get the belt, just like Nyssa's evil wannabe step-mom does to her children!" Then, she was gone into the living room again.

I leaned up against the stove and fought to breathe normally. It felt like I was suffocating. I was worried that my heart was beating so loudly that my mom would hear it and get mad at me for making so much noise. I didn't care what I looked like anymore. It didn't matter if I turned pale and shook. I saw Dawn crying next to me. I was positive that we were going to get it when my mom was done with Alex. Dawn and I were both wrecks, and when Mom saw us, she would unleash her new brand of punishment on us. It was just a matter of time. How much time? I tried to think how much time I had left of my short-lived "good" life I had with my mom. That's when I heard the sounds ... The belt was smacking against Alex.

Alex was crying with every blow. The belt was hitting her on the skin. I hoped it wasn't on her back. I prayed it wouldn't be where she was bleeding already. I felt like I was going to faint.

That's what had made those marks on her back. Oh, God...

Then, the sounds stopped. Footsteps. Mom was walking back to the kitchen. It was all over for Dawn and me. As my mom entered the kitchen, Dawn looked at the floor, and I turned to stare at the kitchen wall. I heard her pull one of the kitchen chairs out from under the table and sit down. I looked at the calendar on the wall and wished that time would stop. Please, just make everything stop.

Time did seem to slow, as Dawn and I waited for my mom's next move. I could hear Alex weeping in the living room. I could hear Dawn sniffling next to me, but my head was turned away from her.

Finally, Mom cleared her throat. Her judgment was coming, "I hope you two know I am not mad at you." She spoke volumes softer than what I had been expecting. She also spoke words I had not expected to hear. She wasn't going to hit us? I turned my head enough to look at Dawn. She had instant color to her face, and she wasn't shaking anymore. We both looked at my mom. Was she toying with us? Dawn obviously believed her, but I knew that my mom was capable of anything. This was made obvious to me over the last eighteen hours.

Mom motioned for the two of us to come and sit next to her. Dawn walked over first, then I followed. I kept my eyes on my mom at all times. Her sudden change of temperament seemed too good to be true. Mom was smiling at us, as she said, "Now, I don't want you to think that I am mad at either of you. But, at the same time, I have to make sure that Alex understands that her actions affect everyone around her." Dawn and I shared a quick look of uncertainty with each other. We had no idea where she was going with this. Mom continued, "So, I am grounding both of you, until Alex can behave herself. Neither one of you will be able to go outside to play after school or watch any television. Understand?"

She seemed stern, but also a bit sorry that she had to tell us what she did.

We both nodded. I could tell that Dawn was as relieved as I was at what my mother said. Grounded? No problem.

Although we hadn't done anything wrong, anything was better than getting the belt. I took a deep breath of relief and felt so happy that I was giddy. I knew it would be inappropriate for me to smile, given that we had just received some kind of punishment. So, I closed my eyes and sank into my seat, hoping my mom would just think that I was being quietly disappointed.

"Okay, then," Mom stood up and walked back to the living room. Before turning the corner, she told us, "You two get started on breakfast," she paused and thought for a second, "Maybe some eggs and toast. Oh, and see if we have any bacon left." Then she turned the corner and was out of sight.

"Okay, Momma," I answered immediately. I went to the fridge to find the needed ingredients. Dawn walked to the cupboard and retrieved the loaf of bread. In less than a minute we had all the food we thought we needed laying across the kitchen counter. The two of us stood awkwardly in the kitchen, looking around for anything else we might need. Anything that we could have missed. Anything to keep us from hearing what my mom could have been doing in the other room to Alex.

I heard my mom's voice getting closer to the kitchen, "You stand like you are supposed to, until you can behave like a human and not a little animal." My mom came into view, pulling Alex back over to what was now "her place." As long as we stayed in the farthest part of the kitchen, we wouldn't have to see her.

Mom walked over to us and we made breakfast like any normal family would. Alex was temporarily pushed from our minds, as we laughed and learned from my mom. When Dawn burned two pieces of toast, my mom didn't even get mad. She just showed Dawn how to scrape off the burned part, so we could still eat it. Dawn scraped too hard and accidentally put a hole in one of the pieces; Mom still didn't get angry. She just laughed and threw the piece away. Then, it was time to serve ourselves and sit at the table to eat.

That meant that we would be right next to Alex. Thankfully, Dawn took the same seat she had the night before and was turned away from her sister. I had to sit where Alex was practically standing right next to me, and Mom sat across from me, where she would be looking at Alex. This didn't seem to bother her or her appetite. The three of us made small talk as we ate. When we were done, we cleaned up and went to the living room. Mom let us watch TV, only because she didn't want to watch the Saturday morning cartoons by herself. I was shocked she was making an exception to a punishment that she had given out only an hour before. But I wasn't going to complain. Happy Mom, happy life.

We had only been watching cartoons for about fifteen minutes, when my mom was up and yelling at Alex for something again. I couldn't figure out what Alex had done this time to upset my mom. All I had seen her do was stand and face the wall. Maybe she hadn't been standing up straight enough.

Inside my thoughts, I began to question my mom's discipline. Something didn't seem right about what was happening to Alex. Although I had never questioned my mom or her methods of discipline, because hers was the only way I had ever known, something inside me felt that she was wrong in how she was treating Alex. But since her standard was the only one I had to go by, I really wasn't sure if other parents did the same things behind their closed doors. As I watched my mom hit Alex again, and yell degrading things at her, my confusion grew.

Something still didn't feel right about this. But, what could I do?

Mom stopped hitting Alex and leaned her hand on the wall to rest. She was actually getting tired from punishing Alex. She walked back over and sat next to Dawn and me on the futon. The three of us sat, staring at Alex. She was hunched over, half lying on the floor.

Slowly, she stood up and walked back over to her place. She turned around and faced the wall that she had been staring at for almost two days. Maybe she was saving my mom the trouble of yelling at her to go back. Maybe she was just getting used to being there.

"Look at her," Mom remarked with disgust in her voice. "She's laughing at me. After all that, she just stands up and waltzes right back over to the wall. She acts like I didn't even spank her."

Mom was getting worked up again. But she still seemed too tired to stand up and continue with the punishment. "Fine." Mom had come to some kind of decision. "Nyssa, take this." She handed me the belt.

"Go and show Alex that she can't laugh at your momma," she ordered.

I stared at the belt and tried to make sense of what my mom said to me. She couldn't possibly mean for me to go and hit Alex. I couldn't. No way. I was feeling light-headed and sick to my stomach.

My mom glared at me, "Did you hear what I said?" she asked.

I nodded, but I stayed sitting and unable to stand up.

"Do you want some of what she's been getting?" Mom was getting closer to my face, as she talked, "Cause that can be easily arranged. As a matter of fact, I think that if Alex doesn't start acting like a normal child, then you two," Mom made sure to look at both Dawn and I, "will be the next ones who get the belt. How about that?" she finished with a wicked smile.

I slowly stood up and walked to Alex. I didn't know what I was going to do. I quickly glanced at Dawn, who was watching me with horror on her face. I looked at my mom and she huffed at me in disgust. She reached out to grab the belt from me, but in a split second, I made a decision that would alter mine and Dawn's lives.

Rather than subject myself to the tortures of my mom, I walked over and hit Alex with the belt. I tried not to hit her too hard but pulled my arm back before striking her, to give my mom the illusion that I had put much force behind it.

"What the hell was that?" my mom asked me. "Look at her, Nyssa. She's laughing at you." Mom pointed at Alex. "She thinks it's so funny that she can do whatever she wants in this house, and you two will get punished for it." My mom was then talking to both Dawn and me, "Can you believe that? She really thinks that's funny. Why else would she continue to act like a brat, when you two are able to behave yourselves?"

I considered all that my mom said. I looked at Alex and didn't know what to make of the expression on her face. She seemed to be grimacing. Maybe it was from the pain she was in. Maybe her face was contorted in such a way, because she was trying so hard not to cry. My mom had seemed more and more upset by the amount of yelling or crying that she did. Or—maybe she was laughing at us.

I couldn't understand why Alex couldn't do what my mom was asking of her. Why could Dawn and I keep out of trouble, yet still be punished for what Alex did? I wondered if my mom was right about Alex deliberately acting up because she didn't feel like "being good." Then, she had the nerve to laugh at us?

"What are you waiting for?" my mom asked me. "She is never going to learn by you just standing there."

I hit Alex a little harder the second time, but I was still careful not to put too much force into the blow. I really didn't want to see her bleed anymore.

"Hit her until you wipe that smirk off of her face," my mom instructed me. She lay back into the futon to rest, while she observed my progress.

I hit Alex faster, but not harder. I aimed for places on her back that weren't already bleeding or covered with raised welts. I couldn't say for sure how long or how many times I hit Alex, but it seemed like an eternity. During my abuse of Alex, I could hear my mom talking to Dawn. She was saying a lot of the same things she had used to try and work me up enough to hit Alex. Dawn was listening to her, just as I had done.

"Okay, Nyssa. Why don't you sit down for a while?" Mom looked at Dawn. "Go and take the belt from Nyssa. I think that Alex would learn better if it were you hitting her." Mom nudged Dawn a little, to get her to stand up.

Dawn and I met in the middle of the room, and I handed her the belt. She took it, reluctantly and we both walked our opposite ways. When I got back to the futon, I looked over to see if Dawn would actually hit her sister. Dawn stood perfectly still, staring at Alex's back. I wondered if that was the first time that Dawn had actually seen the damage that had been done to her sister's back. She seemed amazed and confused.

Before Dawn could lose her momentum, my mom spoke to her, "Dawn, do you remember how much better your mom always treated Alex? Didn't Alex always get babied, and you always got into trouble?" Mom waited for Dawn to look at her and nod. Then, she continued, "And now Alex is still getting you into trouble, when you haven't done anything. She really doesn't care about you. Does she?" Mom finished and sank into the couch, knowing she had said enough.

Dawn hit Alex for what seemed like hours but was actually about as long as I had hit her. Mom finally told Dawn to stop and allowed Alex to go back to her place. Alex had been continuously falling to floor with the last few blows that Dawn had given her. I was pretty sure that Dawn was not hitting that hard, but Alex was more exhausted by her whole ordeal.

Mom was getting tired of having to yell at Alex to stand back up, because it was interfering with her ability to watch her cartoons. So, she let Dawn stop and return to the futon with us. Alex leaned slightly on the wall in front of her, but my mom seemed too entranced by the program to bother with that detail. I was secretly glad that Alex got a very small rest, while my mom was preoccupied.

Later that day, Mom let Dawn and me out to play for a few hours. Although we were supposed to be grounded, she told us that because we had helped her to discipline Alex, we deserved for our punishment to be lightened. We would only be allowed to play for a few hours that day. Dawn and I were so grateful to get out of that apartment. We changed quickly and ran outside to find our friends.

When we were questioned about our whereabouts earlier that day, we told our friends that we had been making breakfast with my mom and watching cartoons with her.

"Wow. Your mom is really cool," Nicole said. "You are so lucky," she sighed with jealousy.

Dawn and I just smiled and agreed; and then ran off to find good hiding spots for our game of hide and go seek. So, the masquerade of our life began...

SOMETIMES THINGS MUST GET WORSE, BEFORE THEY CAN GET BETTER

The next day Tom informed us that Kim asked the court for visitation with her children. Tom had been notified by his attorney the day before but forgot to mention it to my mom.

Apparently, the court had agreed, and she would be picking up the girls on the following weekend.

Mom was furious. "What the hell do you mean, Tom? You sat on this information for a whole day, before letting me know! And she gets to see them after they said she was an unfit parent? What the hell is going on?" Mom was beginning to get worked up, and I was concerned about where she would take those angry feelings to. Then, she looked over at Alex with a concerned look. I wondered if she was thinking about the marks all over Alex's back.

"What am I supposed to do, Tom?" Mom had resentment in her voice, but not as much anger, anymore. "You know that I've had to punish Alex harder lately, because of her disobedience. Kim will have a fit if she thinks that her babied brat isn't being treated like a little princess." Mom was clearly aggravated but keeping her cool.

She seemed to be growing more and more concerned at the situation that was arising.

Dawn and I were sitting at the kitchen table, eating breakfast.

Mom and Tom were sitting on the living room futon couch, having their discussion. Alex was lying in her place. When I had woken up that next morning and saw Alex lying down, I thought that my mom had pitied her and gave her a chance to rest. But, after I had poured a bowl of cereal, my mom had informed me that she had made Alex lay down in the "mess" she had created. As I sat at the table to eat, I could see that she was lying in a puddle of her own urine.

Dawn sat at the table after me, and we ate quietly as my mom and Tom talked. I thought about the fact that the following week the little girl lying on the floor would be back with her mother.

The mother who treated her like a princess. Part of me wanted to let her know what had happened to her little princess. Kim seemed like a messed-up person, but that was her daughter. Another part of me wondered what my mom would do to me, if she found out I told Kim anything.

I was snapped back to reality by my mom's voice. "Stand up, brat." My mom ordered Alex to her feet. "You need to take a bath. Then you can have something to eat, but don't think you're out of trouble. I just think you stink too bad, that's all."

Alex stared blankly at my mom. She seemed either too tired or too weak to answer. She had stood up but was weaving back and forth. I wondered if she would faint right there. Finally, my mom gave up waiting for some reply from Alex and led her to the bathroom. I could hear the water running, while I put my dishes away and got ready to go outside to play. Mom was drying Alex off when Dawn and I finished getting changed and met in the living room. We politely asked my mom what time we should come back in, remembering our restrictions on our play time. She told us to check in with her after two hours. Happily, we left.

While we were playing outside, we asked Nicole to tell us when two hours had passed. She was the only one of us to have a watch. She really like showing it off and telling us what time it was, so she was more than happy to bear the responsibility of being our time clock. She set the alarm on her watch, and we all forgot about it.

We raced around the apartment complex, collected snails and lined them up on the sidewalk to make words, and then picked dandelion flowers and tied them to make necklaces. Nicole's alarm finally went off while we were playing hide and seek. She had been trying to sneak up on us when her alarm went blaring like an ambulance siren. We all screamed. Then, once we realized that it was just her watch, we laughed hysterically. Dawn and I were having so much fun, we half-heartedly started back toward the apartment. Neither of us really wanted to go back inside.

"Hey, Dawn. You want me to see if my mom wants us to come back inside now? She did say for us to check in after two hours. Maybe that means that we won't have to go back in." I motioned for Dawn to stay put. "I'll go ask her. Don't go and hide, okay? That's no fair, cause we're not playing yet," I told her.

"I know," she answered. "Don't worry. I won't hide." She smiled and laughed. I was pretty sure that she wouldn't be going anywhere until she was sure that mom okayed us to stay out for longer.

I ran up to the apartment with a big smile on my face. For some reason, I was pretty sure Mom would let us play for longer. It was such a beautiful day, and we were having so much fun with our friends. I went over in my head how polite I would be to my mom.

I burst into the living room, but no one was there. I heard voices coming from the kitchen, but I couldn't see what was happening from where I was. I walked toward the voices. I could see antibiotic ointment and bandages on the kitchen table. Mom must have been trying to clean up Alex. I also noticed a jar of those awful jalapeño peppers that my mom liked so much. I thought that it was strange that my mom would be snacking on those, as she cleaned up Alex. Then, as I rounded the corner and could finally see my mom and Alex, I heard Mom say, "You better eat it, because that's all you get."

It took me a few seconds to understand the bizarre scene I entered. Alex was standing in front of my mom. She had bandages around her back, but they were also wrapped around her head. The only hole left open in the bandages was a small slit for her mouth. Through this small hole, my mom was pushing a jalapeño pepper. Alex was crying and taking very small bites of the pepper.

She had to be starving to eat those things, I thought. They seemed to be burning her, yet she continued to reach her neck out to eat a little more. I looked around the room and noticed what looked like feces on the floor. The small pile was right in back of her feet. I stepped closer to verify to my brain that my eyes were actually seeing all of this. That's when my mom noticed me.

"Two hours up already?" Mom asked me cheerfully.

"Yeah," I was able to mumble at her. I felt like I had entered into an apartment in another dimension. I could not believe that I was witnessing this horror and my mom could act so cheery.

Mom waved me closer to her and Alex. "Can you believe this brat had the nerve to pee on me while I was drying her off? She was so close to having a nice breakfast. But she obviously doesn't want to make any effort at all to be good. So, I won't make any effort at all to fix her something to eat.

She can just eat whatever is lying around. Isn't that right, Brat?" Mom asked Alex. Alex just kept crying and eating the peppers my mom was feeding her.

"Speaking of whatever is lying around..." Mom reached down with a spoon and picked up a small piece of Alex's own feces.
"This is special for you, Alex." Before I could comprehend what my mom was doing, she had fed it to Alex. Alex couldn't see what it was with the bandages covering her eyes, but she immediately began to gag. Even as she gagged, she continued to chew and swallow. She was starving. I couldn't believe what I had just seen. I stepped back and fought not to lose control. I felt lightheaded and sick to my stomach. I grabbed onto the kitchen table and prayed I would not fall unconscious on the floor. I had to get out of this hell.

"Momma, can Dawn and I play a little longer?" I hurriedly asked her.

Mom thought for a second and answered, "Sure. You two can play until Tom gets back from the store. When you see him pull into the driveway, then you two have to come in. Fair enough?" Mom asked sweetly.

"Yes, Momma. That's more than fair. Thank you." I turned and forced myself not to bolt for the door, but to walk slowly and normally out of the apartment. Once outside, I sat on the top step outside our door. I still felt lightheaded and was having a hard time seeing clearly.

Everything around me was spinning, and I actually laid down on the concrete to try and make things still again. The coldness of the cement felt good on my head, and slowly, I began to see and breathe normally again. As I used the metal stair banister to pull myself to a sitting position again, I struggled to understand what I had witnessed. I didn't care what my mom said. I knew something had to be wrong with her method of "discipline." I just couldn't explain why I felt that way. After all, she was the parent. That meant that she knew what was best. Could Alex really be the demon child that mom said she was? I didn't know what to think or what to do.

"Hey, are you okay?" Dawn was at the bottom of the stairs, looking up at me with worry. I wondered how long she had been there, and if she had seen my near-fainting experience.

"Yeah," I answered, nervously.

Dawn furrowed her eyebrows, "Okay. Well, what did she say?" she asked.

"Uh, she said we could play until your dad gets home," I told her.

Dawn walked halfway up the stairs, toward me. She looked unconvinced. "Is that all?" she asked, with suspicion. She could tell something else happened. I wanted to tell her what I had seen. Dawn and I had become close over the last few weeks. I felt she was the only person who would understand how I felt and what occurred. But I decided not to. I was scared she might freak out. Plus, I didn't want her to hurt anymore for her little sister. The last thing Dawn needed was something new to make her cry again at night. "Yeah," I lied, "that's all. I'm just kind of tired." I explained.

"Well, Nicole and Micky still want to play hide and seek. Wanna go?" Dawn asked.

I nodded and followed her to where our friends had been waiting. I played but stayed with easy hiding places that weren't that far away or hard to get to. I was still scared about my earlier dizzy spell. I also frequently looked up at out apartment window, whenever I had a clear view. I couldn't stop myself from wondering what kind of torture continued, as Dawn and I played our game. Finally, Tom pulled up, and we said goodbye to our friends. We went to help Tom carry some bags up the stairs. As the three of us walked to the door, I prayed that the scene I had seen earlier was over with. Hopefully, Mom had become tired again and had decided to watch TV or anything else besides hurt Alex.

When Tom opened the door, Mom was exactly where I had hoped she would be. She was lying on the couch and watching television. Alex was once again lying in her place. Bandages were no longer around her head, only on her back. Things looked as close to what they had been, before we all left the apartment.

I was so grateful that the episode in the kitchen was over. My mom did not discuss with Tom what she had done to Alex in his absence. My mom and I never discussed what happened that morning. It was as if the whole horrific episode never happened.

And that is how I dealt with it. I kept telling myself it never happened. I pushed that memory so far in my mind that it didn't resurface again for almost seven years afterward. I know it was the only way I could have kept myself from having reoccurring nightmares or crying myself to sleep at night. Thank God for repressed memories.

"So, how did it go with Alex today?" Tom asked my mom, as he put the groceries away.

Mom tiredly looked up at him, "What do you think?" she sighed, "I tried to give her a bath, and she pissed on me. I tried to dress her wounds and she s*** on me. How the hell are we supposed to clean her up? She doesn't want to be clean." Mom got up and helped him put away some clean dishes that had dried on the rack.

"Well," Tom said wearily, "final exams at school are over, so I'll be able to spend more time at home. We'll clean her up by next week." Tom reassured her.

Mom walked over to him and put her arms around him. "It's been so hard without you here. I'm glad those stupid tests are finally over." She hugged him tightly.

I didn't understand why my mom was suddenly being so nice to him. How could she call him a "walking piece of crap" one day, and then be so lovey-dovey with him the next? Her behavior and moods seemed so erratic, I wasn't sure if I could stay on her good side anymore. I couldn't anticipate what would set her off or put her in a bad mood. My haven that had been established with my mom was crumbling to the ground. Maybe staying with my dad and Jay would have actually been a better option.

Then, toward the end of the week, Mom came into my room to talk with me. It was the day before Kim would be coming over to pick up the girls. I could tell this would be a serious talk, because my mom made herself very comfortable on my bed. I sat on the floor and looked up at her.

"Nyssa, I know I probably don't have to explain this to you, because I know you are smart enough to figure this out for yourself—but I just want to make sure. Okay?" she asked me, kindly. I nodded for her to continue. "Alright. Well, when that dragon lady comes to pick up her daughters, she may have questions about the marks on Alex's back. Now, don't worry," she put her hand up in a calming motion, "the marks that you and Dawn put on her back have pretty much healed up. I took good care of them, so they would heal up faster.

But they still look like bruises on her back. So, we have to tell her that Alex got them while playing outside. She falls down a lot. Right?" Mom asked.

I nodded and answered, "Yes, Momma. I understand. Alex falls down a lot." I couldn't believe she was saying that Dawn and I were the ones who put those marks on Alex's back. I knew that Alex had most of the serious marks on her back, before Dawn and I were convinced to hit her.

"Good. I knew you would understand." Mom kissed my forehead and added, "Oh, and there's this thing that some Koreans get. It's called Mongolian Blue Spot. We think Alex might have that, too." I had no idea what my mom was saying but nodded anyway. I just wanted her to leave my room.

Once she was gone, I reflected on our conversation. It was becoming clear to me why my mom had been so sweet to Tom the last five days. She had to be sure that he would go along with this "Alex fell down" story and this obscure condition that Alex would have. Since Tom was not the brightest person, all it took was my mom being nice for him to be onboard with this deception.

What was really bothering me about our conversation was the fact that my mom was blaming Dawn and me for hurting Alex. I started to doubt the severity of the marks I had seen on her before Dawn and I hit her. Had I really seen blood on her back the night before? Maybe Dawn and I really hurt her more. I had been so sure not to hit her very hard and I thought I had not made her bleed, but maybe I was wrong. Maybe my mom was saving me, once again.

I mean, Dawn and I could be in real trouble for what we had done. I really wasn't sure what was real and if I could trust my own perception. Maybe following my mom's lead was the safest thing to do. After all, she loved me.

"Oh, one more thing," she had popped her head back into my room, "If things get too bad, like the police somehow get involved..." she waved her hand in the air, "although that probably won't happen. We'll just say that Dawn was the one who hit Alex. She couldn't stand that Alex got babied by her mom and flipped or something. Okay?" she waited cheerfully at my door for an answer.

I nodded slowly, dumbfounded by what she said.

"Good. Okay, goodnight Sweetie." Mom blew me a kiss before she closed my door again.

Once again, I was feeling a strong bond between my mom and me. I had to help my mom, because she was willing to help me.

We had to be willing to help each other no matter what, because there was no one in the world we could trust to do that. Everyone else had the misfortune of being either scapegoats or the enemy.

Mom was teaching me the difference, more and more each day.

When the day of Kim's visit with her daughters arrived, all of us seemed to be scrambling around the apartment. Mom was busy trying to get the girls to look their best. She spent most of her time on Alex. She picked out an outfit that covered her entire back and most of her neck. She carefully combed what little hair Alex had left (after my mom had chopped most of it off sometime during that last terrible week). I even spent a little extra time getting myself ready. I was anxious to see what this dragon lady looked like.

When the time finally came for her to arrive, we all sat around waiting for her. Half an hour after her visitation was supposed to have started, we were still sitting around waiting for her.

"This is just like her." Tom shook his head. "She thinks that the whole world revolves around her."

Mom had been very calm and composed all day. A little too calm. Almost like she was forcibly breathing slowly and counting to ten over and over in her own mind. She smiled and asked Tom, "Is there any way of getting ahold of her? Maybe she doesn't remember what time she's supposed to be here or something."

Tom thought for a moment, "Let me see if I can track her down," he offered. He walked to the phone to call her home number.

Someone answered on the other end and Tom had a brief conversation with that person. It seemed like he was getting pushed around and wanted to appease the person on the other end. I wondered if he had any backbone at all.

"So, what happened?" Mom asked him, as he hung up and walked back over to the couch with us.

"Well," Tom seemed to not want to tell my mom, but finally did anyways, "Kim wants me to bring the girls over to her. She didn't know she was supposed to come over and get them herself."

Mom put her head in her hands and shook them in disbelief.

"Tom, you know that woman is just being stubborn and lazy. She wants to prove that she still has control over you, too." Normally my mom would have been very upset by a situation like this, but instead she laughed it off. "Okay, fine. Take the girls to her house. What do we care? Right?" Mom asked Tom and me. We both agreed, and Tom left with the girls. Mom and I stayed home and waited for him to return.

Since Kim lived about an hour away, Mom and I spent some girl time together. We painted our nails and watched TV while they dried. We made a gooey s'more treat and talked about things. I was feeling very close to her, and any doubts I had about her judgment in punishment were slowly melting away. She was the coolest person to be around, when she wasn't mad.

"Can you believe those three?" Mom asked. She was referring to Tom and his daughters. "Any doubt about the slow mentality of Polish people should be put to rest after meeting those guys." We both laughed at her mean joke. "I mean," she continued, "none of them can think for themselves. That's including Tom. In fact, he's as bad as his daughters." Mom and I were giggling at their expense. "Oh, Nyssa ... I am so glad I have you here to keep me sane. You are the only one, besides me, who has more than half a brain around here." Mom hugged me, and we laughed some more.

Once Tom got home, our magical time ended, and we continued an uneventful evening. Tom had nothing interesting to say about the transfer of Dawn and Alex to their mother. We had a regular dinner of meatballs, potatoes, and veggies. Then, Mom and I got ready for bed, while Tom got ready to head back out to pick up the girls. Their visit was only supposed to be for half of the day. But, before Tom could call Kim and let her know he was on his way over, there was a knock at the door.

Mom opened the door slightly, enough to see who was outside, when all of a sudden, the door was forcefully pushed open from the other side. Two large men with vests on entered and were both talking quite loudly. There was a woman in a suit with them. I saw the word "Sheriff" on their vests and knew who they were, but the whole scene was chaotic and not what I expected that evening.

"Is this the only minor in the residence?" One of the men asked my mom. The other man was already stepping toward Tom and saying something to him.

Mom was flustered and totally unprepared for any of this.

"Uh, yes. That's my daughter." She took a step back and almost fell into the couch.

"Are you the father of Dawn and Alexandria Suleski?" The other man was standing in front of Tom and asking him sternly.

"Yes, I am. Is there a problem?" Tom asked innocently.

The lady had been standing at the door and surveying the room. She walked over to Tom and answered him, "Yes, Mr. Suleski – there most definitely is a problem." She shut the door behind her and seemed commanding, for a petite lady in a pretty little business suit. "Do you want your daughter in the room while we ask you questions about the marks that were found on the minor Alex?"

She directed the question at my mom.

Mom had regained some of her composure. "No, she can go in her room." She looked at me, and I walked straight back to my room. I had barely closed the door behind me and sat on my bed to take a deep breath, when there was a loud knock on the door.

"Who is it?" I asked.

One of the large men poked his enormous head through my doorway. "LAPD Sheriff's department. I need to ask you a few questions." He walked inside my room, before I had a chance to answer him.

"My name is Steve. Are you Nyssa?" he asked me. He seemed a little nervous or something. He was standing a bit awkwardly by my dresser. He was half-leaning and half- sitting on the top of the dresser. Maybe he was afraid that the dresser wouldn't support all his weight. I thought he was acting a little strange.

"Yes, I'm Nyssa," I answered.

"Your mom said it would be okay if I asked you a few questions about Alex and the condition in which her mom brought her to the police station. Do you understand?" He was a bit too stern.

I wondered if he had ever dealt with children before. Seeing his demeanor as a sign of inexperience with kids, I felt a little more confident talking to him.

"Yes, I understand." I answered, firmly.

At that moment, the other man entered my room. He knocked lightly but entered before I had time to say anything. "Hey," he said softly.

"Hey," I whispered back.

"How's it going?" He seemed to be asking the both of us that question.
Steve answered him, "I was just about to ask her about the marks."

The new guy walked over to Steve and said, "Tammy wants your assistance in questioning them. You know?" There was something unspoken in that last comment. I was a little more worried. Especially for my mom.

Steve walked out of the room, and the new guy reached out his hand to me. "Hi, Nyssa. I'm Peter, and I work for the Sheriff's department. Don't be too scared, okay? I'm not going to arrest you or anything." He smiled and winked at me. So, I smiled back. "I want you to know that your mom gave us permission to ask you some questions, but if you want to stop answering questions at any time, you can do that. Do you understand?" He kept his voice soft and smiled the whole time he talked. I felt very comfortable talking to him. I also thought he was kind of cute.

"Yes, sir. I understand," I answered with what I thought was my cutest smile.

"Great." He looked around for a comfortable place to sit down. He settled on the only chair in my room. It was a metal folding chair, and it wasn't very comfortable, but he somehow made himself look at ease in it and began. "Well, Nyssa. You know that Dawn and Alexandria had a visit with their mom today. Right?" he asked.

"Yes, sir." I still felt quite comfortable talking to him, though I knew some hard questions would soon be coming.

"Well, it seems that she took them to buy some new clothes, and she found some marks on Alex that worried her. Do you know what I'm talking about?" He stood up and slightly turned around.

"They were from here up." He pointed to his middle back. "They went all across both sides of her back." He made a sweeping motion across his back. Then, he sat back down.

"Have you ever seen those marks on Alexandria or know how they got there?" He had soft concern in his eyes, and I felt bad that I would have to lie to him.

"I think I do," I answered. My mind was racing. Was it time for me to blame Dawn? No, I should start small. Maybe it wouldn't come to that. I took a deep breath and tried to remember how I had fooled the two police officers that night at 7-11. They had believed everything I said. They were people, just like everyone else. I relaxed and said, "I think she got them from playing outside and falling down a lot."
He sighed and slouched a little in his chair. "Nyssa..." he seemed at a loss for words. Finally, he said, "You can't get these kinds of marks from falling down." He watched me closely for a few seconds, then said, "You know, I have kids of my own. I know about this kind of stuff." He stopped again and leaned over toward me, "If you're scared to say something, you don't have to be. We're here to help you. Okay?" His concern seemed to be growing. His eyebrows were scrunching together.

"Okay." I knew I would have to say something else. The "falling down" story was not going to work. "Dawn hit her," I blurted out.

Peter sat up in his chair. He tilted his head to one side, as if he was intensely considering what I told him. He slowly leaned toward me again, "You mean, her sister, Dawn?" he asked with some disbelief in his voice.

I swallowed. I wasn't feeling good about this. I hadn't even thought about the consequences to Dawn. Would she go to jail? What would happen to her? I had formed a bond with her, and I didn't want to make anything bad happen to her. But I also needed to protect my mom. Without her, I would be homeless and helpless. I knew she would do the same for me.

"Yes," I said. "Dawn was mad at her because of how much better their mom treated Alex. So, she hit her with the belt. Mom and I stopped her." I finished explaining everything quickly, hoping it would be easiest to just blurt it all out.

Peter sat back in his chair again, "Well," he seemed to be collecting his thoughts, "would you excuse me for a second, Nyssa? I'll be right back." After I nodded, he stood up and walked out.

It wasn't long before he returned with the lady. She was Hispanic looking, but also a little Asian looking. I thought maybe she was American Indian. She was about my mom's age, and I thought she was very pretty. She sat down in the chair that Peter had used and introduced herself by her full name. It was very long, and I only remembered that she said I could call her "Tammy." Her demeanor was polite, but not as friendly as Peter's.

"Nyssa, I just got through talking to your mother and Thomas. They told me their side of what happened." She nodded toward Peter, who leaned up against my closed door. "Peter told me a little of what you said to him. Can you repeat what you told him, please?"

I looked up at Peter, and he nodded for me to answer her. I paused for a moment. What did she mean by "their side?" Had they blamed me? No, my mom would never do that. But, would I be able to repeat exactly what I had said to Peter? I was getting nervous and realized I couldn't remember my exact words. If I said something different, then they might know I was lying. I had to calm myself down. My mom was counting on me.

"I just told Peter how Dawn hit Alex. She hit her because she was jealous of how her mom treated her better." I blurted out for the second time that night.

She looked at me, questioningly, "You mean how their mother treated Alex better than she did Dawn?" She wanted to clarify.

I nodded. There was silence in my room.

Finally, she looked at Peter and nodded. "Okay." She looked back at me and asked, "Do you think that I could look at your back?"

Her question caught me off guard, and I didn't answer. Instead, I looked at Peter.

"I could leave, if you like." Peter offered.

I thought about that offer. No, I was a big girl. I could handle their questions, and I could handle showing them my back. "No, it's alright." I told him. I stood up and turned around. I lifted the back of my shirt and I felt the lady run her hand across the skin quickly.

"Nothing," she stated, and I put my shirt back down. "Okay," she said with finality as I turned back around. "I guess we'll be going." She looked at Peter and he nodded.

I was so relieved. I couldn't believe it had been that easy. I was expecting more questions or something. But, they were already done, and Mom and I were safe.

"Oh, one last thing," Tammy turned around before leaving my room, "You told Peter that you and your mom took Dawn off Alex?" I swallowed again. Why did I go into such detail? I couldn't be sure what my mom had told them. I had screwed up. "Yes, I think so," I answered. Oh, no—I had to be sure—after all, it would have been a memorable event, right? "I mean, I think so, because I remember walking in on her hitting Alex. But I think my mom was already there, and she had been the one who actually stopped her." I was digging myself deeper. What should I do?

She looked back at Peter again and sighed, "Alright. Thank you, Nyssa." Then, they both walked out. They had left my bedroom door open and I could hear the three strangers talking to my mom and Tom in the living room.

Mostly, it was Tammy talking. She said something about them being sorry they barged in, but they thought that a child was in immediate danger. Then, she went on to say they could see that I was fine, and they were not going to take me. She said something about the girls staying with their mom and a further investigation being done. Then they were gone.

I collapsed on my bed. I was so tired. My mom and Tom both came into my room. Mom hugged me and praised me. We went over our stories and found that we were incredibly close, even in details. I was so grateful.

Life got better after the child abuse investigation was concluded. It was decided that the girls would go back to living with their mom, and they could not find any definitive proof as to how those marks got on Alex's back. Apparently, when asked,

Dawn actually admitted to her part in hitting Alex. This made it almost impossible to pin the obvious signs of abuse on my mom or Tom.

Unfortunately, Dawn's honesty allowed our lies to go undetected. It was a confusing irony that I tucked away into my growing arsenal of deceptive techniques.

Without Dawn and Alex in the house, my mom was a lot less stressed, and so our lives were more peaceful. It seemed like our lives were back on track, even with Tom in the picture.

But, what we really needed was a new start...

Dark Secret

STARTING OVER AGAIN

After the girls were taken out of Tom's custody and returned to their mother, my mom decided the three of us needed to make a new start. It made sense to Tom and me. After all, we hadn't exactly had a great start as a new extended family. I was sure the three of us felt the same way.

"What we need is a fresh new start." Mom was sitting at the kitchen table and thinking aloud. Tom was making himself a sandwich (I was sure that was the only meal Tom could make for himself), and I was doing my homework at the table. Every so often, she would peek over my shoulder to see how my math problems were coming along. Then, she would help me with the ones I had gotten wrong (I always had ones that were wrong). After periodically helping me, she would sit back on her chair and sink deeply into her own thoughts, sometimes sharing them with Tom and me.

Eventually she formed a plan, "We need to move." She looked around the apartment and shook her head. "This place is too small and has too many bad memories. Especially for me, since I was the one left to deal with 'the brat.'" She shot Tom a short, dirty look, then continued, "I think Nyssa should go to a different school. This private school she goes to, it seems like it's more trouble than what it's worth. But, if we put her in public school, it should be in a good school district. Don't you think so, Nyssa?"

I nodded, wholeheartedly. Although I had initially enjoyed the challenging and interesting classes that my private school offered me, it was outweighed by the constant teasing and my inability to catch up to the math class of my peers. I was teased every day, because my family didn't have as much money as the other kids' parents. If it hadn't been for my grandmother paying the tuition, I would not have been able to go to the school at all. My self-esteem had gotten quite low, and I had put on a lot of weight because of the stress from school and at home. At twelve years old, I outweighed my own mother.

I was completely sold on my mom's plan for a "fresh new start." It even sounded refreshing.

Mom began letting her thoughts flow, once she saw Tom and I smile and nod. "We should start looking right away. That way we could move as soon as Nyssa's school year is over. She'll have all summer to adjust to her new surroundings and maybe make some friends that go to her school." My mother had come up with this plan so quickly, I almost wondered if she had actually been planning this a while. She touched my cheek and asked me, "What do you really think, Nyssa? Isn't it time to start over?"

I nodded and told her what a great idea I thought it was. I was starving for a change. The apartment did hold too many bad memories, and at the downhill rate my self-esteem was going, I would be three hundred pounds by the time I hit high school. I desperately wanted a big change in my life.

When I was about to graduate from my elementary school, we found a townhouse to rent. It was a bit far from my grandparents' house, which made me uneasy. It had been a few years since we weren't either living with my grandparents or within walking distance. I was very sad to be moving away from them. However, it was also farther away from my dad and Jay. This was a very good thing. Mom explained to me that my dad would get tired of driving so far to see me, and eventually give up this futile custody battle he was still trying to win against my mom. That sounded good to me.

The first time my mom had taken me out to see the townhouse, I was shocked. It was so much larger than our dingy apartment. I was just like a house. I would have my own room, my mom and Tom would have their own room, and we would still have another bedroom that would be used as a computer room or office. I was thrilled! I really did feel like this was a brand-new start for us. I was even beginning to like Tom (a little). I still didn't have very much respect for him, but I least I didn't hate his company, either.

Just before my graduation from the private school I had attended for the longest school year of my life, my mother thought I should get a brand-new look. This would commemorate our new start.

She took me to her stylist, and I got a very grown up hair style. Her stylist showed me how to put hair gel and hair spray in my hair. She even showed me how to blow dry my hair. I felt like a little woman.

Then, my mom took me to get some new clothes. My grandmother had given my mom a couple of her credit cards to buy clothes for me. The only time I seemed to be able to get new clothes was when my grandma bought them.

As we picked out some outfits and I tried the clothes on, I could feel my self-esteem doing loops. The person I saw in the mirror looked so foreign to me. My new haircut added a few years to my appearance. The clothes my mother picked out were more grown-up-looking than I ever imagined I would be wearing at my age. Although I was going to be twelve, I looked like someone who was in high school. Seeing my image in the changing room mirror confused me. I was even embarrassed about looking like I did. The kids at my school had teased me for so long, all I could think was "They're going to laugh at me."

There was a loud knock on the door of my changing room. My mom's voice boomed in the changing area, "Are you okay in there?"

"Yes, Momma," I answered quickly.

She spoke closer to the door this time, "Let me come in. I want to see that last outfit." I was about to lie to her, but I was too scared to try to deceive her. I slowly unlocked the door and let her in.

Her eyes lit up the moment she saw me. "You look so grown up." She sounded very pleased. "You're really developed for your age, you know?" She circled around me as she spoke. She was checking out every angle of the outfit. She continued to go and on about how nice I looked and how the boys would be chasing and ... then I began to cry. At first, I wasn't sure why I was crying.

"What the..." Mom was speechless and totally bewildered.

"Oh, Momma!" I cried and sat on the little bench in the changing cubicle. Mom looked at me, like I was very strange.

"If you don't like the outfit, we don't have to get it. You don't have to cry about it." She spoke softly but seemed upset that I was crying over something like an unwanted outfit.

"No, Momma. I mean, I don't know." I didn't know how to explain myself.

Mom sat down next to me. She sighed and asked, "So, what's this really about?"

I briefly tried to get my thoughts together, when suddenly I began to cry again and blurting out all the feelings and thoughts I had. "Oh, Momma. I can't look like this for graduation! All the kids will laugh at me! I look like I should be a teacher, not a student! My hair is too fancy, and my butt is too big for these clothes!" I placed my head down in my hands and bawled.

My mom's hand squeezed on my shoulder, and she pulled me toward her, to hold me. Then, she unexpectedly laughed. I stopped crying to peek up at her, and she quickly covered her mouth, obviously not intending for me to hear her. "Oh, Nyssa. I'm sorry. I didn't stop to think how confusing a time this is for you." She hugged me and smiled. I wasn't sure what she was talking about.

Hard because of the move? Mom sensed my confusion and explained, "You know that you have the Najera curse. Well, you may think it's a curse right now, but you'll be thankful later. All of the Najera women go through puberty early." I really hoped this wasn't the start of a long talk about "the wonderful changes in our body." Mom continued, "I know it's hard for you to get used to the changes that are happening in your body, but it will all be worth it one day."

Oh, I really wanted her stop now. But she was not done, "You have a few pounds to lose, but you also have curves that most girls your age don't have. Okay, sweetie?" Whew, she was done.

Whenever my grandmother or mom would discuss "the changes in my body," I felt like a science experiment. In my mind, I felt I would be better off not having these "curves" they referred to. For me, that just meant breasts that made me feel awkward and a big butt. No thanks. But I nodded and hugged my mom, to show her that she made me feel better. I just wanted to make it through my graduation without totally making a fool of myself.

The morning of my graduation was a very conflicted time for me. I was wrapped up in the giddiness of my grandma and mom. They couldn't believe how much older I looked, or how great they thought my hair looked. I got a weird feeling that they had just made a new "buddy" for themselves. At twelve, I wasn't sure how I felt about being "buddies" with my grandma and mom. I was also extremely nervous about being seen by my classmates. Part of me didn't want to go, at all. But I knew this day meant a lot to mom and grandma, so I smiled, and we went to graduation day.

When we arrived at my school, I didn't see any other students, at first. As I walked toward the classroom where the ceremony was being held, I noticed a couple of parents eyeing me curiously. I saw that they were the parents of a girl that I had invited over to my grandmother's house (when I lived with her).

The woman came up to me and asked, "Nyssa? Is that you?" I nodded. She and her husband remarked on how nice I looked. They were rambling on about how grown up I was looking, but I was only half listening. I was focusing more on the doors that led to the ceremony area. I politely stood in front of these rambling parents, until my mom and grandma caught up to me. Once all four grown-ups started talking, I slipped away and headed toward my impending doom. I just wanted to get the teasing over with. If it got really bad, I was planning on letting loose and telling them all what I really thought of them. I was moving away anyways—what could they do about it?

The first classmate I encountered was one of my few friends in the school. Her name was Robin. She was a bit overweight, but unlike me, had avoided being teased by having her sister and two cousins (who also attended the school) protect her. She was fun to be around, but I always secretly hated the fact that she never extended her family protection to me. There had also been times when she had stood by, silently, while her cousins picked on me. I had only forgiven her each time, because I honestly thought I would have done the same thing, had I been in her shoes. I reasoned that she needed to let her cousins pick on me, or they would pick on her. Even though she sacrificed me sometimes, she was still the closest friend I had in the school.

When Robin's eyes landed on me, she squinted a little. She seemed to be trying to figure out why I was smiling at her and walking toward her. At first, she obviously didn't recognize me.

When she finally did, she freaked out. "Oh, my god!" She reached out and touched my hair. "You look so different!" She looked down at my tight skirt that was about three inches above my knees. "Does your mom know that you're wearing these clothes?" She giggled and looked around. She seemed ready to hide me, if my mom entered the room.

I laughed. "Yes, my mom knows." I giggled some more. "She's the one who picked them out for me," I explained.

"No!" Robin pushed me, to show that she didn't believe me.

She did that a lot. Sometimes it hurt.

I nodded and assured her, "Yeah. She really did." I was beginning to think my new look wasn't such a bad thing after all.

Robin looked me up and down and asked, "Have you been on a diet or something? You look like you lost some weight." She looked upset. Her parents had tried putting her on a few diets, but after a few days Robin would break down crying, and the diet would end. I never understood why she cried. Maybe she just got really, really hungry.

"No, I haven't been on a diet." I answered her. After thinking for a moment, I added, "I must have been so busy with us moving and all, that I just haven't been eating as much."

Robin's eyes looked a little concerned. "You're moving?" she asked.

I hadn't thought that anyone at this school would miss me. I guess I had taken for granted that Robin considered me her best friend. I was about to assure her we could still hang out, when a group of classmates entered the room. This group consisted of Robin's two boy cousins, Robin's sister, and another girl who I consistently got into fights with. The girl I fought with eyed me suspiciously, then walked to the far side of the classroom. The other three came over to Robin and me, and freaked out (much like Robin had done) once they realized who I was.

Robin's older cousin, Tim, smiled slyly and said, "Wow, Nyssa. I didn't recognize you." He smoothly added, "You still wanna be my girlfriend?" His smile was super flirtatious. This boy had driven me nuts the entire time I went to this school. He had once been my boyfriend (which meant that he tried to kiss me at recess, but I always ran away from him). Then, when I started gaining weight (around the time Dawn and Alex came to live with us), Tim had become my bully. He didn't tease me all the time. In fact, he often stood up for me against his own cousin. Maybe he felt no one else had a right to tease me but him. When he did tease me, it hurt more than anyone else in the school doing it.

Robin's other cousin and sister were about to say something, but Robin's voice cut them off. "She can't be your girlfriend, Timmy." She shot a mean look at me, and finished, "She's moving away."

"Robin..." I began but was cut off by the teacher telling us to get in our seats. Robin hurried off to hers, and Tim shook his head in disappointment at me, before heading over to his seat. I screwed up. Robin thought I was abandoning her. We had talked about going to middle school together and even high school. I was backing out of the promises I made her. Tim would be angry with me, because he was so fiercely protective of Robin. Now, I really had no friends at all. I wanted to cry.

Somehow, I made it through the ceremony without bawling. As soon as it was over, I ran to my mom and grandma and told them everything that had happened. The three of us looked over at the small group of kids that gathered around Robin. Some of them were staring in my direction and others were intently listening to what Robin was saying. She looked like she was crying. I felt like such a monster.
"Don't feel bad, Nyssa." My grandma put her hand on my shoulder. She was looking at me with so much compassion in her eyes.

"Hey." My mom put her hands on my shoulders and spun me around to face her. "We're leaving all this behind. Remember?" she asked. She seemed half-reassuring and half-reminding me sternly.

My mom didn't care much for people feeling sorry for themselves. So, I quickly snapped myself out of my small depression.

"Yes, Momma. You're right. I'll be glad to start a new school." I was convincing myself, as I spoke those words aloud. The truth was, I was going to miss Robin. I was going to miss not being able to see my grandma whenever I wanted. I was really going to miss the familiar neighborhood I had spent most of my life in. But I wasn't going to let any of these weak feelings show in front of my mom.

The three of us headed out of the school and down the steps to the parking lot. As we walked, we talked about my new womanly appearance, the trials of growing up and getting older, and how overrated friendships really were.

Back at my grandma's house, we continued our conversation. The three of us sat around the table eating some yummy cake my grandma had made to celebrate the day. As we talked, I realized that I felt more mature talking so openly with them. Maybe being buddies with them wouldn't be too awful.

Grandma leaned over and smoothed my hair, lovingly. She spoke gently, "You see, Nyssa ... your family will always be there for you. Friends will come and go." She waved her hand around in the air, to signify the fluttering of friendships. "One day they are your best friend. The next day they are making fun of you or getting the other students to hate you." I almost started to cry. My grandma seemed so right and full of such wisdom. It was like she knew exactly what I was going through with my so-called friends.

Mom picked up where grandma left off. "Your family will always be here for you. We stick together—no matter what." Mom stared stiffly into my eyes. "No matter what," she repeated.

I completely believed them. Their 'us vs. them' theory had now been extended further than just "us" vs. my father, Jay, and Kim. I felt I had them to stand with me, and back me up against anyone. I needed to give them that same loyalty. I owed it to them.

IRONIC SIMILARITIES

As my mom, Tom, and I were preparing for our transitions, there were changes in my father's home, as well. My father and Jay had a daughter together. Her name was Monica. At first, I enjoyed having a little sis to hold and play with. But soon, I was resenting the constant babysitting that was required of me whenever I came to visit my father. The relationship between my father and me had grown increasingly distant. The fact that he and Jay went out frequently and left the boys and me to babysit did not help our disintegrating bond.

Tony and Charlie also resented the limits put on their free time. "You're lucky, Nyssa." Tony told me, after my dad and Jay had left for the afternoon.

"Yeah," Charlie joined in. "At least you get to leave in a couple of days."

Tony finished their thought. "We get to stay here and be on- call babysitters." Tony smirked, sarcastically.

Tony and Charlie loved Monica very much but caring for an infant for long periods of time was taxing on two teenage boys.

When I told my mom about having to babysit on my visits, I knew I was adding fuel to the fire. I didn't care. I had lost most of my respect for my father and didn't care much for salvaging a relationship with him. I complained to my mom about everything.

Not only the babysitting, but also that Jay didn't like me taking my allergy medicine. She would sometimes refuse to give it to me. Her reasoning was, since I had been losing weight recently, I must actually be taking diet pills. As a result, when I would get picked up by my mother at the end of a visit at my dad's, I would frequently be suffering from allergy attacks. My eyes would be red and swollen. I would be constantly sneezing so bad that my stomach would hurt.

At first, mom would always be fuming mad when she picked me up in this condition. My complaints of always babysitting would just be the icing on the cake. "Well, why the hell does he keep fighting me for visits with her?" She would scream to my grandma or Tom. "Oh, wait." Mom would answer her own question. "They just need another babysitter. Jay also needs someone she can look down on." It made perfect sense to me. Mom was right, as usual.

Mom reassured me that once we moved to our new home, things would start to change for us. She implied that the move would affect my visits with my dad, and it would be good for us. I was so excited about our move.

After we had fully moved into our new townhouse, the wheels of change began rolling. First, my mom bought three copies of a book on healthy eating. The three of us would read the book and adopt the diet it endorsed. Second, the three of us were going to take a class together. It was a special class that would teach us how to make people feel very comfortable around us, and how to persuade people to see things from our point of view. Mom said this class would help me develop my psyche, as she had promised we would a couple of years ago. I was so excited about these new changes we were making. We would be better people. Better than my dad and Jay. Better than those kids who teased me at my old school. Better than a lot of people. Mom promised.

During that summer, I went through a lot of changes.

Physically, I lost about twenty pounds. I lost the weight by eating all-natural foods that the three of us read about in our new diet book. Tom and my mom both lost weight, too. That alone was a big boost for our self-esteem. We were actually eating more foods, but still losing weight. We weren't hungry, so we weren't cranky. It was great.
Emotionally, I felt stronger than ever. The class my mom had gotten us into did a lot for my confidence. By the end of the class, I felt assured I could handle myself maturely with any adult.

We were taught how to make others feel at ease around us and let down their guard. We were also shown techniques to get others to agree with our way of thinking or make them change their minds about something.

"Let's see Jay make you feel inferior, now." My mom smirked. She knew I was a different person, as well.

My new confidence had led to other changes. I was wearing a little bit of makeup. I was feeling comfortable in my new clothes my mom had gotten me. I could look at myself in my new clothes, with my hair and make-up done, and not be ashamed or embarrassed by what I saw.

Plus, it helped immensely that my mom was happier than she had been in a few years. With Tom's girls gone, my mom had been restored to her cooler self, more fun to be around.

Of course, battles were still being fought at my father's house. Besides still babysitting Monica almost every time I went to visit, Jay was getting more ruthless about what she said to me. I guess she felt there was really nothing more the courts could do to her. Since she couldn't physically touch me, she did her best to hurt me emotionally. But, even that side of her came and went quickly. Sometimes her outbursts would coincide with whether or not my father was home. She would sometimes wait until he left, then suddenly find something that really upset her about me, no matter how trivial.

"Why are you just sitting in the house reading?" she asked one day.

"I like to read," I told her. After reading that book on healthy eating, I found a passion for it.

Jay rolled her eyes at me. She did that a lot to the boys and I, but there would be hell to pay if we did it back to her. "It's not normal for a kid to read so much," she told me, matter of fact. "You should be outside playing or something." She pointed toward the door.

I got off the couch and slowly walked toward the door. I wasn't in the mood for confrontation. I just wanted to get through this visit without incident. But that never happened.

As I passed Jay, she reached out her hand and snatched the book from me. "You'll go outside to play, not read," she instructed me. Then, she added, "But, first you need to go to the bathroom and wipe your make up off." She huffed in disgust. "You look like a hooker."

Inside I was boiling. I wanted to scream at her. I wanted to tell her that I thought she looked like a hooker! But I remembered my persuasion class. I wouldn't let her get the best of me. I took a quick cleansing breath (like I learned in class).

Then, I answered her "Okay, Jay. I'll take the make-up off. But when I go outside, what will I do? Tony and Charlie are gone with their friends, and I don't know anyone in this area." I calmly waited for her reply. I knew she would probably blow up at me. I could see her anger growing. I also knew she couldn't lay a finger on me. Whatever verbal abuse she threw at me, I would just take back to my mom, and it would become more ammunition on our next custody hearing.

As I predicted, Jay blew up. "You think you're pretty cute now. Don't you, Nyssa? You just egg me on, cuz you know I can't spank you like you need to be. Just get in the damn bathroom and wipe that filth off your face," she barked.

I shrugged my shoulders, to show her that I innocently had no idea of what she was talking about. Then I went to the bathroom and washed my face. When I was done, I walked back into the living room and proceeded to the front door. I really didn't know what I was going to do. My father and Jay had just moved to this new neighborhood, and I had no idea what there was to do in this area.

Then, as I was walking out the door, Jay came walking down the stairs. There was something different about her. She was smiling.

Not mischievously or in a sneaky manner—just like she was happier.

"Look, I know that there is really nothing for you to do around here—so do you want to come with me?" she asked. She seemed genuinely nice. I nodded. I had nothing to lose. I really didn't care what I did, as long as it passed the time until my mom came to get me.

Jay's mood had definitely done a 360 since she had told me to take my make-up off. Since the boys were gone, my dad was at work and Monica was at daycare or something, it was just Jay and me. I went with her to pay some bills and do some shopping. I hated to admit it, but I was actually having a good time. Jay was pretty funny, when she wanted to be. She pointed out strange-looking people on the street and said the most hilarious things about them.

On the way back to the house, we had a civil conversation, and I was actually seeing her as a normal human being. "Nyssa, about your make-up..." Jay seemed almost reluctant to finish. Was she truly worried about hurting my feelings? "I think that you wear a little too much eye make-up for your age." She finished. "Maybe you should wait a few years until you decide to wear make-up. Older men think you are older than what you are—and it worries me," she offered.

I nodded and considered what she said. The main reason I started wearing make-up was because my mom told me I put it on very well. I didn't want older men looking at me, though. Yuck. Maybe I didn't need to wear it, yet.

When we were a few blocks from the house, Jay's demeanor turned secretive. She whispered to me (although I was the only one in the car). "Your dad and I are going to have another baby." She smiled at me. I tried to smile back, but I'm sure it came out looking, more like a mouth twitch.

"Oh, wow," I said, at a loss for words.

"Yeah," Jay agreed. "I really hope this one is a boy." She shook her head and explained. "My boys were never as much trouble as you or Monica."

I had heard her say things of this nature before. Whenever she would get really angry at me, she would blame it on my gender, because "Charlie and Tony weren't as much trouble." She had also been using that excuse with Monica, lately.

"Uh-oh," Jay said. She pointed toward the house as we pulled up. "It looks like we're a little late." She commented on my mom's car parked outside the house. "Just run in and get your stuff. I'll tell everyone that you said goodbye," she offered. I nodded and began to open the door. But before I stepped outside, I turned to Jay.

I felt like I wanted to say something to her. Maybe something nice to show her I had a good time. Should I thank her? Tell her I had a good time? What? As I pondered, my mom honked her horn. I decided not to say anything and ran to get my belongings.

After I had gathered my weekend visitation clothes (they were very conservative—so Jay wouldn't complain), I walked to my mom's car. As I walked, I saw that Jay was still sitting in her car. Had she stayed there in order to avoid confrontation with my mom? Was she as confused as I was about our "normal" day together? I just couldn't figure this woman out.

"What was that all about?" my mom wanted to know.

Without waiting for me to answer, she continued, "I've been waiting here for half an hour. Then, I see you drive up with that witch, and you're both smiling." She was sounding more and more upset. "Mind letting me in on your little joke?" Mom was pretty angry, now.

I had to think quickly. If I didn't answer right away, she would know I was trying to make something up. "Momma ... I was just smiling because I saw your car and was so relieved that this weekend was finally over. As for Jay—she's just weird. I don't know why she was smiling. Maybe she was just happy to get rid of me." I shrugged my shoulders, to show I really didn't care why she was smiling.

Mom eyed me suspiciously for a few seconds. Then she smiled, "She is weird." Mom laughed. "That's funny." She began to drive us home, laughing to herself. "She really is weird, huh?" She asked more to herself, than to me.

I thought about the strange and confusing day I had with Jay. Today, she was surprisingly nice and funny. Part of me didn't want to be fooled by what could be a passing mood of friendliness on Jay's part. But I also had to admit that I wouldn't mind visiting more often, if I saw this side of Jay each time I came over.

On the way home, I told my mom how Jay had told me to take off my make-up. I told her how she had taken my book from me and ordered me to go outside in a neighborhood that was foreign to me. I also told her how my dad was at work most of the weekend, so I didn't really "visit" with him very much. I said all the things I knew my mom would want to hear. I did not tell her about my fun time with Jay. I didn't tell her about the good conversations we had.

Although, I did decide to share with my mom what Jay had confided in me. I thought my mom would be interested.

"Oh, Dad and Jay are having another baby," I commented to her.

"What?" Mom seemed especially upset about that last piece of information. She didn't say anything to me after that. The entire ride home, she seemed deep in thought. I knew to leave her alone when she was in a mood like that. Her mind was hard at work and wouldn't take kindly to outside interference. That was fine with me. It gave me more time to reflect on the day's events and my approaching first day at my new school.

By the time the new school year started, I had lost quite a bit of weight. I had also mastered the art of putting make-up on very slightly, so as to not get caught by the teachers (make- up was not allowed in the elementary school—not even for sixth graders). I was so nervous about being the "new girl." But, by the end of the school day, all my nervousness had disappeared. I had easily made friends, even getting in with the "cool" girls who thought I had "cool" clothes. I was not teased by anyone, and I couldn't have been happier. After a few months, my teacher asked me to tutor some younger students in English, because I was so advanced for my age (a positive outcome of going to private school for a while). It got me out of P.E., which I hated, because my allergies would go nuts whenever we played anything out on the grass. Life was good—no—great.

Great things apparently don't last long.

"You're going to have a little brother or sister." My mom was beaming at me. She seemed thrilled. I smiled back at her.

"Oh," I said with a smile.

Mom's smile dissolved from her face. She was obviously upset by my lack of enthusiasm. "Is that all you can say?" Mom asked. Then, she began to rant, before I had a chance to try to redeem myself. "Is that what you said when your dad and Jay said they were having a baby?" Mom let her mouth droop down slightly and crossed her eyes. "Oh." She mimicked me.

"I'm sorry, Momma." I needed to calm her down, before it got too bad. However, I had the feeling that I was too late.

Mom stood before I could finish my sentence. She looked down at me, before heading up the stairs. "Yes," she remarked, "you certainly are sorry."

She had shown a side of her that I had not seen for a while. I especially had not seen her take that tone with me in almost a year. It had been just before Dawn and Alex had come to live with us. After that, she had taken her frustration out mostly on Alex. Since then, it had been Tom who took the brunt of her mood swings. What had changed between my mom and me?

It would take almost two months before I would figure out that pregnancy brought out the worst in my mom. Our "fresh new start" lasted about four months. Now, my mom's fits of ranting and violent behavior would become increasingly more frequent. I hated going home after school. I would walk slowly and ask as nicely as I could to go over to friends' houses. Even "friends" who were really just classmates that lived within walking distance of my house. I made a lot of new "friends" during this time, and none of them knew how crazy my home life could be.

"What the hell is wrong with you two?" Mom was yelling at Tom and me. It was a weekend day, and I had no choice but to stay in the house with my mom and Tom. I could not get ahold of anyone I knew in the area, and it wasn't my dad's weekend for visitation. I had made the mistake of asking them if one of them could drive me to a friend's house that was farther than what I was allowed to walk.

"Today was supposed to be a family day!" Mom screamed.
She put her face close to mine and screamed, "You would rather hang out with your so-called friends, instead of your family? Don't you remember what your friends in your last school did to you?"

She turned to Tom, before I could even nod my head in response.

"And you!" She was now pulling Tom down by his shirt, so that he was face to face with my mom, who was one whole foot shorter than him. "You would rather spend more time at work, than with me?" Tom opened his mouth to say something, but Mom cut him off. "Don't tell me you have unfinished work to do! That's your own fault, not mine! Damn it, Tom! I am not your f***ing mother!"

I cringed to hear my mom cuss.

"It's the work that they gave me as I was leaving yesterday, and...." Tom was quickly trying to explain himself, before he inevitably got cut off again. Which he was.

"B***s***!" Mom screamed. Her face was quite red now. She looked ready to explode. She backed away from Tom, so she could yell at us both equally. "You two are the sorriest sacks of s**** I have ever seen!" Mom had been cussing constantly lately. It felt so wrong to see my pregnant mother spew such obscenities. She was only about two months into her pregnancy, but I had started to see her in a different light once I was told that she was carrying a baby. Now, she was transforming into a pregnant monster.

I thought I could still help the situation. "Momma, what would you like to do today?" I asked as sweetly as I could.

Mom considered what I asked and seemed to be thinking of an answer. Then, she looked at me, menacingly. "You fake little brat," she sneered. "You almost had me."

She wagged her finger at me. "Is that the kind of trick you play on Jay? Kiss her ass sweetly, and she won't suspect a thing." Mom was only half making sense to me. I didn't understand what she meant about suspecting anything. I just shook my head "no" anyway.

Mom paced around the room for a while. Tom and I sat quietly in the living room, watching her pace. "Alright, Tom. You have unfinished work to do?" Mom asked.

"Yes." Tom smiled as charmingly as he knew how.

"Okay, Tom." Mom grinned. "On Monday morning you can go in three or four hours early. I'll be asleep, so I won't care. Then, you can spend the weekend with your family, like a good family man." She nodded, pleased with herself.

"As for you." She pointed at me. "You want to treat me like Jay?" I shook my head, but it didn't matter. She continued, "Then I will treat you like Jay does." She grinned again. Then, she walked over to a tissue box that was sitting on a small coffee table. She picked it up. "Didn't you tell me that Jay used to throw things at you to get your attention? Things like tissue boxes?" Mom waited for an answer. I had to give her one, or risk making her madder.

I nodded. She threw the tissue box at me. I started to cry. It wasn't that it physically hurt , but it felt terrible to see her purposely behaving like Jay in order to hurt me.

"What are you crying for?" Mom screamed at me. "I should be the one crying! My own family wants to desert me! You are both selfish little s****!" Mom grabbed me by the arm. "I should send you back to live with your father. You know, since you don't appreciate your home here." Tears were pouring down my cheeks. I was really scared now. "Yeah, I bet your father and Jay would really love to have you back there now. Especially after all the wonderful things you said about them in court." My heart was racing. Mom laughed at my obvious anxiety. Mom threw one more thing at me, before stomping up the stairs.

Tom and I sat on the couch for a few moments. I'm sure we were both so relieved that she was gone, we just wanted to bask in the quiet and calmness around us. I began to wonder if I should try to head upstairs to my room or avoid the upstairs altogether. Tom decided to use this time to make excuses for Mom.

"I know it's hard to understand, but a pregnancy does things to a woman. It makes her act strangely," Tom explained. I flashed back to when Jay was pregnant with Monica. I also thought about now, since Jay was pregnant again. This was the same excuse my dad used for outbursts that Jay had. Either there was some truth to "pregnancy insanity" or both these men were looking for easy excuses. Just in case, I was not having babies—ever.

"Well, I guess I should try to calm her down. This can't be good for the baby," Tom said. He slowly walked upstairs. I was left in the living room. I was still in a state of fear. I wasn't overly scared about my mom's screaming, or even throwing things at me. I was terrified about her threat to send me back to my dad's house. After all the mean things I had said about Jay (whether true or not), I knew my life would be hell if I had to go back and live with them. I decided that I would run away before I would be sent back there.

Anything was better than living with my zombie dad and his crazy girlfriend.

I heard a crack in the stairway and my heart jumped.

Someone was coming down the stairs. I prayed that it wasn't my mom. But it was.

"Oh, Nyssa!" Mom was crying. She came and sat next to me, throwing her arms around me. "I'm sorry." She wept. I exhaled a sigh of relief and hugged her back.

"It's okay, Momma." I rubbed her back and hugged her warmly.

She sat back on the couch. "This pregnancy thing is a lot harder than I remember." She laughed through her tears. "I know it's hard for you to really understand what I feel right now. Trust me—I don't have too much control over what I say sometimes."

"It's really okay, Momma." I continued to rub her back. I just wanted to be as soothing and relaxing toward her as possible. I was convinced that at any moment she could jump up and start throwing things again.

Mom blew her nose in some Kleenex and leaned against me, as I lightly massaged her back. "I just want us to be a close family. You know, especially with the baby coming." She sniffed, as she told me this. Even after she scared me, I was now feeling sorry for her. I really had no idea what it was like for her and her pregnancy. Maybe it really did make women crazy.

Tom sat next to my mom and pulled her feet up into his lap.

With him rubbing her feet and me rubbing her back, mom became fully relaxed. She looked up at Tom and said, "I think we should tell her about her dad and Jay."

Tom's eyebrows drew together and he sucked in some air, noisily. "Oooh." He seemed unsure if they should tell me.

"Tom, she has to go to the reception next weekend." She strongly reasoned with him.

"Yeah, you're right." Tom nodded.

I couldn't stay quiet any longer. "Momma, what reception?" I asked.

Mom turned herself around, so she could face me. She took both of my hands in hers and said, "Your dad and Jay got married in Vegas a couple of days ago. Your father asked that his visitation for this month be next weekend, so you can go to the reception."

She stopped to let me absorb all that she said.

I was quiet for a few seconds, trying to make sense of what she was saying. Why hadn't my father told me that they were getting married? Did all the family get to go to the wedding—except me? "Momma, was I the only one not invited to their wedding?" I asked.

Mom shook her head. "No, baby." She smoothed my hair, like my grandma did. "Nobody was invited. They were partying in Las Vegas and decided to get married. Just the two of them."

I sat in silence again. I was hurt and very confused. I didn't know what to say. I looked at my mom, questioningly. I needed her guidance and comfort.

Mom took both of my hands again, and sweetly said, "This might make you feel better." She glanced at Tom, who was smiling with her. "Tom and I are planning on getting married next month and we want you to be an important part of our wedding." She was beaming. Tom was grinning so hard, it looked like his face should hurt.

"Important part?" I asked.

"Yes." Mom explained, "We want to write in some vows for you, so you can walk down the aisle with us and take vows that you accept us as your parents." Tom and my mom were obviously very proud of this idea.

I began to cry again. While my dad and Jay were only thinking of themselves, my mom and Tom were thinking mostly of me. I was so lucky to have people who really cared about me. The earlier outburst from my mom had been completely forgiven and forgotten. I couldn't take her for granted, ever. I was sobbing and my mom was holding me, kissing my hair softly.

"Everything is going to be okay," she quietly reassured me. "You will always have your momma—and now you have Tom, too."

I was comforted by the thought of always having my mom but confused about my feelings for Tom. I respected his relationship with my mom, but I couldn't see him as a father figure. He seemed more like an overgrown child than someone's father. But it didn't matter. As long as I had my mom, I would be happy.

Nyssa Rebecca Corbin

FRESH START FOR ALL

The wedding reception for my dad and Jay will always stand out in my mind as the most awkward experience in a family setting.

My dad and Jay seemed very happy and danced almost the whole night (despite the fact that Jay was so pregnant she looked about ready to pop). Both sides of the family seemed happy for them, too.

Some looked forcefully happy, possibly because they had eloped at the last minute to Las Vegas to get married. No family had been there at the actual wedding. Not even my brothers or me. I was admittedly bitter. Charlie and Tony, however, seemed cheerful enough. They danced and laughed with our cousins most of the night. There was one time when Tony noticed me sitting alone, part way through the night and sat down next to me.

"How come you're not dancing?" he asked. "I just don't feel like it," I told him.

He nodded. "Yeah, I know how you feel. It does suck that we couldn't be there when they got married."

I nodded back to him. I didn't know what else to say. It did suck. It sucked that my Dad had clearly chosen Jay over his own daughter, then married her behind my back. The more I thought about it, the angrier and more bitter I felt.

"Well, I'm not going to let it bother me too much." Tony smiled at me, then added, "Come on and dance with us." He held out his hand for me, but I shook my head no, and he shrugged his shoulders and left. For the rest of the night, I sat mostly unnoticed by everyone, eating corn chips out of the bowl at my table and watching everyone "loosen up" and have a good time. If it hadn't been for Charlie and Tony's periodic attempts at getting me to dance, I would have felt completely unwanted. At one point, I thought about walking out of the wedding, just to see if anyone would notice. My pity pit for myself was the deepest it had been in my young life. I was convinced by the end of the night that I was no longer a part of this new family formed by my dad and Jay's wedding.

My mom fed off this self-pity. "Of course, you're not part of their new family." She comforted me through my sobbing and listened to my ranting of the never-ending reception from hell. I did make sure to tell her that Charlie and Tony were the only ones who really interacted with me. "Those poor boys." She shook her head slowly, pitifully. "They're stuck. They really are." She shook her head some more. "But there is nothing we can do for them. Once they get old enough, they'll leave and never look back. Don't you think?" she asked with sorrow in her voice.

I nodded, sadly, and thought about how Charlie had run away once already. I remember my Dad and Jay had found him on his skateboard, on the freeway, headed to Las Vegas (from our L.A. beach community). He told them he was trying to get to his dad's house, so he could live with him. It was a sad memory, and I started to feel even more depressed. I was so sad, my stomach started to hurt. I really wanted to hear some good news. My deep sadness was pretty obvious to my mom.

"Well." My mom looked away for a moment. She seemed to be searching for a starting point. "Okay ... Tom is re-enlisting in the Army." Mom was glowing. Her good news was completely lost on me. Why did this make her so happy?

Mom saw my look of confusion and explained, "Once he re- enlists, we'll have better health benefits, better pay ... well, if you figure that base housing is included ... and we'll get to move somewhere far away. Maybe even a different country!" She was ecstatic.

It took me a few moments to grasp the entirety of what she said. Then it hit me— I wouldn't have to see my Dad or Jay anymore! I hugged my mom as soon as I realized this, and she very aggressively hugged me back. It would be a new start for my family.

I associated new starts with at least of few months of the "good life."

It had worked when we moved to the townhouse; we could just do it again. Maybe the "freshness" of a change would last longer this time.

My mom seemed to be reading my mind. "You know, you could completely reinvent yourself. We could get you some new clothes. Maybe a new haircut. Whatever you like." She was so happy as she offered these suggestions to me. Then she turned a little more serious in her mood. "There are a couple things I need to tell you first." She told me that Tom had recently been voicing concerns over how his ex-wife was raising his girls. I'm pretty sure I stopped breathing, as my mom told me she and Tom had been talking about getting Dawn and Alex to come and live with us again. I suddenly had flashes of the awful things that had been done to Alex and instantly felt that whatever she was getting at her mom's had to be better than what she got while she was with us.

Mom saw my nervous behavior and hugged me close to her. "I know things were a little rough when they lived with us before. But I think things will be much better for us after we move." She spoke in a soft, comforting voice. She rubbed her hands over my hair and continued, "Tom has passed by the complex they live in, and they are always outside playing, unsupervised. Can you imagine? Nobody is watching those girls play! Alex is always dirty, because she still hasn't learned to use the potty. Dawn doesn't pay attention to where her sister is—AND—Kim is working as a prostitute again!"

My mom's voice was filled with disgust. Her eyes were watching me for a reaction, so I also forced myself to look disgusted and blurted out, "Wow! That is gross!"

Really, I still felt that—even with those bits of information— they were better off. I knew what was really bothering my mom. She made it very clear that when the girls were first taken away and placed with their mom, she felt angry about paying so much child support to Kim. I remember her saying Kim was going to spend that money on herself (which I thought was true). But they were still better off with their mom spending all their money on herself and not watching them. This whole idea made no sense to me. Weren't we so much happier now? Wasn't our family getting along better now?

I didn't voice any of my concerns. I knew it would only cause trouble.

JUST TO MAKE A POINT

Before we were to get the girls back, Mom and Tom wanted to get married. They felt it would be more welcoming to the girls to come back to a secure family structure, with parents who were married. I didn't think anything about coming back to live with us could be "welcoming" for the girls. I just knew they couldn't possibly want to come back after what occurred last time they lived with us. But for now, I would have to put on a smile and not offer any resistance to a plan that my mom was obviously excited about.

My mom was excited about the idea of having a wedding.

"Oh, Nyssa—we found this great little chapel down by the harbor. It's right on the water! It's just so cute! Oh," she smiled like she had a secret, "Tom and I have a surprise for you when we get to the wedding!"

Okay, I was a little excited. First, I had never been a part of a wedding before. Second, my mom and Tom were going through a lot to include me in this day that was supposed to be all about them. I realized that my dad and Jay would probably never do that.

In fact, although I really didn't care for Tom at all—I gave him some points for agreeing to share this day so much with me.

When the day came for us to go to the chapel, it was one dramatic scene after another. In the morning, mom had very bad morning sickness and threw up for a long time. Tom waited for as long as he could, then made the mistake of reminding her of the time. "Uh, Mica? I know you're probably not feeling well, but your mom just called and said they're getting ready to leave for the chapel. Shouldn't we get going soon?"

I slowly backed into my room as the door to the bathroom opened, and my mom pulled herself off the floor by the doorknob.

I quietly closed my door, as she said, "So, what do you know about how I'm feeling right now, Tom?" After that she screamed obscenities and cried a little. I sat still on my bed and wondered if the wedding would be canceled. I imagined calling the guest list and explaining that the bride was a screaming, crying lunatic, and we would have to reschedule after her lobotomy. I laughed at my own joke, and immediately there was a knock on my door. I was so startled, I stood straight up, and my heart raced. Was Mom going to think I was laughing at her fit? I couldn't make her wait too long.

"Come in," I said sweetly.

Mom opened the door and leaned on the inside of my door frame. She looked awful. She was pale and sweating. I hurried over to her and helped her to my bed. She sat down and began to cry. "I feel so terrible." She gasped for air as she sobbed. "I don't know if I can make it through the ceremony." She tried to speak more but began to cry uncontrollably instead. I held her and rubbed her back. I felt so bad for having made fun of her earlier. It must be awful to be sick on your wedding day. I felt even worse when I remembered how I was getting a big surprise at HER wedding. I was truly a mean daughter.

"Momma, it will be okay." I thought about what I could do to help her. "Do you want me to get some Tums or crackers for you?" I continued to rub her back.

She looked at me and smiled. "Okay." She said in an almost child-like tone. She lay on my bed, and I went downstairs. I grabbed some Tums, Pepto-Bismol, crackers and water. Pretty much everything I thought might help her. As I was heading back upstairs, Tom asked me what was going on. "I'm helping Mom," I shot back at him and rushed back to my ailing mom. I was angry he hadn't tried to help her. He was such a child.

Back in my room, I nursed my mom for about fifteen minutes.

She took the Tums and ate a few crackers. She sat up and seemingly for the first time, looked at my outfit. "Nyssa, what are you wearing?" she giggled at me. I turned around and looked at myself in the mirror. I was wearing what I thought was the nicest dress I owned. I shrugged my shoulders at her, not knowing what she expected me to say.

"Come on, "she motioned me towards the door and slowly walked me to her bedroom. She picked three of her dresses that she still had from when she was a ballroom dance instructor. They were fancier than anything I had ever worn. Mom lay down on her bed and munched crackers while I tried on her dresses. She liked one in particular and told me I should wear it. It was long and flowing with a lot of brown patterns and straps with animal print on them. It didn't seem right for a wedding—but it was very pretty. Besides, it was her wedding and she seemed happier. "Thank you, Momma." I gushed.

She wrapped her arms around me and hugged me so tight.

"Nyssa, I love you more than anything in the world. You know that, right?" I nodded, too choked up to speak. She smoothed my hair and said, "Don't ever forget that."

With Mom feeling better, we were finally out the door. I looked at the clock and saw that we were running about thirty minutes behind schedule. I didn't mention it to my mom, and thankfully Tom kept his mouth shut, too. When we pulled into the parking lot, we were met by my grandma right away. "Is everything okay?" She took one look at my mom climbing out of the van and said, "Oh, Mica. Are you okay?" She touched my mom's forehead and began to fan her.

"Thanks, Mom," my mom muttered as she sat on the bench outside the chapel. She took some slow, deep breaths and then stopped. "Tom? What are you doing?" she was irritated again. My grandma and I looked at him. He was standing under the shade of a tree a few feet away from us. He seemed bewildered by her question.

Grandma took over for my mom. "Tom, go into the chapel and let the guy know that you're here." She spoke like she was giving directions to a five-year-old.

"Oh." Tom replied and walked into the chapel.

As grandma attended to my mom and Tom was gone, I surveyed the area. It was a cute little area with small shops and architecture that reminded me of some fishing town in Britain. I imagined this was what was called a "quaint" village. The air had a clean quality that gave way to a slightly fishy smell. Nice, but odd. I also realized that there weren't very many cars in the parking lot in front of the chapel. "Grandma?" I waited until she turned towards me, and then asked, "Who is here for the wedding?"

Grandma thought for a moment and replied, "Well, Tata is inside." I was a little surprised. I thought a wedding was supposed to have a lot of people in it and attending it. While I was thinking of the weddings I had seen on TV, I remembered something else—I looked at the dress mom had on. It was nice, but it was no wedding dress.

Tom was wearing a suit, not a tux. This was definitely a different kind of wedding.

Tom came out of the chapel and said, "He's ready for us, whenever you feel up to it." Tom smiled, and I was somewhat surprised by how appropriate that comment was.

Mom smiled and nodded. We all got up and walked into the chapel. My first reaction to the place my mom and Tom would marry was shock. It was incredibly small inside. There was barely enough room for thirty people. I guess it was a good thing not many people were here. It was also fairly old looking inside. Not really in a way that adds character, but just in a way that made it look slightly dingy and spooky. The man who would marry my mom and Tom fit the chapel completely. He was old and spooky and made me feel uneasy.

The man smiled at me and grabbed my arm with his skinny fingers. "So, this is Nyssa? What a beautiful young lady." He hissed when he said "s," and it made me think of an old movie I had seen about vampires. The head vampire spoke with a European accent and hissed when he said "s."

"I will walk you through the ceremony, then we can begin. Yes?" Again, the hiss. I nodded. His hand was still holding onto my arm. I was increasingly more uncomfortable at this, and imagined him pulling me into the basement for his vampire friends to attack me. I wanted to hurry this along.

After he explained my role in the wedding, I was on the verge of tears. My mom and Tom were to walk down the aisle, then wait for me. I would then walk down the aisle and join them at the altar.

Then, this man would marry my parents and ask me if I accepted them as my parents. To which, I would reply "I do." Then, he would introduce the three of us as a new family. I was actually IN the wedding with them! I couldn't believe it!

The actual wedding went fairly quickly, but at the same time, seemed in slow motion. I noticed odd details about the ceremony. I remember Mom cried and her nose ran. Tom smiled the whole time, and I could see the discoloration in his front teeth. The man talking had funny-smelling breath. Then it was over.

Grandma offered to take me for the weekend, so my mom and Tom could have some time alone. But Mom refused. "I don't feel well enough to have a honeymoon. Besides, Nyssa is an important part of this family, and she shouldn't be dropped somewhere for the weekend." She smiled warmly at me and I finally broke down.

I cried and cried. I was overcome by how much my mom loved me. Sure, sometimes she got angry—but she loved me most in the world. I knew that. She had shown me that. There was no one else in the world I could trust more than her. No matter what happened, I would always remember that.

Nyssa Rebecca Corbin

OPERATION: TOM SCREW'S UP

I had to admit: My Mom and Tom made staking out someone's home pretty fun.

I really had no idea what was in store when my mom informed me we were going to get Dawn and Alex back. I thought it would involve a court preceding or a phone call to Kim. Maybe she didn't even want the girls anymore, and that's why she let them roam the neighborhood all day. Well, apparently, she had no intention of giving up her two girls or two child support checks she received each month. So, we had to trap her.

Step One: Stake out the area where they live and take pictures of the girls playing unsupervised. Pay close attention to Alex's clothes, which would definitely be dirty.

Step Two: Confront Kim with those pictures and threaten to take them to the police, unless she agreed to give up custody of the girls.

Step Three: Take the girls home. Move to Tom's first duty station. Live happily ever after.

Well, things got a little messed up part way through Step One.

The first official day of our surveillance was an adventure itself. My mom and Tom had warned me we were going into the city of L.A. Although I had lived near the city all my life, I had not ventured into it more than a few times with my mom. Not only were we going into the city, we were going into a part of the city called Koreatown—or Ktown to those who lived there. My mom warned me that it was incredibly dangerous, dirty, scary and no one spoke any English there.

Tom began to interrupt her, and I thought he was going to argue that last point she made, but she cut him off. "No one speaks our language there," she repeated. I was thoroughly freaked out.

A couple of hours and three doughnuts later, I was okay. We were parked outside of a run-down looking apartment complex.

There were iron bars and fences around the entire building. Actually, a lot of Ktown looked like this. Not as dirty or scary as I pictured it, but more iron around every building than I had seen in my life. I was more intrigued than scared. I peered out of the back window of the van as I munched my third doughnut and wondered if the people who I saw passing by would understand me if I leaned out the window and asked them a question. I felt like I was in a foreign land. Weird.

Halfway through the day, I began to get bored. I had done all my Mad Libs books, I had four doughnuts for my breakfast/lunch, and I really needed to use the bathroom. My mom was just starting to discuss the possibility of Tom dropping us off at the 7-11 for a five minute break, when she stopped in the middle of her sentence. She gasped slightly and whispered, "There they are."

Tom and I whirled around at the same time and saw them. Dawn looked like she had grown taller since the last time I had seen her. Alex was still very small, but healthier looking. Her once pale complexion had a little more color to it. Dawn opened the gate for her sister and Alex stepped out of the confines of the complex. They both looked up and down the block. They talked for a minute, maybe discussing which way to go. Dawn pointed one way and Alex nodded. Then Dawn grabbed her sister's hand and started walking. Alex skipped lightly alongside of her.

The three of us in the van watched the two girls walk up the block, away from us, until my mom snapped us back into our mission. "Grab the camera—take a picture of them—get Alex's butt – it looks soiled," she barked her orders so fast; I think Tom tried to obey all of them at the same time. He grabbed the camera and took a picture of the van's floor as he tried to pull the camera in his direction. The flash went off and startled my mom who instinctively threw out her hand and knocked the camera out of Tom's hands. It then flew across the front cab of the van and slammed into the radio.

When it finally hit the floor, it made an odd whirring noise. My mom yelled something at Tom, and he picked up the camera to examine it. After a few moments, he said, "I think it's broken." Mom snatched the camera from him and began pressing buttons on it.

"Uh, you guys?" I felt they needed to know something.

"What!?" My mom was losing her temper trying to fix the camera.

"The girls just turned that corner." I pointed in the direction that I had last seen them.

"S***!" My mom yelled and opened the van door. "Come on! We have to follow them!" She began walking very fast down the street. Tom and I jumped out of the van and caught up with her. I wasn't sure what we were doing following them with a camera that didn't work. However, I knew better than to question my mom when she was worked up about something. She was without a doubt, worked up at this moment. She was breathing hard and walking fast. I had to jog to keep up with her. She was perspiring, even though it was cool outside, and her eyes were large with agitation. I wasn't sure if this was the best thing for her to be doing, in her pregnant state.

When we reached the corner, the three of us rounded it at full speed. Apparently, we all expected to find the girls part way up this block. Instead they were standing less than ten feet from the corner, and we almost plowed right into them. The girls had stopped to talk to a girl about Dawn's age who was on a bike. Dawn, Alex and the third girl stared at us with surprise. For a while, it seemed that time slowed down, and the three of us and the three of them were trying to make sense of what was happening.

Then—Dawn's face showed fear as she recognized my mother, and she grabbed her sister's hand. They began to run. The third girl saw Dawn and Alex run from us and sped away in another direction on her bike. I had a moment to think about how awful it felt to have kids running away from you in terror, when my mom was off again.

"Come on!" she yelled back to Tom and me. "We have to talk to them!" She was running now. Tom and I ran after her. Tom passed me quickly with his tree-like long legs and soon passed my mom. I was having a hard time catching up to my mom and was starting to get concerned about her running so fast and having a baby inside her jostling around, when I noticed that Tom had stopped. My mom caught up to him, while I was still jogging toward them.

I could see Tom holding the gate open that led into the apartment complex. My mom held the gate for me and ordered Tom to continue chasing after the girls. He did, and when I reached the gate and went inside with my mom, we had no idea where Tom or the girls had gone. There were five or six large apartment buildings inside the gated perimeter. Inside each building looked to be a maze of apartments. My mom and I wandered around for a few moments, until my mom heard Tom's voice. We walked in the direction of his sound and found him talking to Dawn and Alex next to an entrance to one of the buildings.

"I'm so sorry we scared you!" my mom began at once. She put on a very concerned face and went on, "We have been so worried about you guys! Your mom won't let us see you, and we didn't know if you were okay or not. Isn't anyone watching you? Someone could take you both right off the street!" My mom opened her eyes wide and was actually making them well with tears.

I couldn't believe how believable she was! She had taken a failing mission and made it brand new. She was trying to win the kids back over. I had doubts this would work, until I saw Dawn's expression. She seemed confused, but not afraid anymore.

Dawn looked at the ground and whispered, "My mom is at a friend's house. We just wanted to play."

My mom moved a little closer to her and spoke softly, "Of course, you did. There's nothing wrong with that. The only thing wrong here is your mom not being here to look out for you." My mom bent over to be at eye level with Dawn. "Thank goodness we came to make sure you were alright." She reached out and touched Dawn's shoulder.

141

Dawn looked at her, still seeming confused. I'm sure she was struggling with her memories of my mom and trying to compare them with the concerned woman she saw before her. Alex, however, was not confused. She pulled Dawn's hand toward the door and mumbled something that sounded Korean. My mom didn't lose sight of the prize.

"Oh, go ahead," she motioned toward the door. "We don't want to get you into trouble. We just wanted to make sure you were okay." My mom smiled as warmly as she could to Alex. Alex tugged her sister's arm and looked away from my mom. "Oh," my mom offered, just before they went inside, "Would it be okay if we came to visit you again? Maybe we could all go out for ice cream or something?" My mom gave them a hopeful look.

Dawn smiled shyly and answered, "Yeah, I guess so." Then the door closed, and they were gone.

The three of us were fairly quiet walking back to the van.

Tom kept shooting goofy smiles at my mom, but she didn't greet any of them. I had a sickening feeling about my mom ignoring Tom. I knew she was either extremely angry or disappointed in him. Neither one would be good. Just as I was beginning to dread our return to the van, my mother put her arm around me and kissed me on the head.

"You did great, sweetie," she murmured near my ear. I breathed deeply and felt instantly better. I was okay. She was not mad at me.

When we got back to the van, my mother walked up to the driver's side and got in. Tom looked at me with "What's this?" written all over his face. I shrugged my shoulders and got in the back. Tom got in the passenger side and opened his mouth to talk.

He was immediately cut off. "Give me the keys." My mother said calmly. Too calmly.

Tom knew this was a bad sign. "Look." He tried to talk but was cut off.

"Give me the keys and shut up." My mother again sounded perfectly calm and focused. Tom handed her the keys, and we drove out of the neighborhood. I was relieved when we pulled into a 7-11 parking lot. I had only temporarily forgotten that I had to use the bathroom, while we were chasing the girls. I felt that my bladder was about to pop. The three of us went inside and used the facilities. While my mom was washing her hands, I decided to speak to her. I was just going to test the waters a little and see how receptive she was. "So ... Tom screwed up, huh?" I tried to seem casual as I was washing my hands next to her.

My mom didn't answer right away. She walked over to the hand dryer and started it. She began talking, and I had to move quickly next to her to hear what she was saying over the roar of the hand dryer.

"Tom is so stupid, I swear. Here you are, twelve years old, and you have more street smarts than him. I can't believe the army is taking him back!" She laughed at her last comment and I laughed with her. I had assumed at this point, that she was angry about the camera incident in the van, but there was probably something else, too. Maybe she was mad that she had to take charge of the conversation with the girls, as well. Whatever it was, I was so grateful it wasn't me facing her anger.

Tom was already sitting in the van when my mom and I returned. Once seated, my mom calmly turned to him and said, "Give me your wallet." Tom looked unsure but reached into his back pocket and handed her his wallet. She rummaged through the contents and asked, "Do you have any other cash on you?" Tom reached into his pocket and produced some change. She reached out her hand, and he gave it to her. "Get out," she continued to speak in a monotone voice, showing no emotion.

Tom glanced around the area and turned toward her pleading, "Please, Mica. I know you're upset. I just don't understand–"

He didn't get a chance to finish. "You don't understand much, Tom. You don't understand how to work a camera. You don't understand how to talk to children. You don't understand how the world works. So, consider this a lesson in street smarts. Get out of the van and find a way home— without money, your ID - AND without calling my mom."

She was still talking quite calmly, but I knew that wouldn't last long. Mom's switch was about to flip on, and I just wanted Tom to get out of the van before he tripped it.

Tom had his hand on the door handle but was still hesitating and looking around the area. I didn't blame him for hesitating. In the parking lot alone, there were two cars parked next to each other with seriously bad-looking gang- bangers playing loud music and staring hard at all who entered the lot. There was a homeless man picking through the garbage near the corner of the lot, and there was a man screaming into the pay phone on the side of the store. I thought the screaming man was delusional, because he would hang up the phone then pick it up and yell into it, without having put any money in it. Two of the gang-bangers watched the screaming man and laughed loudly at him.

Tom seemed to be taking in this entire scene, as well. He apparently thought he should try one last time to talk to my mom. "Mica..." he realized too late that he had made an awful mistake.

My mother grabbed Tom by his hair (which was still shoulder length and in a pony-tail), and pulled his head in an unnatural angle toward her. His hand grabbed at his own neck. I knew he was in pain. My mom spoke with a quiet anger that made her voice hoarse.

"You will get out of this van or I will NOT be a part of your life anymore," she took a slow breath and added, "You will not see this baby, either. You worthless piece of crap." She inhaled deeply and released her grip on him. He stepped out of the van and walked into the 7-11. I could see his head over the food aisles and followed it back to the men's bathroom. Mom shocked me with a wicked-sounding laugh.

"He probably crapped his pants," she offered as she pulled away from the store. I forcefully laughed with her, but inside, I felt sick and worried. I didn't really care for Tom, but this "lesson" seemed very harsh.

During the drive back to the townhouse, Mom began talking to me about why she had done this to Tom. I almost got the feeling that she was trying to convince herself that she had done the right thing. Maybe as we were driving out of that part of town, she noticed all the scary people and dirty places I noticed.

Maybe she was beginning to doubt her decision. Or maybe she just wanted to make sure that I was on the same page as her. No matter what—I was on the same page—no way was my butt going to be left in the middle of "the hood."

"You know, Tom really needs to wake up and stop being such a screw up. I mean, we're having a baby together now. He has to grow some brain cells, whether he likes it or not," she went on like this for the entire ride home. I didn't talk at all. I just nodded my head and listened to every word she said. When we got home, Mom made some weird health nut sandwiches, and I ate every bit of it. We didn't talk about Tom at all, once we got home. We eventually went to bed, as though Tom was away on business.

The next morning, I got up and poured a bowl of cereal. I was usually up before my mom, and I enjoyed how quiet the house was at this hour. I was getting out the milk, when I heard a rattling at the door. Having just woke up; I actually forgot about Tom being dropped off in L.A. and grabbed the first thing I could throw at whoever was entering our home. The door opened, and Tom slowly dragged his feet through the door. He looked at me, then glanced at my weapon.

He smiled a weary, goofy smile and said quietly, "I used the emergency key—please don't throw onions at me."

I looked in my hand and saw I had grabbed an onion off the counter and was holding it like a baseball. I felt foolish and placed the onion back. Tom was going up the stairs by the time I turned around. I listened to him slowly pad across the floor upstairs to the third bedroom that was used as an office. He was going to sleep there. Good choice, I thought.

After they both woke up, the day went on as usual. I never found out how Tom made it home alive. Mom didn't yell at him again for whatever he had done that day. We never talked about that incident again.

There would be many things like this—events we pretended never happened. Things we pushed under some imaginary mat and forced ourselves to forget about. Like Alex getting beat. Like the lies we told the family court judge about my dad and step-mom. We were getting so accustomed to letting unpleasant things disappear into thin air that nothing we did really seemed so bad anymore. My mom and Tom were certain it would never catch up to us—but I was so afraid that one day it would.

GREAT NEWS

It wasn't long after our incident in Koreatown that Dawn and Alex came over for a visit. I'm not sure why Kim agreed to the visitation. Mom told me that Kim wanted a break from taking care of them. Tom said she wanted to appease us with visitation, so we wouldn't seek full custody in court.

Apparently, Kim really liked the child support money she got and didn't want to jeopardize losing it. I figured the truth of this visit lay between what both of them said. In any case, the girls came over for about three or four overnight visits, spaced out throughout a one-month period. It was after the last visit that our whole world turned inside out.

"The girls are moving back in with us!" My mom seemed overjoyed. I was very confused, although I didn't show it. If this was something that made my mom happy, then I did not want to look like I wasn't happy. I smiled and nodded my head approvingly. I wanted to say something positive, but I didn't know what to say.

Inside, I was completely shocked.

My mom hugged me and pulled me into the bathroom. Once inside, she closed the door of the bathroom and lowered her voice to a whisper. "Kim agreed to a cash settlement for signing over full custody rights to Tom. I told you she only wanted the money," she whispered close to me. Then she opened the door and peeked outside. Satisfied that the girls were occupied with something in some other room, she closed the door again.

I had sat down on the toilet with the seat closed and attempted to take in what my mom was saying. Mom squatted next to me and continued, "We aren't telling anyone about the money. So, this is just between us. Right?"

She looked fixedly at me, and I nodded. She then left the bathroom to go check on the girls. I continued to sit on the toilet and grasp the reality of what was happening.

My mind was reeling with memories of last time the girls lived with us. The awful things that had taken place between my mom and Alex. The way my mom was so angry all the time with everyone in the house. Currently, I had become used to and even happy with, this new living situation. I kissed my mom's butt, and she mostly yelled at Tom. Now, we had bought two children who had previously set my mom into the deep end. Mom being pregnant would make this even easier to achieve, this time.

I knew it wasn't the girls' fault, but I hated our lives when they lived with us, and I knew they had to hate the time they lived with us, too. I realized the girls were in a similar position as me, at that point. The three of us could not say anything about the choices being made for us. My mom and Tom were calling the shots, and we were just kids. Sure, my mom talked to me about things that most parents didn't discuss so openly with their own kids—but I was still just a kid. Practically property.

When I snapped out of my despondent trance, I realized I had been in the bathroom for at least five minutes. I didn't want my mom to think that I had been sulking or crying or anything remotely negative, so I flushed the toilet. Then I washed my hands, put my game face on and opened the door. My mom was sitting on the couch with the girls. She was telling them about Kentucky. This is where Tom had gotten his first orders to. This is where we were moving in about two weeks. It was to be a temporary move, for Tom to get the training he needed before we moved to our final destination for the next few years—Germany. I had lived in Germany with my father for a few months when I was younger. My dad had worked there, and I still had fond memories of the time I spent there with him. But that was way before he met Jay and things started to change.

Mom was still sitting on the couch with the girls and telling them about all the states we would pass through on the way to Kentucky. I leaned against the wall and half listened to her describe the wonders that we would see; the Grand Canyon, some mountains in New Mexico, some other historical something in Texas. I was watching my mom's mouth move without hearing the words she was saying. I couldn't believe we had the girls again, and we were moving to a state I knew nothing about, so very far away. I felt sick to my stomach. This was not a good plan and there was nothing I could say or do.

Tom brushed by me as he walked down the stairs and entered the living room. He showed my mom some paperwork he was taking over to his lawyer. She skimmed through it (although I'm sure she read it, because she was a speed reader) and handed it back to Tom. She nodded her approval to Tom and turned back toward the girls, who had patiently waited to hear more about our fascinating trip. Tom left quickly and didn't return until after dinner that night.

Everything had been finalized, and the girls were now able to move to Kentucky with us.

There was an added complication to this trip; just before Tom had gotten his orders, Mom had gone to the hospital because she thought she was having contractions. It had been a scary experience. It was too early for the baby to come, and the terror on my mom's face had made the situation more frightening for me. I wasn't used to seeing my mom scared because something was out of her control.

After doing some tests on her, the nurses told her what she felt was normal, and the baby looked fine. My mom became angry that she was being brushed off and began to cause a scene. The nurses calmed her and eventually a doctor came in and wrote her a prescription for something. This seemed to make my mom feel better, but the doctor warned her that there were side effects, and she should be careful to watch for them. Mom didn't seem to mind and was more concerned about the "false" labor pains that she had felt.

The meds apparently made her very tired at times—usually right after she took them. This situation added to my feeling that this trip with the girls was not a great idea.

As if we didn't have enough complications, within the first few days of Dawn and Alex living with us, Alex wandered off. She was only gone for about twenty minutes, and she had just walked next door, because these were the only neighbors she knew—but it still upset my mom greatly. She held Alex close to her and told her she could never walk off without telling someone again. I thought that the whole scene seemed odd to me. I mean, if Alex had really been misplaced, why had my mom not gone straight over to the neighbor's house to see if they knew where she was?

Instead, we walked around the entire complex "looking" for Alex. Mom didn't want us yelling for Alex either, since they would only disturb all our other neighbors. Part of me wondered if my mom had allowed Alex to walk off, knowing she was going somewhere safe, just to confuse Dawn and Alex into thinking she was extremely concerned for their well-being. I knew it was a weird thought, but Mom was conniving.

But, as I looked at everyone in the room, once the news of our move was shared, I could see how thrilled they were with the news. I looked over at Dawn and Alex and wondered if they were faking, like me. Alex seemed not to really understand what was happening. All she knew was that she got ice cream every night she had stayed with us, so far. Yay for ice cream!

Dawn was harder for me to figure out. We had not been alone since they had come for visits, so we weren't able to talk openly to one another. I wondered what she was really thinking as she smiled at my mom and her dad and kissed them good night. Was she remembering the horrors of last time we all lived together? Were things really so bad at her mom's that living with us would actually be better?
Maybe she felt helpless like me.

It would be a long time before we would be able to openly talk to each other. Years would pass before we would talk about our feelings and trust each other not to tell my mom what was shared between us. In those few years, so much would happen to our family.

THE TRIP THAT WOULDN'T END

Gazing out at the vast desert of California can either fill you with a peaceful tranquility, or you see it as an empty, dry terrain that depresses you. At this time, I was feeling a little of both. We were traveling across the country to our new home.

All our "loose ends" (as mom called them) had been taken care of. This included working out a new visitation schedule with my father, signing some last-minute paperwork with Kim, and mapping our trip out to Kentucky. As I sat staring out the van window, several hours into our trip, I thought back on the events of the last week leading up to this trip.

My last visit with my father had gone well. Jay and my dad had voiced their opinions about me moving several visits before and knew that nothing they said during this last visit was going to change what was happening. The paperwork for the visitations between us had already been signed. My grandmother's expensive new lawyer had pushed the needed paperwork through the court fairly quickly. My father only insisted on a week during my Christmas break and two weeks during the summer. This amounted to a lot less time than he currently got with me, so my mom agreed. I wasn't thrilled about spending more than a few days at a time with him and Jay, but I figured I could suck it up, if it meant I would only have to do it twice a year.

During my last day with my dad, I hoped to spend some time with him alone. We hadn't done that in a long time, and I really missed it. I still felt angry at him for choosing to be with Jay, but he was my dad. Instead, there was a small family gathering at my grandmother's house. It was nice to say goodbye to my aunts, cousins, grandmother and close family friends. Jay was on pretty good behavior, because my grandma and aunt would confront her if she was too out of line. My grandmother was most vocal when she didn't like Jay's attitude, so I stuck close to her during the barbeque.

There was only one awkward moment at the end of the day.

My mom was very late picking me up and had called to let my dad know that it would be late in the evening when she would arrive. My dad had already planned to go out with some friends. So, instead of rescheduling whatever he planned, he decided to have Jay stay with me until my mom arrived. Before he actually left, he had a heart-to-heart talk with me. I think it lasted about two minutes.

"You know I love you?" he asked. I nodded.

"You know that you are very special to me?" I nodded.

"I will always be your daddy, and I will miss you so much."

He looked at his watch and hugged me goodbye. I hugged him back and fought to keep my composure. I was getting so mad at him, I wanted to cry. Why didn't he stay with me until my mom came?

Then, he was gone. My sisters were asleep. My brothers were spending the night at friends' houses (that seemed to happen a lot). Jay and I were alone, together. I was in the dining room, where my dad had left me as he hurried out the door. Jay was sitting in the living room, which was one room over from where I was. I sat very quietly in my seat and hoped she would forget I was there.

Maybe she had fallen asleep on the couch. I closed my eyes and prayed that she would leave me alone. No luck. "Nyssa? Could you come here, please?" she sounded very nice, and I really hoped that she was having one of her "good moments" that I witnessed on several of my visits. I knew I couldn't ignore her, so I got up and went into the living room. I expected to see her sitting in the recliner that was "her" seat. Instead, she was on the couch. I knew this meant she wanted me to sit next to her. Crap.

She patted the couch next to her, "Come and sit with me."

I sat next to her, and she began immediately, "Now I know that you and I have had our rough times together. I know you don't like me very much. But I have to tell you that what your mom is doing is not a nice thing." She shook her head. I wondered what the heck she was talking about.

She continued, "You know your mom is only using you to get back at your dad. She can't stand the fact that she doesn't have control over him, that he moved on with his life—with me."

She touched my shoulder and I consciously made an effort not to recoil. I really thought she was off her rocker, and I didn't care to understand the nonsense she was spewing at that moment. However, I did want to make it through the day without an incident with her, so I sat very still and tried to look like I was interested in what she had to say. She seemed encouraged by my behavior and went on.

"Don't you think it was weird that your mom decided to get married right after your dad and I did? And what about her getting pregnant? That happened pretty close to us announcing we were going to have another baby. Remember? Your mom is just trying to make your dad and I feel inferior. That's why she's taking you away." She sat back into the couch. She seemed to be giving me time to absorb all of what she just told me. I tried so hard to think what I should do to avoid a confrontation, but not agree with the garbage she was trying to feed me.

"Okay," I muttered. I gave her a half-smile and nervously glanced around the room. I didn't want to look at her. I was so completely uncomfortable and just wanted my mom to pick me up already.

Jay sighed and I could feel her leaning back into the couch.

After a while, I had to turn around and look at her. I was too curious about what she was doing back there. She was reclining on the couch with her legs stretched out and her hands resting over her eyes. She looked exhausted and slightly frustrated. She sighed again and removed her hands from her eyes.

"I hope one day you think back on this and realize that what I said was true." With that, she stood up and walked into the kitchen. I could hear her opening a can of soda, and when she didn't reappear, I assumed she was drinking it in the kitchen. I stayed in the living room and soon the doorbell rang.

Jay came and gave me a quick hug before opening the door, then I was gone.

Now, as I sat in my mom's van, on the way to a state I knew very little about, halfway across the country, Jay's words echoed in my head. Was I dwelling on what she said, because I thought she was out of her mind? Maybe I was thinking about it, because it made me mad she thought she had my mom so figured out. But no, I wasn't really mad about our conversation. I was wondering if there was any truth to what she had said.

When I really thought about it, the timing of the weddings and babies were strikingly similar. My mom announced her plans after I told her about my dad and Jay. Was she really just trying to hurt my dad? Was she mad she didn't have the pull with him she did before Jay came along? Was she now using me as the knife to inflict her final jab? Even us moving to Germany, the only foreign country my dad had been able to take me to ... did she feel the need to "one up" him by also moving me there, but for a longer period of time?

All these questions were giving me a headache. I closed my eyes and let the hum of the engine lull me to sleep. I would have plenty of new challenges awaiting me in Kentucky. A new school, new neighborhood and new friends. Anything beyond that could wait, for now. But I didn't realize that more serious drama was already beginning on this lovely family trip out to our new home.

"Tom, pull over right now!" Mom screaming at Tom woke me to a state of panic in the van. My arms flailed in front of me and I sat straight up in my seat. I quickly searched around me for the source of my mom's panic. We were not in an accident. The van was not on fire. My mom didn't look like she was having the baby. But what was that smell?

I followed my mom's gaze and saw that she was glaring at Alex. I blinked my eyes hard to focus my sleepy eyes better and realized that Alex was soaked from the waist down. Had she spilled something? My next thought answered that question.

Alex had peed on herself. She still had problems going to the bathroom. A long car ride was probably the worst thing to do with this child.

"Tom, just pull off right here!" My mom was getting ready to attack Tom.

He pulled off, but remarked, "There's no place to eat here."

Mom rubbed her now protruding belly and yelled, "Jesus, Tom! Your daughter just pissed all over the floor in here, and all you can think about is food?!"

Alex was crying and looking toward Dawn and me for comfort. Dawn kept her eyes on the book she was reading. She clearly did not want to get involved. Neither did I. However, I could see my mom was getting more and more aggravated at having to yell at Tom and deal with Alex crying on the floor of the van, at the same time.

"Mom?" I took a deep breath and hoped I was doing the right thing. "Do you need me to do anything?" I asked.

My mom looked at me, like she didn't realize I was awake.

She looked around and saw that we were pulling into a gas station.

"Yes. Could you help Alex out of the van? I need to find her another pair of clothes." She seemed a little more at ease and that seemed to calm the whole van down. Alex's crying turned into a light whimper.

Dawn looked around at the situation a little more freely. Tom —well, I didn't really care.

Fifteen minutes later, we changed Alex, all took bathroom breaks, and went up the street to the local am/pm for their cheap burgers and nachos. This was to be our staple meal every day for the next six days we traveled. At 99 cents a burger, it was the cheapest meal my mom found.

Since my mom calmed down, we were able to laugh a little about what happened. "What is wrong with you, Tom?

Seriously." My mom laughed, as she asked him. "You truly are thinking about food every minute of the day, aren't you?" She threw a French fry at him, and we all laughed.

Tom brushed the fry from the front of his shirt and said, "I couldn't help it. We hadn't eaten in over four hours. I was starving."

His mouth was full of burger as he spoke. I thought he looked so pitiful.

My mom turned back toward me and touched my shoulder.

"Thank you for helping me." She whispered it close to my ear. I nodded. My mouth was full of food, and I knew I shouldn't talk.

"See, Tom? Nyssa knows her manners. She doesn't talk with food in her mouth." Tom just smiled a goofy smile, and everything seemed loose and fun.

But I knew that things would be changing again. I had not forgotten that Alex had peed in the van and my mom had been very upset by it—again. It had been over a year since they had been taken away, and now I feared that the same problems were arising again. These familiar problems would have familiar punishments. I knew this was the path we were headed down.

The next day, we stopped at the Grand Canyon to see what my mom called "the most beautiful place in Arizona." Apparently, we ended up on some back route that wasn't meant for most tourists (at least ones with three children and a pregnant lady). Mom got frustrated with Tom and told him to pull over down a gravel road, and we would hike over a small hill where we could see the Canyon. Once we parked in a makeshift parking area, the problems started immediately.

"Tom! She peed again!" Mom was furious. Since no one else was in the parking lot, she was free to yell and rant. There was one other car in the lot, but it was empty. I thought that was a good sign. These people went to see something nearby, right? That meant this hole we were here to see must be close by. But first, we had to deal with our current situation.

"Oh, Alex." Tom looked at her with dopey disappointment, then just stared at her.

"Ooooooohhhh, Ah-lecks," Mom mimicked him. "Is that your solution to this?" She pushed passed him and took Alex by the arm.

"Tom, you are so useless. When we get to the Canyon, do us all a favor and jump in—kay?" My mom was pulling Alex to the back of the van to change her. She changed her quite roughly and complained about running out of clothes for her before the trip was over. Finally, with Alex changed, we found what looked like a trail and began following it.

Mom walked with Tom, up in the front of our group. Dawn and Alex walked in front of me, and I was last in line. That was fine with me; I was away from the major sources of drama. I thought.

As I walked behind the girls, I saw urine run down Alex's leg. Part of her shorts became dark with wetness, but she continued to walk normally in front of me. I couldn't believe what I had just seen. She had peed herself ten minutes ago. How could she be doing this again? And how could she just walk like nothing is happening? Or—better yet, what was going to happen when my mom found out about this?

I looked ahead at my mom and Tom. We had actually been walking up this hill for a while, but I had lost track of time worrying about what Alex had done. My mom was looking a bit winded, and we still had more than half the hill left (turned out—it looked a lot smaller from down in the parking lot). Mom found a fallen tree to sit on and ordered Tom to go to the top of the hill and give us a report. With Tom gone and my mom resting, I knew it was a matter of time before she saw Alex's wet shorts. I had to think fast.

"Oh, I'm sorry, Alex," I said, before I realized what I was doing.

"Mom, Alex told me she had to potty, and I told her to hold on for a minute. I guess she couldn't wait." After I finished, I was happy with my "on the spot" improv.

Mom looked extremely frustrated and put her head in her hands. I began to rethink what I had done. Was she going to be mad at me, now? Just then, Tom came down the hill and nearly took out Dawn because he slid on some gravel. "There's just more mountains on the other side of this one. I don't think we're in the right place."

He seemed not to notice my mom's despair or Alex's wet shorts.

Mom lifted her head slowly, "Everyone back to the van." She was so calm that I knew she was about to blow. Everyone walked back to the van. We might have stood a chance by following mom's orders, but Tom had to mess things up. "Are we going to another place to see it?" he asked.

Mom didn't speak. Tom looked at me, and I shook my head with a pained look on my face—it read "please, shut up."

Tom shrugged his shoulders, and we all hiked back to the van in silence.
Once there, my mom turned around and let loose. "I hate you all! Alex just peed and now she purposely peed on herself, again! Nyssa, I don't believe you for a second! Tom is so oblivious to everything, and Dawn is the mindless zombie child! I planned a perfect trip for us, and you are all ruining it!"

She slammed the door open and suddenly glanced over her shoulder. It was then we all realized the occupants of the empty car were walking toward their car. They had been close enough to hear my mom screaming at us. I was so embarrassed.

Mom calmed down with strangers around and placed a towel on the floor, then told us to get in the van. Once we were down the road, Mom turned around and addressed Alex, "You sit down on the towel. If you can't control yourself, you're not sitting on my van seats." Alex crawled onto the floor and sat cross legged on the towel.

This caused a whole new problem—Alex got car sick from the strong vibrations on the floorboard. She threw up, and Mom freaked out once again. This trip was never going to end.

It was during this trip that I prayed to God every day that He would not let the same situation occur in our household that occurred the year before. I prayed before I went to sleep. I prayed while we drove across the endless country that led to our new home. I prayed while we ate, with my eyes wide open. I begged God to control my mom and protect Alex. I wanted protection for Dawn and me, as well, but I knew Alex needed a supernatural power on her side to make it through my mom's harsh character.

I never told my mom that I prayed. My mom and Tom were into a lot of different "spiritual" ways of life and belief systems, but Christianity was not one of them. My mom seemed to favor astrology with some Wicca mixed in. Even at a young age, I knew that this was very strange and did not mention it to many people. I learned a little about God through my grandmother, who had been raised Catholic. That is, until my mom and her began joining séance meetings. Then she was more interested in talking to dead people than God.

As the tensions grew in the van, the number of prayers I sent up also grew. Toward the end of the trip, I was praying about every thirty minutes. I would read a chapter of one of the books I had brought, then I would pray. Mom would start screaming and throwing things and I would pray. Eventually, I was praying and making promises I could never keep. I prayed, "Please Lord, protect us from this woman, and I will never be bad again. Please Lord, make Alex stop peeing on herself, and I will never tell a lie in my life." It's no wonder He didn't answer those prayers.

I was pretty sure Dawn felt the same way I did. We started our trip out full of hope for our future in a new place. We finished the trip scared of my mom, angry at Alex for not having control over her bodily functions, frustrated at Tom for not being a man and protecting us from my mom, and basically depressed about what the future would hold for us. It was glaringly obvious that nothing had changed from a year ago, except now we were far away from anyone who could possibly help us. I didn't even have my dad to go visit when things got really bad between my mom and Alex. I'm sure at this point, even Dawn was wishing she could see her mom walk up to the van and take them both back to their small apartment in a very dangerous neighborhood. Instead, we were stuck. I didn't even know where Kentucky was on a map. Great.

WELCOME TO KENTUCKY

The countryside of Kentucky was strikingly beautiful. It was just beginning to change into autumn, and the hills were still lush and green, but some of the trees were changing colors to the most amazing reds and golds I had ever seen. After being inside the van for more than a week, I longed to be outside in this awesome display of nature. The van smelled of urine, fast food and sweat. I felt I was suffocating in the funky smells of our road trip.

"Tom needs to check in on base, then we can find out where our new home is." Mom was beaming with excitement as she told me and Dawn the current plan of action.

She turned back to Tom and rambled on a bit, "Do you think we'll move into housing this week? That neighborhood over there has such nice-looking brick homes; will that be like the one we get? Is the family hotel really nice? Will they give us enough money to stay in a hotel out in town? The town seems nice and quiet enough. Maybe we should check it out tomorrow; I mean after we take it easy this evening and get some sleep."

On and on she went. Tom seemed pleased she was so happy and excited about our living arrangements here. He smiled and nodded toward her as she talked.

Little did any of us know that only a couple hours later, we would be stuffed into a one-room military hotel that resembled the cheap Motel 6's we stayed at on our way to this base, Fort Knox.

We could only stay here for a week, then we would have to find our own housing off base. My mom had been upset to learn that there was a waiting list for base housing, and it could take up to a year before we were able to move into one of those cute little brick houses that we had seen earlier. Until then, we would need to find housing off base.

I didn't think this was such a bad thing, until my mom started screaming, "We have how much allowed for rent every month?" Obviously, it was much less than she had expected. She was so furious by the turn of events, that she hit Tom on the side of the head.

I couldn't stand being cooped up with this hostility any longer. I knew I was risking a lot, but I had to ask, "Mom? Could I please go outside and look around? I promise to stay close to the motel." Surprisingly, she murmured, "I don't care. Just take Dawn with you. The less people invading my space right now, the better."

She lay down on the bed and told Tom to rub her feet. I grabbed Dawn, and we headed to the door. Alex followed us with her eyes, longingly. Dawn and I knew better than to invite her along, so we ignored her and went outside.

It was early evening, and the fresh, cool air was what I needed to revive myself. I took a deep breath and enjoyed the smell of the clean air. I assessed the area around me. The door we exited from emptied into one side of the parking lot. A family was trying to get themselves out of their truck and into the motel. They seemed to have a difficult time with their luggage and younger children. The mom yelled something out, and two boys jumped out of the truck. One was about my age and the other was a little younger.

The boys helped their parents carry some bags into the door that Dawn and I were still standing near, while their mom and dad attended to two younger children. Soon, they were all inside the building.

Dawn and I had been momentarily entertained by this family, and when they were gone, it was quiet and awkward. Dawn and I smiled at each other nervously. We hadn't been together in a long time. We both looked around the parking lot and surveyed the surrounding forest. All was quiet. We glanced sheepishly at each other again and smiled. I didn't know what to say, and clearly, she didn't either.

Just when I was about to ask Dawn what she thought we should do, the two boys from a few moments earlier came out the door. The older boy had a skateboard, and the younger one had a soft bean bag type ball that he threw up in the air and bounced off his head. They stayed in the parking lot, only a few yards away from where Dawn and I were. We sat on the curb and watched them for a while. We tried not to stare, but since we weren't really talking to each other, we had nothing to do but watch these two boys.

Finally, the older one skated over to us. "Hey," he said, with a smile.

"Hey," I answered back. When I didn't hear Dawn say anything, I glanced at her. She was staring at her feet.

He didn't seem to mind that she hadn't answered him. He asked, "Did you guys just get here, too?"
I nodded.

"Where from?" he asked.

"California," I answered. Then I thought I should ask him, just to be polite. "How about you guys?"

"We just drove up from Georgia." He pointed toward his brother and their truck. Then he looked surprised and asked, "Are you really from California or was your dad just stationed there?"

"No, this is our first base—or station, I guess. We lived in California," I explained.

The boy looked excited. "You mean like where Hollywood and Los Angeles are?" he asked in disbelief.

I nodded again. I didn't get why this boy was so worked up about California. To me, it was just one of the fifty states and happened to be the one we were from. I was about to tell him that it was really no big deal, when he turned toward his brother and yelled, "Get over here Todd! These girls are from California!" His brother scooped up the ball he was playing with, using the tip of his shoe. He ran over and asked, "Are you from Hollywood?"

Dawn and I looked at each other and giggled. What planet were these guys from? "No, we're not 'from' Hollywood. We live about thirty minutes away. Um, I mean lived." I was about to ask them if they knew anything about this base, other than there was a bunch of gold kept somewhere. But they just wanted to talk about California.

"Have you ever seen a movie star?" the younger one asked.

"Um, yeah." I was struggling to remember the names of actors we had seen while eating or shopping, when I heard my mom's voice.

"Dawn and Nyssa—time to eat!" Mom was standing at the side door with her hand on her hip. I was very uncomfortable with her demeanor. Dawn and I got up and said goodbye to the boys. We walked into the room and saw that there was no food set out. Was it too much to hope that we were actually going out to eat? Yes, it was.

Mom sat on the bed and told Dawn and me to sit across from her. "Look, I know you are both anxious to make some new friends, but you need to be careful about who you are talking to." I didn't see what could have been wrong with those boys, but I kept my mouth shut. "Don't give people you just meet too much information about yourself, especially boys."

Mom looked tensely at us when she spoke those last few words. When she was done talking to us, Dawn went to use the bathroom. Mom whispered to me, "I don't really care if you make friends with boys; I know you can handle yourself. I am more worried about Dawn. Just keep an eye on her for me. Okay?"

She winked at me, and I nodded with a smile. Mom obviously trusted me the most in the family. It made me sad to think that she treated me more like an adult than her own husband. But I guessed that wasn't my fault.

We made sandwiches in the room for dinner that night and managed to make it through the evening without any major incidents. I think my mom was too exhausted from the long trip to get worked up any more about our situation. We all fell asleep, with the hope of finding a new place to live tomorrow. Mom and Tom in their bed, Dawn and I sharing another bed, and Alex on the floor.

Mom said she couldn't be trusted not to wet the bed. I guessed that made sense.

The next day, we ventured into town to look at a few apartments and homes for rent. My mom had decided on a town that was closest to Fort Knox, so it would be the closest to where Tom worked. It was called Radcliff, and that was about all we knew of it.

I was interested to see what this new community had to offer. My mom seemed more and more irritated at having to do all this footwork to find a place to live. She had been looking forward to the commanding, little-brain-effort required approach that the military took to moving its soldiers around. I was beginning to feel that it worked well if that soldier didn't have a family attached to him.

Whatever. I was still fascinated by the new and unknown, and this town was definitely new and unknown to me.

"Hey, there's a Walmart." Tom pointed out.

Mom looked at Tom with the most uninterested look and said, "Fine. What's a Walmart?" She sighed and acted like she couldn't care less.

Tom thought for a moment and explained, "Well, it's like a Kmart meets a grocery store. Er, something like that." He seemed unsure of his explanation and shrugged it off.

"Really?" Mom seemed mildly interested. "Maybe we could stop by on the way back to the base. Ya know, just to look." I was happy to see my mom interested about anything in the town. Maybe she wouldn't be a mean grump all day.

The first part of the day was rough. The few apartments we looked at were either too small, or Mom didn't like the look of the neighborhood. I didn't see anything wrong with the neighborhood, but I guessed by watching the area that if there were a lot of teens riding bikes and skateboards around —that must mean it was a bad neighborhood.

The one house we went to look at was too expensive (why did we even go, then?). By lunchtime we were all pretty tired, hungry and forlorn. Where would we live? We decided to eat at Wendy's and passed a trailer park on the way there.

"There's a trailer park. I thought I saw a 'for rent' sign up in that first trailer," Tom remarked.

Mom huffed and snarled, "There is no way that we are living in a trailer. It is bad enough we moved out here to the middle of BFE. Now we're going to act like trailer hicks, too?" She made herself chuckle, and we all laughed nervously.

Lunch went quietly after that. It wasn't until Dawn and I returned from using the bathroom that Tom smiled and told us that we would be checking out that trailer park, after all. I looked at mom for approval, and she just shrugged a "Whatever" shrug. I thought she was getting too tired from running around in her pregnant state to even put up an argument. I didn't know much about trailer parks, so I really didn't care either way.

When we got to the trailer park, Mom and Tom went inside with Alex, while Dawn and I stayed in the van. It was getting colder outside, and Dawn and I did not have very good coats. October in California was not as cold as October in Kentucky. Dawn and I huddled on the bench seat and watched kids playing around the trailers. It wasn't until I started drifting off to sleep that I realized that they had been in the rental office for a while. Was this a good thing?

When they finally returned, Tom had his big goofy grin plastered all over his face, and my mom looked upset. This was not a good combination. As Mom loaded Alex into the back of the van, I noticed an Asian lady walk over to the glass door at the rental office and wave. I waved back, thinking she was waving at Dawn and me.

"Don't bother, Nyssa. She already saw the both of you out here. Alex is the one she is waving to." She spoke in her monotone voice she used to keep from blowing up. I looked at the window and saw she was still watching us. It wasn't until Alex turned around and waved to her that she began waving again. Okay—so she only likes little kids? Mom explained, once we got on the road back to the base.

"That woman is Kim's evil twin. And you know that must be bad, because Kim is the devil." Mom went on to explain that the owner's wife was a Korean lady who was infatuated with Alex. She had looked out the window at Dawn and I and said we were "okay," but Alex was a little "doll child." Mom looked at Dawn and asked, "Sound familiar?" We all knew this was what Kim had always called Alex, and that she favored Alex over Dawn, because she was her "doll child." Dawn nodded and looked down.

Tom began talking, "Well, the good news is that we have a trailer to move into tomorrow. The price is reasonable, for now, and it's right across the street from a middle school. So, you can walk to school like you always liked to do." Tom was smiling at me in the rearview mirror.

"Cool," I answered, with little emotion. I was wondering if this Korean lady would agitate my mom to the point of her kicking this lady's butt. I knew that was a sad possibility.

On the way back to the base, we stopped at Walmart and were all shocked at how huge the place was. "Why don't we have these in California?" my mom asked in awe. We bought a few groceries to make a dinner back at the base motel. The ride back was happy, with the hope of us moving into a bigger place. Although the trailer park wasn't where we had been expecting to live—anything was better than all of us living in one room with one bathroom.

Nyssa Rebecca Corbin

Dark Secret

MAKING A NEW HOME

Once we had moved our belongings into the trailer, we realized what little we had. Our large household items were still with the military and would not be unloaded until we moved on base. So, we only had what things we had brought with us on the trip. The trailer came with a couch and three basic beds. But that was it.

I don't think Dawn and I really cared. It was so roomy compared to the motels we had been staying in, and we both knew it was temporary. We made the best of it by playing card games, drawing and listening to music in our room. Our room was partially divided by a half-wall, so we had some privacy, but were also able to spend some time together, without my mom breathing down our necks.

At first, Mom didn't seem to notice all the time Dawn and I were spending together. She had been preoccupied looking up information about what schools we would be attending and where we could get cheap household items (like a T.V.). It really wasn't until Dawn and I began to include Alex in our card games that Mom became concerned.

"What are you guys doing?" Mom asked, after getting off the phone with someone from the base. She had been trying to get us all physical exams, so we could enroll in our schools. She didn't seem angry, but something about her tone told me she was at least annoyed by us at that moment.

"We taught Alex how to play 'Go Fish.'" I tried to think of a way to make this appealing for my mom. "Dawn and I wanted to keep her busy while you were on the phone. And she is really funny when she plays. Wanna see?" I handed out the cards and thought my mom would find it amusing, maybe even cute to see Alex say "Fish!" and try to give us cards that we didn't ask for as a consolation for her not having any matching cards. It had cracked the three of us up. But Mom wouldn't give it a chance.

"She needs to keep practicing her writing. She will never be okay for school unless she can at least write her own name legibly," Mom remarked while getting more paper out for Alex to write on.

Alex had been scribbling on paper most of the last few days. Sometimes it resembled her name, sometimes it just looked like doodles. Mom used that time to point out what an awful mom Kim had been. "I taught Nyssa to write her name and the alphabet by the time she started preschool," Mom boasted. Apparently, school had not been that important to Dawn and Alex's mom. Maybe Mom would bond with Alex while trying to help her get ready for school.

Or, maybe she would find another thing to ignite her anger toward Alex. My mom hated incompetent people, even children.

Once Alex was given more paper and told to practice her name, Mom turned toward Dawn and me. "Both of you get a notebook and a pencil." She sat on the couch and looked exhausted. After Dawn and I picked out a notebook each from our new school supplies, we headed down the hall and back to my mom. We stood in front of her, and she quietly told us to sit on the floor in front of her. We briefly looked at each other, questioningly.

My mom took a deep breath and began. "I know this trip has been difficult. I know this isn't what we expected would happen when we got here ... But I want you to realize how lucky you are to still be here. Nyssa, you know how awful things got at your dad's house. How your dad chose Jay over you, time after time. How mean and uncaring Jay was to you, and how she always favored her own boys over you. And Dawn, you remember how much more your mom loved Alex than you. You remember how many good things she would always say to Alex, but not you. Do you both remember that?" Mom asked.

We nodded and looked down at the floor. We felt guilty, somehow. "Just so you guys don't forget those things, I am going to have you write some things down. Ya know, to keep them fresh in your minds." She said sentences aloud and we copied them. Mine said, "I was never happy living with my dad and Jay. I love living with my mom and Tom. My home here is happy, safe and loving." Then, I copied those few sentences fifty times.

Dawn's sentences were similar to mine. As Dawn and I went to our room to write, I realized how quiet the trailer had become. No more games—the three of us had writing to do. Maybe Mom just wanted the place quiet. Maybe Dawn and I had inadvertently made it harder for my mom to make her phone calls. Whatever the reason, I was sure she had a good reason for giving us these sentences to copy. Besides, writing good things over and over couldn't be bad—right?

After a while, the silence was broken by my mom yelling, "What, are you an animal?" Dawn and I looked at each other.

We knew Alex had wet herself. There was screaming, a pounding sound, and then Alex's soft crying. Dawn and I didn't say anything.

We finished our writing and later that evening showed my mom. She smiled at us, and we smiled back. Neither Dawn nor I paid very much attention to Alex standing in the corner of the living room. Things were going fairly well for Dawn and me, and I'm sure neither of us wanted to jeopardize that.

Mom got off the phone with Tom, who was on his way home from the base. He had been gone for a few days for some special training having to do with his re-enlistment. Mom sounded so happy to have him coming home. She seemed overwhelmed at trying to register us for school by herself. She hung up the phone and had a big smile on her face.

"Tom was able to get tomorrow off, so he can be with us when you guys are registered for school." She seemed happy to have him along. She explained that she made quite an impression on Tom's supervisor. She convinced him that her pregnancy was very high risk, and that she needed a lot of assistance.

Then, she suddenly realized what time it was. "Oh, girls, I am so tired. Could you make dinner? Nyssa, tell Dawn what you need her to do." We both popped up and went into the kitchen.

Things were so good when Mom was happy. Dawn got out the ingredients for Hamburger Helper, and I started the electric wok with some water to boil. I showed Dawn how to use the can opener for the vegetables and we were just about to start cooking the meat in a different pan, when mom yelled from the living room. Dawn and I looked through the opening over the stove to where my mom was, to see her with her head in her hands and still sitting on the couch.

This is when I got a clear look at Alex. She was standing in the corner, facing out toward my mom, with her arms outstretched in front of her. She was standing on top of an opened garbage bag, presumably to "catch" any more of her accidents. I wondered if she had been that way the whole time she had been in trouble (since her last accident several hours earlier). Her shaking arms told me that she had. Just then, I heard the trickling sound of Alex peeing on the plastic bag at her feet. Dawn and I stood silent in the kitchen. What were we supposed to do?

"Mom?" I asked quietly. I thought I could help her, before she completely lost it. She looked up at me, cold. I continued, anyways. "Is there anything I can do?" I was sincere in my question.

Anything to get back that happy mom of thirty minutes ago. Mom shook her head. "No, Nyssa. Tom will deal with this, this time. I'm done for today." She leaned back into the couch and closed her eyes.

Being pregnant seemed to be very draining. That was good for Alex, this time. I reasoned that it would be better to have to deal with Tom than my mom.

I returned to the kitchen to finish dinner and took a quick peek over at Alex. She was shaking and silently crying. She continued to keep her arms up, but the constant tension on her arms seemed unbearable. She may have also been feeling the coldness from the wetness on the lower half of her body. I felt so bad for her, but I had to focus on finishing dinner. Sympathizing with her too much would only make things worse.

Dawn was in a daze, staring at her sister. "Dawn, get the plates out for dinner." She looked at me with tears in her eyes, then walked over to the cupboard and began pulling out our dishes.

Just as I was plating the food, Dawn and I heard the van pull up. Tom was home. I took a deep breath and hoped this situation would blow over quickly, and we could get on with dinner. Part of me knew that was asking too much.

Tom opened the door with a big grin on his face. He seemed happy from his earlier conversation with Mom and the news that he didn't have to go to work the next day. But Tom knew something was wrong when he wasn't greeted by a return smile from my mom.

She continued to lay back into the couch with her eyes closed. Tom saw Alex standing in the corner. "What is this?" he asked, to no one in particular.

Mom opened her eyes and slowly sat up straight. "You wanna know what this is? Your daughter feels that her new home is a giant toilet and she can go wherever she pleases. It's too much trouble to say you have to go, isn't it, you little brat?" Mom sneered at her.
"No, Anna," Alex whimpered back to her. This was her and Dawn's new name for my mom, given back before we left California. Back when they were getting ice cream every day and bribed to want to come with us to Kentucky.

My mom looked coldly at Tom and said, "You need to deal with this, I'm done for today." Then she closed her eyes and sat back into the couch again.

Tom walked over to Alex, turned her around and spanked her. Then he shook his finger at her, "I will spank you every time you pee on the floor. Do you understand?" Alex was crying, but she managed to say, "Yes, Daddy." Then, Tom started to walk over to my mom. Alex collapsed in her own puddle, exhausted from her hours of punishment.

"Are you kidding me, Tom?" Mom looked at him with disbelief. "You think she is taking you seriously? Look at her." All of us looked at her. Dawn and I were still in the kitchen, we did not want to get too involved in this. Alex was beginning to calm down and seemed to be catching her breath, still seated in her own puddle.

"She's laughing at you. Look at her." Mom pointed at Alex. I didn't see what mom was talking about. Alex definitely was not laughing, but maybe I was at a wrong angle to see her.

Tom walked over to Alex and said, "This is not funny, young lady. I will spank you again, if I have to."

Mom began to laugh. "Really, Tom? Cause I don't even believe you, so I know she thinks you're a big joke. Look at her. She is smiling at you." Again, we all looked at Alex, who still looked the same as before. Except now, she looked a little more scared. I'm sure she sensed, like Dawn and I, that mom was leading up to something.

Mom raised her voice and said, "You are the man of this house, and your five-year-old is laughing at you!"

Tom grabbed Alex by the arm and faced my mom, "What should I do?" he asked.

"Be a man!" she shouted. "Should I spank her again?" "She'll just laugh at you again." "What should I do?!"

"BE A MAN, TOM!"

"What do you want me to do?!"

"LOOK! SHE IS LAUGHING AT YOU!" Mom yelled.

Then, Tom lifted Alex up over his head, and she screamed as Tom dropped her on the living room floor. She yelped as she thudded on the ground, then buried her face into the carpet as she cried.

The extreme quiet in the trailer, after such escalation, seemed so strong. Dawn and I stood silent in the kitchen. I realized that Alex could really be hurt, but for the first time since knowing Tom, I was too afraid of him to say anything. My mom had used him as her tool for discipline, and I was extremely scared.

Mom had Tom clean up Alex and the floor, then he joined us for dinner. Alex ate after us, alone at the table. I glanced over at her, when my mom wasn't looking, and she seemed to be eating her food very quickly. I thought that was a good thing. I mean, if she had been hurt badly, she wouldn't just be sitting up, eating like normal.

I turned my attention toward Tom and my mom talking about the next day's events. We had to get physicals and turn in paperwork to the schools the next day, so we could start as soon as possible. School was a good thing. With all of us out of the house, Mom could relax and have no one to piss her off. I really wanted us all to start school. I sat on the couch, next to my mom and Tom and thought about the outfits I could put together with the limited clothes I brought with me. I thought about how I would wear my hair. I thought about how I could make friends.

Then, a strange sound interrupted my daydreaming. A wet, choking sound made me look up toward Alex, who was still sitting at the table. Her body lurched forward, as she made the awful sound again. Mom yelled at her, "Get up! Go to the bathroom!"

Alex stood up and started walking toward the bathroom, but only a few steps from the bathroom door, finally lost what little dinner she had eaten only minutes earlier. When she was done, she stood there and stared at the mess that was now in the middle of the hallway.

Mom screamed at Tom, "You're useless! Why didn't you do something?" Just as Tom opened his mouth to answer her, she said, "Shut up. Don't say anything. Don't do anything. You seem to be good at that." She stood up from the couch and said, "Dawn, get some paper towels and a plastic bag to clean up that mess. Nyssa, get some clean clothes for Alex. At least I know you two will help me." As she walked toward Alex, Dawn and I went quickly to obey our orders.

After finding some clean pajamas for Alex, I stood in the door of the bathroom and waited for my next set of orders. My mom was sitting on the side of the bathtub, while Alex kneeled in front of the toilet. She seemed to be finished throwing up, but my mom wasn't taking any chances.

"She keeps making sounds like she's going to puke again," my mom explained to me. I nodded and stood in the doorway, like an obedient soldier, holding the clothes my mom had requested. I watched Dawn scrub the hallway carpet, attempting to get all the vomit out of the carpet fibers. She was so focused on her task, she didn't notice that I was watching her. I turned to look back into the bathroom, when I heard Alex's familiar puking sound. I saw her body lurch forward again, but she was slightly to the side of the toilet. If she threw up, it wasn't going to make it into the toilet.

Mom grabbed Alex by the back of the neck and pushed her head into the toilet. "This is where you throw up!" she yelled at her.

Once Alex's head went into the toilet, I instinctively turned my head away from the awful scene. I was looking at Dawn, who was staring back at me with terror in her eyes. Even with only being able to hear the sounds from the bathroom, I was sure Dawn knew what was happening. I pointed to the floor where she had been cleaning, and she nodded. Wiping away her tears, she picked up all the paper towels and put them into the plastic bag. She glanced at me one more time, before heading to the kitchen to throw the bag away.

I didn't want to, but I knew I had to face my mom at some point. I turned back toward the bathroom. Alex was sitting in front of the toilet, quietly crying. Mom was wiping off the rim of the toilet with tissue, and then she flushed it.

"Thanks, Nyssa," she said, as she took the clothes from my hand. I nodded and asked if she needed anything else. She smiled and said, "No, Nyssa. You have done more than enough." She hugged me and kissed me goodnight.

I escaped to my room, just as Dawn was doing the same. We didn't say anything to each other, as we both got ready for bed. The events of that evening had tarnished any joy or excitement we had felt about going to our new schools the next day. I tried to remember the things I had been daydreaming about earlier. My outfits, how I would make friends ... anything that would keep the image of Alex being thrown on the ground out of my head, or Alex having her head shoved into the toilet. Anything else to fill my thoughts, so I could fall asleep. I wondered what Dawn was thinking about in her bed, just five feet away from me. I wondered if I should ask her, but finally fell asleep.

READY FOR SCHOOL

The next day, we awoke to the smell of something yummy cooking in the kitchen. Dawn and I crawled out of bed and followed the smells coming from the front of the trailer. Once we were in the kitchen, we saw that my mom made eggs and pancakes. Since mom wasn't much of a morning person, this was a special treat.

Dawn and I ate well and complimented mom on her food.

"Oh, I'm glad you like it. I wanted to make sure you all got a good breakfast before we start our day of running around and registering you three for school." Mom smiled and sipped on her coffee.

I looked around when she mentioned the "three" of us and became aware of the fact that Alex was not around and had not eaten with us. I felt a little uneasy. Where was she? I continued to eat and struggled to come up with a way to ask about Alex, without sounding too concerned. Thankfully, Alex walked out from the back of the trailer then.

"Did you pee in the toilet?" my mom asked her.

Alex nodded and smiled.

"Good." Mom motioned for Alex to come toward her, so she could brush her hair. She spoke softly to her, "You know you have to use the toilet at the school, or you can't play any games or have any friends there—right?" Mom was very gentle as she slowly pulled the brush through Alex's shiny black hair.

Alex spoke quietly, "Yes, Anna. I remember." Her broken English would have normally upset my mom, but she didn't seem to notice it at that moment. Alex's "baby talk" was always a reminder to my mom that Kim treated Alex like a baby, and now it was my mom's job to "fix" her.

"Good." Mom gently turned Alex around and said, "You want to go and play at school, right?"

Alex nodded more vigorously this time.

Mom smiled and told her to go sit on the toilet again.

"Okay, girls. You both need to go and get ready. We are leaving in forty minutes. Nyssa, you can have the shower. If Alex is still in there, just ignore her. I would rather she just sit on the pot until we leave, than piss herself while we're out. Dawn, get changed. You can take a bath tonight. Okay, go on, you guys." She shooed us out of the kitchen and we both headed off to get ready.

When I walked into the bathroom, Alex was indeed still sitting on the toilet. She kicked her feet slightly back and forth, as her toes didn't even touch the floor. She smiled at me, and I thought she looked cute. As I warmed up the shower and prepared to enter it, Alex passed a little gas. She covered her mouth quickly, but a little giggle escaped. I laughed quietly (so as not to alert my mom) and entered the shower. Alex seemed so different this morning. So comfortable and happy. I smiled to myself and thought how nice it would be if this continued. Maybe Alex needed to go to school, so they could teach her things that would make her annoy my mom less. Maybe my mom needed that time away from Alex. Today could be the start of a solution to this family problem. I was very optimistic.

Getting our physicals was really a joke. We walked into the military hospital and walked out less than an hour later with sheets of paper that said we could start school. Mom joked, "That's the military for you, sign this—move along." I laughed, although I didn't really get the joke. Things were going so well that day, I just wanted to stay in this joking happiness, no matter what.

With the four of us ready (and on time), we left for the first stop. Tom had been able to go with us to help my mom register all of us. It seemed that my mom was really milking this whole pregnancy to get her way with the military. The few times we had gone on base for something, she made sure to exaggerate her sickness and tiredness in front of others. She really was more tired than usual, but not to the dramatic level she showed in front of Tom's coworkers and superiors. In any case, she got her way in having Tom with us for the day to assist her.

Since my school was right across the street from the trailer park, we went there first. I was extremely intimidated. First, it was a lot bigger than any school I had gone to before. My mom and some lady from the office encouraged me to walk around the building while they talked. "It's really not so big." The lady smiled at me and handed my mom a paper to sign. With Dawn and Alex sitting in the office and looking at books, and Tom reading plaques on the wall, I wandered out into the hall. I found a bathroom and used it. All was quiet, since it was class time. I walked down the hall and turned around to head back to the main office.

That's when I heard, "Who's the White girl?" come from down the hall. I looked over to see several girls staring at me. It was then I became aware that I had not seen any other "White girls" since arriving at school thirty minutes before. I was instantly nervous about being so different than most of my classmates. Was this going to be a problem? I had never faced any "racial issues" before. These three girls didn't look like they wanted to be my friend. Was it because I was a "White girl?"

Would it make a difference if I told them my grandmother was Mexican? I could feel myself getting flushed with embarrassment, as the girls continued to stare at me while walking past their classroom door.

"Are you done with those erasers?" A teacher called to the girls from the classroom and they went back inside. I exhaled a sigh of relief and walked briskly back to the office.

Mom was finishing up the paperwork and said she needed to take the girls to the bathroom. Tom followed her into the hallway, then stopped suddenly when he realized he couldn't go into the girl's bathroom. He awkwardly walked up the hall and found some trophies to look at. With everyone gone, that left me alone in the office. The secretary peeked over at me and smiled.

"Did you get to walk around?" she asked nicely.

"Yes." I smiled and tried to think of something positive to say. "It's very quiet," I remarked.

She laughed, "Oh, that's because it's class time. It's much louder when it's not class time."

We both laughed. I was concerned she would ask me more questions, and I was not sure how I would answer them, so I said, "I should go help my mom," and began walking toward the door.

"Okay, see you later, sweetie." She waved with a smile, and I left.

Mom and the girls were exiting the bathroom when I closed the office door. Mom still seemed in a good mood, so I assumed Alex had not had an accident. That was very good news.

We all got into the van and headed out to Dawn's school. On the ride over, I confided in my mom about my fears of getting lost in such a big school and of being an outcast because I was a "White girl." This made my mom laugh.

"Oh, Nyssa. You'll be fine. Those girls were probably just not sure of you because they didn't know you. This is a new and different situation for you, and it will only make you stronger and better able to adapt. You won't get lost, and you probably won't be the only 'White girl.'" she reassured me.

I smiled and agreed, although inside, I was the most nervous I had ever been about starting a new school. I had done it so many times in my life, but none were as different as this. The fact that we were halfway across the country added to my anxiety.

But I continued to smile and was determined to make my mom proud with my "ability to adapt."

Dawn's school looked newer than my school. Dawn seemed excited, as she and my mom and Tom left the van and walked in the front door. I stayed with Alex in the van, so Mom would not have any distractions and could finish the paperwork as quickly as possible. Alex stared outside the van and watched the kids playing during recess. I was preoccupied with my own thoughts about my new school and what I would wear for my first day (the next day).

Some time passed, before I realized that it had been awhile since Alex had used the bathroom. I quickly turned towards her and blurted out, "Alex, do you have to pee?!"

Alex seemed frightened by my sudden outburst and looked down at herself. A dread filled me, as I wondered if I had just scared her so badly that I made her pee on herself. After a few agonizing seconds, I realized she had apparently been looking at herself to assess if she actually had to go.

"No. I don't," she answered with a smile, and turned back around to look out the window.

I was too nervous about her having an accident to let her go this long. I convinced her that we should just try to go, and we began to leave the van. Just as I was locking the doors, I heard my mom's voice.

"Is everything okay?" She was walking up the path, with Tom and Dawn in tow. I explained that I just wanted Alex to go potty before we headed out, and Mom offered to take her. She complimented me, "That was very mature for you to think of that. Thank you." That one comment was enough to ease some of my nervousness.

While mom and Alex were in the school, I asked Dawn about her new school. I was not prepared for what she did—talk non-stop.

"It's so neat. I already made a friend and my teacher is really nice, and we do all kinds of art things, and the kids seem soooooo nice, and my class looks really neat..." And on and on she went.

I had to admit that I was feeling a little jealous. Okay, very jealous. Why couldn't I be that excited, instead of so nervous? I was glad when Mom and Alex got back, because then I didn't have to hear about how great Dawn's new school was.

Mom settled Alex and herself in the van and said, "Okay, now it's time for Alex's school. Are you excited, Alex?" Mom asked.

I had never in my life heard my mom talk like that before. She sounded like a female Mr. Rogers, and it was honestly creeping me out. I understood that this was better than her yelling and played along.

"That is exciting," I added. Alex nodded and smiled. I was genuinely happy that things were going so smoothly. I should have known it wouldn't last for long.

Dawn and I stayed in the van, while Alex was registered for school. Again, Alex's school looked newer than my school. But, instead of letting it be a negative thing, I thought "my school has history." I tried to change my outlook in order to be less nervous. I thought about how good things would be once we were all in school.

Mom could relax during the day, we can all have our stuff going on, and then family time will be special and less stressful. It made so much sense.

I turned toward Dawn and tried to make up for my earlier hard feelings against her, "So, you said you made a friend?" I asked.

Dawn nodded. Then she began rattling off this story about how this girl came up to her and started talking to her. She went on and on, even explaining what the girl looked like. I just smiled and nodded.

I told myself, "I am happy for Dawn. This is good for our family." I hadn't noticed Mom, Tom and Alex, until they were opening the van door and getting in. Dawn stopped her story abruptly.

I could tell something was wrong. Mom's smile had left her face and was replaced with a firm look of coldness. Tom seemed uncomfortable and nervous. Alex wasn't as happy as before but seemed a little oblivious to Mom's noticeable disapproval of whatever had happened in that school. She buckled Alex in the seat and sat down in the driver's seat. She paused before starting the van.

I thought she might fill us in on what had happened, but she didn't. Instead, she drove us quietly back to the trailer. Her quiet calmness seemed so eerie compared to the happiness of an hour earlier. Nobody dared to talk. Tom sat still next to my mom. Dawn, Alex and I sat quietly in the back of the van, not even making eye contact with each other. What could have gone wrong?

After we were back in the trailer, Dawn escaped to our room, Alex sat on the floor with her paper and crayons and began to draw.

Tom had gone to the kitchen and started making tea for my mom.

Mom sat on the couch, in her usual tired and pregnant way and rubbed her eyes slowly. That's when I noticed she was crying. I didn't know what upset her, but it was hard not to feel bad for a crying pregnant lady.

"Mom, what's wrong?" I asked.

"Oh, Nyssa..." she took a deep breath and cried for a few more seconds before she explained. "The school said they couldn't let Alex enroll because of the marks on her arms. I tried to explain that they were bug bites she scratched too much, but they said she had to get them checked out by a second doctor, then they could let her in." She was sobbing now. "This is going to be like last time." She gulped for air.

"She won't be able to go to school, and I will be stuck with her all day. I know it!" She was wailing, now.

I sat down next to her and held her hand. I tentatively rubbed her back, not sure if I would be helping or invading her space. She continued to cry but had downgraded to a softer cry. Tom watched us from the kitchen but seemed unsure about coming over to help. I glanced at him and wondered why he had even come with us that day. He really had not been any help at all. Mom always took care of everything, and he just followed her like a lost dog.

Mom and I sat there for a while, until mom noticed something that made her sit straight up. I followed her glare and realized that Alex peed on the floor. She was looking up at mom and me. With both of us staring at her, she began to cry.

I felt mom's body tense up, then she slowly whispered, "Nyssa, go to your room. You don't need to be a part of this." Then, her demeanor changed, and she smiled a little. "Why don't you go get your school stuff and clothes together for tomorrow?"

I welcomed the chance to escape the drama in the living room, but worried about what would happen to Alex. I thought about how well she had done all day about going pee in the bathroom. I reasoned it was because we worked so closely with her. The last two hours, we had forgotten to take her. That was probably why she had an accident. But, was it normal for a five-year-old to need that much supervision? I wasn't sure what to think. It was hard for me to imagine that Alex would purposely wet herself to anger my mom, when she knew it would only result in severe punishment. I wish I knew how to fix whatever was happening with Alex. Finally, with little noise coming from the living room, I was able to put the whole situation to the side and busy myself with my first day of school.

I packed my backpack with items I thought I would need. I was sure I wouldn't need all the notebooks or pencils that we purchased the day before. Just a couple pencils (in case one broke), maybe three notebooks (in case different teachers wanted me to have a notebook devoted only to their class), and a couple folders for homework.

I lifted my backpack to see how heavy it was. Not bad. Then, I realized that I would be receiving books from my teachers. That would weigh it down. Would it be too heavy? No, we got lockers at school. I probably wouldn't take all my books home, so my backpack shouldn't be too heavy.

My backpack dilemma was interrupted by, "Nyssa, could you please start dinner?"

My mom's voice came from her bedroom. I glanced down the hall and saw my mom folding laundry on her bed. "Okay, Mom," I answered.

I started my specialty—Hamburger Helper. This time it was a creamy sauce (stroganoff or something). Paired with canned vegetables, it was a fairly nutritious meal that Mom felt comfortable with me making unsupervised. I finished dinner and called through the trailer, "Dinner's ready!"
Dawn came first and said, "This looks yummy," as she sat down.

Tom came up the hall from the main bedroom and said, "You are getting really good at cooking, Nyssa." I thanked them both, and we waited patiently at the table for Alex and my mom.

After several minutes of waiting awkwardly at the table, I called, "Mom? Did you hear me?" After a brief silence I heard my mom's heavy swollen feet coming down the hall. She sat down at the table and said, "Oh, this looks good. I am so hungry." She smiled at me and touched my shoulder. It felt good when she was proud of me. "Oh," she added casually, "Alex won't be eating with us right now." Then she started eating.

Since it was not abnormal for Alex to have to eat separately from us, I didn't think much about what she said and began to eat. During our meal, I briefly wondered where she was being punished, because I could see she was not in the living room—her usual punishment place. I imagined her standing in the corner in my parents' room, and resumed eating.

Dinner went very well, with Mom asking both Dawn and I questions about our new schools. I felt like such a normal family, just me and my sister, talking to our mom about our feelings and such. It was really cool. Tom just ate and smiled at us as we talked.

Dawn and I lingered at the table long after our food was gone, and I'm sure Mom knew that we enjoyed talking to her. There came a point when Mom said, "Okay, you guys. I have some laundry I need to finish folding. We can talk again tomorrow, after your first day at school." She smiled at both of us. I wanted to capture that moment forever.

Once Mom left the table, Dawn and I quickly cleared the table and got back to obsessively packing for our big day. Dawn had also finished packing her school supplies but readjusted them once I told her she had packed too much. I explained why she wouldn't need so many things right away and she agreed. Once she dumped half her pencils and notebooks, she sheepishly asked, "Could you help me pick out my clothes?"

She was staring at her feet and I wondered if it was hard for her to ask for help. I had gotten the impression from my mom that Dawn's mom didn't care so much for her. Then, with my mom discouraging stupidity (that included asking for help and/or asking too many questions about things), I wondered how many times Dawn had tried to figure things out for herself, when she really wanted to ask for help.

"Sure, I can help you. What were you thinking about wearing?" I asked. Her face lit up and she showed me a cute shirt that we had just bought at Walmart and some jeans she had from when she lived at her mom's. I explained that the weather was a lot colder here then we were used to. Maybe a cute sweater would be better. In the end, we compromised with her outfit, plus a sweatshirt added for warmth. We stood back and looked at our accomplishment laid out on her bed.

"Do you want me to help you pick your clothes?" Dawn asked, with more confidence in her voice. I thought about it for a second and realized it couldn't hurt to get a second opinion on my outfit.

"Sure," I agreed. I pulled out my clothes, and she said they looked good. Then, she asked, "Where are your underwear and socks?"

I laughed, having not pulled them out like Dawn did when she chose her clothes, I thought she would just assume that I had intended on wearing them—I just didn't need to see them with my outfit. But, to make her feel better, I opened my underwear/sock drawer and found only socks. I looked through other drawers and found that I had no clean underwear. I looked at Dawn, who was now laughing so much she was snorting. I smiled and said, "I guess I better go ask mom for 'chonies.'" We always used this Spanish slang word, and it made Dawn laugh. Sure enough, it made her laughing fit worse, and she flopped onto my bed snorting as I left the room to ask my mom for clean underwear.

As I walked into my mom's bedroom, I could see that there was a lot of clean, folded laundry on her bed. Tom was in the kitchen doing dishes, and Mom was alone in the room. She smiled when she saw me come in. "What do you need, Nyssa?" she asked sweetly.

I smiled and asked, "Do you think I really need to wear underwear to school tomorrow?" I knew this was my mom's kind of humor.

"Ha!" She blurted out in a loud laugh. "Are you serious or is this your way of asking me for chonies?" She was still giggling a little at my joke.

"No, I'm just kidding. I'm nervous enough without being panty-less at this new school. I just need some undies." I grinned.

My mom's demeanor calmed but remained soft. "Oh, Nyssa. I know you're really nervous about tomorrow. You have to trust me on this—you will be fine. You are smart and pretty, and you always make friends very easily." She put her hand on my shoulder. She smiled warmly and handed me the underwear. I don't know how she did it, but I did feel better. I made friends in all my other schools, why wouldn't I make friends here?

I was about to offer my mom a hug, when she made an awful face. She smelled the air, and her face contorted more. I thought maybe hyper-sensitivity to smell that accompanied her pregnancy was bothering her, but then I smelled something, too. It did smell bad. Mom followed the scent over to her bedroom door and said, "Oh, no."

She bent over a black plastic bag that was sitting in a large shallow box. The bag had not been closed, but the top of it had been folded in such a way I couldn't see inside. Now that my attention was also focused on the bag, I could see it moved slightly. I walked a little closer to make sure I had seen the bag actually move, and that it wasn't my mom moving it. But she was still staring at it, with the back of her hand covering her nose and mouth. She had not touched it.

Suddenly, she took a deep breath and opened the bag to look inside. "Oh, you little nasty animal!" She gasped and closed the bag with her hands. She grabbed another bag off the dresser and flung it open. She placed the second bag on the floor, holding one end open. She then rolled the first bag into the second bag.

She picked a bag tie off the dresser and tied up the bag.

While she did this, she yelled toward the bag, "You want to sh** all over the place? Then you can live in your own filth, because I'm not going to deal with it anymore!"

With that, she pulled at the tie she made, and satisfied that it would hold, turned toward me. I quickly took a step back to the bed, to place myself in my original position.

"So," Mom sighed deeply and asked, "Can I see what you're wearing tomorrow?" She seemed quiet and calm again, but I wanted to get out of that room.

"Yes, Momma," I answered.

She turned and walked out of the room, toward my bedroom. I followed behind her. I slowed drastically as I neared the bag that I now knew held Alex. I had walked right by that bag when I came in the room but had no idea she was there.

Now, I struggled to bring myself to pass it again, since I knew she was right there.

I stared at the bag as I walked by, careful not to draw attention to myself. I could see my mom entering my room, and I was not far behind her. Then, as I was feeling a slight relief at almost being passed the bag and out of the room of insanity, I heard a sound come from the bag.

Time froze.

I heard a deep gasping sound emitting from Alex's bag. It was not a sound I had ever heard her make before. It seemed too deep and strained to come from a little girl like Alex.

I continued my journey and was finally out of the room. I was so relieved when I was sitting on my own bed, showing my mom my outfit. I tried to throw myself into that moment with her and forget about what I heard. Mom approved of my clothes and kissed me goodnight.

Once she left, I gathered my clothes together and tried to get ready for bed as fast as I could. I was so deep in my own world, I hadn't noticed Dawn talking to me.

"I said, did you find some underwear?" She was looking at me intently, as if she couldn't understand why I was so spaced out.

I nodded and said, "Yeah, I did. I'm really tired. I think I need to go to bed." I wanted to end any further conversations with her that night.

She seemed confused. "Oh, Okay. Well, I'll be quiet," she offered.

I curled up in my bed and struggled to make sense of what happened. One part of me wanted to go to sleep and forget about it. But I also wanted to convince myself that what my mom had done was okay, even though I felt strongly inside that it was very wrong.

I could trust my mom; she had always been there for me. Even when my dad or my friends had betrayed me, my mom had always been there to support me. She had a bad temper sometimes, but it was only because she was pregnant or when someone was being bad or stupid. Then, people deserve to be treated harshly. Right?

But Alex was so little. This felt like it was too much for her. I was grateful I hadn't actually seen her in that bag.

What would she have looked like? Then, there were those sounds she made. What could have caused her to make such awful sounds? I imagined myself where she was just then. Closed up, in that black bag, there would be nothing but darkness. Darkness ... and her own feces and urine. I couldn't imagine how awful it smelled or how scary the darkness would be. I wondered if she had been crying so deeply it caused her to sound the way she did. What kind of anguish would a child have to feel to cry like that?

I was awake most of the night. I bounced between rationalizing what I had seen and heard, reasoning why my mom chose this method of punishment, and wanting to forget it all and go to sleep. It seemed like forever until I finally fell asleep, exhausted.

OCTOBER 26, 1989—PART ONE

When I woke the next morning to my alarm, I was initially struck with confusion. Why was my alarm going off? I turned off my alarm and lay back down in my bed. I had not set my alarm for several weeks. I had not needed to set my alarm, because I had not started school yet.

School! I sat up in bed and realized (with my heart thumping in my head) that today was the first day of school! I jumped out of bed and scrambled to the bathroom to begin my morning routine that I adopted earlier in the school year. Shower, blow dry, light make up and lotion my knees and elbows (they got so dry, they cracked painfully). Only this time, it was for a new school in a new state! I was so nervous to look my best, that I really lost track of time and didn't know how long I had been in the bathroom, until my mom knocked on the door.

"Nyssa, are you almost done? Dawn and I need to use the bathroom. We also need to leave here in fifteen minutes. Okay?" She sounded slightly stressed, but not too bad.

"Okay, Mom. I'm coming out." I had really spent a lot of time re-spraying my hair and tweaking my make-up. I guess it was good enough. I opened the door and rushed to my bedroom.

I had decided at the last minute to change my pants. I knew it was getting cold, but I really wanted to wear a skirt. I took out a skirt that my grandma bought me before we left. It was an incredibly puffy and ruffled skirt that was very "in," because Madonna had made it "in." I didn't really understand how that worked, but I desperately wanted to be accepted at my new school, so I put it on.

"Okay, girls. Let's go." Dawn rushed from the bathroom to the bedroom to get her backpack. I grabbed mine, and we both headed to the front door. Tom was standing there.

"Are you guys ready for your first day?" Tom grinned. I saw that he was ready to go, and realized that he would be taking us to school. I wasn't thrilled about that, but I knew he had to go to work, too. It would be more convenient for him to take us.

"Of course, they're ready, right?" Mom smiled at us, and we agreed. She hugged us both and we were gone for our first day of school.

The ride to school was fairly uneventful. Tom tried to make small talk. Dawn and I were not very interested in talking. Anyone could have seen how nervous we both were. As we pulled up to my school, I wished Dawn a good first day, and she said, "You, too."

Then I walked into the school and watched Tom drive off. That was it; I was officially on my own. I took a deep breath and walked to the main office.

When I walked in, the secretary smiled at me. "Good morning, Nyssa. You're here early." I explained that my step- dad had to go to work and still needed to drop off one of my sisters.

She nodded at my explanation and handed me a sheet of paper.

"Well, that just gives you more time to see your classes. Oh, and if Chris gets here early, I can have him show you around."

"Chris?" I asked. I hadn't been told about any "Chris."

"Oh, I was going to tell you yesterday, but you left to go help your mom. Chris helps us in the office for first period. He's a nice boy. I was going to have him walk you to all your classes, so you'll know where they are." She smiled warmly.

I felt much better. Someone my age would walk me around the school and show me where all these classes were. Cool. As I sat waiting for Chris, I looked over my classes. Each class was a combination of a letter and some numbers. I hadn't used that system in my other school and was a little intimidated, until I remembered that Chris would help me. It was going to be okay, I reassured myself.

As time passed, more kids came, and the halls got louder and more crowded. Then, the bell rang, and all the kids filtered into their classes. It was very quiet. The only noise was from the secretary typing. Finally, that stopped. She peeked over her desk and seemed startled.

"Oh, Nyssa. I had forgotten you were still here. I can't imagine where Chris is..." She stopped mid-sentence, when a boy walked into the office, very much out of breath.

"I'm sorry, I'm late. My brother's bus was late, and I had to run here." He was panting as he put his backpack behind the secretary's desk. He took a deep breath to slow down his breathing.
"Oh, that's okay Chris. We have a new girl. I was hoping you could show her where all her classes are." I could tell that the secretary really liked this young man. Maybe he worked hard in the office and was really respectful to her, or something.

I suddenly felt self-conscious as Chris looked at me. "Oh," he said, "Sure. What's your name?" he asked. This made me more self-conscious. I didn't like telling people my name for the first time. They never got it right, and kids my age usually made fun of it.

"Nyssa," I said as clearly as possible.

"Nyssa?" He had actually said it right. I nodded.

"Are those your classes?" He pointed to the sheet of paper I was holding. Again, I nodded. He held his hand out and I gave the paper to him. He looked it over and said, "This isn't too bad. Most of your classes are in the same hallway. Here, I'll show you."

He started out the door, and I looked back at the secretary. Was it okay for us to just leave? Apparently, it was, because the secretary smiled and said, "Have a good day, sweetie," and returned to her typing.

I followed Chris out the door, and we walked upstairs. "I'll walk you to each of your classes in order, that way you won't get too confused." He talked while we walked, looking down at the paper, then up at the door numbers to make sure he had the right room.

He seemed nice, just focused. I thought he was probably a good student. Cute, but not really my type. "Here is your first class." He pointed to the door in front of us. Because it was open, the teacher looked over at us.

"What do you need, Chris?" she asked. Then she saw me.

"Oh, do we have a new student?" she asked.

Chris nodded. I stood frozen, seeing that part of the class was staring out the door at me. "Yes, Mrs. Steer. She has this class now, but I'm going to show her where her other classes are. Then I'll bring her back." I was impressed how well he spoke in front of a bunch of people and to adults, as well.

"Okay. See you in a little bit." She waved, and I nervously waved back. A few of the students laughed, and I quickly put my hand down. I followed Chris while my face grew red with embarrassment. Had I just made myself look stupid by waving? Why did those kids laugh at me? I was so sucked into my own obsessive world, I hadn't noticed Chris talking to me.

"Did you hear me?" Chris asked. I shook my head "No." He sighed and repeated himself, "I said not to worry about those kids that laughed. They might give you a hard time because you're new, but they'll stop if you show that it doesn't bother you. Don't let it get to you, ya know?" Chris finished.

I nodded and smiled. I did feel better. We moved on to the next class and the next, until we had walked to all my classes. He went over the best way to get to my classes, then asked, "Do you think you know where you're going now?" I nodded and he asked, "Do you want me to walk with you back to Mrs. Steer's class?" I really did want him too, but I didn't want to seem like a baby, so I thanked him and told him I could handle it.

"Okay, see you around, Nyssa." He waved and walked down the hall to the stairway, then he was gone. I stood in the hallway and wished I hadn't told Chris I could handle it. The hall was so quiet.

As I walked back to my first class, I felt each step I took echoed in the hall. I walked by classrooms that were completely quiet. Maybe they were taking tests. I felt like half the class looked up from their work to see who was clacking their feet in the hall. By the time I got to my class, I was at the height of being self-conscious about everything.

The teacher saw me at the door and motioned for me to come in. The class was quiet and most of the students were working on something at their desks. However, when I came in and stood by the teacher's desk, I felt all eyes fix on me. I positioned myself so I wouldn't be facing the class.

"How do you pronounce your name, sweetheart?" Oh great. I hated this part.

"It's 'Nyssa.'" I said. I thought I heard a "What?" come from the back of the class, followed by some low giggling.

"Oh, Nyssa. How pretty." She made a note of something in her roll book, then pointed to an open seat for me to sit in. I walked to the seat, without making eye contact with anyone.

Once in my seat, a boy sitting next to me said, "Mmm-mmm. New girl is fine." I looked up and saw him smirking at me, with a smile I had never seen from someone my own age. He was cute, but I was very creeped out by his behavior.

The girl behind him laughed quietly and said, "I bet she doesn't date ugly players, like you." Then she smiled at me. I smiled back and was grateful for that small token of kindness.

I thought the uncomfortable situation was over, until he asked, "Do you?" He was looking right at me. What was I supposed to say? I didn't want to say "No," because then I would be calling him ugly. I definitely didn't want to say "Yes" either.

I opened my mouth to say something, when the girl behind him spoke again. "Dante, just shut up and leave her alone, before I tell Tina." She was firm, but not yelling. Dante looked like a wounded dog and went back to his work. Again, she smiled at me, and again I smiled back.

"Okay class—I'm sure you have all noticed our new student, Nyssa. This is her first day, so I hope you all make her feel welcomed. Nyssa, why don't you tell us a little about yourself?" She asked, with the whole class looking at me.

BRIIIIIING! The bell went off.

I had never been so relieved to hear the class bell. Students around me began getting their books together.

"Well, Nyssa? Just tell us where you are from and why you moved here." The class settled down once they realized that we weren't excused yet.

With the class looking impatient, I blurted out, "We moved here from California because my step-dad is in the Army." The class approved of my answer and began to get out of their seats.

Mrs. Steer spoke again, "Wow, all the way from California! Well, I hope you like it here." She scanned the classroom, as some students were slowly making their way to the door. "And I hope our young men and women here make you feel welcomed today." She seemed to be giving the students a look of warning as they passed her desk to leave. As I walked by, she said, "Have a great day sweetie, see you on Monday." She smiled at me as I left. I smiled back and nodded.

Out in the hallway, I became momentarily confused. The hall looked so different with a sea of middle school kids pushing their way through to get to their next classes. I found my class schedule and began walking down the hall and looking up at the door numbers, trying to match a classroom to my schedule. I hadn't figured out the purpose of the letter before the numbers, or why the numbers weren't always in numeric order. I then tried to remember which way Chris had taken me, after my first class. But, I couldn't. I clearly had not been paying attention when he had been walking me around. I looked back at my first class down the hall and wondered if I should go back and ask the teacher. She seemed nice.

"Do you need help?" A girl with glasses was standing by the door of the classroom in front of me. I probably looked pretty pathetic standing there for so long, just looking up and down the hall. I thought asking her for help would make me look more pathetic to my fellow students, but with the halls emptying fast, I figured I would look worse being late for my next class.

I showed her my schedule, and she pointed to the classroom two doors down. "That's math with Mr. Tradell. He's hard, and he's got a scary toupé." She smiled, and after realizing she had made a joke, I smiled and giggled nervously. "Hey," she continued, "I could meet you after class, and we can go to the next class together. You have Social Studies with me." She smiled at me and handed the schedule back. I was so shocked by her generous invitation that I stood there for a minute.

"Or not..." she finally muttered. She turned her body to return to class, when I blurted out, "Oh, that would be great. Thanks!" I realized how desperate I must have sounded and grimaced slightly.

"Okay, cool," she replied. "You better hurry or you'll be late. See ya after." Then she returned to her class. I was so thrilled at having a friend; I turned and walked slowly to my next class, smiling and enjoying that comforting feeling that accompanied not being a total loner.

BRIIIIING! The halls were instantly emptied and doors were shutting. Crap! I was late!

I got to the classroom door just as a student was closing it. I walked into a quiet room, where all the students were already working on something and the teacher was reading a book. I walked over and handed him my schedule. He didn't smile. He looked through his attendance book, marked something down, then handed my schedule back to me. He pointed to a basket at the front of his desk, "When you come in, you need to take one of these practice sheets and go to your seat to finish it."

He looked back down at his book, but continued to talk to me. "At quarter after, the sheets get passed up, whether you've finished it or not. Then class starts." He glanced up from his book and said firmly, "Don't be late. The door closes when the bell rings, and there are no exceptions." Then he returned to his book. I stood for a moment, looking out at all the eyes staring at me.

I had to ask, "Where should I sit?"

He looked up at me with astonishment, "Preferably somewhere there is an empty seat." Half the class burst out laughing.

I avoided eye contact and found an empty seat to sit in. After finishing my math sheet, I spent the next five minutes thinking what a mean old man Mr. Tradell was. I remembered what the girl in the hall had said,and checked out his hair for the first time. I almost burst out laughing. It was the biggest comb-over-looking toupé I had ever seen. I put my head down on my desk to avoid laughing and making more of a scene than I had a few minutes ago.

Math class was pretty uneventful after that. I didn't understand half the things the teacher said but was able to do most of my work by reading the directions from the book. When the last five minutes of class came and the kids around me were packing their things, I began to think about the girl in the hall. Would she remember to meet me? What if I couldn't find my next class? I was starting to get myself worked up again, when the girl sitting diagonally from me turned around and smiled. It was the girl from my first class that saved me from the super-hormonal Dante.

"Hi," she said.

"Hi," I managed to repeat back.

She tilted her head and asked, "Are you really from California?"

I nodded. I was beginning to see that this was an interesting topic for some people and expanded on it. "Yeah, I grew up around the L.A. area."

Her eyes widened and several other surrounding students turned around in the seats to hear our conversation. "Have you ever seen a drive-by?" she asked in a scared whisper.

I shook my head immediately. "Oh, no." I had to think of something just as interesting as big city crime. "But I have seen a few movie stars." Her eyes widened more and now the kids sitting within two seats in every direction were asking, "Like who? Yeah, who?"

I had just started naming the few celebrities I had seen in my life, when the bell rang. A few of the kids groaned, and I realized it was because they wanted to hear the rest of my list. I felt really good.

The girl who originally talked to me said, "Hey, what do you have after this?" I told her and she said, "I have class right next door, I'll walk you there." She seemed so nice, I was so happy to have a friend, and then I remembered the girl from the hall. As we walked out of our class, I saw the hallway girl standing outside the door.

She saw me walk out with the other girl and said, "Oh, hi Monique."

She seemed agitated to see her walking with me.

Monique looked over at her and said, "Can I help you with something, Latisha?" There was definite attitude there. She sounded much different than her friendly self of a few minutes ago.

I quickly pointed to Latisha and said, "She was going to walk me to the next class, because we both have it." I looked at Monique and hoped this wasn't a problem.

"Oh," she mumbled. "Well, I better go meet my friend anyways. I guess I'll just see you later. Bye, Nyssa."

She said my name right! I didn't want to get in the middle of whatever was going on between these two, but I liked the first impressions I had from Monique, so I added, "Okay. Bye, Monique ... and thanks for that whole Dante thing." I smiled, like it was an inside joke between good friends.

She laughed and replied, "Anytime, girl. Dante is trouble."

She paused and looked at Latisha. Then, she lowered her voice, "But I'll tell you more later." She waved goodbye and walked away from us.

I wanted to redirect us away from that awkwardness, so I asked Latisha, "Is our class close by?"

Latisha mumbled, "No, it's at the end of this hall." She didn't seem as friendly as she had earlier. What was the deal with those two? I didn't want to pry, so I remained silent. We got to the class, and I checked in with the teacher. This time went so much more smoothly, because class hadn't started yet. Students were too distracted with coming in and finding their seats to worry about me.

The teacher seemed really nice, and she asked me, "Is there any seat in particular that you would like?" I scanned the classroom and saw Latisha waving her hands. She pointed to the seat next to her and mouthed the words, "Here, here." I turned back to tell the teacher, who was smiling and said, "How about next to Latisha?" I laughed and walked back to the empty seat as the bell rang.

Social Studies was very interesting, and I had to say this teacher was my favorite. The whole class really seemed to like her and the things she was teaching. Time went by fairly quickly, and soon, we were packing up our backpacks for the move to the next class. I finished packing and looked over at Latisha. She was talking to another White girl who was sitting in front of her. They were laughing about something, and I got the impression that they were pretty close friends. Latisha and the White girl noticed that I was staring at them and smiled.

"Hey, is your name Nessa or something?" Latisha asked. "It's Nyssa. Like Nissa," I said.

"Oh, well this is Rachel." She pointed to the White girl.

Rachel was very petite, with short dirty-blonde hair cut just below her ears. She smiled and asked, "How do you like Radcliff Middle?"

I shrugged my shoulders. "It seems okay." I wasn't sure how to answer. I really hadn't formed a solid opinion yet.

Then, Latisha whispered to Rachel, "Monique is trying to be friends with her." Rachel looked at me with concern.

"Do you have someone to eat lunch with?" asked Rachel. I shook my head "No."

"You should eat with us, cuz there are some things we need to tell you." Latisha seemed very serious as she told me this. Rachel nodded in agreement.

"Uh, okay." I answered. I hadn't even thought about lunch. I could have been all by myself for lunch! I was so grateful for their invitation.

Just as we were ready to leave, the teacher, Mrs. Nassbaum said, "Oh, class—I almost forgot. We have a new friend in our class. Everyone, say hello to Nyssa." She waved towards my direction; and part of the class said, "Hi, Nessa," and another part said "Hi, Neesa," and a few people said "Hi, Nyssa."

Mrs. Nassbaum smiled and said, "It's 'Nih-sah' everyone." There was a group, "Oh..." Then the bell rang. "Have a great weekend my friends!" she sang out as we filed out of class. The students wished her a good weekend, and some asked what her plans were. I had never really seen a teacher so close to her students. It was lunch time and kids were actually staying back to talk to her for a few of their own minutes. She was obviously a favorite at this school. I was glad I had her.

Once we got down to the cafeteria, I realized I had a new problem. I didn't have any lunch. I was strangely uncomfortable about eating in front of others. I normally skipped lunch at school, unless I was able to walk home and eat. Since this school didn't allow that, I would be skipping lunch. I wondered how weird my new friends would think that was. Thankfully, Rachel never ate lunch either. Latisha brought a small sandwich that took her two minutes to eat, so that left a lot of time to talk. The three of us talked for the whole lunch hour.

In a nutshell, Monique was one of the "loose" girls at the school. She had slept with most of the basketball team and some of the baseball team. She seemed nice at first, but she would backstab her friends for any list of reasons, the least of which was looking at a guy she liked. Chris (who had walked me round school that morning) was indeed a "nerd." Although he was very nice and smart, he didn't have many friends because, well—he was so nice and smart.

Oh, and I had to be careful because as the new "White girl" at the school, I was not only fresh meat, but a different kind of fresh meat.

"What does that mean?" I had to ask. I had never been compared to food before.

Rachel looked at Latisha, like "You better handle this."

Latisha began, "It's like when you eat a sandwich every day for lunch." She unintentionally looked at her lunch bag, "sometimes you start to feel like something different."

Rachel giggled, "Like pizza."

Latisha laughed, then became very serious. "I'm trying to be straight with her, Rachel. You're gonna mess me up." She took a breath and attempted to finish her thought. "Sometimes you may wanna try something, just because you never tried it before." Latisha was making me uncomfortable. I didn't want to be the "new and different meat."

Just then, Rachel burst out, "Like pizza with white sauce!" She was laughing so hard, she doubled over and laid on the lunch bench.

Latisha also burst out laughing and smacked Rachel in the arm, "You messed me up! What's wrong with you?" Yet, she continued to laugh and rolled her eyes. "Rachel makes a joke out of everything. She'll crack you up." She smiled at her friend, and I was glad I had met them.

I was having such a good time at lunch I really didn't want to go to another class. But it finally came to an end. I was also given the bad news that I didn't have any other classes with either of them. Yuck! So, we exchanged phone numbers, and they said we would hang out again on Monday. That seemed so far away.

The rest of the afternoon passed without much incident. I had learned from my first two classes that it saved a lot of drama if I arrived on time. So, I walked quickly down the halls and asked a few students for directions. That only backfired one time; it was my last class and I was so tired from my first day of school, it was welcoming to think I was almost done.

I asked a boy at his locker if he knew where my class was. He smirked at the boy next to him and said, "Oh, yeah. Here, follow me." He smiled at me, and I followed him down to the end of the hall. Once we got to the stairs, he turned around so quickly I bumped into the wall behind me. He then placed his hand on the wall and leaned in toward me. He was quite a bit bigger than me, and I had no room to get around and away from him.

"What's it worth to know where that class is?" His grin was slimy and wicked. I began to breathe heavily and wondered if anyone would come to rescue me—the bell was about to ring and the halls would be totally empty. What could I do?

"Mikey! Get off that girl!" The voice sounded familiar, and once "Big Mike" got off of me, I saw Monique walking up the stairs. She looked angry. "What the hell is wrong with you?" she yelled.

I thought she was speaking to me, so I answered, "I just wanted to know where my class was." I felt like I was about to cry.

Monique took my hand, "Not you—I was talking to this big ape." She motioned to my aggressor and finished, "You better stay away from her, or Tyron will kick your butt!" Mike looked upset and walked away.

Monique sighed and asked, "Where is your next class?" I told her, and still holding my hand, she led me to within a few feet of the door. Before letting go of my hand, she said, "Don't trust the guys around here. They ain't no good." She shook her head sadly, let go of my hand and walked away. I realized once she was gone that I had been so upset by the incident, I hadn't thanked her. I would have to remember to say something to her on Monday. I knew Rachel and Latisha had said she had a bad reputation, but why had she been so nice to me then?

The last class was a joke. I was late, but no one seemed to notice. In fact, no one seemed to notice even when the teacher was teaching. The man teaching was small in stature and seemed afraid of the students in his class. Notes were passed, things were thrown, and conversations went on as if there were no class at all. I noticed some kids using it as time to finish other schoolwork and thought I might try that. Before I could really start, a few kids from my earlier class with Monique noticed me and asked me to finish my "celebrity list." I talked and made a few new friends. Then it was time to go home.

I felt drained. Even though our trailer park was only across the street and up the hill, I was not looking forward to walking any distance, anywhere. But I knew I would feel better once I got home.

I could lie down on my bed. I could eat—oh, I could eat! I had not eaten breakfast or lunch and I felt so hungry I would eat just about anything! The thought of food renewed my energy, and I was able to walk home. The trailer was actually a welcome sight at that point. I knew I would feel better once I got inside.

OCTOBER 26, 1989—PART TWO

When I opened the door to the trailer, I felt instantly exhausted. My first day of school had been incredibly draining. I was sure it didn't help that I had not eaten all day. The expression on my face must have been pretty sad because Mom immediately commented on it.

"Wow. You look like you haven't slept in days. Was it that bad?" Mom really did look concerned, so I began to explain my day. I sat on the couch next to her and rambled on for about thirty minutes. She half-listened to me, and half- finished writing a letter to my grandmother. I didn't care if she really listened or not, it just felt good to talk about everything.

"What? You didn't eat at all today?" Mom gasped. I had mentioned how hungry I was and why. "Go get yourself a little snack, and we'll start an early dinner. Tom's getting home a little earlier anyways, and I am feeling pretty hungry myself." Mom rubbed her giant belly and smiled.

I sank into the couch, while Mom went to put her letter stuff in her room. I really was so hungry, but I was also so tired. I felt like I could take a nap right then. As I wrestled with whether to get a snack or take a nap, I briefly wondered where Dawn was. Had her day been as eventful as mine? I was pretty sure elementary school wasn't as dramatic as middle school, but I couldn't really remember.

I forced myself up and off the couch. I dragged my weary body to the kitchen and leaned against the counter. The thought of eating some warm Hamburger Helper made my stomach sound like a wild animal. I reached up to the cupboard and started pulling out the needed pots. Now, I just needed to decide between cheesy or creamy...

The thudding of my mom's feet coming down the hall startled me. I looked down the hall and watched my mom walking very fast toward me, with the scariest look on her face. I didn't know what to make of it, as I had never seen her look that way before. She seemed scared, sick and in shock.

I quickly wondered if she was going into labor, when she blurted out, "Alex is not breathing, I have to call Tom." With that, she passed me on the couch and continued to the phone in the kitchen. She dialed some numbers and began to talk. I didn't hear what she was saying. Not because I was physically too far away from her, but because I was mentally too far away. My mind felt like it was in a haze. It felt like the night before when time slowed down as I walked by that bag —Alex's bag. I focused on what my mom said to me and tried to make sense of it. How could Alex not be breathing? She would have to be...

"Nyssa?" Mom was standing in front of me, bent over so she could see eye to eye with me. How long had she been there? I felt like I was going to be sick. She repeated herself, "Nyssa?" She was obviously looking for a response from me. I nodded, afraid if I opened my mouth that I would throw up.

Mom knelt in front of me, keeping her eyes locked on mine.

She placed her hands on my legs and quietly began to speak, "I really need you to help me right now. Okay?" She was pleading with me in a way I had never seen her do before. I nodded.

She took a deep breath and started, "Something happened to Alex, and she is not breathing. There is nothing we can do for her, Nyssa." She made a choking sound and struggled to continue, "If we call the police, they will take you and Dawn away, and we will never see you again." Now she was crying.

"I need your help, Nyssa. We need to figure out what to do, now." She held both my hands and looked at me with tears in her eyes.

I couldn't understand what she was saying. It seemed so unreal. I nodded anyway. Mom collapsed in a hug and held me for a few minutes, crying. Every thirty seconds or so, she would make a comment like, "I know I can trust you, Nyssa." Or "I love you so much, Nyssa."

Eventually, she slowly got up and headed back down the hallway. I watched her enter her room and partially close the door. I heard some movement, but I couldn't make out what was being moved. I listened in the quiet stillness of the trailer, until I heard the sound again. I thought I knew what it sounded like – the box from last night being slowly pushed across the floor.

A realization hit me like a ton of bricks. Alex had been in those two bags and the box not only all last night, but also all day! This day! This day I had been at school, obsessing about trivial things and struggling with stupid little problems. Alex had been in her own personal hell all that time.

The door to the trailer flung open, and Tom flew in, looking pale and in a panic. His breath was labored, and he asked, "Where's your mom?" I was still in a daze and turned my head to look down the hall toward their room. Tom walked slowly by me, staring at me in shock. I must have looked pretty scared, myself.

Then, he flew down the hall and entered their room.

I returned to my catatonic state on the couch and wondered if I was actually dreaming. I couldn't tell how much time passed; thoughts and feelings jumbled in my head, along with my perception of time. But at some point, Tom came stomping down the hall and was blurting out a slew of statements:

"We have to call the paramedics. This was an accident. This can't be happening. We have to call now, maybe they can save her."

Although he was not yelling, there was urgency in his voice that I had never heard from him. He began walking toward the kitchen for the phone. Mom went over and grabbed his arm, hard.

"No, Tom!" Mom yelled. Tom turned to her, with utter confusion plastered all over his face. "If you call them, then they will arrest us! They won't understand that it was an accident! The kids will get taken away!" Mom was screaming and crying, but Tom seemed unsure.

Mom stood in front of him and looked him straight in the eyes—just like she had done to me, earlier. "Our baby will never know us, Tom." She spoke more calmly. "She will be taken away, and we will never see her." She finished slowly and Tom softened his demeanor. She had convinced him.

Tom took a very deep breath and asked, "What do we do?"

He glanced over at me, as though I may have an idea as well. I looked at the floor.

Mom stood in front of the both of us and began, "We have to get rid of the body. Then, we can call the police and say she wandered off again. Remember, she did that before?" She nodded calmly and said, "It can work." Then she looked at Tom. "But we need to do this now." She emphasized now. He got it and nodded his head.

Mom looked at me, "Okay?"

I knew I would need to answer her verbally on this one, so I said softly, "Okay." The three of us all nodded awkwardly at each other, with really nothing left to say. The two of them went down the hall and into the bedroom.

Tom bent down, like he was going to lift something. Fearing I would see Alex's dead, frail body, I turned away and looked at the front door. I heard movement in the hall, and when I thought it was quiet enough, I again looked down the hall. I quickly caught a glimpse of my mom holding the end of something before they were in the bathroom and the door was closed.

Had I seen her carrying Alex's feet? Did that mean Tom was carrying her upper body? The shower came on. I guessed they were cleaning her. Why would they do that? The bathroom door opened, and Tom came out alone. He did not make eye contact with me, but went outside and soon returned with a large box that our new vacuum cleaner had come in. It had been in the van, because Tom was going to dump it somewhere on base. Now, Tom was taking it to the bathroom. I understood that Alex was going to be put into this box—but then what? I didn't have to wait long before I had the answer.

Mom opened the bathroom door this time and held it open for Tom. He exited, carrying the box. It was noticeably heavier this time, though not too heavy for Tom to carry by himself. He walked down the hall and mom got in front of him, so she could open the front door for him. After he had left the trailer, Mom sat on the couch next to me. She grabbed my hand and stroked it softly as she spoke.

"Nyssa, I need you to stay here, in case Dawn comes home. If she does, tell her that Alex wandered off, and we went to look for her." Mom touched my cheek and finished, "I know I can trust you with this, Nyssa. You are my special girl." She squeezed my hand with a little smile, and I forced a smile back to her. Then she left with Tom. I heard the van pull out from our gravel lot, and all was totally quiet.

I sank back into the couch. I was so glad to be alone for a moment. I couldn't believe all the events of this afternoon really happened. Then a sudden thought hit me—Dawn! Mom had told me to be here in case Dawn came home. Where was she? I hadn't seen her since I got home. My stomach wrenched terribly, as I wondered if something had happened to her, as well. After what happened to Alex, I was afraid to think of what else my mom was capable of. Should I go out to look for Dawn? Should I wait at the trailer? I reasoned I should do exactly what my mom asked me to do. I didn't want to cause any more turmoil.

I lay on the couch and scrunched into a fetal position. My stomach was hurting so bad. I knew I couldn't eat any food at that point, or I would throw up. In desperation, I laid on the floor with my back flat on the floor. When the pain didn't stop, I flipped over to lay flat on my stomach. After a minute or two with no relief, I again put myself in a fetal position and prayed for help.

As I was finishing a pleading prayer, I heard footsteps clanging on the metal front porch. I barely had enough time to sit up before the door opened, and Dawn entered. She looked puzzled and asked, "Were you just lying on the floor?" She was out of breath and began talking before I could answer. "I saw Daddy and Anna leaving. They said Alex is gone again. Is she still gone?" She glanced around the trailer, as she waited for my answer.

"Yes," I answered slowly. "She's still gone." I began crying for the first time since coming home to a twisted reality. Dawn seemed surprised and put her hand on my shoulder.

I cried harder, and she reached out to hug me. Having never hugged each other in the entire time we had known each other, it was awkward and strange. Dawn reassured me, "It's okay. We'll find her. I'll go back out with my friends, and we'll ride around the park."

She seemed to be begging me to stop crying with her reassurance, so I forced myself to stop. I didn't want her to feel bad for me. I should've been the one feeling bad for her. She had no idea of all that had transpired since she had been out riding bikes with her friends.

"Okay," I answered Dawn, taking a deep breath to control my emotions. She seemed glad I was done crying and left the trailer.

I went out to the little porch and watched her get on her bike and ride out to where a few other kids on bikes were waiting for her. Then they all rode off together.

The fresh air outside felt good. I leaned on the trailer and breathed the clean air to calm myself. The air was so fresh, it seemed somehow sweet and comforting. It was pretty chilly out, definitely colder than what I was used to. I didn't care. I didn't want to go back into that trailer—ever. But then, I heard a phone ring. I listened more carefully and knew it was our phone. I didn't want to go in and answer it. But what if my mom was trying to call me to see that I had stayed in the trailer, like she asked me to? I quickly went back inside and answered the phone.

"Hello?" I was more breathless than I thought I would be. I felt a little dizzy and weak.

"Hello? Is this the Suleski residence?" The man on the other end had a strict tone that sounded like he could have been from the base. Maybe Tom's work was calling to check on him.

I took a deep breath to steady my voice. "Yes, this is."

"This is Sergeant Bailey with the Radcliff Police Department. Are you missing a child from your residence?" He asked bluntly.

Oh crap! How did the police already know about this? What should I say? My mom wasn't home yet. What would she want me to say?

"Hello? Are you still there?" The Officer sounded less blunt and more concerned.

I had to think fast. "Uh, well she's wandered off before. My parents are out looking for her and I wouldn't say that she is really ... missing." Would that be enough to explain my initial pause?

"Okay." The Officer paused for a moment. "Could you give us a description of what she was wearing? I have here that she is part Asian and has short black hair in a 'bob' haircut. Is that right?" I agreed with his description. "Will you have your parents call the Radcliff Police Department, as soon as they get home?" he asked.

"Oh, sure," I answered, relieved. I had bought us some time.

I hung up and went back out on the porch. Maybe the fresh air would help my dizzy spell. It did seem to help, although it seemed even colder outside than it had been earlier, and I wasn't sure if I should stay. I didn't want to get sick. Mom hated having colds in the house.

I stood up slowly to force myself back inside, when I saw Dawn and her friends riding up on their bikes. One of the kids pointed towards me, and I saw a police car following them. Was this the cop that called me? Why was he here? Where was my mom? I was freaking out.

The police car pulled into our driveway, and the guy that got out identified himself as a Sergeant. Was he the same person that had just called? "Are your parents home, yet?" He seemed in a hurry.

"No," I answered. "My parents are out looking for my sister. They will probably be home soon."

The Sergeant looked confused. "Have they been out for a while looking for her?"

"Uh, I don't know. I think so." I mumbled. I realized what I had done wrong. Parents who have a missing child stay out for a long time looking for them, right?

He quickly pulled out a little notebook and continued, "I have a basic description of her—Alex. Right?" Before I could answer he asked, "Do you know what she was last seen wearing?" His rushed tone was making me too nervous to stop and think before I spoke.

"Well, my mom was the last to see her. I don't know what she was wearing. And yes, that's her name." I hoped I had not said anything I wasn't supposed to say.

The cop looked a little upset at not having a description of her clothes. He finished by saying, "Please have your parents call the Radcliff P.D. as soon as they get home. Okay?" I nodded, and he rushed back into his car and drove off. He seemed very concerned for Alex. I shivered in the cold and wished my mom would hurry up.

I returned to the quiet trailer and tried to busy myself. I put some dishes away. I wiped down the counter and kitchen table.

Anything to keep my mind off how awful I felt. Finally, I heard a car pull over the gravel that was our parking space and peered out the kitchen window to see the van.

Relief spread throughout my body, until I realized that the Sergeant's police car was pulling in next to them. I watched him quickly come around his vehicle to my parents and asked them questions in the same manner he had asked me, with urgency for a lost little girl.

I watched the three of them walk around the trailer and realized that they were going to come inside. I quickly sat at the kitchen table, so they wouldn't see that I had been watching them through the window. Mom came in first and saw me sitting at the kitchen table. She squinted her eyes at me, and I realized I was sitting in a dark room. That did seem strange.

As Tom and the Sergeant stepped inside, Mom walked over and turned on the light for me. She sat down across from me and said, "It's okay. Everything will be alright." She spoke calmly, and there was no longer the stress of earlier showing on her face. I believed her. I had to. I wanted this day to be over.

Tom closed the door, as the Sergeant left. Tom said, "There will be more officers and stuff coming during the night. It's almost bedtime. I'll get Dawn, and the girls should try to get some sleep."

He walked outside without a reply from either of us.

Mom held my hand and stroked it slowly. "Look, Alex went out to play, and we haven't seen her since. She went out before you even got home from school, so you didn't see her at all today." She smiled. She was trying to make it easy for me.

I was grateful. I couldn't handle remembering a bunch of things to say. Mom stood up to hug me. I stood up to make it easier for her. She whispered near my ear, "It will all be okay." I hugged her strongly and began walking back to my bedroom.

As I slowly dragged my feet across the living room floor, the front door opened again. It was the same Sergeant from earlier. He asked my mom if it would be okay for Dawn to walk with an Officer named Heslip. "Officer Heslip is actually the one who alerted us about Alex being gone," he explained.

"Oh really?" My mom answered. I wasn't sure if she would secretly be detesting this officer, who had cost her time needed to cover her crime.

"Yes," Sergeant Baily said, "Officer Heslip was flagged down by a neighbor who was out looking for Alex, and he alerted the rest of us."

Mom took a deep breath, "Oh, well … thank goodness for that." Her voice seemed entirely too monotone for what she was saying.

"Well, the officer would like Dawn to show him a couple of places that Alex was familiar with around here. Would that be alright?"

Mom nodded, and Sergeant Baily went back outside. I could hear the muffled voices of Tom, a few men and Dawn. I guessed she would be coming to bed later. Once inside the quiet of my shared bedroom, I heard what sounded like the muffled voices of a few officers entering the trailer and talking with my mom and Tom.

As I was pulling out my pajamas for the night, Mom entered my room in a slight panic. "Do you have any of Alex's clothes in here?" She glanced around my room and looked questioningly at me.

I shook my head, "No." Why would I have Alex's clothes in my room? What did Mom want with her clothes at this particular time?

Mom moved her face close to my ear and whispered, "The police are bringing in a dog to pick up Alex's scent. They want something of hers for the dog to smell." She glanced toward my door, as if to see if someone would hear her next sentence. She returned to her position right next to my ear and hissed, "I don't want them to get something with a fresh scent on it."

It was then that I understood. My mom was looking for Alex's clothes that would have either none of Alex's scent on it, or a mix of scents. Anything that might confuse the specialized dog that was being brought in to find Alex.

Mom peeked out my door and looked down the hall.

Satisfied that no one would see her, she motioned for me to follow her, and we walked to the back of the trailer and into her bedroom. She picked up a small blanket that had been washed and set it aside. "Hopefully they'll use this." She stopped and seemed to ponder something for a moment. Then, she began pulling more of Alex's clothes out of the hamper. "Just in case..." She seemed to have a back-up plan forming in her head.

I sat down on her bed, as she walked from one end of the room to the other. I felt dizzy and hoped I wouldn't pass out.

Mom found a very large plastic storage bag and shoved some clothes that she picked out from the clean laundry basket into the bag.

She walked over to me and ordered, "Touch these."

I reached my hand into the bag and touched Alex's tiny clothes. Mom reached her hand in and rolled it around, as well.

"Let's see how they like these." She seemed entirely too satisfied with tricking the police officers. "I'm going to put these somewhere. You can go to bed now."

Relieved, I slowly dragged myself to my room. I caught a glimpse of my mom heading toward the door and heard the door open and shut, as I entered my own room.

As I changed my clothes and was beginning to look forward to lying on my bed, there were voices and footsteps coming up the porch. It was more than Dawn, Tom and my mom. I sat on my bed and listened. As the door opened, I heard another officer and maybe someone behind him. From their voices and the few words I could make out, I figured out that law enforcement had returned with a dog handler and asked for something with Alex's scent on it.

Mom immediately got up and said, "Oh, I know something you can use." She said something else that was too low for me to hear. A moment later, I heard someone pad up the hall and stop where the folded blanket had been left. A muffled conversation followed, and from the few words that I could make out, the officers did not seem to like the blanket for what they needed. I heard my mom leave the trailer and thought I heard the van door open. Why did she put the bagged clothes in the van? Wouldn't the officers think that was strange? I imagined my mom had a good excuse for why the clothes were in a bag and in the van. She always had a back-up plan.

I needed to go to sleep. I needed sleep more than I had ever needed it before. I could hear my parents talking to people in the living room. Answering questions and asking their own. I heard people talking outside the trailer. Maybe neighbors or maybe more police. I thought I heard the "special" dog that had been brought in. The sound of an excited bark seemed too close to the trailer to be a coincidence.

I crawled into bed and curled up in the blankets as tight as I could. Dawn came into the room, also ready for bed. She sat on her bed and looked at me. She continued to stare at me, and I put together that my side of the room was too dark for her to see I was still awake and staring back at her.

"Are you okay, Dawn?" I felt I had to ask. Pretending to be asleep seemed harsh.

She leaned over to see me better. "Oh, you're awake?"

"Yes," I answered.

Dawn lay down in her bed and explained, "The police guy asked me to show him where Alex and me played sometimes. He asked me if I played with her today." She paused. I wasn't sure what to say to that, so I waited. After a moment of me debating whether she was done, she finished. "Do you think they'll find her?"
I blurted out, "Of course they will." I hated myself. I needed this conversation to be over. "Goodnight, Dawn."

"Goodnight, Nyssa." She rolled over, and we were done for the night.

I wanted so desperately to fall asleep. My body felt like I had been in a car accident. I hadn't eaten all day. Awful thoughts and images raced through my head. I tried to remember how I had finally been able to fall asleep the night before. Then I remembered why I had not been able to sleep the night before.

Alex had been in the bags. She had made that awful sound. That awful sound! Had I heard her struggling to take her last breath? Was that when she died? I felt responsible. I had heard her—yet I did nothing. What could I have done? Mom would not have let me call the police or an ambulance. But maybe she would have loosened the tie.

Was this my fault, too? I wrestled with these tormenting ideas most of the night. When I finally fell asleep, the sun was starting to rise, and the voices around the trailer had not stopped.

Dark Secret

THE SEARCH FOR ALEX

Things around the trailer got increasingly more chaotic over the next couple weeks. People were constantly filtering in and out.

Police officers, detectives and eventually (when a sighting of Alex was reported across state lines) even FBI agents were some of the strangers walking around our trailer. At the end of the day, Mom would usually fill me in on what was currently going on in the investigation.

"So, today they wanted a current picture of Alex for some 'missing child' posters. But I told them we didn't have any because all our stuff was in storage. So, we had to call Kim for a picture." Mom told me this info in a very matter of fact way. Like she was telling me the current scoop on what was happening on a T.V. show.

At first, I didn't understand why she had said we didn't have any pictures. We had taken pictures on our trip out from California. I thought about those pictures and knew why mom had not offered them. Alex didn't look happy in any of them. She was either crying, visibly upset or told to get out of the picture altogether.

That would clearly not make my parents look as innocent as they were trying to seem.

Mom was wiping the countertop, and I was sitting at the kitchen table, as she continued, "It's actually a good thing we had to call Kim. Now the police want to question her. She would be the type to kidnap her favorite daughter." I didn't know what to say.

Kim seemed like a terrible mother and person, but she had not done anything to Alex. Not like my mom and Tom. My lack of response seemed to concern Mom. "Are you okay, sweetie?" she cooed to me.

I smiled and nodded. She returned to wiping down the entire kitchen. "Oh, I almost forgot," Mom looked at me with a smile.

"There is a group of ladies that have gotten together and want to bring us dinners for a while." She sighed with relief. "That will really help, right? Now you don't have to make dinner most nights."

She smiled and rubbed my shoulder as she walked by me.

People were bringing us food? They must feel sorry for us— because they think Alex was kidnapped or wandered off or something. How could we accept their food? I hated what was happening. An innocent person was being investigated, and nice people were taking the time to make meals for us. What would be next? I could not have imagined.

Someone gave us a T.V. when our second dinner was delivered. It was partly because they felt bad that we didn't have one, and partly so we could see Alex's story being broadcast on the local news. Tom even said a few words to a camera crew and we would see it that night.

Mom and Tom spread out the food, and we all served ourselves, then we went to the living room to watch T.V. and eat the food generously prepared for us. The food was so good; we were only half-watching the television. We were all going on and on about how delicious it was. Then Alex's name came from the news anchor. We became extremely quiet and watched intently. The anchor spoke briefly about the search, then Tom appeared on the screen. He looked nervous and spoke quickly.

He urged anyone who knew where Alex was or thought they saw her to call the authorities immediately. I'm sure Tom's pleas were heart-wrenching for all parents watching the news that night. For me, it was gut-wrenching. The lies were getting bigger and more devious, and now even broadcast over the television. My dinner didn't taste as good as it had a few minutes earlier. In fact, my appetite was gone.

As Mom rubbed Tom's back and told him what a great job he had done, I excused myself and went to get ready for bed. Dawn came to the room, as I was starting my diary entry for the night.

I immersed myself in my writing to avoid Dawn, purposefully. I didn't want to talk about Alex with her. I felt an overwhelming mix of negative emotions every time we talked about Alex. I felt envious that she knew nothing of what really happened to Alex. She didn't have to live with the things I had witnessed and then have to lie about them.

But I also felt deeply guilty she didn't know. Alex was her biological sister, and she was worried she was out in the world, all alone. Either way, I found it easier to avoid talking to her altogether. Dawn saw I was writing and quietly got ready for bed.

Writing my diary entry was partly for my benefit and partly for my mom's. I knew that my mom occasionally read my diary. She accidentally mentioned something that I had only written in that diary, and I pretended not to hear her. She did not repeat it, probably because she realized she had seen it in my diary and didn't want me to know she looked through my stuff. Knowing this, I wrote things in my diary that I knew she would want to read. Things about not really liking Dawn, and thinking Tom was a goof, but that she was the greatest mom in the whole world. I also wrote that I was worried about Alex being missing, and I hoped she would come back soon.

Writing this actually was therapeutic for me. It was a lot like the sentences that mom had Dawn and I write. When we wrote them, it made the words more real to us. Writing that Alex was actually missing put a slight doubt in my head as to what was real. I knew it was fake, but at that point I would have rather believed something that was totally false than the painful truth.

When I was done writing, I placed my diary in my sock drawer and hoped Dawn had already fallen asleep. But she spoke as I was adjusting the blankets. "Are you mad at me?" Her voice was like a mouse. I thought about the question that her pitiful tiny voice asked and knew I had been cold to her since the day the search started. I knew it was because it made me feel bad to talk to her now, but I also knew it wasn't her fault. What was I supposed to do?

"No, I'm not mad at you." I knew I had to give her a logical explanation for my behavior. "I'm upset about Alex." Strangely, that was true, just not the way she would think.

"Oh, me too," Dawn answered quietly. Then she rolled over, and I thought I heard her crying. Crap! I was such a terrible person!

How could I not tell her? How could I not comfort her in the least, just because it made me face what I was doing? I rolled over and began to cry, too. I thought about the hopeless situation in the trailer – Mom and Tom plotting their next deceitful move, Dawn feeling all alone and not knowing where her sister was, and me having to deal with it all.

I cried more and thought to myself, "There can't possibly be a God. He wouldn't let this happen, if He was real." With those thoughts, I would not pray again for almost three years.

The next few months were more of our family portraying the poor victimized people who had lost a loved one. It became a little harder to do this, when suspicion began to fall on my parents. There were several detectives from Radcliff P.D. who had become quite familiar to our family, because of their constant presence. They wanted to set up multiple interviews or schedule times to meet up and ask my parents about developing issues related to the search.

Detective Gruber and Detective Kirby were two of the detectives whose names would constantly come up around the dinner table. To me, it seemed that they were completely dedicated to finding Alex.

Detective Gruber was a little older and spoke with a rasp and tone that made you think he was really a "no nonsense" type of person. Detective Kirby was much younger and seemed to be assisting Det. Gruber. Part of me deeply respected how much they wanted to find her, while at the same time I wished they would give up. I hated that we were lying to them but saw no other way to help them and my mom.

The FBI also had an agent who was well known to my family. He had worked on missing child cases before, and this made my mom very nervous around him. It was during his first visit to introduce himself that my mom began faking contractions. The fact that my mom was willing to put on such a show in order to avoid all contact with this man told me that she feared him the most.

Agent Lewzader was a tall man, about as tall as Tom, at six foot-two inches. He had a very deep voice, which, added to his appearance, would have normally scared most children. But the soft tone he used when talking to Dawn and me immediately put us ease. That is, until my mom began screaming in pain on the couch, and Agent Lewzader and his partner left, to give her time to rest.

By the time the FBI became involved, it was obvious that the Radcliff P.D. had their doubts about what really happened to Alex. They had Tom take two polygraph tests and said he failed one of them. They said they found discrepancies in the stories that my mom, Tom, and I told them. That didn't surprise me, since the three of us hadn't had time to come up with a detailed account for that evening. Many things were apparently not adding up for the authorities. It was at this time that my mom found an attorney to answer any additional questions the FBI or Radcliff P.D. had.

These added stresses were making Mom more and more outrageous. She came up with mean nicknames for the "main three," as she called them. "Grubby Gruber," "Baby Kirby," and "Lurch" became her new names for these men who wanted to know what happened to a little five-year-old girl. She also became convinced that our trailer had been "bugged" by the FBI and refused to say anything about Alex while we were home.
"I know Lurch bugged the bathroom when he said he had to 'go'," Mom stated to me, while we were shopping at Walmart. "Just don't say anything about Alex anymore. It isn't safe."

Mom also began bad-mouthing the group of ladies that formed to help us "in our time of need." They called themselves "The Friends of Alex Suleski" and did just about anything my mom asked or got us anything my mom mentioned we needed. They seemed very concerned for Dawn and me and would have bought us, given us or made us anything.

Although my mom liked them coming around and doing nice things for us, I believe they made her jealous, and she would say the most awful things about them as soon as they left.

Faking a contraction episode became an art form for my mom, as well. Several times she acted like she was going into labor when she was either being questioned by authorities, or "The Friends" had stopped by for something. She would always refuse an ambulance and explain she was being treated for premature labor and this type of event happened quite often. It would really scare the crap out of anyone who witnessed it. This was exactly what she wanted. It was hard to think a pregnant lady who suffered from severe early contractions could be capable of anything heinous. Once the person or people left, she would actually laugh and make fun of them.

Finally, whenever we had to do something in public for Alex's search, Mom would act like she didn't really care to have much attention put on her. However, she would go to great lengths to pretty herself up before such events.

On November 26, the night of Alex's sixth birthday and one month after her "disappearance," the Friends thought it would be a good idea to have a candlelight vigil to honor her birthday and to keep Alex's face in the news. Mom went on and on about how the emphasis should be put on Alex, and she hoped Tom or her would not have to talk too much to the TV crews that would be there.

However, the day of the vigil, we ran around town until my mom found a hairdresser she liked. Then, she got a double foil—which was apparently very expensive and not recommended for pregnant ladies. Then, we went to a nail salon, where she got her nails done and finished just in time to make the vigil. Tom did speak to the crews, and Mom was right next to him the whole time. When we watched the broadcast later the next day, Tom commented on how nice Mom looked, and she actually smiled so hard she beamed. Jekyll and Hyde had nothing on the manipulative master that my mom was.

I grew increasingly scared of what my mom was capable of and strived even harder to please her and stay on her good side. I really didn't see that I had any other alternative. I didn't know enough about foster homes to know if Dawn and I would be safe. I really didn't think that going back to live with my dad would be a wise choice. That left trying to make the best of mom's scary behavior.

I really felt Mom had been a lot nicer to me since October 26, and even treated me like I was her little best friend. She was blunt with me about what she thought and felt about other people. While the content of what she said bothered me sometimes, I thought it also meant that she trusted me and liked to talk to me.

That was good, right?

THE SEARCH DWINDLES

By the time the search for Alex was beginning to wane, it was becoming clear that part of the town thought my parents had something to do with her "disappearance." Mom became increasingly suspicious of The Friends of Alex and their questions about what had happened to Alex. Since they all heard my mother's account of that day, she reasoned that they were working with the police and trying to trick her into saying something incriminating.

My mom also said she heard people pointing and whispering about us while we were shopping around town. I wasn't sure if my mom was mentally cracking under the pressure of concealing what happened, or her demands as a mom with a newborn that never slept were messing with her sense of reality. Thankfully, that was a big change that happened and helped to distract us from our stressful situation.

My mother had a baby girl they named Novi Chrysta, on November 28, just two days after the candlelight vigil for Alex. My mom's tradition of different names continued.

It had been a terrifying experience of driving my mom to the hospital in the middle of the night, with her writhing in pain in the back of the van. I knew she was not faking this time, because there was no one to fake for. When we arrived at the military hospital, she had Novi less than 20 minutes later. Despite having been up all night at the hospital, Tom decided to take us to school. I hated him. He really couldn't think straight without my mom to guide him.

I arrived at school, tired and feeling wilted. Friends said "hi" using my new nickname I was still struggling to get used to. Once the search began, my parents thought it would be a good idea to have new first names so reporters couldn't ask for us at school. I jumped at the idea, having always disliked my strange name.

After a couple hours of thinking about it, I decided on Rebecca. I reasoned that even the nicknames for Rebecca would be okay, so it was a good choice. Having other students call me by that name was still taking some getting used to.

At school, I met with Rachel like I usually did before classes and told her my mom had the baby. She seemed excited for me and hugged me. She hugged me a lot. I had never had a friend who did that. After spending the next half-hour telling Rachel about the exciting night I had, I remembered I had something else to tell her.

"Rachel, we got permission to move on base," I blurted out. "We can still see each other and I'll call you every day." I tried to smooth over the bomb I had dropped. I knew this would be hard. Rachel and I had become very close. I felt more comfortable with her than I ever had been with any of my friends, ever. I knew she didn't realize it, but she helped me through a lot of the garbage I had gone through the last few weeks, by just being a great friend to me.

Rachel's eyes teared up. "Oh, Becky," she decided to call me that when I switched my name to Rebecca. "When are you leaving?" she asked.

My eyes teared up. I didn't want to go. "I think I have two more weeks here."

Rachel hugged me again and brushed some tears away. "I can't believe you're leaving," she said softly.

A few girls saw us crying and hugging and came over. "Are you okay? Is it about your sister?" one of the girls asked with a concerned look. I had quickly become well-known in the school once the search for Alex was underway. Many of the students had been extra nice to me. Even the girls who "had problems with all other girls not in their clique" were pretty nice to me.

I shook my head. Rachel answered for me, "She's moving on base and going to school there." She hugged me again and wiped more tears from her eyes.

The two girls looked sadly at each other, and the same girl said, "Oh, I hope everything goes good for you there." The second girl touched me on the shoulder and said, "Yeah, if anyone messes with you, just let us know." Then they both nodded at me and walked away.

Normally the fact that I didn't recognize either of the girls would have made the encounter very strange. But, many of the students at the school felt so bad for me that they been abnormally nice.

I finished out my two weeks at Radcliff Middle and spent a lot of time at Rachel's house. Mom knew I wouldn't be able to see Rachel as often and was generous with the time I could spend with her. I rode home with her after school, and Tom would pick me up on his way back from work. I spent the night on the weekends, and even went to church with her. I was moved by how devoted she was to being a "Christian" and wondered if this was why she was such a nice person. It was enough for me to wonder if being a part of a church could help people be decent, but not enough to take back my feeling that God was not real.

At the end of the two weeks, we moved on base. We had a new member of the family, a new house (three times bigger than the trailer) and new schools to go to. I had been so programmed to think that a new start meant old problems went away that I was very upset when problems seemed to get worse.

Now that Dawn and I had separate rooms, we really didn't talk at all. This was more convenient for me, but I knew it had to be harder for her. She didn't really talk to my mom or Tom. Mostly this was because they didn't really talk to her that much, but it was also because when she did talk, Mom made her feel like an idiot.

Dawn became increasingly shy and wouldn't look people in the eye. I'm sure she had issues that she wanted to talk about but had no one to talk to. I thought I should try to talk to her a little and decided to invite her into my room. I wanted to show her how I had set my daybed up. I really thought it looked cool and was desperate to show it to someone. Plus, I figured Dawn wouldn't talk about Alex when I was just showing her my bed. Mom was in the room immediately.

"What's going on?" she asked, concerned.

"Oh, I wanted to show Dawn my bed." I pointed in my room, toward the bed.

"Really?" Mom seemed unsure.

"Yes, look." I showed them both my bed. Then, after the three of us had stood there for a while, Mom looked at Dawn and left.

Mom sat on my bed and sighed. "Look," she began, "I know you probably just wanted to show someone your bed, but you need to be careful around Dawn. If you accidentally say anything strange around her, we might get into trouble. I mean, seriously, the cops want to accuse us of abusing her, because she's so skinny! Can you believe that? Just cause she's built like her dad?" Mom seemed appalled, so I faked exasperation and rolled my eyes.

I was secretly relieved when Novi started crying from Mom's bedroom. This meant our conversation was over—for now. She squeezed my shoulder and gave me a warm smile, then left to attend to Novi.

I knew what she meant. She didn't want me discussing anything having to do with Alex to Dawn. I didn't think she had anything to worry about, since I dreaded the very thought of having to speak to her at all about Alex. But I didn't want to have to explain that to my mom. There were too many ways that scene could play out badly. I could imagine her accusing me of feeling guilty and being a "weak link" that could not be counted on. Nodding and agreeing with my mom, while offering no extra information, seemed the safest bet. So, that's what I did for the next few months.

Life went on without Alex. I became used to my new school on base, just like all the other "new" schools I had been to. I made friends and even had a boyfriend. Although Rusty was my boyfriend, we were more like best friends. We didn't hang out much outside school (my mom felt that would reflect negatively on our family, which she said was "always being watched"). So, Rusty and I ate lunch together every day at school, walked together to almost every class, and talked on the phone at least once a week. I felt as close to him as I did with Rachel—who I still talked to as much as I could.

He cared about me a lot. I knew there were girls at the school who would do things with him that I did not, but he still chose to stay with me. I didn't understand that decision, but I appreciated it.

As the cold winter weather gave way to the spring, my mom eventually let Rusty walk me home sometimes. It was during these long walks home that I wanted to open up to him about things at my house. Things that happened. I even thought how wonderful it would be to have him and Rachel over and tell them everything. The enormous weight that would be lifted and the deep breath I could finally take afterwards. But, I didn't.

I settled into a comfortable close friendship with him and Rachel. We talked about going to high school together. Rachel and I would become cheerleaders, and Rusty would continue playing football. It was going to be so much fun. Life was going to be normal.

That idea was shattered when law enforcement knocked on our door, on April 15, nearly six months after Alex had been gone.

It happened so fast—my mom and Tom were led out in handcuffs, Dawn and Novi were taken by social workers, and I was taken away in a separate car. Taken away from my hopes of having a normal life, with normal friends who cared about me.

After a brief time being questioned by a Radcliff Police officer in an "interrogation" room, a social worker entered. She smiled and did not seem concerned with questioning me about Alex.

"Nyssa, I have to tell you that while we wait for your grandmother to fly in from California to take custody of you, you will be placed in a foster home." She saw the concern on my face and touched my hand. "Oh, sweetie. It won't be so bad. I have a really great family for you to stay with, just for a day or two. I know your grandma is trying to get here as fast as she can." She smiled again, and I nodded.

I thought of something my mom had yelled at me as she was being put into the back of the police car. "Can my sister Novi stay in the same house?" I asked the social worker.

The lady smiled again and answered, "Yes. I already worked that out." She shook her head, still smiling and remarked, "Your mother has been most vocal about that." I grinned a little as I thought, "I bet she has."

As we left the building and headed out to the car that would take me to my foster home, I thought of what my mom had yelled before being driven away. I had been at the doorway watching her, when she turned and looked at me. She yelled, "Take care of your sister! Don't get separated!" I knew which sister she was referring to. It was the only one she considered to be my sister.

The social worker and I stopped and picked up Novi nearby and continued on to our temporary home. I could tell she had been crying, and I snuggled with her in the backseat. She put her little hands over her car seat to touch my arms, and I wanted to cry. I had not lost control of my emotions since the police had taken my parents. Now, as I sat cuddled with my baby sister, I felt a wave of sadness come over me.

It wasn't right she should experience this and not understand why. How scary it must be for her to be ripped out of her familiar surroundings and not know what was going to happen next. Suddenly I was struck by the similarities between Novi and Alex. She didn't understand what was happening or why. I couldn't contain myself anymore, and I cried. Because Novi was asleep in her car seat, I gently pulled away from her and cried toward the window. I did not want to wake her.

A DOSE OF ANOTHER FAMILY

Our foster home was not scary like I thought it might be. But I definitely thought it was strange. The family was made up of a stay-at-home mom, a dad who was gone most of the day, and three adopted children. I was going to sleep in the same room as the one little girl they had. Nelly was about Dawn's age and offered to sleep on the floor, so I could have her bed. She seemed nice. Novi was going to sleep in another room that was reserved for infants and toddlers this family occasionally cared for.

I spent some time going through the bag that the social worker packed for me from my home. She had actually done a pretty good job. Two of the outfits were ones I liked, but the third one was actually a sweat suit my grandma had made for me a couple years back. She had used Minnie Mouse fabric, and I had been forced to have a serious discussion with her about how I was no longer five years old. She had taken it quite well. I only kept this hideous outfit in case of emergency. Like, I needed to help my mom paint something, or someone stole all my clothes and I needed to not be naked.

Now, I was faced with having to wear it on what was probably going to be my last day of school here or pretend I didn't see it and wear the same outfit twice. That first part wasn't an option I was seriously considering, so I pushed the Minnie Mouse blob back into my bag. Nelly came in and began making her bed on the floor as I was laying out my clothes for the next few days.

She watched me as I looked over the two usable outfits I had, and quietly laid her blankets on the floor next to her bed where I would be sleeping. When she was done, she sat on the makeshift bed and watched me some more. Feeling a bit awkward, I struggled to think of something to say. I finished getting my things together and asked, "Where can I change?" I held up my pajamas to show her what I meant. She pointed down the hall, and I could see the shadows of what looked like a bathroom. I said, "Thanks," and headed toward that room. It was the bathroom. I was somewhat relieved.

This was the first quiet moment by myself since my parents had been taken away earlier. It was nearly bedtime, but it felt much later. The day had been so unusually long.

I changed my clothes, washed my face and realized I should probably go check on Novi. She had been sleeping in her car seat when we arrived, and the mom of the house had taken her to another room to finish sleeping. The mom seemed nice enough.

When she had shown me to my room, she hadn't talked much. I didn't know what to make of that. Was she uncomfortable because she knew who I was and what my parents were being accused of? Was it odd to have new children coming in and out of your house? Maybe she was just a quiet person.

"Nyssa?" Nelly called to me from the other side of the bathroom door. I opened the door and smiled.

"Oh," she seemed a bit startled by the door opening so quickly.

"Sorry," I said. "Do you need to use the bathroom?" I asked.

She shook her head. "I just wanted to know if you read before you go to sleep?" I must have looked confused, because after watching me, she began to explain. "We can read for thirty minutes before we go to sleep, and it's almost thirty minutes before we are supposed to go to sleep, now."

I nodded my head that I understood. Then I answered, "No, I don't read before bed. I think I'm going to check on my little sister. Then I'll be back up, okay?" Nelly smiled and went back to her room. I headed downstairs.

Walking down the stairs, I could hear a male voice and the mom's voice. They were quietly discussing something. As I got closer, I could hear Novi's babbling and cooing sounds coming from the same area. I followed the sounds to the dining room and found Novi in a highchair, wearing a bib, and being fed some mushy stuff by the mom of the house.

I was a little shocked. Novi had only been breast fed by my mom and had not started to eat any kinds of food, yet. This mom obviously didn't know that.

The dad of the house looked over at me. "Hi," he said toward me.

"Hi," I answered back.

The mom turned around and remarked, "Oh, you're changed for bed. Good. It's bedtime in twenty minutes. You can read or relax until then." Then she went back to feeding Novi. The dad had nothing further to say to me. I was beginning to feel this couple didn't care for me much. That made me angry.

"You know, Novi doesn't eat foods yet. She is only breast fed." I informed the mom. She turned around again and said, "But, she's over six months. She should be at least starting some cereal once a day. It's good for her, and it will help her sleep better. That's why I'm giving it to her before bedtime." Then she turned back to Novi. She felt the conversation was over. I was getting more and more ticked off.

"Well, she just got done taking a long nap. I'm sure she won't be going to sleep any time soon." This lady didn't know me or my sister. She wasn't going to tell me what was best for us.

The mom turned around again, as the dad mumbled something to her. I couldn't hear what it was, but it made the mom rethink what she was about to say. She half-smiled at me and said, "It's about time for bed. Why don't you go get comfortable?" I was too tired to try and think of something smart to say.

"Okay, goodnight," I said to the parents. The dad nodded and the mom murmured "goodnight" quietly. I walked over to Novi and kissed her on top of the head. She tried to touch me with a gooey baby cereal hand, but I moved away.

I slowly walked back to Nelly's room and climbed into bed. She was deep into her book, so I turned over and hoped she would think I had immediately fallen to sleep. I didn't want to talk to any more people in this house. I hated what happened, and I hated feeling uncomfortable in a strange house. I hated not knowing what would happen to my parents or my sisters or even me.

A small voice called up to me, "Is your sister okay?"

It seemed ridiculous to pretend to be sleeping, so I answered, "Yes, she seems okay."

I heard some rustling of Nelly's book. I thought she was putting it away. Great, now she really wanted to talk. I took a deep breath and told myself that Nelly seemed like a nice girl, and I needed to be nice back—even if I didn't feel like it.

"So," Nelly began, "are you and your sister going to be here for a while?"

"No," I immediately answered. "We're here until my grandma can fly in from California to get us."

Nelly seemed disappointed. "Oh, I thought you might stay. It's nice here. I get my own room, and my brothers share another room." She pointed down the hall. I knew her brothers weren't there; I heard the social worker talking to the mom and knew the boys were sleeping over somewhere else that night.

I was facing toward her, but I closed my eyes. I really was very tired. I remarked, "I'm glad tomorrow is Sunday. I could really use the extra sleep."

Nelly laughed. "You take naps during the day?" she asked.

I opened my eyes and laughed a little. "No, I mean that we don't have to get up for school in the morning."

Nelly laughed a little, too. "Oh, yeah." Then she got quiet and said, "But, we do have to get up early for church." The footsteps coming up the stairs cued her to put her book under the bed I was using and snuggle up in her "floor bed." The dad peeked his head through the door and said, "Goodnight."

Then shut the door before we could say anything. Real warm. The reality of what Nelly told me was sinking in. I was going to have to get up early and go with this stranger family to a stranger church in the morning. I tried to make myself feel better by thinking, 'This might be like the church Rachel goes to. That wouldn't be so bad."

Nelly made a yawning sound in the dark and said quietly, "It's too bad you won't be staying. It would be fun to have an older and younger sister around." She rustled in her bed a little, then got very still. I lay there, not knowing what to say back. Eventually I heard her heavy, even breaths and was glad the conversation was over. Now, if I could only fall to sleep.

The next morning, I awoke to Nelly kneeling over me asking, "Are you awake yet?" Even in my sleepy state, I noticed she was dressed nicely. Like she was dressed for church. Oh, crap. I sat up and smelled breakfast.

"Nelly, did everyone eat already?" I asked her in a slight panic. I didn't want to make this family late for anything. I didn't want to give them any reason to dislike me any more than they already did.

Nelly shook her head. "No," she answered. That was good. I searched through my clothes and picked one of my nicer school outfits to wear. I was making sure I had everything to go to the bathroom and change, when Nelly said, "You still haven't eaten. But everyone else has." Double crap! I ran to the bathroom and got ready as fast as I could. I knew I didn't look as well kept as I would have liked, but I didn't have time to worry about that. Besides, I probably wouldn't know anyone at the church anyway.

I walked into the dining area and saw a single plate at the table. It had French toast and sausage on it, with a glass of juice next to it. I wanted to make sure this was for me, before I ended up eating the dad's breakfast. I walked around the downstairs and found the mom sitting next to Novi on the floor. Novi was in some sort of bouncy chair and had the cutest dress on. The mom was handing her toys that she dropped onto the ground. The mom seemed to have a lot of patience for this game.

"Excuse me," I began. The mom turned toward me. "Uh, I just wanted to know if that breakfast had been left for me, or if it was someone else's."

The mom thought for a second, then said, "Oh, yes. Everyone else has eaten. Nelly said she tried to wake you, but you wouldn't get up. So, we left it for you." She glanced up at the clock and with slight concern in her voice, said, "You should probably hurry.

We have to leave here in five minutes." Again, she didn't seem rude; just lacking emotion.

I quickly went back to the dining room and ate as much of my breakfast as I could, before the dad came down the stairs and everyone came to the front door. It's like the dad's footsteps meant for something to happen in the house. No words were spoken, just footsteps—then appropriate response. I tried to follow the example and got up and went to the door. I figured we were ready to leave, when the dad looked toward the table I left.

The mom said, "Oh," and ran over to clean up my dishes, with Novi on one hip. I ran after her and grabbed my glass. I whispered, "I'm sorry," as we put all the dishes in the sink. She smiled and nodded, and we both went back to the door. The dad seemed pleased that all was in order, and we filed out of the house and were off to church.

The ride over to their church was completely silent. Nelly did not start any conversations with me, the wife and husband did not talk to each other, and even Novi seemed distant and maybe even tired. The only sound in their van was the soft church music coming from their radio. Maybe they were all listening to it, and I shouldn't interrupt their routine. I looked out the window and remained quiet for the entire ride.

When we arrived at the church, I was a little shocked.

Rachel's church had been a large, but plain-looking building. The only distinguishing architecture had been the wooden- looking cross protruding from the top middle portion of the front of the building.

The foster family's church was very different from Rachel's. The building was tall and grand, with many stained glass windows all painted with religious art. I thought the steps looked like a fancy stone. Was it marble or something? It reminded me of the type of churches you would see on television. Inside, the stage looked fantastic! There was gold melted into amazing candle holders and what looked like the stand where the pastor would talk. As we filed into our pews, I could no longer hold in my awe.

"This is your church?" I asked Nelly.

Nelly smiled and nodded her head. "I go into the kid's area before the service starts. Are you coming, too?" she asked, hopeful.

The mom heard our brief conversation and answered, "I think they will stay here with us, since this is their first time here."

She saw the disappointment on Nelly's face, and then added, "Tommy and Brian should be there. The Thompson's brought them from their house."

229

Nelly seemed a little happier. She kissed her mom goodbye and waved to me, as she met up with another girl coming up the aisle, and they both disappeared around a corner. That left the mom, Novi, and I sitting in the pew together. The dad had gone off to talk with someone or something. I didn't really care, I felt uncomfortable when he was there anyways. I didn't think he was violent or anything, it just seemed like the mood changed when he was around. 'Time to be serious and non-emotional. Dad's home."

Something like that. I didn't get it.

I decided to take this time to try and talk to the mom. While I didn't really care if she liked me or not, I did want to feel more comfortable around her while I was living in her house. "You have a really pretty church," I commented to her.

She smiled at me and said, "Oh, thank you."

I was encouraged by her genuine-looking smile and struggled to find something else to say. Just then, Novi yawned and began wiping her face tiredly into the mom's shoulder. "Oh," I began, "she usually takes a morning nap around this time," I offered.

The mom sat Novi up and gave her a little stuffed bear to play with. "Well," she countered, "It's better for her to take one big nap during the day. Then she will sleep better at night." She looked at me and seemed to realize that she may have been too harsh. She continued, "If she is constantly taking little naps, she will not know how to sleep for more than an hour or two at a time. At her age, she should be learning how to sleep for longer sections of time. Does that make sense?" She was softer in her tone with me. We were having an actual nice conversation.

I nodded and was going to ask her how she knew so much about babies, when the dad showed up. He walked past me and sat on the other side of his wife. All was silent again.

I took that time before the service started to ponder what the mom said. It did make sense. My mom always let Novi sleep whenever she wanted. She woke up several times a night and took as many as four naps during the day. It was difficult for all of us. At night, we were constantly awakened by her cries, then playing. During the day, it was hard to know if Novi would be sleeping, so it seemed like we always had to be extra quiet. I wasn't sure if it would ever end. Now, according to this lady, it was supposed to end, but someone had to train Novi. I wrestled with the idea that my mom didn't know everything.

Once the service started, I didn't have any more time to think about the matter. We sang a few songs (they were a little slower paced than Rachel's church), then things got complicated. Some people bowed down on little pedestals that were part of the pews in front of us, some people got up and walked down to the stage to eat something and interact somehow with the pastor, and all the while, words were said that didn't quite make sense to me. I was sure it was English, it just seemed mixed up or something. At first, I tried to fit in by copying what people around me were doing. I knelt down on the pillowed beam in front of me when I noticed the dad doing it.

The mom grabbed me by the elbow and pulled me back up. She was shaking her head and whispered, "Just sit." I was deeply embarrassed and hoped no one else had seen me. Apparently, there was a very precise way of doing things at this church, and I didn't have a clue or was not qualified to participate. I sat and sulked until all the formalities were finished and it was time for us to sing a couple more songs, then it was over.

The mom and dad talked briefly with a few other people, then we walked down to get Nelly and her brothers. Her brothers looked about five and eight years old. We all piled into the van and assumed the "quiet ride home" routine. As we pulled out of the parking lot, I looked back at the beautiful church. I was surprised I had not enjoyed myself as much as I thought I would in such an amazing-looking building.

I thought of something my grandpa Tata had told me. "Don't judge a book by its cover". It made sense to me. Not only did it apply to that church, it made me think of this family I was with. Someone looking from the outside might think they were just an ordinary family. They might not know that the kids were adopted, and the mom was really smart, and the dad was ... well, a cyborg. You don't really know what's happening on the inside of a book, until you read the individual pages.

Part of the way to the foster family's house, I smiled to myself. I had a pretty mature epiphany for my age, and I was feeling a little self-righteous about it. Then, a terrible reality hit me. The book I was in looked pretty bad to those seeing it from the outside. But it was even worse than anyone could imagine. I leaned back in my seat and fought the urge to cry.

THE GRAND JURY

My last day of school was emotional and strange. I sat in the backseat of the foster family's van and steamed over the idea that I was being made to go to school. Everyone would know that my parents had been arrested over the weekend. Why did I even have to go?

As we pulled up to the school, the mom glanced at me in her rearview mirror and said, "I know this isn't going to be easy." She seemed to feel sorry for me. She started to say something, then changed her mind and said, "I hope you have a good day." She smiled, and I thought about how dumb that was for her to suggest this would be a "good day." I kissed Novi goodbye and left the van.

Immediately, my friend Suzy ran over to me. "Rusty's been looking for you. We heard about your parents. I am so sorry. Who was that? Do you have an aunt you're staying with? Are you okay?" She wasn't giving me time to answer, but it didn't matter anyway. I just shook my head, not wanting to explain that I was in foster care. I did, however, have one concern.

"Where is Rusty?" I looked around the front of the building for his familiar face but didn't see him.

"Oh, I think he's looking for you at your first class. He asked me to come out here and wait for you." She looked very concerned for me. I felt bad that she was worried. Somehow it made me feel guilty, and I didn't want to be around her anymore.

"I guess I better go to class. I don't want to be late," I said, then quickly walked away.

Suzy yelled, "Will I see you at lunch?"

I yelled back, "Yeah, sure." I was determined to be lost in the sea of students going through their lockers and rushing to their classes. Instead, the hall went quiet and pairs of eyes locked onto me as I walked down the hall. I tried to ignore the stares and walked as "normally" as I could to my class.

When I rounded the corner to my first period, I saw Rusty standing by the door. I was thankful he was at the far door, because I could use the second door to enter without talking to him. Having slipped in through the other door, I quietly slid into my seat. Again, I ignored the awkward silence and curious stares as I looked up at the clock to see how long it was until class started. It was a whole two minutes. Thankfully, the time passed without an incident ... until class started. Rusty's friend Nick had first period with me and walked past me intentionally before heading to his seat.

"Didn't you see Rusty out there waiting for you?" When I didn't respond, he shook his head and went to his desk. Later, during the class, Nick passed me a note that said, "Rusty will meet you at your locker after this class." Crap! I didn't want to deal with having to tell him that I was leaving or have him look at me with the same pity that everyone else was. How was I going to avoid him all day?

Yes, this day would surely suck.

After class, I stayed in the bathroom until the bell for the next class rang. No one was in the halls when I came out. I entered my next class tardy, but I didn't care. For the next class, I took the long way. I knew Rusty wouldn't be in the far hall, and he wasn't. I had made it to lunch without having to speak to him. But, now what? I walked into the counselor's office and asked to speak to the head counselor. I had talked to her before, and I felt she was my last hope.

I entered her office, not knowing what I would say. Then, I sat in the chair across from her and began bawling. I felt so stupid, because I wasn't sure why I was crying.

The counselor passed over a box of Kleenex. She had tears in her eyes, as well. I was struggling to think of what I would say to her, when she sighed deeply and began to talk. "Nyssa, I have to let you know that whatever you tell me, may be shared with the authorities. If you really want to, I would love to speak with you. I just have to tell you that." She thought I was there to talk to her about my parent's being arrested.

I shook my head and took a deep breath to calm myself. "No, I just wanted a place to stay for lunch. I don't want to be around all those kids." I sniffled as I spoke.

The counselor was taken aback. She thought for a moment.

"Well, you are welcome to stay here for lunch. I don't have anything planned; I will just be eating my ham and cheese." I was overcome with relief and began to cry again. The counselor drew her eyebrows together and asked, "Are kids teasing you out there?" I shook my head "No" immediately. She seemed unsure. "You can tell me if someone is bothering you about what's happening."

I half-smiled and whispered, "I know." The lunch hour passed quietly. At first, I was not sure how to pass the time. Doing homework when this was my last day seemed ridiculous. Then, I remembered that the foster mom had packed me a lunch. My mom never packed me a lunch or gave me money for food at school, so I normally just skipped the meal altogether.

I opened the brown bag and found a peanut butter and jelly sandwich, an apple, a string cheese and a juice box. I smiled to myself as I thought, 'This is exactly what I imagined a typical packed lunch to be.' I ate the cheese and apple. I also finished the juice but couldn't bring myself to eat the sandwich. I knew I still had the second half of the day to get through, and Rusty was in my last class. My stomach began to feel twisted.

The warning bell rang for the next class and the counselor looked up at me. "Just get through the next few classes, sweetie. This day won't last forever." She touched me on the shoulder as she led me to the door leading to the hallway. I could hear the bustling of students on the other side. I drew a deep inhale, thanked the counselor and entered the hall. I quickly began walking to my class, staring at the floor and not making eye contact with anyone. This was a bad idea.

"Becky!" I heard Rusty's voice, then saw his shoes and knew I had to eventually look up. I glanced at him, then quickly looked away.

"I have to get to class, I'll be late," I murmured. I tried to sidestep him, but he moved with me and was still blocking my way.

"What do you mean?" He huffed in frustration. "Where have you been?" He sounded concerned, but also upset. I felt a crowd of people watching us in the hallway. I had to get out of there.

"Look," I whispered, "I had to go see the counselor. Now I have to get to class. I will see you later." Then I walked past him with force enough to bump him in the shoulder.

A girl who was known for being a bully sang out, "Oooooh, it looks like Rusty just got dumped." I felt awful leaving him to deal with that but felt instantly relieved when I heard several other people telling her to shut up. Now I just needed to figure out what I was going to do for my last class.

When I entered my last period of the day, I had no idea what I would say or do. I was so grateful when the teacher began to immediately speak, and Rusty and I had no time to talk. I could see him out of my peripheral vision staring at me, but I kept my eyes locked on the teacher.
By the end of the class, it had become obvious to Rusty that I was ignoring him. I could sense his frustration in the way he was breathing, the way he was handling his book, even the way he was sitting in his seat. I officially didn't care anymore. I just wanted this day to be over. The bell rang and I grabbed my bag and headed for the door.

When I didn't see Rusty following me, I felt more at ease and stopped by my locker to grab my personal belongings. I walked down the hall, keeping my eyes on the prize— the door to the outside pick-up area. I knew Rusty took the bus and would not be out in the pick-up zone. But, to my surprise, he was standing in my usual waiting spot, staring at me. I saw my foster family's van and decided I would use that as an excuse for why I couldn't stay and talk.

Before I could say anything, Rusty spoke. "You know—I just wanted to be there for you." Then his eyes welled up with tears, and he walked away. As he walked away from me, I could see him wipe his face with his sleeve, then straighten his body as if to compose himself. He walked around the front of the school, never looking back.

I was jarred back to reality by the voice of the foster mom.

"Nyssa, are you okay?" The van had pulled up to where I was, and she had rolled down the passenger window to speak to me. I hadn't even noticed; I was in such a daze. I didn't answer her but climbed into the van next to Nelly and Novi. The boys were in the next row of seats. Novi's smiling face made me feel better, and I pushed all the uncomfortable feelings of the day down somewhere deep, to deal with it later.

When we got to the house, the social worker was waiting for us. She explained that my grandma was now in town, and we would be brought to stay with her. However, we would not be flying back to California with her. Apparently, my parents had to go before a grand jury to answer some questions about Alex. Dawn and I would also have to testify at this grand jury.

I guessed I looked quite frightened, because the social worker tried to convince me it wouldn't be so bad. "It's just a small group of people who need to hear what happened to Alex, so they can decide whether or not to pursue charges against anyone." She stopped and looked a little uncomfortable. "Look, I'm sure you'll be fine." Maybe she wasn't supposed to give legal advice. Was that considered legal advice?

Whatever was happening next, I was so glad to be leaving the foster home and going to stay with my grandma.
Sitting in the social worker's car, I snuggled with Novi until she fell asleep. The foster mom had fed her a bottle while I gathered my things, so she was ready for a nice long car nap. I thought about how weird that family had been; Dad was a cyborg who ran the house with his iron fist, mom was a moody woman with no guts to stand up for herself, a daughter in desperate need of a friend in the house, and did I really need to get started on that church?

However, I was drawn to think of some other qualities I had seen while staying there. The dad was the opposite of all that Tom was—he had a backbone and seemed to keep a sort of order in his house. I didn't think he was mean or abusive, just a strong male figure who maybe wasn't used to showing emotion.

The mom seemed to know a lot about domestic issues. She took good care of her kids and family, although she seemed to lack the ability to show much emotion, as well. I wasn't sure what to really think of the foster family who had taken care of my sister and me. This was my first experience being exposed to a family other than my own, for an extended length of time. It would be a time that I would reflect on often in the next few years.

I was overcome with relief when I saw my grandmother and Uncle Pat at our house. A few of the Friends of Alex were also at the base housing we lived in. They wanted to help us in any way that they could and offered to watch Novi during the day while we would be at the grand jury hearing. I was beginning to feel that this grand jury thing would last a while. I was feeling more nervous about this group of people I would have to speak, and even lie to. What if even one of the people didn't believe me? What would happen to my parents then?

Sleeping that night was very difficult. My grandma seemed out of sorts trying to get Novi to sleep. Novi was crying and sleeping for only a couple of hours at a time. I finally got out of bed and told her that the foster mom had given Novi some cereal before bedtime, and it seemed to help her sleep better. I also thought about how my grandma had let Novi sleep most of the day and that might have messed up her "sleeping schedule," as the foster mom had said it would. I decided not to mention the second point after grandma blew off my suggestion of giving Novi cereal.

"Oh, I don't know Nyssa. I don't think your mom was doing that, so I don't think we should change things like that." She seemed very reluctant to change what she knew my mom would want for her kids. I didn't blame her. I guessed if Mom found out someone was taking over her role and changing it, she probably would have been pretty angry. Nobody who knew my mom like Grandma, and I did wouldn't want to take on that scary drama.

After a sleepless night, one of the Friends came to pick up Novi. Grandma, my uncle and I got ready to head to the building where the grand jury would be. On the drive over, they were giving me "pointers" about how to handle speaking to this group of people.

"You want to make sure to make serious eye contact with all the people in there, Nyssa. That will show them that you are not scared and are telling the truth." My uncle Pat was very serious about his advice to me, but I had to practice extreme self-control in order to not smirk at him.

My mother had three brothers. The two older ones had done very well for themselves. One was a retired LAPD Officer, while the other was the head of a music department at some well-known university in Virginia. Her younger brother, however, was kind of the joke of the family, on account of him spinning the grandest lies about his life experiences. Although he had joined the army, he had never completed boot camp. He said he injured his knee and received a medical discharge, while my other uncle (who was a Vietnam veteran) explained to my mom and me that he was sure Pat faked the injury because he couldn't make through the required training.

Incredibly, this didn't stop Pat from claiming that while he was in boot camp, he was involved in "special operations" that were highly classified. He claimed to be a part of secret battles against—of all countries—Canada. Even I knew how ridiculous that would be.

"Okay, Uncle Pat," I said with the most serious expression I could make.

Grandma had advice next. "Just know you don't have to be scared, baby. Tell them the truth, and nothing bad will happen." She smiled at me and reached through the opening over the middle console to the back seat, where I was. I held her hand and marveled at how bad her advice was. She had no idea that telling the truth was exactly what I had to work to avoid.

The large government building made my stomach turn. Now, I was starting to feel nervous and intimidated. Through the metal detectors and up the elevator, we sat on wooden benches in a long hallway for most of the morning. Something was happening in the room where this grand jury was, but I wasn't sure what. Were other people talking to them before me? Would police be there to tell them about the discrepancies in our stories? This would make it harder for them to believe me.

I asked my grandma, but she didn't know anything either. Uncle Pat offered to find out what was taking so long. He walked off down the hallway, like he was on a mission.

"Your Uncle Pat will find out what is going on." Grandma believed everything Pat said and doted on him more than any woman should on her grown son. I thought he was probably going downstairs to buy a Danish and hang out for a while. He would probably come back with a wild story about a covert operation being conducted in the men's bathroom. The humorous thought relieved some of my nervousness.

A little while later, Uncle Pat was still not back, and I was being called into the grand jury room. Grandma hugged me and whispered, "You can do this," before I followed the bailiff into the room.

As I walked in, I immediately felt like I would throw up. The grand jury was a group of people sitting in a horseshoe shape. The seat I was led to was directly in the middle of this giant half-circle made of people. The person asking me questions was sitting in front of me. All eyes would be on me during every question I answered. This was the most nerve- racking moment of my life. I was beginning to doubt my ability to hold up to such scrutiny.

It wasn't until several questions were asked, and I answered, that I was able to really look at several of the jurors. The few who sat in my direct line of sight looked like your average everyday people.

One man looked like he could have been a mechanic or a construction worker of some kind. He seemed strong, but his eyes seemed kind. He looked about my mom's age, and I imagined he had a family of his own. Maybe even a daughter my age. The lady sitting next to him looked like an elementary school teacher. Not the mean kind, but the kind with never-ending patience. I imagined she really liked her job, and so really liked kids.

Adding my own thoughts about the lives of the people in the room made it easier for me to answer the questions the way I was supposed to. When I began to cry (I cried for the loss of Alex, but it fit with what I was being questioned on), a few of the jurors also cried a little. Tissues moved all around the room, and I knew I would be okay. I wanted these people to feel sorry for me. How can you take parents away from a girl you feel sorry for?

When I was done being questioned, Dawn came down the hall to speak before the jury. I had not seen her since we were separated into different foster homes. She smiled at me, and we hugged. We began to talk, but the bailiff nicely reminded us that the jury was waiting.

"I'm sure you can talk when she is done, okay?" he offered. We nodded and went our separate ways. When I got to the open hallway, Grandma popped off the bench and came to me.

"Are you okay, baby?" She didn't wait for my answer but pulled me toward her and hugged me tight. "It wasn't too bad, was it?" she asked.

"No, it wasn't as bad as I thought. I just answered their questions." I realized something that I felt needed to be addressed. "Grandma, why isn't Dawn staying with us now that you're here?" I pulled away from her slightly, so I could see her as she answered me.

"Oh." Grandma seemed unprepared for this question. "Well, I thought I would have my hands full taking care of Novi and didn't think Dawn ... well, the social worker said she was having a good time with her foster family, so..." She trailed off and sat back on the bench. I sat next to her and didn't know what else to say. Uncle Pat stood next to us, also quiet.

I couldn't stand the awkward silence anymore. "Grandma, will Dawn be coming with us after this grand jury thing?" I was feeling a little upset that Dawn was such an outsider. Maybe the fact that Alex died and she didn't know made me have more sympathy for her.

Grandma fidgeted a little. "Well, I hadn't really thought of that. I guess when your parents are released, then you'll all be back together." She smiled at me. I nodded and let it go. I guessed I would have to wait and see.

When Dawn was done being questioned, she came out and sat on the bench next to me. We made small talk about how many people were in that jury room and how hard it was not to cry during some of the questions. It was lunch time, and Dawn pointed down the hall to a couple who were sitting on another bench. "I think we are going to McDonald's for lunch. Do you want to come?" She looked hopeful at me, and I had to admit, McDonald's sounded really good.

Plus, I realized that I missed Dawn and wanted more time to talk to her. Mom wasn't around to keep us from having a conversation; maybe I could take advantage of this and actually have a nice talk with her.

I looked at my grandma and asked, "Can I go with them?"

"Oh," Grandma seemed uncomfortable with the question. "I think we had something else planned for lunch." She looked over at Dawn and said, "But, I'm sure we'll see you later." Dawn looked at the floor in disappointment. I put my arm around her shoulders and gave her a quick squeeze.

She looked at me and nodded, as if saying "It's alright." Then she walked down the hall to the friendly looking couple waiting for her. The woman immediately put her arm around Dawn and comforted her as they walked into the elevator and were gone. "Well," Grandma seemed to take a sigh of relief that the awkwardness was finished. "How about we get some food on the way back?"

So, just like that—Grandma was able to wash away all that was unpleasant with a kid's meal from Wendy's that I got to eat in her rental car. The rest of the day was spent watching television and viewing in an oddly detached way the news being reported about my parents.

Grandma had not been in Kentucky during the search for Alex, so she was not used to seeing our pictures and hearing our names broadcast over the nightly news. She and my uncle were glued to the T.V. I grew tired of hearing the same story being reported and played with Novi until I went to sleep early.

I was actually able to sleep easier, having no pressure on me to face a jury the next day. My part was over; hopefully Tom wouldn't mess up his. I knew Mom could handle herself.

It wasn't long after that day that I was told that my mom and Tom would not be facing charges in Kentucky for anything having to do with Alex's disappearance. My grandmother, uncle and I were practically jumping for joy. That was, until we were told that they would be facing kidnapping charges in California. We were told that Kim claimed we took Dawn and Alex out of the state without her consent. She said the girls were supposed to come with us for a vacation but were never returned to her. We were outraged.

"Oh, honestly," Grandma began. "She didn't notice until just now that the girls were gone? She doesn't give a rat's ass about those girls! She is just as evil as Tom said she was!" Grandma sat to catch her breath and calm down.

I choked back tears as we prepared ourselves for the flight back to California. We packed what we could take on the plane with us and were told that the rest would probably be shipped out to us by the military at a later time. Having moved so many times in my life, I really felt bitter at never having the time or place to have things that were meaningful. I looked around my room for the last time and realized that my bed, dresser and clothes were really the only things I had. I had packed most of my clothes, so that only left the two pieces of furniture. I guessed it didn't matter if I never saw those again either.

Dawn had arrived a few hours earlier and packed her things, as well. We met in the hallway, and I thought she might be feeling the same as me. "We're not leaving much, are we?" I said with a smile.

She smiled back and whispered, "No."

The trip to the airport and the flight itself were largely uneventful, except for Novi crying during most of the flight. It was explained that her ears were not "popping" like they should, and it was hurting her. We gave her juice, but she didn't want to drink.

Grandma and I took turns carrying her up and down the narrow aisle, but that seemed to annoy everyone on the plane.

Finally, the flight was over, and Novi slept deeply on the ride to Grandma's house. I was feeling as good as I could, considering my mom and Tom were still under arrest. I was going to my grandma's house, which had always been a safe place for me. No matter what was going on between my mom and dad or other people they were seeing, my grandma's house was always the same. Good food, encouraging words and no drama.

I thought it would be good for Dawn to be with us, too. It wouldn't take long for my parents to be set free. After all, it had not taken long in Kentucky, and these charges actually seemed fraudulent and insane to me.

In the next few days, many events happened that changed the calmness I thought I would receive once in my home state.

First, my grandmother put her house up as collateral for my mom to get out of jail. This did not sit well with my mom, who felt Tom should also be out with her. There were some tense moments between the two women, before it was interrupted by more news.

The court felt it would be better for me to stay with my dad during this new trial. I cried and begged, but it didn't seem to matter. I had to stay with him, indefinitely. Lastly, my sisters Dawn and Novi would be staying with my Uncle Sokie and his wife Linda. This was my mom's older brother who had been a police officer in LA. I had even heard he was somewhat of a legend in the department for some undercover work. I was confident Novi and Dawn would be safe with him. However, I was a little nervous, since I did not know Linda or her kids from a previous marriage.

Whenever my grandmother and mom talked about her, it was always with a twinge of disapproval—something about my uncle buying her a business and her being much younger than him. I knew my uncle was a funny guy, but would he know how to care for an infant and a displaced little girl? Once again, decisions were being made that were out of our control. Once again, Dawn and I would have to put on a brave smile and suck it up. This time, we would be dragging our little sister down the "It'll be alright" road we always seemed to be on.

THE MOCK TRIAL

Staying with my dad was just as uncomfortable as I thought it would be. Sure, the first couple of days went well. But I felt they were putting on their best behavior because I was being checked on by a social worker, and I was speaking to my lawyer every day at the trial. This was a bit of news that made me feel better about the whole situation. I had my own lawyer who I met when the charges were read and a start date for the trial was agreed upon. He seemed very nice and spoke to me like I was his equal.

"Wow, would you look at that? We have the same birthday!"

He pulled out his driver's license to show me. "Do you think they matched us up like that on purpose?" He laughed and so did I. He even leaned over to my dad and Jay's lawyer before the trial started and said, "Can you believe we have the same birthday?" The other lawyer seemed disinterested but faked a small smile and went back to looking through his papers. My lawyer whispered to me, "I guess he didn't think that was as cool as we do." I laughed. I was so glad this guy was my lawyer.

This new trial was set up differently than the one in Kentucky. It wasn't a grand jury, so we were in a regular courtroom with a judge who would listen to everyone's testimony. My lawyer told me that this was a good judge, and he would see the truth. I felt confident that this trial would end well for us.

Later that day, I made the mistake of sharing this feeling with my dad. We were on our way back from the first day, and it was a long ride back to my dad's house from this courthouse. I was happier than I had been since coming to stay with him and Jay. Dad must have seen me in the rearview mirror and asked what I was thinking about. I told him I thought it wouldn't be long before these charges were dropped, and we were all back together again.

Jay made a sound from the passenger seat, but I couldn't hear if it was a word or not. Dad glanced at her and smirked. He looked into the rearview mirror and spoke to me. "Do you really think your mom and Tom are innocent of the charges, or do you just want to be back with your mom again?"

I spoke quickly, "They didn't do this. Kim is crazy."

Jay mumbled something else from the passenger seat, and I could feel my face growing flushed. Why didn't she speak up or shut up?

Dad seemed to sense my anger toward Jay and whispered something to her. Jay threw up her hands, as if to say, "Fine then."

Then, Dad turned back to the mirror and said, "Okay, sweetie. I'm just glad we get to see you for a little while." He smiled, and the rest of the ride was uneventful.

When we got back to the house, I ate my dinner quickly and rushed to escape to my room. It was actually Monica's room, but she was sleeping in my dad and Jay's room so I could have my own 'space'. I went to take out my diary to write about the first day of the trial, when I saw that it wasn't where I had left it.

I grew frantic and searched through all my belongings. When I had looked everywhere I could, I lay on the bed and tried to remember the last time I used it. I definitely used it at my grandma's house. Maybe I left it there. I wasn't going back downstairs because I was bored, so I looked around the room and found some of my sister's books to read. They were childish but passed the time until bedtime. Then I went to bed without saying goodnight to anyone.

The trial seemed very long and drawn out. All the different lawyers asked questions. This added to the amount of time each witness was giving their testimony. I had a lawyer, Dawn had a lawyer, my parents each had a lawyer, and even my dad and Jay had a lawyer. It seemed like some of them asked the same questions, just worded differently. I thought that at this pace, the trial would never end.

I knew I would be one of the first witnesses called to testify. My lawyer had already warned me and was surprised by my matter-of-fact reply. "Okay," I had said.

"Wow, Nyssa. I am really impressed by your maturity in all this," he remarked with amazement. I really liked this guy. He was so nice to me.

I was extremely relieved that I would be giving my testimony in closed chambers. My lawyer explained this meant it would be in the judge's office and not in the open courtroom. My dad and Jay would not be there. This was more good news. I was beginning to feel like the two of them suspected my parents strongly in Alex's disappearance. Jay especially made comments to people on the phone, and even to Dad, about the "strong" case against them.

I didn't want her to hear anything I said, then share that information with others. I really felt she would use it to paint me in a bad way to relatives on my dad's side.

My testimony in the judge's chambers was much like the other times I had to answer questions about my parents, Alex and our home. Although this was a trial about whether they kidnapped the girls, once Alex was brought up, so were the circumstances surrounding her disappearance. So, that is mostly what I answered questions on.

Then, something different was thrown my way. The prosecutor introduced a new piece of evidence.

Apparently, when I answered a question about the contents of my diary, he was able to counter what I said by introducing a full, book-sized copy of my diary. My heart sank in my chest. I desperately tried to remember everything I had ever written and if there was anything that could be used against me now.

Everyone in the room was given a copy of my diary. I was so humiliated. Every boy I ever had a crush on, all the questions young girls ask about themselves as they grow older, all my insecurities and weaknesses were being read by total strangers. I was asked about several entries where I said I hated my mom. I had forgotten about those entries. I honestly couldn't remember what had been done or said to make me upset, so that's what I told them.

Then, I was asked about an entry I made about a week before Alex disappeared. In it, I had talked about how Alex had thrown up on the floor, and my mom had pushed her head in the toilet. I REALLY forgot that I had written about that.

Normally, I had been careful not to write about anything that could get my mom or Tom in trouble. Partly, it was because I wanted to pretend like those things really didn't happen, and partly so if my mom read through my diary (which I was sure she did) she would not throw it away because it contained incriminating information about her. How had I overlooked this entry? Why had I written it?

As I asked myself these questions, the prosecutor was asking them aloud.

"Uh, I didn't mean that my mom pushed her head into the toilet. I meant she just put her ... so her head was bent over the toilet ... and she would stop throwing up on the floor." I was satisfied with my answer.

The prosecutor asked a few follow up questions, then had no more. I was done. The judge was very nice to me the whole time I was questioned, and I was grateful for that. I was not grateful, however, for my diary being passed out to all these people.

Walking with my lawyer out of the judge's chamber, it became clear to me that my step-mom was the one who gave the prosecutor my diary. I was furious! I felt I reached a whole new level of dislike of that woman. I turned away from her and my dad and avoided them as much as I could during the trial. At lunch I didn't talk at all, and they seemed not to know what to say either. So, we ate quietly and went back for the second half of the day.

Dawn was also questioned in the judge's chamber, and one other person was called to the stand. It was a police officer, or detective or something. He testified in the open court, so we all got to see. It was much like I had seen on T.V. Except this was real, and my life would change forever based on the ruling of this trial.

Finally, the end of the day came, and we drove home. I steamed quietly in the backseat as my dad and Jay made small talk up front. When we got back to their house, Jay went into the house first, and Dad placed his hand on my shoulder.

"Jay really thought she was doing what was in your best interest. I know you don't see that, but I know it's true." He was waiting for a reply. I had none. I wasn't going to argue with him. He was wrong and didn't realize it. Soon, this would be over, and I would be gone, and my dad and Jay could live in this la-la land of being vindictive and calling it "In someone's best interest." I was done caring.

The next day was a Saturday, and my dad and Jay decided to have people over and barbecue. I decided I would hide out in my room and only come down when it was time to eat. All was working out well, until my dad called me down to eat. I was really looking forward to eating—the smell of the cooking meats had been wafting up the stairs to my room for a long time.

I walked down the stairs and headed towards the dining area. I could see to the other side of the room where the sliding door was that exited to the patio, and where the barbecue was cooking the meat.

Suddenly, I heard my step-mom yell out "What?"

I looked out toward the patio and saw Monica talking to her mom, and whatever she was saying sent Jay into a rage. Jay looked up from the barbecue and stared straight at me. I stopped dead in my tracks. What had I done? Jay took a step forward and slammed open the door.

"You wanna tell my daughter that I'm a mean bitch?" Jay screamed at me.
I instinctively took a step back and my gaze focused on the greasy spatula Jay was holding like a sword. "No ... I didn't..." I tried to say more, but once she took another step inside the door, I was done trying to explain anything. I turned and ran out the door as fast as I could. I ran up the block, then turned a corner and ran even faster.

I heard my dad screaming, "Nyssa! Wait!" He seemed far away, so I continued to run. I would run away. I would keep running, and they would never find me. It seemed like my only option.

"Nyssa! Please!" He sounded closer this time. I turned and looked. He was only about a half a block behind me. I couldn't outrun him. I stopped and collapsed on the ground. I sobbed like a baby. My whole body shook, and tears streamed down my face faster than I could wipe them away. Dad sat next to me on the curb and struggled to catch his breath.

"I think you should go out for track or something," he said between gasping breaths.

I continued to cry and blurted out, "I didn't say that about Jay!" I had thought it many times, but I wouldn't have said it. I especially would not have said it to my little sister Monica, who would have run to tell her mom.

Dad put his hand on my back. "Okay, let's go back, and we'll talk about it."

"No!" I yelled at him. "She is not going to listen to me! She never listens to me! She hates me!" I was not going back to the house to "discuss" anything with that mad woman!

Dad tried to calm me and convince me that we needed to go back to the house and "talk" about the situation. I became more and more adamant that I was not going back to the house. Finally, in desperation, I blurted out, "I wanna call Uncle Sokie. Maybe I can stay with him and my sisters."

Dad seemed concerned about this incident being relayed to anyone, so he immediately suggested, "Hey, how about you go and stay with Grandma Bita?" This was my grandmother on his side. I thought this option over: Grandma Bita always stayed pretty neutral in situations concerning my parents and step-parents, she had enough room for me, and I didn't want to impose on my aunt and uncle who were already caring for my sisters.

"Okay, I guess that's okay," I told my dad. He seemed very relieved. We walked back to the townhouse, and he went in first to explain things to Jay. I heard her raising her voice, and I thought I might have to make a run for it again, but soon my dad came out and told me I could go and pack my stuff. I threw my few belongings in my bag and we drove to my grandma's house.

Dad went into the kitchen with her, and they talked for a while. I wondered how he was explaining the earlier incidents to her. Was he watering them down a bit? Grandma would not have liked any adult losing control of themselves with one of her grandchildren. I decided I wouldn't offer any information, unless she specifically asked me. I just wanted this drama to be over and my life to get back to normal.

So, after dad left, Grandma and I ate dinner and watched some Wheel of Fortune, and then I went to sleep on the couch. It seemed like a normal visit to Grandma's house, and I was briefly able to distance myself from all the garbage in my life. I wondered if Grandma didn't ask me any questions so I could do just that.

The next morning, my aunt who lived with my grandma woke me before she left for work. I guessed she had come home after I fell asleep and was told why I was there. She nudged me and said, "Hey. Pest. Time to get up. Your dad will be here in about an hour to get you and we all know it takes you forever to get ready ... so, get up." I turned over on the couch to see her grinning down at me. Because she was the youngest of my dad's siblings, she had the most immature attitude of them all. Again, it was a welcome distraction.

I moaned and answered, "It doesn't take me forever. It only takes me an hour to get ready." I smiled back at her.

She laughed and headed for the door, "Well, then you better hurry your butt up, because an hour is all you have." She waved goodbye and left.

I didn't want any extra stress this morning, so I hurried to get ready. My grandma made me a quick breakfast, then my dad arrived to take me to the trial. Jay was not with him. On the way, Dad explained that Jay would not be coming unless she had to testify. She needed to work, anyway. I didn't care why she wasn't coming. I was just glad she wouldn't be there.

The trial continued, day after day. I slept at my grandma's house and visited with her and sometimes my aunt (she went out a lot after work). Dad picked me up, and we would spend the day watching people testify. It seemed like it would never end. Then, the lawyers finally said they had no witnesses. The judge seemed satisfied and decided to render his verdict.

He stated that he felt the charges had not been backed up enough, and he had to dismiss all charges against my mom and step-dad. I couldn't believe it. I hugged my lawyer, who was happy for me, but seemed uneasy to be hugging me. After I pulled away from him, he patted me on the shoulder and mumbled something about finding out what would happen to me. He took off to talk to someone else. I sat and smiled to myself. I looked around the courtroom and took in the different emotions. Some people were clearly disappointed. Some people seemed relieved it was finally over.

Then, there was my dad. I smiled at him, and he just nodded and looked away. Was he crying? What was his deal? My lawyer came back and told me that I would ride back to my dad's house and get my things. Then, I would be released back into my mom and Tom's custody. I was so relieved; I wanted to hug him again, but I remembered how weird that had been for him, and I put my hand out to shake, instead.

"Wow, Nyssa—you are really mature for your age. I know you are going to do great things when you get older." He smiled and shook my hand. I really enjoyed him being my lawyer, and his last comment made me feel encouraged in a way I hadn't felt in a long time. We parted ways, and I followed my dad to his car.

I was so happy to be going home and fully in my own world, that it was quite a while before I noticed how silent it was in the car. I thought maybe my dad was upset because this meant my mom had custody of me again, and he would have to work out visitation to see me—on her terms. I tried to think of something reassuring to say to him. I didn't want to leave things on a bad note, and I wanted him to be happy like I was.

"Dad?" I waited for him to respond, but he seemed glued to watching the traffic in front of him. I continued anyway. "Dad, I'm sure we will see each other more. I mean, I don't think we are going back to Kentucky. You know?" I waited for a response. When he didn't answer, I turned and looked out the window. I just had to get back to Grandma's house and get my things, then this would all be over. I leaned back in my seat and smiled as I watched the buildings zoom by on the side of the freeway.

"Do you think your mom and Tom had anything to do with Alex disappearing?" He asked me the question so suddenly, I had to replay it in my head to be sure that I heard him correctly. He didn't wait for me to answer. "I mean really— they had the girls taken away once for abuse, their own stories about what happened to Alex don't even make sense, and what you wrote in your diary about what your mom did to Alex..." He shook his head and looked down for a second. I thought he might cry.

I opened my mouth to answer him, but I was still trying to process all the things he was saying. Finally, I asked him, "Do you think they did it, Dad?" I didn't clarify what "it" was. I couldn't bring myself to say anything more.

Dad was quiet for a while. Finally, as we turned down his street, he parked in front of his house and said, "Grandma already brought your stuff over, and your mom or someone will be by to pick you up soon." He took a deep breath and locked eyes with me. "And yes—I think they did it."

I gasped and began to cry. I stepped out of his car and walked up to the door. I waited to hear him turn off the car and follow me. Instead, I heard the car take off. I turned around, and he was gone. I stood in front of the door to my dad's house and bawled. I sat on the small step and cried so hard I soaked the sleeves of my shirt as I used them to wipe my face.

Finally, Jay opened the door and convinced me to come inside. She hugged me and told me that everything was going to be alright. How could she say that? She didn't even know why I was crying. Why would she say that? Didn't she still think I called her a foul name? Why did she care about me?

I realized I didn't care at that point and hugged her back.

After soaking the front of her shirt with my tears, I went to the bathroom to clean up. I was horrified at my own reflection. I hoped my mom would think I was crying tears of joy because we were together again. She would be very upset if she knew I let something my dad said get to me so bad.

I heard the doorbell ring and rushed out to open the door. When I saw it was my mom, I grabbed my bag off the floor and walked outside. I didn't say goodbye to anyone. My mom looked back and said, "Thanks" to Jay as she closed the door, and Jay answered with, "You're welcome."

Mom didn't ask me why I had been crying. She just hugged me for a long time before getting into my grandma's car and held my hand while she drove. When we got to my other grandma's house, everyone went on and on about how great I had done with my testimony. Then, over our first dinner together in weeks, we made fun of the witnesses against my parents. Everything was so carefree and fun. I didn't want to ruin things by telling anyone what my dad had said to me. At that point, I didn't care if I ever talked to him again.

That night, I struggled to fall asleep with my grandmother in her bed. The bed itself was extremely comfortable. It was a king-sized bed with a feather comforter that you could sleep on top of. It was really like sleeping on a cloud. The problem was her pet chihuahua, named Pullita (little flea in Spanish). The dog had allergies or something, because it wheezed as it breathed and occasionally had fits of snorting before it would go back to wheezing. In the quiet of the night, these were horrible sounds to have coming from the foot of the bed.

Lying in the bed, not able to sleep, I found myself replaying the events of my last car ride with my dad. Why was he so convinced they had done something to Alex? Was it because he didn't believe me? Was that what upset me so much? Or, was it because he had sat through the trial like everyone else and formed his own conclusion based on the evidence given? Oh, what did it matter?

Determined to go to sleep, I forced myself to "quiet my thoughts" like I had been shown by one of the "Confidence Building" seminars my mom and I had gone to. Then, just as I was drifting off to sleep, an ambulance passed by in the distance. The siren was barely audible to me, but apparently unbearable for my grandma's dog. Her chihuahua began barking and snarling like a wild animal, to which Grandma mumbled, "Oh, Pullita."

This repeated itself several times through the night, and I never got more than a couple hours of sleep. Well, at least I was home.

TIME PASSES

The next week was full of new adjustments. Tom had to fly back to Kentucky to have the military "dishonorably discharge" him.

We would not be going back to Kentucky or continuing in any way to live a military life. This meant we would be starting all over again. I had really lost count of how many times my mom and I had to do this. Would there ever be a time when we picked a life and stayed with it? As I was getting older, I was beginning to see that it could be done. My dad and Jay were doing it, most of my friends and their families seemed to be doing it. Even that strange foster family had established traditions and placed roots in their community. I was feeling a little bitter at having to start from zero again.

Grandma offered for us to stay with her (like she always did), until we got ourselves back on track. Since Tom had no job, and we had no money and very few possessions, this seemed like a very generous thing she was offering us. We could all be with her and my grandpa (Tata) for a while. Mom didn't see it that way.

"Oh, don't get me wrong—Grandma can be a very nice person. But she always has another motive for doing what she does," Mom explained to me. The two of us were shopping with my grandmother's credit card for a few outfits for me to wear to school. I commented to my mom about how nice Grandma was, to let us use her department store credit to get some clothes.

She seemed to sneer at the idea of Grandma being genuinely nice.

"Look," Mom saw the confusion on my face and began to explain, as we sorted through jeans on a rack. "Sometimes Grandma helps so that people will see her as a martyr and feel sorry for her. Sometimes she does it just to point out how much better off she is than others." Mom seemed angry with this last comment, so I tried to change the subject.

"Oh, Mom," I pulled out a pair of cute little jeans to show her. "These would look really nice on you." I knew flattery could go a long way with her, and I was trying to change the mood.

Mom looked at the jeans and said, "Well, I probably shouldn't get too much. But those would look nice on you."

I looked at the little jeans and thought she was kidding. I began putting them away. "What are you doing?" Mom asked me.

I stared blankly at her. Did she not realize that those jeans were a size four? I blurted out, "Mom, those would never fit me." Then I looked down at the ground and hoped she wasn't going to use this time to take out her frustrations with Grandma on me by making fun of me.

"Nyssa, what are you talking about?" She reached in and grabbed the jeans off the rack. She looked at the jeans, then looked at me. She looked at the embarrassment on my face and then realized something. "Nyssa? Do you even know how little you are?"

I didn't answer her, and she grabbed my arm and the jeans and took me to the changing room. "Come on, I want to show you something." I was really hoping it wasn't how awful those jeans were going to look on me.

Once at the changing room, Mom made me try on the jeans.

After I had them on, she made me come out to the common mirror area. She turned me around and stood next to me. "Nyssa, you haven't been overweight for a long time. You're the same size as me." She stood at the same angle as me, and I saw what she meant.

Why did I keep thinking I was fat? What was wrong with me? Mom seemed to understand my confusion. "Oh, Nyssa. You are just a typical young girl. You think you are fat, or not pretty enough, or whatever other things drive young girls crazy." She hugged me and said, "If you ever feel that way, come talk to me. I will let you know what's real. Now, let's get those jeans! They are so cute on you!"

I smiled and felt like a load had been lifted from me. Not only did Mom show me what was true, but she would always be there to show it to me—in all areas. I felt a rush of love for my mom as we finished shopping and headed home. Any nagging thoughts I had about her bad-mouthing Grandma were gone.

"Oh, I almost forgot..." we were close to Grandma's house, and I was rummaging through the bag of clothes. Mom continued, "Tom and I think it would be best for Dawn to stay with Uncle Eddie in Virginia for a little while. We have so many things going on right now, one less child would be helpful, and Uncle Eddie might be able to actually do something with her." Mom smiled at her last comment and pulled into the driveway.

At first, I was saddened that they thought of her as such a burden. But then I realized, she would be with my uncle. This would be so much better for her than being with us—more specifically, my mom. Uncle Eddie had an awesome house, and no children of his own. Dawn would love it there. I nodded and laughed at Mom's last comment, as we went into the house. She probably didn't realize that I was happy for Dawn, not because we were getting rid of her. But, so what? Maybe this new start would be the best one of them all.

It didn't take long for my optimism to dwindle.

Dawn went to stay with Uncle Eddie, clear across the country. Tom went back to Kentucky to receive papers that basically said that he was not needed or ever wanted back in the military again. Mom began filling out paperwork to collect unemployment, although my grandma told her she wouldn't get it, because she was married to a man who was capable of working and many other reasons. Mom filled out the papers, anyway. Then, she took me with her to the welfare office, since I didn't start school until the next day.

The welfare office was in the city, which scared me. My last encounter with the city had been when we went to Koreatown. I envisioned a dirty place with more homeless people, drug dealers and crime than I had been raised around. It was as I pictured it. The inside of the building was not much better. The floors looked like they hadn't been cleaned in years, and the chairs were barely holding together. After we stood in line for a very long time, we took some seats in a far corner to wait for my mom's name to be called.

"Don't stare," Mom whispered to me.

I didn't realize it, but I had been staring at a man sitting slumped over about five seats down from me. He looked like he could have been sleeping or something, but he moved his head slowly and looked around. Then, he dropped his head back down and closed his eyes. I turned to my mom and asked, "What's wrong with him?" as quietly as I could.

Mom shrugged her shoulders and whispered, "He could be drunk, I guess." Then she reiterated, "Don't stare at people. Look at the T.V." She motioned upward, and I looked at the fuzzy screens placed in security-type boxes, firmly bolted into the concrete wall. What kind of place was this? A drunk guy getting ready to pass out in broad daylight, and T.V.s that had to have their own security? I began twitching my leg with nervousness, and Mom asked, "Do you have to pee?" I looked at the badly rusted door to the women's bathroom and quickly shook my head. I was not going anywhere secluded in this building.

We spent hours waiting for my mom's name to be called. We got a snack out of the vending machine, and I did venture into the bathroom, but only after Mom said she had to go. It was worse inside than I had thought, and my mom went into the stall with me to fully cover the toilet seat with half a roll of toilet paper before I could go. Finally, it was time for us to meet the caseworker and talk to her. She was a short, stern lady who didn't smile at all. She sat us down at her desk and began asking my mom questions.

"Where is your current husband? Where are you living? How long have you been looking for work and unable to find any?"

And so on.

I was prepared for all the lies Mom would tell. She had told me on the way over that she was going to say that Tom was not living with us, that we were living with my grandma but paying rent, and that she had been looking for work for a few weeks and was not able to find any. Nothing she was saying was truthful. She explained to me that if she went back to work, she would have to pay for childcare for Novi and that would take most of her paycheck—so what was the point of working? Since we needed money while Tom looked for a job, she reasoned that this was the only way for us to survive. Since my thirteen-year-old mind didn't have any other ideas, I agreed.

When the lady was finished listening to my mom and writing in her notebook, she closed the book and took a deep breath. She spoke in a tired monotone voice, like she had been doing this job for a long time. "Look, Ms. Suleski—I cannot recommend you for unemployment benefits at this time. You have not been looking for work for long, you are living with your mother, who would not let you or your children starve, and you are not in danger of being out on the street."

She saw my mom was getting ready to talk, and she cut her off. "If you would like to reapply after the required wait period, you may. But, my case on you is closed for now. If you would follow me, please." She stood up, and the two of us followed her back to the waiting area. "Goodbye," she said in her robot voice and closed the heavy metal door between us.

I followed my mom to the car and didn't say a word. I knew she would be upset about this. That woman had told her "No" to something she wanted. She also did it with an attitude! I don't think that lady knew how lucky she was that she hadn't done this to my mom on the street somewhere. She probably would have ended up in the hospital or worse.

Mom waited until we were almost home to talk briefly about what happened. "Look, don't tell Grandma what happened. She'll probably just say 'I told you so.' I'm going to tell her that they are looking over my case, and I'll have to go back in a few weeks for another review. Okay?" I nodded in agreement and figured that was probably when she would be able to go back and reapply anyway.

Mom had been planning this out on the way home, apparently.

Grandma smiled when Mom told her "the news" and said, "Oh, good. I hope it all works out. That would really help you guys out."

Once Grandma left the room, Mom mimicked how she talked. "Oh, good—I hope it all works out." She said in a whiny tone, as she rolled her eyes. "She's just waiting for me to fail. I promise you that." Mom seemed so certain of this fact, I believed her. I didn't want to think bad thoughts about my grandmother. After all, she had been there for us so many times when we needed her. She never seemed to ask anything in return.

Yet, Mom knew her better than me, and she seemed right about so many other things in life. Maybe Grandma was secretly a mean person. Well, I would have to keep my eyes open this time and see if I could find out for myself.

Starting school at Madrona Middle School was like all the other times I had to start at a new school. Full of embarrassment (why do teachers make you introduce yourself?), uneasiness (are those girls looking at me because they want to be friends with me or tease me?), and unexpected events (you want to eat lunch with me and that guy thinks I'm cute?). The only extra event I had this time was a meeting with the school counselor. She was made aware that one of my sisters was missing and wanted to talk to me.

As I entered the counselor's trailer, she immediately stood up and greeted me, "Oh, Nyssa. It's so nice to meet you. Now, do you prefer to be called Rebecca instead? I wasn't clear on that." She led me to the couch and chair on one side of the trailer. I quietly answered, "Rebecca, please," as I sat on the couch. I had been to enough counselors to know that they always took the chair.

She sat down and began asking how my first day was going. She looked at my schedule and pointed out a few teachers she knew quite well and especially liked. She seemed happy about my new friends, as well. I was really beginning to like her.

I told her about my friends, and she knew one of them. "Oh, she's a good girl—you'll like her," she smiled. I really felt good about meeting this counselor. Then, she said, "Well, I just want you to know that I know about your sister's sudden disappearance in Kentucky, and if you ever need to talk to anyone about that—or anything else— well, my door is always open."

I nodded and said, "Okay."

"Well, okay. I guess you can head back to class, if you want." She stood up when she saw me stand up and walked me to the door. "It was so nice to meet you, Rebecca," she said warmly, as she led me outside.

"You, too," I responded. I meant that. There was something different about this counselor. I didn't feel like she was trying to get information from me. She seemed more interested in what I felt like talking about. I had never been to a counselor like that. The ones my mom brought me to seemed motivated to get as much incriminating information they could about my dad and Jay. The ones the court required seemed interested in what happened to Alex and how that "made me feel." I really liked this lady, Mrs. Sandborn. Maybe I would come back to see her again.

The rest of the school year was as normal as it could have been, given our circumstances. I didn't speak much about my time in Kentucky, so few people ever knew about Alex. This helped me develop normal relationships and go through normal pre-adolescent experiences. Not that these were any fun. By the end of the school year, I was ready for high school and a different, more mature environment that didn't center around what clothes you wore or who had a crush on you.

At home, Mom eventually collected unemployment, which was spent on computers and furniture for their room in Grandma's house. Grandma tried to tell them that I only had four outfits for school, but Mom just sneered that they were four good outfits, and Grandma should mind her own business.

Tom eventually found work doing teaching or something of this nature—I never asked, because I didn't really care. His paychecks were split between saving for when we moved out and paying for their legal expenses incurred during the trial. So, basically, we were still fully relying on my grandma to feed and shelter us.
I was having a hard time finding the "secret meanness" that Mom implied my grandmother possessed. If I needed lunch money, I would ask Grandma. If I needed new tennis shoes because mine were falling apart, I asked Grandma. If I wanted to go see a movie with my friends but had no money —I could always ask Grandma. She did nothing but help me. What was I missing?

The summer I was preparing for high school was stressful, but not for the reasons most kids have. It was during this summer that I spent a lot of time over at my two best friends' houses. This trend led to a drastic shift in the way I perceived the world and the events in my own life.

My best friend Samantha lived only a couple of blocks away from my grandmother's house, and we walked home together every day from middle school. If I wanted someone to hang out with on short notice, she was very convenient and funny. She was one of the girls who never had hang ups about "acting cool." She would make a funny face and make everyone laugh, while still maintaining her status as a pretty girl. I wasn't sure how she did it.

Then, I began spending more time at her house. She lived with her mom, who was raising her alone. She had an older brother, but he already moved out. Her mom was especially interesting to me.

Not because she was a single mom, but because of the way she acted with Sam.

"Hey, Sam," she said warmly and gave her a big hug and kiss. We had gotten back from hanging out at the park up the street. Every time I had seen Sam and her mom meet, they were very affectionate and sincere with each other. This was in contrast to my mom, who could be very lovey at one moment or totally removed in her emotions the next. I would not count on getting a loving hug from my mom every time we met.

Sam began to tell her mom about our day at the park, as she popped us some popcorn for a snack. I was shocked by how much Sam told her mom. She told her every detail of our day, even the fact that some neighborhood boys had been there and one of them had a crush on me. I blushed and looked down at the floor.

"Oh, Becca," she put a hand on my shoulder, "don't be embarrassed. That's what boys do at this age. They like girls —really like girls." Then she sat down next to me. "Can I give you some advice?" she asked. I nodded.

"Just be careful how nice you are to guys that might like you – they may think you're leading them on." Then she added, "Oh, and it's okay to be picky. You know, you don't have to get a boyfriend just because everyone else is doing it."

"Okay, Mom. I think she gets it," Sam said, as she handed me a bowl of popcorn.

Sam's mom smiled and left the room. I was surprised at the calm tone she used with me, considering this would have been such a serious issue in my own home. My own mom would have told me exactly what to say or do with this boy. Her "advice" was always more like step-by-step directions that were the only right way to do anything. This was why I had not shared everything in my life with my mom. Anything involving boys would lead to instant drama in the house—no matter how innocent the situation.

The more time I spent with Sam, the more situations I witnessed that were very similar. Sam would tell her mom everything, and her mom would give her sound advice. She would not blow up at her or accuse her of things she imagined she was doing. She seemed to be guiding Sam through this time in her life, while giving her the opportunity to make a good or bad choice. To Sam's credit, she made good choices more often than bad.

Okay, but this was only one other mom I knew. Maybe she was an exception to the norm. But then there was my other best friend...

My other best friend was a pretty Japanese girl named Tori. Besides being a great listener and fun to be around, I liked going over to her house because it was like stepping into a different culture. Her house was decorated with Japanese furnishings, and her mom was always making Japanese food. Every new food item I tried, I liked.

Tori's mom seemed totally devoted to helping her and her brother. Whenever Tori or her brother needed something, her mom would help with a smile. She seemed to have a quiet satisfaction about seeing her children happy. This happiness did not seem based on things she was doing or buying for herself. This honest selflessness was so foreign to me, I almost wondered if it was just a huge cultural difference. Yet, Sam's mom also had this trait.

Why was my mom so different?

As the summer went on, and I spent most of it away from my grandma's house, I began to question many of the realities I had accepted in my life. My mom's selfishness and extreme moodiness were not acceptable, but terrible character flaws. They were not "typical" of a loving mother and wife.

Also, I began to realize that when she was nice to me, it usually coincided with her needing something from me. This usually meant she needed me to back her up on something that, had I enough time to think for myself, I would not have agreed to. I was being manipulated. I had been manipulated.

This raised the most uncomfortable of all my realizations ... What happened to Alex could not be rightfully justified. It had not been "an accident." The cover-up afterward had not been "necessary" to protect Dawn and me. What happened to Alex was wrong. The problem was, I was the only person out of the three witnesses who felt that way. What could I do?

Feeling that I had no one to confide in, and the fact that it would be my word against my mom's, led to me to decide that, currently, there was nothing I could do. My mother was a master liar and would make me look like a maniac of a child if I ever had to go against her in a court.

Or worse, she would blame what happened on me. Maybe she would argue that she actually covered for me and something I had done to Alex! My mother was evil enough to do something like that in order to save herself. Feeling like I had no other choice, I decided to wait and see if an opportunity would ever present itself for me to be free from this nightmare.

As hopeless days passed, I struggled to adjust to my new high school schedule. I had to wake up extra early in order to walk the two miles to school. Then, I would walk home, do an enormous amount of homework, and get on our recumbent exercise bike that was kept in the garage. Keeping very busy made it a little easier not to focus on the warped reality I lived in. This left only dinner time that I had to spend with my family. I struggled to seem like nothing had changed. I read my mom's mood and acted accordingly.

I just needed to buy some more time, until I could figure out what to do.

My mom interrupted our normally quiet dinner to announce, "Dawn will be coming back to live with us." Mom saw my confused look and explained, "Look, she is being spoiled out there. She takes voice and violin lessons from Uncle Eddie. Can you believe that? We can't afford to give you the voice lessons you deserve. Do you really think she can possibly appreciate that?" Mom huffed and continued, "She so easily gets on a high horse about herself, and Uncle Eddie doesn't understand. So, she will be coming back."

I shrugged and remarked, "Okay." I figured acting indifferent to Dawn was my best option. While I ate the rest of my dinner in quiet reflection, my mom and Tom discussed where Dawn would sleep and what school she would attend.

I wondered how much Dawn had changed in the past year. I had seen a picture of her from a few weeks ago and she looked taller and older. Maybe we could talk and help each other through the dysfunctional maze that was our home. Of course, we would need to hide any friendship or alliance from my mom. I could not imagine how angry my mom would be if she thought Dawn and I were nice to each other behind her back. The more I thought about that, the more I realized how crazy that was. Didn't most parents want their kids to be nice to one another? Why had I not seen how odd that was before?

As I cleared my place from the table and washed my dishes, I looked up at my mom. She was still eating and talking to Tom. I stared at her profile and tried to reconcile the conflicting views I had of her. I was beginning to see her in a whole new light that exposed her conniving, evil nature. However, I remembered her supporting me during times when no one else was around for me. I felt torn inside.

"Everything okay?" Mom felt me looking at her.

"Oh, yeah." Everything was far from okay, and I had no idea it could get any worse.

DAWN RETURNS

In early April of 1991, my mom and Tom were working out how to get Dawn back to California, and they had come up with an extraordinary plan. They were going to drive out to get Dawn, with a small stop in Kentucky.

Mom pulled me aside one day and whispered their plan to me. "We have to stop in Kentucky to make sure all of Alex is ... well, destroyed." She looked around the kitchen to make sure no one else was around. She was extremely paranoid to mention any of the real details of what happened that day. Even in the privacy of my grandmother's home.

"Oh, okay," I whispered back. Then, a thought occurred to me. "What about Novi?" I really hoped she had not planned to take my little sister with her on this disgusting mission.

Mom allowed her voice to become louder than a whisper, "Oh, well—we'll leave her here. That trip is too long for her. But I'm going to need for you to help Grandma with her." She looked sternly at me. "I don't want her to have too much influence on my little girl."

I nodded, although I had no idea what she was talking about. Novi was just a toddler and barely talking. How bad of an influence could Grandma be? Anyway, I was grateful that Novi would be staying behind and offered to help Grandma whenever I could.

Mom hugged me and went upstairs to start packing and preparing for the trip. They would leave as soon as they could. I sat in the chair at the island in the kitchen to collect my thoughts.

This had been the first time Alex's remains had been mentioned since the day of her death. I remembered Tom telling me something about putting "the box" somewhere where there were a lot of leaves in the woods. I had not asked for any specifics of this location, because I had hoped to just convince myself that it had all been a nightmare and Alex had, in fact, been kidnapped.

I even came up with a story of a poor childless couple who desperately wanted a little girl of their own. I tried to insert this story into my memory bank but found the action much more difficult than I anticipated. I guessed it was hard to fool yourself about traumatic events that etched themselves into your mind.

The next morning, the two of them left for their cross-country journey. I had to go to school, so I did not see Grandma or Novi until the late afternoon. Grandma looked exhausted. I played with Novi in the living room, while she made dinner. Then, the three of us ate quietly at the kitchen island. My grandfather, Tata, usually ate much later, because he stayed up watching TV much later. Grandma had explained to me once that older people need much less sleep, so this was normal. I understood but felt a little sad that Tata always ate by himself.

After eating silently for a little while, Grandma asked, "So, do you know why your parents decided to drive all the way out to Virginia, instead of just flying Dawn back?" She looked quizzically at me, as I shrugged my shoulders. "I mean, Uncle Eddie even offered to pay for the ticket. It's not like they're in a position to be spending more money than what they need to. They are supposed to be saving to move out." She was quiet for a moment, and then seemed to realize something. "Yet they always have money for computer stuff and for your mom to get her hair done at that salon."

I knew what she was trying to say, and I agreed with her. But I hesitated to say anything. I didn't want my mom to find out somehow that I was talking about her behind her back with my grandma. I even found myself looking around, in the same paranoid fashion my mother used when talking about Alex.

Grandma seemed to read that I was uncomfortable with the whole conversation and remarked, "Look, you don't have to say anything. I know you understand because they never spend any money on you, but they always have money for what they want—more specifically, what your mom wants. It's not okay, Nyssa." She smiled at me warmly and finished. "At least you have your fairy Grandmother here to help you when you need it."

I smiled back and dinner was finished.

As I spent time with Novi before bedtime, I thought about what my grandmother had said. Was she someone I could confide in about what happened to Alex? Was she being manipulative in the same way that my mom was? I wasn't truly sure what to think about Grandma, so I decided not to take a chance on sharing too much about my mom with her. I would wait it out a little longer.

When my mom and Tom finally got back from their trip, they had a different vehicle (apparently Tata's van had finally broken down somewhere on their trip) and a totally different- looking Dawn than who I remembered.

She was definitely taller. In fact, she was almost the same height as me. Her hair was longer, which I had not seen on her in several years. And, she looked older in the face. More like a young adult and less like a child. She hugged me and smiled. I hugged her back but pulled away slightly when I saw my mom eyeing us.

Then, Dawn did something I had never seen her do the entire time I had known her. She began to talk—a lot.

"How have you been? You look so much older. I like how you have your makeup. Are you still singing? I started taking violin lessons with Uncle Eddie. Are you in high school yet? I think I'm going to go to your old middle school. Do you still know anyone there? Oh, hi!"

Dawn only stopped talking "at" me to say "Hi" to Grandma. Grandma hugged her and remarked on how great she looked.

"Oh, Nyssa, I bet she could fit into some of your clothes," Grandma commented.

Mom had been holding Novi since they all walked in and finally joined the conversation. "Oh, Uncle Eddie said she just had a growth spurt and needed some new clothes. He offered to take her shopping before we left, but we were in such a hurry, we told him, 'No thank you'. Nyssa, if you have something she can wear for a little while, that would be great. I think she only has a few sets of clothes."

I nodded. "Oh, sure. I'll go look right now." I wanted to help Dawn, but I also knew that my own selection of clothes was quite sparse. If the two of us were going to be sharing clothes, we were going to wear out what we had that much quicker. I tried not to focus on my own selfish desires and found a pair of shorts that were a little too tight for me, two tops that I thought she might like, and a really cute pink dress that was too short for me to wear anymore. Since she was a little smaller than me still, I thought she would be able to fit into the smaller items.

When I brought the clothes downstairs, Dawn was talking to Novi. The two of them seemed very comfortable around each other.

Almost like no time had passed. My mom was watching them like a hawk and jumped on me when I came downstairs.

"Oh, good. You found some things." She held them out for Dawn and said, "Here, go try these on."
I thought Dawn would be exhausted from the trip, but she didn't complain. She walked over and got the clothes. "Thanks, Becca." She smiled at me and went to the bathroom to try the clothes on. Mom was instantly over at Novi's side, and I thought I saw her sigh with relief. Was it so bad that Dawn was just talking to Novi?

When Novi was younger, my mom had always limited the amount of time Dawn interacted with her, especially compared to me. I had assumed it was because Dawn was younger than me, and Mom was concerned about Dawn not handling a baby correctly. Now, Dawn was older and so was Novi. Why would my mom continue to have a problem with them playing together?

"Oh, look!" Grandma exclaimed. We all looked toward the bathroom and saw Dawn standing in front of the door. The shorts and shirt looked pretty good on her.

"That looks nice," I said with a smile. I instantly looked toward my mom to see if I had been too nice. But her eyes seemed locked on Dawn. "Hey. Not bad," Tom remarked.

"That is a very cute outfit Dawn," Grandma encouraged her.

Dawn smiled at everyone and said, "Thanks!" Then she spun around and went back to the bathroom. I assumed she was going to put on the dress. I looked back toward my mom. She was the only one who hadn't commented on Dawn's outfit and seemed somehow upset at the attention that Dawn was getting. Surely, she had to realize that it was mostly because Dawn had been gone for so long.

But, no—I didn't think she did. Either that, or she didn't care for any reason why Dawn should get this much attention. I looked toward Tom to see if he sensed the anger from my mom that I did. Of course, he was totally oblivious. He sat at the dining room table and stared off into space, clearly in his own world until Dawn re-entered the room.

I believe there was a collective gasp when Dawn came out in that pink dress. She looked great. I had never seen her look so pretty before.

I blurted out "Wow!" before I could censor how loud I was. Thankfully, I wasn't the only one.

"Oh my, Dawn! What a beautiful dress on you!" Grandma gushed.

"That looks really nice," Tom told her, with a smile.

Dawn beamed and walked toward the mirrored wall in the dining room to get a better look at herself.

Then, I heard mom laughing. We all looked over toward her and saw that she was turning red with laughter. She continued to laugh, as we all looked at each other for answers as to why she was laughing so hard. Finally, she wiped a tear away from her eye and took a deep breath. "You all are hilarious. Just hilarious." Mom stood up and walked over to Dawn. I had a sickening feeling that this was going to be unpleasant.

Mom continued to talk as she walked. "I mean, really—by what standards does this dress look good on her? You mean compared to a bean pole?" She chuckled at her own joke. She stood facing the large mirror side-by-side with Dawn, much like she had with me when we had gone shopping the year before. "Really, this dress just hangs off of her like it's hanging in a closet." She looked at Dawn's behind "She has no rear end." She looked at Dawn's stomach area. "She has no waist." Then, she looked at Dawn's upper body. "And she's got no shape up top, except for massive shoulders."

Dawn's eyes were welling up with tears. I wanted to yell at my mom to stop but was too scared of the consequences. I looked at Tom, but as usual, he was useless. He sat staring at his feet, hoping to avoid any confrontation with my mom at all.

Finally, Grandma began to speak, "Oh, Mica, please..."

But Mom cut her off abruptly. "Don't even, Mom. At least I'm honest with her, not filling her head with a bunch of BS."

She stared at my grandma as if daring her to continue. My grandmother just shook her head and walked upstairs. She was disgusted with my mom but not willing to take her on.

Mom turned back to Dawn, "Give that dress back to Nyssa. You won't be wearing it." She then turned around and walked back toward Novi, shooting me a warning look that said, "Don't give her that dress again." I looked at the floor and understood.

Now, I was officially as useless as Tom. I hated this feeling. I didn't know if it was my newfound set of morals, the hormones I had been told were raging inside me, or a combination of the two—but I was not going to be useless anymore. I had to find a way to stop the monster that was my mother. She was clearly going back to her old ways with Dawn. Dawn was quite possibly going to be the new Alex. The quiet scapegoat for whatever was ailing my mom that day. This couldn't happen again.

Over the next week, I watched as my mom systematically broke down Dawn's spirit. First, she had Dawn sleep downstairs in the dining room. She was alone on the bottom floor, except for Tata, who slept in the far-back bedroom. But my paralyzed grandfather would be of little help if someone broke in the front door—which was less than five feet away— and scooped Dawn up. Even at fourteen, I knew this was a dangerous sleeping arrangement. But my mom just explained that there was no more room upstairs for Dawn.

This was a flat-out lie. There was an empty bed in my grandmother's sewing room and plenty of room in the master bedroom where Grandma and I slept. However, no one called her on the discrepancy.

Mom was also making fun of Dawn whenever she had a chance. She would pick on her hair, her mannerisms, or whatever Dawn said—when she dared to talk. Finally, Dawn became the shy, quiet, self-conscious girl I remembered before she left to live with my uncle. Was the reason she was that way always because of my mom? I felt awful for Dawn. And still useless.

Soon after Dawn came back, an event happened that shifted my frame of mind away from feeling useless.

By the end of Dawn's first week back, Mom seemed extremely tired from having to focus so much negative energy at one person. When Mom was tired or stressed, this meant that Mom was also very moody. I tried to avoid her altogether but living in the same house with no room of my own to retreat to made that difficult.

It was after dinner, and I had spent thirty minutes on the recumbent bike in the garage. I knew I needed to rinse off and get to bed soon, so I turned off the lights in the garage and headed inside. Once I opened the door to the house, I knew I should have stayed on the bike longer.

My mom was screaming at Tom in the kitchen. She was holding Novi on her hip and Novi was clearly getting upset by my mom's yelling. Before I could make out what the argument was about, Tom said something to my mom that threw her into a rage. She put Novi on the floor and rushed at Tom. She punched him in the face over and over, causing his glasses to fly off and hit the table before landing on the floor.

Novi screamed like I had never heard her scream before, as she watched the one-sided boxing match between her parents. I rushed over and scooped Novi up as fast as I could. I turned around so Novi would not be facing the violent fiasco, but she turned her head to see if it was still happening.

When she saw Mom was still pummeling on her dad, she began to scream again. Tears poured down her face, and she was an abnormal color of red. I had never seen her so upset. Every ounce of me felt this was wrong and a two-year-old should never be that scared of her home. I began to grow angry.

"Give her to me." Mom was standing behind me. She had finished with Tom and wanted me to hand over Novi. She was red and shaking. I couldn't just hand Novi over to her.

"No." It took a second for me to realize I had uttered that word to my mom. I was scared, but firm in my belief that I couldn't hand Novi over to her.

My mom gasped at me, and asked, "What did you just say?"

I knew that my next words to her had to be chosen carefully.

I wanted to reason with her, somehow. "I think you are too upset to comfort her right now. Let me hold her a little longer." I watched her to see if she would agree.

At first, her face seemed blank. It was as though she could not process what I was requesting of her. Then, she reached out and pulled me by the top of my hair. Her grip was incredibly strong, and I nearly dropped Novi. Tom raced across the room and grabbed Novi from me. Novi began to scream again as Mom dragged me by my hair back to the garage. She slammed the door behind us and pushed me onto the floor.

The pain coming from the top of my head was so sharp, I felt like the room was spinning. Just as I was regaining my senses, Mom was hitting me on the sides of my head. It hurt so bad and disoriented me completely. It seemed like when I was figuring out what direction she was coming from and preparing to defend myself, she would land another blow and I would be lost again. I was beginning to black out, and I briefly wondered if I was dying.

Then, the room was completely quiet. I lay down on the cold garage floor and struggled to make the dark tunnel in my vision widen and clarify. The spinning took a little longer to subside, but the cold floor seemed to be helping me to focus and feel more normal again.

"You need to sit up," a voice said to me from the door of the garage. I was so confused; I actually wondered who was there with me.

"Okay," I answered and slowly pulled myself into a sitting position. I instantly felt dizzy again and leaned against a stack of old newspapers. Reality began to set in, and I saw my mom sitting on the steps leading into the house. I realized that she beat me into near unconsciousness. She showed no emotion, and her eyes seemed to look right through me. How could she not feel sorry for what she had done?

Mom got up from the steps and walked over to me. I wondered if she was going to hit me some more and decided I would grab a piece of a cement block that was near me and hit her with it if she did attack. Instead, she squatted next to me and sneered, "Don't you ever step between me and anyone in this house again. Got it?"

I nodded wearily, and she got up and walked out of the garage. I could hear Novi still screaming before she closed the door.

Alone in the garage and faced with what happened, I broke down. I cried and cried. I held my head and cried because of the intense pain. I cried because of the crazy woman who ruled our house and our lives – my mom. I cried because I still felt useless. Despite her petite size, my mom worked out daily and was incredibly strong.

I was no match for her. I couldn't stop her.

Images of Dawn's and Novi's faces flashed before my eyes.

That anger I felt earlier began to grow again. I knew I was the only one in the house who could end my mom's tyranny. I began to feel determined and strong. As I got to my feet and held my throbbing head, I thought of the things I had working for me.

I knew what my mom and Tom had really done to Alex. I knew my mom's selfish nature well enough to know how to stay on her good side and make her feel comfortable around me. By the time I reached the downstairs bathroom, I was a different person.

I rinsed my face of tears and snot and looked at myself in the mirror. Mom hit me on the sides of my head, so my face was unblemished by the abuse. I smiled at myself as I thought, "I will find a way to stop her. I will not be useless anymore."

Then, an overwhelming nausea swept over me, and I rushed to the toilet just in time to throw up. I felt better afterward and went to the kitchen to find some ibuprofen for my aching head.

"Um, goodnight," a small voice said as I passed the bed in the dining area. I squinted through the dark and saw Dawn lying in the bed. She must have come to bed while I was in the bathroom. She had been up in the sewing room reading a book when all hell broke loose earlier. I wondered if she had any idea what transpired while she was upstairs. It didn't matter. I knew, and I would be talking to her about it later. I would be talking to her about a lot of things later.

I smiled and said, "Goodnight, Dawn." Then, as an afterthought, I added, "Hey, maybe this weekend, I'll come down and sleep in the living room. You know, so you're not down here by yourself."

"That would be great! But ... will your mom let you do that?" Dawn seemed excited, but worried about being the center of any conflict with my mom.

"Don't worry about it. I'll figure something out." I smiled at her again and went to retrieve my ibuprofen. I took the maximum amount, then quietly went upstairs to bed.

All sides of my head hurt, and it was impossible for me to find a comfortable position to sleep. Although it was hard to fall asleep, I felt light and liberated. I was still scared. In some ways, I was more scared than I had ever been. I was working on a plan to take down my mom, and she had shown me that she wasn't afraid to take me out. But somehow, I felt free knowing that I had "right" on my side. I didn't know how to explain it, even to myself. It was like something was telling me I was not alone.

This same feeling was telling me that my mom would have to answer for her evil deeds. Was it God? I didn't know. I hadn't entertained the idea that God cared about me for a long time. Yet, as the medicine started to work and I drifted off to sleep, I prayed for the first time since before Alex died.

"Dear, God," I thought, "please be with me. I'm scared. Amen."

OUT-BLUFF THE MASTER

That weekend, I asked my mom if I could sleep downstairs. I had thought carefully about how to approach her and had come up with an idea. "Grandma's dumb dog has asthma or something and keeps me up all night with its awful wheezing sound," I told her.

Mom laughed at the jab I had taken at Grandma's precious little dog. "It is a pretty stupid little thing, isn't it?" She laughed some more.

"Yeah," I continued. "And it barks at every police car or ambulance for miles around!" I laughed with her.

Mom laughed hysterically. "Oh, no." She pushed the words out in between laughs. My plan worked, and Mom let me sleep downstairs. She only had one warning for me: "Don't mess around with Dawn. She needs to sleep." The laughter switched off like a light. It reminded me of the switching off she had done from hitting me a few days earlier to laughing it up with me now. That was okay, I could play her game.

"Oh, I don't care about Dawn. As long as she doesn't start wheezing, too!" I smiled, knowing my mom would love that joke.

"Oh!" She laughed so hard her eyes watered. She could barely breathe enough to squeeze out, "Maybe she'll start barking, too!" Mom immediately burst into uncontrollable laughter and had to sit. I faked as much laughter as I could, then excused myself to the bathroom.

Step one was in motion. This first step required me to become close enough to Dawn to see if I could include her on the rest of the steps, which I hadn't quite worked out, yet, and possibly tell her the truth about Alex. She deserved to know, and I owed it to her to tell her.

That night, I made a bed on the couch and said goodnight to everyone upstairs. Grandma gave me a little guilt trip for leaving her all alone in her room again. I came down and saw Dawn was already in bed. I said goodnight to her and lay on the couch. I lay there for a while, wondering if I should say anything to Dawn. The house was very quiet, and I didn't want to take a chance that Mom would hear me talking to Dawn. I figured it was enough for Dawn to know that I had kept my promise to come down and sleep with her.

Baby steps to the goal. I felt calm and was able to fall asleep quickly.

I awoke to Dawn standing over me. "Becca? Are you awake?" Although she was whispering, I was startled to find her so close to me.

I sat up quickly. "What's wrong?" I asked.

Dawn shook her head. "Nothing," she answered. Then, she looked down at her feet and said shyly, "I wanted to thank you for coming down here last night. I wasn't scared to sleep." Hearing a noise coming from upstairs, Dawn hurried away from me before I could say anything back.

While Tom came downstairs with Novi to eat breakfast, I thought about what Dawn had said. She was scared to sleep at night? Of course, she was. She was in a house she had never lived in before. She was sleeping just feet away from the front door. I was sure that the fact that the door was half glass didn't help. I was uncomfortable walking by the door sometimes, because anyone from the main street in front of us could look in and see me. I definitely wouldn't want to be sleeping there. How awful it must be for her to feel terrified every night as she tried to go to sleep.

Besides feeling sad, I also felt relieved. Dawn had seen my gesture of goodwill and had received it like I had hoped. Baby steps to the goal.

After another week, I had come up with another plan. A bolder plan. I needed to get time alone with Dawn. This was never going to happen in the house.

"Mom?" I found her in the garage lifting weights. That's just what we needed, a pumped-up maniac mom. I guessed Tom was upstairs watching Novi. She looked up briefly from her bicep curls. "Mom, can I ask you something?"

She set her weights down and took a swig of water from her bottle. "What is it?" She was usually pretty focused when she was working out, and I hoped I was approaching her at the right time.

"Mom, I have a small problem." She nodded for me to continue, as she loaded weights onto the chest press machine.

"Well, I need to go to the library to research a president for my history project, but no one can go with me today. Tori is out of town for the weekend, and Sam has a tournament. I know you don't like me walking alone, so is it okay for Dawn to tag along with me? I mean, I wouldn't ask if I had any other option." I rolled my eyes to show my disappointment at having to resort to bringing Dawn with me.

I watched Mom carefully, as she considered what I said. She sat on the chest press bench and said, "Yeah, I guess that's okay. Just make sure she doesn't space out and wander off or something." Mom laughed a little and laid on the bench under the weights.

I laughed with her and headed for the door, before she could change her mind. "Yeah," I added, "I'll have her get a kiddie book and sit at the table while I study."

Mom laughed some more, and I left the garage. I practically ran upstairs to tell Dawn, again afraid that Mom would change her mind and we would lose our chance. I found Dawn in the sewing room reading, like usual. I wasn't sure if Tom would hear me, so I kept my voice low and calm. "Hey, Dawn. I need for you to walk with me to the library."

Dawn's eyes lit up. "Okay." She put her book away and followed me downstairs. I grabbed a notebook and a pencil, although I didn't plan on writing anything at the library. I was just going to check out a few books, as quickly as I could, so Dawn and I could use the rest of the time to talk.

We left the house and began walking quietly to the library. Dawn smiled and looked around while we walked. It was a beautiful day, and I wondered if she had been able to go outside at all. Well, except for at school. School—that was a good place to start.

"So, Dawn ..." she looked at me with a content smile. "Uh, how do you like Madrona Middle?" I thought this would be a good place to start a conversation with her. I liked the school and had hoped she would, too.

"Oh, it's great. I really like my teachers! Well, except for Mr. Blackstone. It's not that I don't like him; it's just that..." She was struggling to explain, but I knew what she meant. I had been in his math class, too.

"It's just that he's so boring?" I offered.

Dawn laughed. "Yes! I mean, does he have to talk like a robot? My friend Sarah says he's an animatronic. Ya know, like at Chuck E. Cheese?" Dawn laughed again, and I laughed with her.

That was a really funny comparison! His monotonous tone and demeanor did make him seem like a robot of some kind.

By the time we reached the front of the library, she had told me all about her new friends and named all her teachers. Since I had been in most of the same classes, we had a lot to talk about. I wanted to continue our conversation, but I knew we needed to be fast in the library to have the time to talk. If we were out for too long, my mom was sure to be suspicious.

I explained to Dawn that I was going to pick out a couple of books quickly, and then we could walk up to the park. I figured we could take the back way that cut through the civic center buildings, so Mom wouldn't see us laughing and talking while we walked.

Dawn seemed ecstatic and agreed to be quiet and out of the way while we were in the library. We hadn't been in the library long before I realized that I had forgotten where some of the books were kept. The three-story building was going to take a while to comb through, and according to their computer, my books were in three different sections. Only one of the sections was familiar to me.

Dawn saw me looking around confused and asked, "Do you need any help?"

I was concerned about her getting lost, but also realized that we were running out of time. "Okay," I showed her one of the cards with information on where a book about Zachery Taylor was. "I don't know where this book is. Do you think you can ask a librarian to show you?" Dawn nodded and smiled. She turned and began to walk away when I stopped her. "If you get lost, just ask another librarian for help. Please don't talk to anyone who doesn't work here, and I'll meet you back at this front entrance. Okay?"

She smiled and giggled. She clearly thought I was babying her but agreed to my terms and walked away. I watched her pass by two librarians without asking them for help. I was beginning to regret letting her help me.

But then she stopped at a large stone tablet in the center of the library and studied it. She seemed satisfied with what she saw and walked toward the elevator. She pressed a button and rode the elevator to her destination. It was only when she was out of sight that I remembered the stone tablet was a map of the library.

Smart girl.
After I used the same map to find my other elusive book, I found Dawn waiting for me exactly where I asked her to. I took her book and checked out what I needed. Once we got outside, I asked her, "So, you know your way around a library, huh?"

She blushed and said, "I saw the map when we first came in. I thought it might help me find your book."

I was impressed that a twelve-year-old would remember something like that, then use the information so wisely. Dawn was definitely more mature and smarter than I had given her credit for. Then again, it was hard to give someone any credit when they were constantly being belittled in front of you.

"That was pretty smart of you," I told her. She blushed again and looked at her feet.

I pointed to the road that we would be taking back. I thought about the maturity she had shown earlier and decided to be honest with her. "I think it would be better if we walked down this street, so Mom doesn't see us talking and laughing and stuff," I explained.

"Oh, yeah. I get it," she answered. This was good. Dawn understood some things about my mom that most people didn't. We needed to be careful around her. I was beginning to feel that Dawn was up for the task ahead.

We made small talk some more, then found ourselves in front of the police station. Seeing the police vehicles and knowing that this was a building full of people who upheld the law, instantly made me feel guilty. I knew something that I should share with them. But, I couldn't yet. I looked at Dawn as she went on about her pet cats back in Virginia. I wanted to share what I knew with Dawn. But I knew it was too early. I had to feel out our relationship a little more. I needed to be patient.

We continued our walk around the park and back to the house. As we approached the last block, I felt the need to explain some things to Dawn about our "library trip."

"Dawn, I told my mom that I needed you to walk with me to the library, because I couldn't find anyone else. We can't look like we were having a good time or..." I was about to continue when she interrupted.

"I know. It's okay." She smiled at me. "Can we do this again?" She seemed to understand the façade that was needed for my mom. I was thankful she did.

"Yeah. I'll try to think of another time for us to go out. It might be a little while, though. I don't want Mom to get suspicious," I said.

Dawn smiled, slyly. "Yeah, cause we don't want her to know that we are friends or anything." She giggled.

By the time we entered the house, we were totally calmed down. Dawn went straight upstairs and back to her book. I went straight to the dining table and opened my books from the library.

Mom was in the kitchen preparing dinner. She looked over at me after a while and asked, "So, was it so bad?"

I shrugged as nonchalantly as I could and answered, "I guess not. Dawn was quiet enough with her books." I tried to think of something mean and witty to say. I had it. "She would totally get lost in that building if I hadn't been there, though. I mean, how hard is it to go to the kid's section and come right back?"

Mom laughed. "Yeah, she gets that brainless gene from Tom." Then she went back to cooking dinner. Mission accomplished.

A week later, Dawn and I were able to go to the library again. I wasn't feeling bold enough to ask for her to accompany me anywhere else, and I figured Mom wouldn't say no if it was school related. She agreed (after we made a few mean jokes about Dawn together), and my sister and I were off on our second outing together.

We followed the same schedule as before; Dawn helped me find a few books to check out, we checked out as quickly as we could, then we walked the back way home so we could talk. Our conversation didn't consist of anything mind blowing, but it was feeling more natural and not forced. Dawn and I were really becoming friends and real sisters. I felt hopeful that it wouldn't be long until I could confide in her about Alex and our parents.

But, as we came back to the house and resumed a "whatever" attitude toward each other, I knew we weren't ready yet. I was not even sure what we would do after I told her. Mom would be too much for even the both of us to take on in court, or in any situation. I refused to give up hope and continued to pray that if there was a God, He would take pity on Dawn and me and reach down to help us.

That next week, an unexpected event occurred.
When I got home from Sam's house, my mom was waiting for me. Panic gripped me, as I wondered if she knew my plans to take her and Tom down for what they had done to Alex. But once reality set in, I knew that couldn't be what she wanted to talk to me about. After all, I hadn't talked to anyone about my plans—I didn't even know what my plans were. Plus, her face seemed more concerned than angry. The more I watched her picking her words carefully in her head, the more I realized how phony my mom seemed when she acted concerned for anyone other than herself. Her emotion seemed forced.

"Look, Nyssa ... Your dad called here a few minutes ago." Mom reached out to grab my hand. It seemed so rehearsed. "He's checked himself into a drug treatment program, and he's staying at some hospital or something." Mom waited for a moment while I digested what she had said.

Dad called? He had a drug problem?

Mom continued, "He wanted to talk to you, and I told him he could call back in a couple of hours."

My head was spinning. When had my dad taken drugs? I asked my mom if she knew that Dad had a drug problem, and she shrugged and said, "I know he took some drugs a long time ago, but it seemed like everyone was doing it back in the 70s. But I didn't know he was still doing them."

"He's going to call back?" I asked. I hadn't talked to my dad for almost two years. My last memory of us interacting was that dreadful car ride home after the trial. I had been so mad at him for accusing my mom and Tom of doing something to Alex. How ridiculous that seemed now. He saw through their lies and told me something I had not wanted to hear, even though it was true. I was nervous to talk to him. What would we talk about?

Mom placed her hand on my shoulder. "Just be careful when you talk to him. He has a way of making someone feel sorry for him and let down their defenses. Don't forget how many times he picked Jay over you and how long it's been since he last talked to you." She was prepping me for my phone conversation with my dad. I thought how odd it was that I never noticed her doing this before.

When I was younger, she would do the same thing, but I never thought there was anything wrong with it. Now, in a more mature state of mind, I saw how manipulative it was. Still, I would play along—for now.

"I know, Mom," I answered. "I won't fall for any of his tricks. Besides, I'm just curious about this whole drug thing." She nodded and smiled at me. Then, I waited for my dad's call.

Right before bedtime, the phone rang, and my mom quickly answered it. She said, "Hello," and "She's right here." Then, she hugged me and handed me the phone. She sat on the bed that Dawn was using and made herself comfortable.

Great—she was going to watch me have this conversation. Like I wasn't nervous enough.

"Hello?" I whispered.

"Sweetie?" Dad's familiar tone and pet name for me instantly made me want to cry. But I knew I had to keep my emotions under control at all costs. I had an audience who was watching me like a hawk.

"Yeah, it's me," I answered. I rolled my eyes at my mom, and she smiled.

"Hey..." There was an awkward pause before my dad finally said, "Look, I know your mom probably already told you I am in a hospital for drug abuse treatment. Right?" he asked.

"Mmm-hmm," I answered. I figured the fewer words I used, the harder it would be for my mom to know everything we were talking about.

"Well, I just wanted you to know that as part of my treatment, I need to face some of the things I have done in my life and ask for forgiveness." Dad continued with nervousness in his voice. "I would really like to see you in person to do this. Do you think that would be okay?"

"Uhhh." I looked at my mom and didn't know how to answer. I didn't want her to know I was eager to see my dad, but I didn't want him to think I didn't want to see him. I really wanted to scream, "Yes!" But instead, I mumbled, "I have to talk to my mom about that."

My dad's voice sounded sad. "Oh, I understand. Of course, you should talk to her." My heart ached. I was sure he assumed I was still fully under my mom's control, and after talking to her, would not be interested in seeing him at all. But, with my mom watching me, I could not explain to him that this was not the case.
"Sweetie—whatever you decide, just know that I always love you, and I'm sorry for not calling you all this time."

"Okay."

"Well, goodnight."

"Goodnight."

I hung up the phone and looked at my mom.

"Well?" She obviously wanted to know all the details of our short conversation. I slowly sat on the bed next to her, using that small amount of time to strategize how I would approach this situation with her. I had an idea.

"He said that as part of his treatment, he's supposed to apologize to people or something. Ya know, for the bad stuff he's done. He says he wants to meet with me in person, so he can do that." I shook my head like the whole thing was just weird.

Mom smirked, "If he's got to apologize to everyone he's wronged, he'll never finish his treatment!" We both chuckled. Then, Mom got serious again. "So, did you want to meet with him?"

I knew she would ask that last question. I went over my answer in my head, as I acted like I was confused and shrugging my shoulders. "Well, I don't really want to visit him—especially after all he's done...." I had to choose my next words carefully. "But, I don't want him and Jay blaming me for his not being able to complete the treatment. Can you just see that happening?" I asked my mom.

Mom's eyes got big, "Oh, definitely." She nodded her head, "Yah, you should go. I'll call him and work out a time that Tom and I can take you. We won't be his scapegoat, that's for sure."

So, it was settled. She hugged me and said goodnight. I told her I would be going to bed in a minute, that I needed to take some Tums first. She smiled. "Talking to your dad always makes me sick, too." She smirked and walked upstairs.

I grabbed some Tums, because truthfully my stomach did hurt. I was sure it was because out-bluffing my mom was giving me an ulcer or something. I chewed them quickly and went to get a glass of water to wash them down. Dawn suddenly appeared from the living room and said, "Goodnight."

With the strange events of the last few hours, I had lost track of her. Apparently, when my mom made herself comfortable on Dawn's bed, Dawn sat in the living room and waited for her to leave. I didn't blame her.

I said "Goodnight" back and smiled. I wanted to talk to her about what happened on the phone with my dad but didn't want to chance my mom hearing us talk. I finished my water and made my bed in the living room, about fifteen feet away from where Dawn slept. As I finished laying my blankets out and crawled under them, she whispered, "I'm glad your dad called you. I mean, if you're glad."

I listened carefully for any sounds coming from upstairs that would indicate my mom heard Dawn. After making sure that all was completely quiet, I whispered back, "Yes, I am." Then I smiled at her, and although the lights were out, the moonlight shone through the glass-front door, and I could see she was smiling back.

DAD'S RETURN

On the way to visit my dad in the hospital, my mom was constantly jabbering. She went on and on about all the bad things she felt my dad had done. She went on and on about the "kind of person" who becomes addicted to drugs. Finally, she went on and on about how I needed to stay strong and not be sucked into his sappy pitifulness. I just nodded my head and tried not to scream for her to shut up. I was really only half-listening to her, as I tried to wrap my mind around the idea that my dad and Jay used drugs. Was this why my dad seemed distant at times? Did it affect Jay's personality, as well?

When we got to the hospital, Mom went in with me and Tom stayed in the car. Dad was waiting in an inner lobby area. It was a shock to see him after so long. He had put on a little weight, which for him was a good thing. He looked older, although it had only been a couple of years. I wondered if he had been through a lot in those years.

He hugged me and said, "It's so good to see you, sweetie." I hugged him back but was careful not to seem too happy to see him.

I stepped back to put some distance between us. Dad looked at my mom and said, "Thank you for bringing her. I really appreciate that."

Mom nodded. "Of course. It was the least I could do," she said, with the phoniest sweetness.

Dad began to give us a tour of the facilities. As we walked around the building, I was struck by how different this "hospital" was from any other I had been to. It was like a day camp and hospital hybrid. Dad showed us the cafeteria, the dorm room area, and the basketball court. He was especially happy about the basketball area.

Mom actually laughed when Dad began introducing us to all the people who were playing basketball. When he was done with his introductions, he asked her, with a smile on his face, "What's so funny?"

Mom shook her head and chuckled, "Oh, some things never change." My dad had always loved basketball, but I didn't see the humor in that.

However, Dad laughed a little and said, "You're right."

This exchange somehow put my mom at ease because she suggested Dad and I take a short walk together before we had to leave. Dad seemed as surprised as did I. "Just have her back in the lobby in fifteen minutes. We have to get home to the baby," she explained. Dad eagerly agreed, and I began to walk off with him. Then, just before we rounded the first corner, I shot my mom the best "I'm uncertain" look I could. She gave me a thumbs up, and I was out of her sight.

Dad and I walked through a garden area that he had shown us earlier and took a seat on a bench inside the door to the dorm area. "It should be quiet in here," Dad remarked.

I nodded, not really knowing what to say. Thankfully, he began the conversation.

"Look, I know this must all be a shock to you." I nodded. "Well, I wanted to explain some things. See, Jay and I have had some serious problems with drug abuse, and in my case, also an alcohol addiction, for a while now. We realized we were really going down a detrimental path and it was affecting those around us—people we cared about..."

Then, my dad did something I had only seen him do a couple of times in my whole life. He began to cry. But, just as quickly as it began, it stopped. He took a few deep breaths and wiped his face before he continued.

"I hope I have not destroyed my relationship with you, and that you can forgive me for some of the things I have done and said in the past, and most of all—for not calling you for so long." His eyes welled up again, and his face cringed with pain. "I am so sorry," he whispered. Again, he took deep breaths and wiped his face, desperate to regain control of his emotions.

I began to answer him, but when I opened my mouth to talk, a sob escaped instead. I cried and my dad held me. Comforting me must have helped him calm down, because he composed himself and was telling me, "I am so sorry, for everything."

We sat on that bench for what seemed like a long time. He hugged me and continued to apologize. Finally, a couple of guys came around the corner, and I tensed up and pulled away from my dad. He must have realized someone was coming and turned to look.

The two men looked at my dad with recognition, and one of them said, "Oh, hey Ben. Are you playing ball tonight? I heard not many guys are gonna show up..."
Then, the second guy nudged the first one and looked at me.

The first guy spoke again. "Oh, I'm sorry. I didn't know you had a visitor."

"It's okay," my dad said with a smile. "Hey, this is my daughter, Nyssa." He put his hand on my back.

I was a little embarrassed at being caught in such an emotional state by people I did not know. I also felt self-conscious that I probably looked terrible from crying so hard. However, my mom always taught me that a first impression was extremely important, so I took a deep breath and said, "Hi. It's nice to meet you." I looked them both in the eyes and shook their hands firmly.

"Wow, Ben," the first guy spoke once more. "She handles herself better than most grown chicks I know." The second guy hit the first in the arm and gave him a "Did you really just say that?" look. This flustered that first guy.

"Uh … I mean, yaw know. She seems mature and…"

My dad laughed. "It's okay. I know what you mean." He looked at me and said, "She's always been one who could handle herself well." I don't know why, but when he said that, I looked at the ground and wanted to disappear. Sensing the awkward moment, the two guys excused themselves and told me it had been nice to meet me. I smiled and said, "You, too." I really wanted to leave.

My dad sensed that we had accomplished enough for one night and said, "Well, we should probably go meet your mom. It was nice of her to bring you to visit me, and I don't want to keep her waiting." We held hands and walked down the hallways to the main foyer. As we got close, I dropped my hand from my dad's grasp, and he put his hand in the pocket of the light jacket he wore. I thought maybe he understood that it would not be the best idea for my mom to see us being so close. I hoped he didn't think I was ashamed of him, or anything.

Once we met with my mom, the two of them exchanged some pleasantries ("Thank you for bringing her." "Thank you for not taking too long." "You look well…") Then, we left.

On the ride home, Mom asked me what happened. I knew I had to give her details, so I told her that we mostly talked about what the facility was like. I also told her about the two guys that came toward the end. I completely left out the part about me crying and my dad apologizing. She seemed to believe me.'

"The two guys were talking about basketball, huh? Yeah, your dad is never going to change when it comes to that. A lot of things take a back seat when it comes to his beloved sport." She shook her head in disappointment, and I nodded in agreement. The rest of the ride consisted of her retelling some of the many stories she had about the times my dad disappointed or emotionally hurt her in some way. I had heard all these stories before but letting her repeat them gave me time to nod my head and reflect on my visit with my dad.

Things had gone so well. My dad seemed changed, in a positive way. I felt more comfortable around him than I had in years. It had been a great visit—except that awkward moment with his friends. Why had it sucked the confidence out of me to hear my dad compliment me? He had always been the type of parent to compliment his kids, even if he had not spent a lot of time with them. Even my own mom would state that I was mature for my age, so why had I frozen earlier?

Realizing I needed to do more than just nod my head as my mom droned on about my dad, I put this question to the side and interjected with "Really?" and "I can't believe he did that!" to let my mom feel I was completely in tune with how awful my dad was. Once we were home, I ate dinner, making sure not to give Dawn too much attention, and retelling the account of my visit that I told my mom earlier to my grandmother.

Afterward, my mom, grandmother and I all made fun of what a basketball nut my dad was. Dawn tried to join in by laughing, but my mom made her feel stupid by telling her she didn't understand what we were talking about. The three of us then smirked at Dawn.

When it was time for bed, I laid in the living room, trying to get my body to relax and fall asleep. I thought about how I could trick my mom into letting me have an outing with my dad, without making her think that I wanted to see him. I wondered if it would be too soon to set up another outing with Dawn. I didn't want to arouse my mom's suspicion on that front, either.

Oh, crud—I had forgotten about my math test the next day. I would need to wake up extra early to study.

Then, it hit me. I knew why it had bothered me to hear that my dad thought I "could handle" myself well. It was because I didn't want to. I didn't want to be constantly worried about what I was saying and to whom. I didn't want to be organizing a plan to bring my mom and Tom to justice, save myself and my sisters, and reconnect with my dad. I just wanted to go to school and maybe have a part-time job or something. I couldn't help but feel jealous that my friends didn't seem to have problems that even resembled my own. Although I was determined to see my plans through, I was growing resentful at having to plan them at all.

Once again, as I had begun to routinely do, I prayed. I prayed that God would help me not lose hope. I prayed that He would show me the next step. He had put my dad back in my life. Was this a sign to me? What did it mean? I needed to know that there was an end in sight to the madness I lived in. Soon after I prayed, I was finally able to go to sleep.

Toward the end of the week, Mom approached me with some interesting news. "Your dad called yesterday and asked if he could take you out for lunch this weekend." She waited and seemed to be searching my face for some signs of how that made me feel. I stayed stone-cold and shrugged my shoulders.

She nodded, "Yeah, I thought that's how you would feel. But I think you should go out with him. I don't want him to have any excuse for not paying child support." I shrugged my shoulders and continued doing my homework, like it didn't really matter to me. She seemed satisfied by my reaction and said, "Okay, I'll call him back and tell him he can have you for lunch this Sunday." She went upstairs, and I was finally able to smile. There it was—my chance to be alone with my dad and see if he could be the one to help me end this horrible façade.

Once Mom came back and told me that the plans were definitely set, I felt bolder and asked if I could take Dawn to the library once more. I showed my mom a project that I needed to work on (even though it wasn't due for another three weeks) and explained it would take longer this time, because I needed to look up newspaper articles. Dawn would merely need to sit and read books, while I got my information together. Mom seemed unsure, but then agreed, "Only on the condition that you get all your library work done in one day. You don't need to be making multiple trips out with her."

"Okay," I sighed. "But, if it's only one trip, it could take a long time."

"That's fine," she smiled. "As long as you get all your research done in one day."

"Thanks, Mom." I hugged her and gathered my things. I also asked my grandmother for some money, in case we needed to get lunch from the vending machines at the library. She gave me five dollars, and Dawn and I were on our way. I could not believe how well that all worked out!

It was Saturday, the day before I would meet my dad. My mom obviously didn't realize I could use the library at school to do most of the research for my paper, so I wouldn't need much from our city library. Plus, she had given us all day! This was it. I knew this was the day I would talk to Dawn about everything.

I explained to Dawn that we were going to make a quick stop at the library, then we would be going to the mall.

"The mall?!" Dawn squealed.

"Yes," I motioned for her to calm down. "But my mom thinks we are just going to the library all day. Okay?" Dawn nodded and smiled.

Once inside the library, Dawn helped me to locate a few articles I needed for my paper. We made copies of them, so I could use them later. We also checked out two books, even though I really didn't need them. Then, we were free to walk up to the mall. The mall was only a few blocks away, but this gave us about fifteen minutes to talk. I recognized that I would need to find a way of easing Dawn into all I was about to tell her. So, I began slowly.

"I'm sorry about the way my mom talks to you sometimes. I know that sucks when she does that." I was hoping this would give us some open dialogue about my mom.

"It doesn't matter." Dawn suddenly went from smiling and looking around, to quietly staring at the ground. "I know she's never really liked me, anyways." She pushed her glasses up, as they began to slide down her nose.

I tried to fully process what she said and find another opening to where I wanted this conversation to go. "Well, I don't think it's that she doesn't like you. It's more like she just always needs someone to take out her anger on. Ya know?"

Dawn looked up and seem to ponder that idea. "Yeah, I guess so."

I wanted to keep the conversation going. "It's like how she used to treat Alex. Remember?" I took a deep breath and waited for her reply. Dawn and I had not talked about Alex since she had "disappeared" several years earlier. Did I drop Alex's name on her too suddenly? Would she clam up now?

My apprehension was gone when she quickly nodded in agreement. "Yeah, I remember that. Anna was mad all the time at Alex." She lifted her face and started to walk differently. Were those memories making her a little angry?

We reached the mall entrance, and I suggested we go the Orange Julius on the second floor for something to drink. Both of us were very thirsty after walking and sitting down with our drinks would give us more time to talk. Dawn squealed again at the idea of getting a frothy, cold juice drink. The money Grandma gave me just covered two small drinks, and we sat at a table in the eating area. I liked this small food court, because it was never busy.

It was at the far end of the mall that never got much traffic. We were the only two people sitting in the eating area. I thought we were in the perfect place for me to tell her what I had been trying to build up to. Dawn was smiling and enjoying her drink across from me. I waited until she was halfway through with her drink. Watching her enjoy her simple outing with me made it even harder to confess to her.

"Dawn, I need to tell you something very important." I paused, and she turned her full attention to me. "You remember how my mom and your dad treated Alex, right?" Dawn nodded and clenched her jaw. "Well, you also remember that we told the police Alex had been kidnapped?" Dawn nodded and squinted her eyes in confusion.

"Well..." I wanted so desperately to find the right way to break it to her. Instead, I blurted it out. "Alex didn't just disappear. Something happened to her, and my mom and Tom got rid of her."

I sat back in my seat, feeling an incredible sense of relief I had not experienced in years. I really felt like an enormous weight had been lifted and carefully watched Dawn's face. I worried I had just burdened her with that same weight. She seemed to be absorbing the information I had given her. Her eyes welled up, and one tear fell. She wiped the tear away and took a deep breath.

Then, she did something I never expected her to do. "That makes sense," she quietly said.

She still seemed sad, but more composed than I thought she would be. "I guess I always thought that they did something. I just didn't want to admit that they could do that to her," she explained. She looked off and began drinking her juice again.

At a loss for words, I too began drinking my drink. We sat there quietly drinking. When we were done, we sat there playing with our empty containers nervously. The few awkward moments that passed seemed like a long time.

Dawn's eyes widened as she seemed to have a sudden thought. She looked me straight in the eyes and asked, "What are we going to do?"

This is what I had hoped to talk to her about. I really only had one idea. I quietly answered, "I think we should tell Grandma. She knows how crazy Mom can be firsthand, and I know she'll believe me. She'll know what to do." This seemed like the easiest course of action.

Dawn seemed unconvinced. "Are you sure? I mean, I know Grandma and Anna don't always get along, but that is still her daughter. It just seems like she might not help us too much."

"Well," I began, "I guess I have another idea. I just don't know if it will work right now." I looked around the food court like a paranoid thief. I was nervous to even say my idea aloud. "I think we might be able to trust my dad. We could tell him."

Dawn's eyes narrowed. "You mean your dad that is in the hospital for doing drugs?" She had heard my mom describe him as such since he re-entered my life. I could understand her confusion.

"Well, he got treated, and he's not doing drugs anymore." I watched her relax her face as I explained, "He also knows how my mom is, and I think he always thought that Mom and your dad had done something to her."

Dawn seemed surprised. "So, he kind of already knows?"

I had not thought of it that way, but I guessed she was right. I shrugged, "Yeah, I guess so."

Dawn smiled at me. "Okay."

I smiled back. "Okay."

We threw our trash away and began the trip back home.

Dawn guessed bits and pieces of what happened to Alex, based on her memory of the days before she died. I did not give her the awful details of Alex's last night alive, and she didn't ask. We talked about my growing relationship with my dad and when we thought would be a good time to talk to Grandma. We decided that I would approach her alone, and I would wait until Mom and Tom had both left the house. By the time we reached the house, it felt like a new chapter of our lives was starting.

The next weekend, I got my chance to talk to my grandmother alone. Mom and Tom left to look at computer stuff (they were very into new technology and computers). I didn't expect them home for at least a few hours. I told Dawn it was time, and she nodded and went upstairs to give Grandma and me some privacy.

I approached my grandmother in the kitchen. She was getting out ingredients to start some Menudo. I instinctively made a yucky face when I saw the familiar ingredients for the Mexican soup my grandmother made several times throughout the year. I thought that cooking Menudo always made the house smell like vomit. I quickly composed myself before Grandma turned around and saw me.

"Oh. Hi, mija," she said sweetly. She hummed as she put things into the pot that waited on the stovetop.

"Hi, Grandma." I leaned on the counter and watched her prepare her soup. Once it began cooking, I knew I would have about an hour before the barf smell permeated the entire house.

Grandma continued to hum as she filled the pot, set the fire under it, and began to clean up. Once she was done, she suddenly looked up at me. It was like she hadn't realized I had been standing there for so long. "Is something wrong, muneca?" She always seemed to have more Spanish nicknames for me when she was cooking Mexican food.

"Well, I kind of wanted to talk to you about something..." I hadn't planned out word for word how I would expose my mom and Tom to my grandmother. How do you plan out something like that?

"Ooohhh," Grandma breathed. "Is it something juicy?"

Oh, it was "juicy," alright. But not in the way Grandma was thinking. "Well, I'm not sure if you would say that. But ... well, could we sit in the living room and talk?"

Grandma eyebrows furrowed with concern and she nodded.

We walked into the living room and sat down. I sat on the love seat, while she sat across from me in the oversized lounge chair that my grandpa sat in, on the rare occasion that he joined us at all and was not cooped up in his bedroom.

"What's the matter, bonita?" Grandma asked.

I decided it was probably better not to overthink how I would have this talk with her. I mean, the facts were the facts, and I was so sure that Grandma would be able to help us.

"Well, I guess I should just tell you." I took a deep breath. "You know how this whole time everyone thinks that Alex is missing or kidnapped?" I waited for her to nod. "Well, she isn't. I mean, Mom and Tom did something to her and got rid of her body." I finished and waited for her shocked reaction.

Would she ask for the awful details? Would she cry? Maybe, like Dawn, she kind of already knew that something wasn't right about the whole situation. However, her reaction was unlike anything I had planned for.

"Oh, Nyssa…" She looked around the room, checking to see who would hear her next words to me. "We cannot tell anyone this. You know that blood is thicker than water, and we have to stick together, no matter what." She sighed and looked around the room again, although it was obvious the two of us were the only ones there. "Does anyone else know?"

Because I was still trying to process the first few sentences that she spewed at me, I didn't answer her question. I was dumbfounded. Quickly, I realized she was waiting for me to answer her. I knew then that she would not be someone who could or would help us. Trying my hardest to mask my immense disappointment, I lied to her and shook my head. I did not want her to know that Dawn knew what was now "our" terrible family secret.

Grandma nodded with approval. "Good. Nobody else should know about this. Okay?" She was looking at me carefully. I knew it was important that I put the same game face on with her as I did with my mom.
"Oh, of course," I answered. "I just thought you should know. You know, because you're Grandma and everything." I smiled through my disgust with her.

She smiled back. "Thank you, muneca. I hope you always come to me with whatever you have on your mind or in your heart." She hugged me and kissed my cheek. I resisted the urge to pull away from her.

As she went back to cooking her soup and preparing another dish to accompany it, I quietly went upstairs. I was taking a big chance talking to Dawn in the house, but I had to let her know what happened. As soon as I walked into my grandma's room and saw Dawn innocently reading her book on the bed, I knew I had to keep her hope alive. I put on a little smile as she looked up at me.

Quickly, I whispered, "Grandma can't help us, but I will talk to my dad tomorrow when he picks me up. It's going to work out." She seemed confused but smiled at my cheerful demeanor and gave me a thumbs up.

I continued to loop around the connecting sewing room that went from my Grandmother's master bedroom to the second bedroom that my Mom, Tom, and Novi slept in. I was allowed to watch television in there when they were gone, so I turned the volume up loud enough for my Grandma to hear where I was and changed the channel to something I would normally watch.

But I wasn't planning on watching anything. Instead, I lay on the bed and relived the moments of my conversation with Grandma.

How had I misjudged her so badly? Was she just like my mom said she was? And in that case, was she just like my mom?

A distant memory revived itself in the back of my mind. When I was about eight years old and my parents were just starting their nasty child custody battle over me, my dad said to me that my mom was turning into her mom. He said my mom had always hated how manipulative her own mother was and always swore she would never be like her. Yet, over time, she became the person she despised. The scariest part of the whole memory was the realization that I too, could become a monster like them. Would I even realize I was turning into a vile, controlling witch of a woman who lacked true compassion and love?

Just as I was feeling sick to my stomach, I heard the beads on the downstairs door rattle against its windowpane and knew that my mom and Tom were back. I pretended to be asleep, hoping they would not bother me. But, when they came upstairs, my mom nudged me until I opened my eyes and began telling me all about the marvels of future technology that were somehow available today. I smiled and nodded, as she talked and talked. I kept telling myself that I just needed to get through one more day. As I listened to her drone on and on, I studied her face. Phony smile, eyes without emotion, and the capacity to be completely cruel.

That night, I prayed that God would never allow me to turn down the same path that my mom and grandma had turned down in their lives. I prayed that I would know the words to speak to my dad the next day, and that he would know the right steps to take to help us. I was feeling more and more every day that God was the only one with the power to make these things happen, and He was the only one who wouldn't let me down.

FINDING ALLIES

The next day, my dad picked me up as usual. For the last few weeks, my dad had been picking me up once a week for his basketball games. He played in what he called an "old man league." We usually got something to eat and then went to his game.

Afterward, we would talk for a while in the parking lot of the gym, before heading back to my grandma's house. Mom was happy because she figured we weren't getting a lot of quality time if I was just watching him play basketball. My dad and I were happy, because we were able to fit in time to talk right under my mom's nose. This evening, there was no basketball game. I had neglected to tell my mom this bit of information, as did my dad. This was going to give us a lot of time to talk.

As my dad pulled away from the house, he asked me, "So, what do you want to do?" Before I could answer, he said quickly, "I'm guessing Carl's Jr. for dinner."

I smiled and nodded strongly. Dad knew that Carl's Jr. was my favorite place to eat. While we drove to the location that we liked best, I glanced over at my dad. He always seemed so happy during our visits. He laughed a lot, and this made me laugh a lot, too. I felt sad that this visit would be different. Dad had no idea that I was about to confess something so serious to him, as was evident by him singing along to the corny song playing on the radio and smiling at me.

I waited until we finished eating and were in our after-dinner- talking-time. This was the time we usually talked about new things going on during the week and sometimes about problems we were having. I think my dad found that when he opened up to me about issues at work or with my sisters or brothers, it was easier for me to tell him the issues I was having at school or with my mom and Tom. I was at a point where I was telling him about fifty percent of what was happening at home, which was more than I told anyone else.

After making small talk for about thirty minutes, my dad asked, "So, are you going to tell me what's on your mind, or should we wait til later?" He smirked with one side of his mouth. I realized he had picked up on my behavior and knew something was "off" that evening. He left me a perfect opportunity, and I needed to take it.

I sighed, "Okay, I do need to tell you something." I looked around the restaurant and saw there was nobody near us. Then, I told him in the same manner that I had told Grandma. I just blurted it out. No details, just a few hard facts.

"Wow." Dad used his hands to wipe his face in a massaging motion and took a long drink of his Coke. He seemed to be choosing his words carefully. "I was not expecting to hear that information from you tonight." He smiled nervously. "I thought this was just going to be a typical visit. But I guess not." He laughed, also nervously. Seeming at a loss for words, he blurted out, "Maybe we should go back to the house and talk to Jay about this."

I wasn't sure what Dad's plan of action was, or if he even had one. But I could see he was shaken up about what I told him and that gave me hope. That was the reaction a normal person would have. Not the way my grandmother reacted.

About fifteen minutes later, we were sitting in my dad and Jay's living room. My relationship with Jay had also begun healing since she had gone through her rehab program. She and my dad had come to one of my choir programs, which Mom never came to, and she talked to me when she came to one of my dad's games to drop something off to him. All our interactions had gone really well.

Now, after giving me a hug, my dad told her to sit down. The three of us sat, and my dad told Jay what I revealed to him at Carl's Jr. Jay began to cry. She reached out and hugged me as she sobbed.

"I'm so sorry that happened," she choked out as she cried.

Suddenly, a great wave of emotion overtook me, and I began to cry, too. We cried for the injustice that had been done, for the ugly secret that had been kept, and most of all, for Alex. For once, someone else was crying for what really happened to her. I was overwhelmed. We cried for what seemed like a long time. Realizing that we didn't have all night, I pulled away from Jay slowly and looked at my dad.

Dad sighed heavily. "What do we do?" he asked for me.

Jay suddenly remembered something. "Do we still have that card for that FBI Agent? What was his name?"

Dad put one finger up to tell us to wait a minute. I heard him rummaging through something in the kitchen, then he moved to the dining area. Finally, there was silence and he returned with a single small piece of paper. He smiled and said, "I found it."

The three of us talked about calling this FBI Agent. His name was Agent Lewzader, and I remembered him instantly. He had been involved in the case in the very beginning, when the FBI investigated. He had traveled to California to testify in the kidnapping case against my parents. Watching him testify, I could see how deeply he believed that my mom and Tom had done something to Alex. If anyone would help us, it had to be him.

Dad went into the kitchen to use the phone. I could hear him leaving what sounded like a message on an answering machine. He came back into the living room and shrugged. "I guess we'll see what he says when he calls back."

There was an awkward silence, as we all wondered what to do next.

Dad looked at me with serious concern in his face, "Hey," he furrowed his eyebrows together. "Do you still like ice cream?" Jay and I laughed, and the tension was finally broken. Jay went to scoop some small bowls of dessert for us, while my dad asked me about school and my friends.

When we finished our treat and decided it was time for me to be getting home, the phone rang. My dad quickly got up and answered it. He began having a conversation with the person on the other end, and when I heard my name—I knew Agent Lewzader called back.

Suddenly, an unexpected nervousness washed over me. I lied to this person. I was a roadblock in helping him find the truth about Alex. I tapped my foot uncontrollably on the floor, as I listened to my dad give a brief summary of what I told him.

"Nyssa?" Dad was calling me from the other room. "Can you come here, please?"

Jay touched me on the shoulder and smiled. "It's okay," she whispered.

I nodded and walked over to my dad. He handed me the phone and I squeaked out, "Hello?"

Agent Lewzader identified himself and asked how I was doing. "Fine," I whispered tensely.

"Well, Nyssa, I'll get straight to it—your dad told me you shared something very important with him. Do you know what I am talking about?"

"Yes," I forced myself to speak more confidently.

"Do you think you can tell me what you told him?"

"Yes." I was feeling less anxious and more determined. I repeated most of what I told my dad and Jay, but with a little less detail.

When I was done, there was silence on the phone. I almost wondered if we had been disconnected and I would have to repeat my horrible story yet again. But then, a sigh, and "Nyssa. You are a very brave young lady for doing this. I want to tell you I am very proud of you, as I'm sure your dad and step-mom are right now." He sighed again and asked, "Can I talk to your dad again?"

I handed the phone over to my dad, who listened for a moment and then answered, "Great. See you then."

He hung up the phone and looked at me. "Uh," he thought for moment about what he was going to say. "Agent Lewzader said he would be flying here ... tomorrow." We looked at each in disbelief. Tomorrow?

Time was getting away from us quickly, and my dad and I headed back to my grandmother's house. We talked about how I could get out of the house to see him again, if the agent wanted to meet in the next few days. We both knew Mom did not like me seeing my dad more than one time every week. Maybe we could tell her I was visiting another relative in my dad's family. We knew we had to be careful and not let my mom know. Then, I remembered another complication.

"I told Grandma yesterday," I muttered.

Dad's eyes grew big. "What did she say?" he asked.

I gave him a summary of what happened, since we were only a few blocks away from my home. He shook his head sadly. "I have a feeling that there is a long history of dysfunctional thinking passed down from generation to generation."

I became quiet as we entered the driveway. Dad sensed my uncomfortable, quiet demeanor and added, "But, you're lucky..." I looked at him, questioning. "You take after my weird side of the family." He grinned and gave me a big hug. I hugged him back, and he promised to contact me as soon as he could.

I felt as happy as I could feel, having to re-enter the Najera Home for the Insane. The only person who made any sense in the house was my grandpa, and he always stayed in his room. Like an instant epiphany, I thought I understood why my grandpa kept to himself. Not only did he not approve of my grandma's condescending put-downs toward him, but he also couldn't stand the dysfunction. I was sure of it. I decided I would spend more time with him, before he was gone and it was too late.

I must have been very deep in my own thoughts, because I didn't see my mom watching me as I entered the house and went straight to the cabinet that held my blankets. Since it was almost bedtime, I was going to lay my blankets on the living room floor before I washed my face and changed. The sound of her voice startled me.

"So, how did it go?" She stepped out from the kitchen, so I could see her.

"Oh," I gasped, quietly. I pulled myself together quickly and answered her as calmly as I could, considering she had appeared out of nowhere and scared me half to death. "It was alright, I guess." I shrugged and finished pulling out my blankets. I walked over to the living room floor and began laying the blankets in the order that I liked to sleep on. Puffy blanket first, then bottom sheet, then a flannel blanket to cover myself. I tried to focus on what I was doing and not on the fact that I could feel my mom's eyes watching me.

She had not said anything else, just stood very still and watched me. This made me incredibly nervous, given what happened at my dad's house. Did she know? No, there was no way she could know. Would Grandma have told her that I talked to her? No, that would cause more problems between the two of them. I was being paranoid. Yet, she still stood staring at me as I finished my bed and started up the stairs to retrieve my pajamas. I had to play this whole awkward scene off, or I would risk seeming guilty of something.

I stopped at the bottom of the stairs and looked over at my mom. "Is everything okay?" I asked with the greatest concern I could fake in my voice.

Mom smiled and motioned for me to come back from the stairs. Her easy smile and the calm way she sat at the kitchen counter, told me she was clearly in a very good mood, and I had nothing to be worried about. She had no idea I confessed all her sins for her—to my dad. I sat across from her at the counter and breathed a quiet sigh of relief. Now, that I was not freaking out about her demeanor, I was able to really look at her. She seemed so incredibly happy about something. She was glowing with excitement. I sat, confused, waiting for her to let me in on her joyous news.

"Well, I wanted to wait for Tom before I talked to you about this, but he is taking forever to put Novi down to sleep, so, I guess I'll start." She was like a little kid who couldn't wait to reveal a great big secret. "Tom may have found a job. Actually, he has found a job. A really, really good job." She beamed like a laser ray, as she finished her news. "The most exciting part is—it's in Australia!" She smiled so large it was creepy.

I smiled back, so she wouldn't be upset by my lack of super- excitement. But inside, I was still trying to digest the information she had given me. Tom had a job—good. Us moving to Australia—not good.

I smiled even bigger to hide my concern. "Wow," I said. I needed to add more than that. "That's incredible news," I finished.

Mom reached out and hugged me. I squeezed her back, although inside I felt sick. I glanced around and realized that Dawn was not around. "Does Dawn know?" I asked her.

Mom pulled away and said, "No, I told her to stay upstairs until I came to get her. We can tell her later. What will she care, anyways? You know what is so cool about all of this?" Mom didn't want to talk about Dawn, so I moved on with her.

"What?" I asked.

Mom sat back in the chair and began, "So many things. I mean, we get to go to Australia! How many people do you know that can say they have even visited there? Now we get to move there!"

She gasped dramatically at her own words. Then, she added, "And it'll be the fresh start that we need!" That last sentence made my stomach lurch violently. I remembered those exact words as they echoed in my head. She had said that very same thing when we had been on our way to Kentucky. Once again, we were being isolated, and Mom would have all the control. This couldn't happen.

Just then, Tom came down the stairs. The two of them laughed and smiled while they relayed the information that they had about the area we would move to in Australia. I think they talked about Tom's job, as well, but I was not really there. My body nodded and smiled while my brain struggled to come up with a plan to stop this from happening. I had to get in touch with my dad.

Eventually, we all went to bed. Dawn came down and was allowed to go to bed, not knowing the important newly shared information. She didn't yet know the outcome of my conversation with my dad, either. How could she just lie in her bed, several yards away, and calmly go to sleep? It was because she had to. She didn't have a choice. I remembered her telling me that some nights she lay in bed for a long time, unable to sleep because of how close she was to the front door. As I said my extra-long nightly prayers (extra for all that happened that day), I added in a prayer that Dawn would not be restless that night but that she would sleep. I figured it was all I could do for her.

The next day, I tried to go about my day as normally as I could. All through school, I could only think about the day before and wonder what I should do. As I was walking home, I saw Sam. We hardly got to walk home together anymore, since our school schedules were so different. Some days she stayed later, and some days I stayed. The moment I saw her running across the street to join me on our walk home, I felt the relief of a plan.

"Hey! Long time, no see! You walk here often?" Sam grinned at her own joke, and I laughed. She had no idea how much I needed her help that day.

We walked and talked about school stuff. We caught up on things that had happened in the few weeks we had not spent time together. She was shocked, but happy that I was visiting with my dad again. "I'm so glad he got help. I hope things work out." She touched my back and smiled. She was such a good friend, I almost started crying. I knew that would alarm her, so I took a deep breath and began to work on my plan.

"Hey, is it okay if I call my dad from your house?" I needed a good reason, so I lied to Sam. "I was supposed to call him from the school, but I forgot. Now he might be worried that something happened to me, if he doesn't hear from me soon."

Sam nodded quickly. "Sure." She was quiet for a moment, then she asked, "But, since you only live a few blocks away, why do you want to use my phone? I mean, by the time we get through my security gate and make our way to the back of my complex to my apartment, then walk up the three sets of stairs, you could already be home." She made a very good point that I had not thought of.

"Well," I struggled to come up with something. I looked at her and saw that she no longer believed me. I couldn't lie to her anymore. As we approached her complex, I knew I didn't have time to explain everything to her that very moment, either.

"Look, I'm sorry Sam. I promise that I'll tell you everything, on another day. Right now, I need to call my dad and get home as fast as I can." I struggled to keep my composure. If I couldn't use her phone, I didn't know how I was going to contact my dad. Maybe I should have taken some change from my grandma's purse and used the pay phone at school. Why didn't I think of that sooner?

Sam watched me squirm in extreme emotional turmoil, then touched my back again. "Of course, you can use my phone. You can tell me later what's going on. K?" She opened the security door to her complex, and we both went in.

When we entered her apartment, she pointed to the phone, and I lunged for it. I began to dial my dad's number and turned to see where Sam was. She pointed to the kitchen, and I knew she was signaling to me that she would be starting an afterschool snack while I talked in the living room. I was grateful she was giving me some space.

The phone rang several times, then my dad answered. I blurted out everything that I remembered about my mom and Tom telling me about moving to Australia. He mumbled, "Crap," before taking a deep breath. He waited for a moment, as if assessing this new information and the things he needed to tell me. "Well, Agent Lewzader and another detective from the Radcliff police department are in Los Angeles. I think they are meeting with some FBI at the office out here. But then, they want to meet with you right away."

A wave of relief washed over me, and I began to cry. He told me he would find a way to contact me, and we hung up. I sat on the sofa and cried, until I thought how puffy my eyes were going to look and began to make myself calm down. I couldn't let my mom see anything was out of the ordinary. I also needed to leave very soon.

"So, you want some popcorn or something?" Sam asked quietly. I hugged her and apologized for having to leave so suddenly.

"It's okay," she hugged me back, "but you owe me some quality girl time, when we can unload—or maybe just you can unload." She smiled at her little joke, and I laughed. I was so grateful for her friendship.

I let myself out of her complex and hurried home. I was still within a normal time frame for coming home at this time of the year.

There were choir performances or other after school activities, so my mom would expect me home no later than 4:30 p.m. I walked in the house at 4:15 p.m. I walked into a very quiet house, which was not normal for that time of day. I followed the sounds of voices up the stairs, to my mom and Tom's room. I heard my mom's laughter, and Tom and Dawn's voices. I found that combination odd, but I really didn't want to be involved in whatever they were doing. I had my own things to think about. Just as I had turned to walk back down the stairs, the door to their room opened.

"Oh, good. Nyssa's home. She can help us." Mom smiled at me. "I thought I heard the front door open. Come in and help us out." She motioned for me to come inside the room. I took a step inside and regretted even coming home at all. Tom and Dawn were sitting on opposite sides of a small table placed at the foot of the bed. On the table sat a Ouija board. I didn't want any part of anything having to do with ghosts, but I knew I couldn't refuse.

To my mom, Tom, and Grandma, speaking to the dead was perfectly normal. Several times a year, they would hold "psychic prayer groups" that would meet at the house. They would "astro-travel," attempt to see into the future, and use Ouija boards to talk to dead people. I always played along, although the whole thing gave me the creeps.

"Here, come and sit in Dawn's spot." My mom waved Dawn away and pointed for me to sit down. Dawn quietly got up, looking dejected and sad. Mom said, "I think Dawn lacks the ability to do this. But I know you can." She smiled at me. The few times I used the board with my grandma or her at their weird parties, we received favorable replies. Apparently, to my mom, this meant I had a special talent for it. Creepy. But I smiled back and sat down. Now, more than ever I needed my mom to trust that I was on her side.

After I sat down, I noticed Novi playing on the bed behind my mom. She was making a stuffed bear fly over her head and land on a pillow. She did this over and over again, and the innocence of her play made me wonder, on a scale of one to ten, how dysfunctional was it that she played only a few feet from where we were attempting to contact dead people? This whole situation seemed very wrong.

Putting on my poker face, I smiled and grabbed one edge of the triangular-shaped piece that floated over letters to convey messages from the great beyond. Immediately, the piece began to move. Because Tom was touching the other end of the piece, I wondered if he was moving it. My mom seemed excited and grabbed a notepad she had nearby with a pen.

She asked, "Who is this we are talking to?" Apparently, ghosts do not speak proper English.

The letters spelled out, A-U-N-T-H-E-L-E-N. The name of a family friend we had all called "Aunt Helen." She was not really an aunt to any of us, but she was especially close to my grandmother, and so was given the name. Right before she passed away, she led the "spirit parties" at my grandmother's. She seemed to have a new way of communicating with the dead every time she came to a gathering, and this made her a big hit at these séances.

Then, Mom asked, "Can you tell us why you are here?" The board spelled, "F-O-R" and then lurched toward me.

The force was so strong, I began to feel even more assured that Tom was actually moving the piece around.

Mom asked, "You have a message for Nyssa?"

The board pointed to YES.

Mom grinned and squeezed her arms together in excited anticipation. "What do you want to say to Nyssa, Aunt Helen?" she asked.

The spelling piece quickly raced across the board and stopped only for a second on what seemed like random letters. Mom scribbled the letters down as they showed themselves, and I peeked over at her notepad to see the secret message from beyond— which I was sure was actually from the child-like man sitting across from me. It was hard to make out the separate words, and I decided to wait and see what my mom read to us in the end. Then, the piece stopped moving.

Mom put slashes between certain letters to make words out of the collection that had been shown to us. Then, she read, "Good job getting rid of..." she paused to make sure she was reading it right, then finished with a confused look on her face. "...bad people?" She looked over the list of letters again, and I began to feel light-headed.

How on earth could Tom have produced something like that? Was this a trick? Did my mom already know that I told my dad everything? But, as I watched her struggle to make sense of the message, I realized she really didn't know. She read it again, "Yes, that's what it says. 'Good job getting rid of bad people.'"

She looked up at me and I quickly blurted out, "Oh, yeah. There's this girl at school that's been bullying everyone, and I told the Vice Principal, so she is probably going to be in trouble now." I came up with the story before I had time to really think about what I was saying. But the satisfied look on my mom's face told me she bought it.

"Oh, okay. Well, maybe she can tell us something else." She was referring to my "Aunt Helen" who somehow was using the board to speak. Mom looked at the board and asked loudly, "Can you tell us about Nyssa's future husband?"

"Mom!" I knew my mom and grandmother hoped I would be married shortly after high school, because they didn't want me to end up an "old maid." But this idea was not on my list of things to do in the near future.

Mom smiled as the piece began to move and laughed as she copied down the letters as they were shown. In the end, we ended up with "The Orient." Having been around elderly people like my grandparents, I knew this meant Asia. I had no idea what this answer meant. The confused look on my mom's face meant she didn't have a clue, either.

"What do you mean, Aunt Helen?" Mom asked abnormally loud, as if Helen was sitting in the room with a hearing aid and cupping her ear with her hand—"Huh? What didja say?" I didn't get it.

The piece began to move wildly around the board, not really stopping on any letter in particular. Mom asked again, "What do you mean?" Mom stood up and bent over the board to project her voice better. She was practically yelling at the Ouija. "Is Nyssa going to meet her husband in Asia? Is that what you mean?" The whole scene was obscenely insane.

The board suddenly became still, and Tom and I both looked questioningly at each other. Mom asked us, "What happened?" We both shrugged. I wanted to say, "We musta had a bad connection," but knew my mom would not appreciate my joke.

The three of us sat back and talked about what happened. Mom wanted to dive right into the questions about my future husband. "Isn't that great? I mean, Australia is practically in Asia. So, moving there must be meant to be." Tom smiled and nodded in agreement. He loved hearing about destiny and things that were "meant to be."

After half-heartedly joining in on their conversation, I asked my mom if I could leave to work on some homework. She agreed, and added, "Can you believe Aunt Helen affirmed our move to Australia?" I smiled and gave a thumbs up. As I walked downstairs, I really couldn't believe the comment that came right before the one my mom harped on.

Why would the Ouija spell out that comment about bad people? Had I subconsciously made it do that? Was someone or something really communicating through that wooden board? Was it on my side or trying to sabotage my plan by telling my mom? I decided to try and forget about the whole situation, before I had permanent heebie-jeebies.

I worked on some homework and went to get on the recumbent bike in the garage. After riding the bike for twenty minutes, I had cleared my head and was really hungry for dinner.

When I opened the door, the smell of grilled meat and steamed veggies made my stomach growl. I helped set the table, and we all began eating. I ate quietly, while Tom and my mom discussed options for the Australia move.

Suddenly, Mom looked at me. "Oh, your Aunt Beverly called and asked if she could take you shopping for school clothes tomorrow. I said that it was okay with me, but I didn't know if you already had plans."

I knew instantly where this was going. My dad obviously didn't want to arouse suspicion by making another date for me to visit with him and talk to the FBI agent. My aunt was just a cover and would probably be taking me to see my dad once she picked me up. I saw my mom was waiting for a reply, and calmly said, "No, I guess not. I mean, I was going to meet Rachel at the park, but I could use some more school clothes."

Mom smiled. "Yes. And that would be less we have to buy. We have a lot of expenses to think about for this move." She went back to eating and I struggled not to show my excitement for the rest of the meal.

Dad was keeping the wheels moving and doing the best that he could. I was sure of it.

Dark Secret

THE END IS NEAR

When it was time for my aunt to pick me up, my mom informed me that plans had changed, and my dad would pick me up and take me to the house my grandma and aunt shared. I figured my aunt wasn't able to get the time off to be part of this charade and wondered if this would tip my mom off in some way.

"I just hope this visit is what your dad said it would be – a shopping trip with your aunt and not a sneaky way of getting more time for himself and being deceitful about it." She squinted her eyes suspiciously at me. At least she only thought that my dad wanted to spend more time with me and didn't suspect anything more.

I rolled my eyes. "I'm sure Dad knows better than to try something like that. I mean, what would we do?" I was always trying to keep up the "my dad doesn't interest me in the least" attitude for my mom.

Mom stopped squinting at me and smiled. "Yeah, your dad would probably just take you to a basketball game. He doesn't really do anything else. Right?" She laughed at her condescending comment.

I laughed also and escaped into the bathroom to brush my hair. I stayed in there, brushing my hair and re-applying make-up. I was trying to stay away from my mom. I was increasingly nervous she would suddenly realize I had told my dad about her and Tom. Maybe I would look too nervous or say something awkward, and it would all come together for her. She would instantly realize I betrayed her, and she would need to "take care of me." It seemed like forever before I was relieved of my paranoia, when I heard the doorbell ring.

As I walked to meet my dad at the door, I heard my mom warning him that she had approved this trip for my aunt. Dad reassured her that he was only dropping me off and that he had other things to do that afternoon. She seemed to accept his statement and hugged me goodbye. Finally, I was free. I sighed deeply once we were in the car.

Dad looked at me with concern. "Are you okay? You look sick or something. Do you think your mom thinks that something is up?" He sounded a little paranoid and stressed.

I shook my head. "No, I don't think she knows anything. She just doesn't want us spending any extra time together. And I'm okay. Just really nervous." I squeezed my hands together in my lap and took some long, deep breaths to calm myself down. Dad put his hand around the back of my neck and squeezed.

"Well, Agent Lewzader is here, with a detective from Radcliffe. I don't know if you remember him or not. I think his name is Detective Gruber. They're both at the house with Jay right now."

Dad looked at me when we were stopped at a red light. "You know, they really want to help you any way they can. They will know what to do." His calm tone helped me relax a little.

After a fifteen-minute ride to my dad's townhome, we began walking up the sidewalk to his front door. Instantly, I began to feel unbearably nervous. What if they were mad at me for not telling the truth? What if they said there was no way they could help me?

What if they blamed me for covering for my mom and Tom? I slowed down and slightly bent over to accommodate the cramping feeling growing in my stomach. Dad put his arm around me and guided me to the door. "It's going to be okay," he whispered right before he opened the door and we walked in.

As we entered the house, the two men sitting on the couch stood up to greet us. My step-mom was sitting across from them and walked over to hug me. The men took turns shaking my hand. Agent Lewzader knew he did not have to remind me who he was, so he just said, "It's so nice to see you, Nyssa." Then he turned and said, "I'm not sure if you remember Detective Gruber. He was involved with your sister's case from the beginning but didn't show himself around your home very often."

Detective Gruber smiled and shook my hand. "I really didn't want to badger your family; I only wanted to find Alex." He was incredibly sincere in what he said, and I felt guilty as I remembered the mean things my mom said about both these men. I remember the cruel nicknames she had given them and how she made fun of their inability to close this case. Every day, it seemed, I was gaining a clearer picture of who my mom really was, and how warped a reality she convinced me to believe.

As we sat down, I became incredibly nervous again. How would this meeting start? The last time I saw Agent Lewzader, I was in court and lying to everyone there.

"So," Agent Lewzader started, "I thought we could give you a chance to tell us what you told your dad. If that's okay with you." His calm demeanor helped me start my story. I went through the actual events of the day my sister died, trying not to miss any of the details I could remember. My step- mom cried and had to excuse herself. I began to cry, and my dad held my hand as I finished. I was asked a few follow-up questions, and they looked at each other. It was obvious they wanted to ask or tell me something that was not easy for them. I felt like throwing up.

What could possibly make an FBI Agent and an established police detective nervous?

"Well, Nyssa," Agent Lewzader took a deep breath and explained, "What we have here is basically your word against theirs. I mean, we," he pointed to both himself and Detective Gruber, "feel strongly that you are much more believable to a jury than your parents. However, it would make a stronger case if we could gather more evidence."

Here, he paused again. Looking me directly in the eyes, he asked, "How do you feel about wearing a recording device and talking to your mom about the events of that day?"

I instantly began shaking my head, "No, no. I can't. She'll know. No." I could feel my whole body shaking but was helpless to stop it. I began crying uncontrollably.

Detective Gruber eyes slightly teared up, and he quickly wiped them. "It's okay, Nyssa. We won't make you do anything you don't want to do. It's okay." He seemed upset that something they said made me cry. I struggled to calm myself, feeling bad I couldn't do what they needed me to do.

After a few quiet moments passed, Agent Lewzader asked another question. "What about Tom?" He watched my reaction carefully, again.

I took a deep breath and answered, "Yeah, I think I could that." I noticed I wasn't shaking or crying anymore. I felt better and realized I really could do that. "Yes, that would be much easier."

Agent Lewzader smiled. "I am so glad to hear that. That would really be a lot of help." He spent the next ten minutes walking me through what would happen when I wore the wire. He suggested a few ways I could bring up the events of that day, but I didn't feel completely comfortable with any of them. He asked for any suggestions I had, and I shared one that was based off a problem that I had soon after Alex was gone.

"I could tell Tom I have been having bad dreams about the police finding evidence against them and taking them away." I knew this would make Tom feel bad and want to open up to me.
Agent Lewzader saw where I was going. "And then you could ask him for reassurance as to where they disposed of her. Because you want to make sure that we won't find her."

"Yes," I answered. I couldn't believe this was actually going to happen. I felt numb.

Detective Gruber had been quiet most of the time, but as we were wrapping up our meeting and my dad was preparing to take me back home, he said, "Nyssa, I want you to know that we think you are incredibly brave to come forward now. We know this must be very hard for you. And it must have been very hard this whole time—just keeping this all to yourself. Everyone is very proud of you." His kind words made me cry. "Oh no," he seemed worried, "I didn't mean to make you cry."

I smiled through my tears and said, "I thought you were going to be mad at me. I knew what really happened and didn't tell you the truth." I wiped my face, struggling to explain. "I just thought you all would be mad at me."

Detective Gruber smiled. "Oh, no. We don't blame you one bit. You were only a child and scared, too. We know that." He leaned forward and whispered, "If truth be known, your mom scares the crud out of me, too." He winked, and I laughed. Everyone in the room laughed. A joke like that might have seemed inappropriate to someone looking in from the outside, but it was just what we all needed to be pulled out of the dark reality of what had been talked about that afternoon.

Agent Lewzader shook my hand and Detective Gruber asked if he could hug me, which I quickly agreed to. My dad and I were soon on our way back to my home. Because I had no clothes to show for my supposed "shopping trip," we had to come up with an explanation. We decided to tell my mom that my aunt got home late, and we were only able to go to one store. I didn't find anything I liked, so she wanted to take me shopping again the following week, which coincided with the day I needed to be back at my dad's to have the wire put on. We agreed I would be the one to explain all of this to my mom, since my dad worried she would not believe him. Driving up to my grandma's house, I went over the story in my head and mentally prepared myself to face my mom.

When we went into the house, my mom was cooking dinner. Dad stood awkwardly at the door. Mom walked over and asked, "Where's her clothes?"

Dad shrugged, "I guess my sister got off work late, or something. Nyssa just ended up hanging out with my mom most of the time."
Mom asked, "Did they shop at all?"

Again, Dad shrugged. "I'm not sure. I didn't ask. I'm sorry, but I gotta run to the bank before it closes." He waved to me, "See you next week, maybe?" Then he left before I could answer him. I was impressed at how well played that little scene went. He seemed just disinterested enough to seem real to my mom.

Mom closed the door and shook her head. "Your dad sure is weird. So, what happened?"

"Well," I began, "Beverly didn't get off work until later than she thought she would. We ran out to one store, but I couldn't find anything there. Really, they had a lot of 'old lady' clothes." I rolled my eyes, and my mom laughed. "So, we left to meet Dad back at the house. Aunt Bev feels bad she wasn't able to take me to more places, and she said she wanted to try next week—if that's okay with you. She said something about taking a half-day at work, so we would have plenty of time." I tried to look like I could care less what answer my mom gave, while watching her mentally digesting the information I had given her.

Mom was quiet for a minute, then she said, "Well, I guess it's okay. I mean, even though you didn't go shopping, you just hung out with your grandma. You know I don't have anything against her. And it would still be helpful if Beverly could buy you some clothes, so ... I guess it's okay." She smiled at me. "Are you okay with that?"

I wasn't sure if my mom was trying to gauge my eagerness to hang out with my dad's family or if she was just in a really good mood and genuinely wanted to know how I felt. Either way, I shrugged and answered, "Yeah, I guess." Mom smiled at my response, and I helped her finish dinner. It had all worked out.

That night, as I lay on the living room floor where I slept, I waited for all the sounds of the house to die down. I heard my grandma go to her bedroom. Then, I heard my mom and Tom turn off the T.V. upstairs, as they decided it was time to go to sleep. All was quiet in the house, as I slowly crawled out of bed and moved across the room toward Dawn's bed. Not wanting to startle her out of a sound sleep, I made a small "Psst" sound.

She immediately whispered back, "I'm awake."

"Can you come by my bed?" I whispered as softly as I could.

I figured my bed was far enough from the stairs that our voices would not carry up to the bedrooms. Without answering, Dawn slowly removed her covers and quietly tip- toed behind me. We snuck back over to my bed on the floor and sat on the blankets.

"So, you know about us moving to Australia?" I asked her.

"Yeah," she answered, "they told me right before they brought the board out. They said they wanted to 'seek guidance' on the move." Dawn turned her head questioningly. "Is Australia far away?"

I nodded my head quickly, "Yes, it is VERY far away."

Dawn wiped her eyes, and although it was very dark in the room, the moonlight shone on her enough for me to see that she was crying. "Yuck," she muttered. Dawn never complained, so this was almost like a cuss word for her.

Wanting to give her hope, I began to explain, "I told my dad, and he is helping us." Dawn looked up at me as I continued. "An FBI Agent and a detective from Radcliff came out, and I talked to them. They all want to help us." I could see Dawn's face light up in the moonlight, and I briefly thought what a pretty smile she had --- then a noise came from the stairway.

We both turned our heads towards the stairs, and I struggled to quickly process the sound I had just heard. I realized that someone upstairs had opened one of the bedroom doors. I turned to Dawn, to see her looking back at me. Her eyes were wide with fright. I quickly placed one hand on her shoulder to calm her and motioned with my other hand toward her bed. She nodded and swiftly bear crawled over to her bed. She slid under her covers, as I pulled my blankets over me, as well. We were both completely still, as footsteps came down the stairs and a light came on in the kitchen.

After some rummaging in the refrigerator and one of the cabinets, the light turned off and the footsteps headed back upstairs. I never knew for sure who came down that night, but I prayed a long nightly prayer of thanksgiving that Dawn and I had not been found out, before finally falling to sleep. I felt good, knowing that Dawn might get a good night's sleep, having finally received some hopeful news. I put the specifics of my upcoming "wire mission" out of my mind and focused on our new-found hope.

Sleep came easier that night than it had in a long time. During the next week, we had our typical ups and downs.
Mom was really stressed out with all the planning for our move and was quick to take her frustration out on whoever was nearby. However, she was also very excited about our move and was extremely fun to be around, if you caught her at the right time. The only reason her Jekyll and Hyde routine was not driving me insane was because I was now hopeful. I believed the people who said they wanted to help Dawn and me. I was beginning to see the powerful force behind having hope. It made everything in my life more bearable, even my mom. Dawn even seemed less impacted by my mom's cruel comments and back-handed remarks. We had hope.

I used that hopeful attitude to build myself up for the day I would have to talk to my step-dad about Alex while wearing a wire.

Earlier that week, my dad and I had our usual visit. Instead of going to his basketball game, we had gone to the local FBI office to meet with the agents who would be monitoring the "undercover operation" that I would attempt. The local agent was named Gallagher, and he went over the timeline of what I could expect, as Agent Lewzader had done. I was feeling more comfortable each time I heard the plan, and the fact that it stayed the same. I was introduced to the female agent who would attach the wire to my body and shown the device that I would wear.

Agent Gallagher assured me that I would be watched at all times. He said cars would be parked in many locations with other agents that would be fully committed to watching me and assuring my safety. I was shocked at the lengths that were being taken to keep me safe.

Then, the day of my aunt's "shopping trip" had come. My Aunt Beverly had actually taken some time off so she could pick me up from my house and drop me off. This seemed to put my mom more at ease. She waved to my aunt and kissed me goodbye, as she ran upstairs to do some Australia-related things. My aunt and I got into her car and headed to my dad's.

We made small talk but considering we had not seen each other in more than two years, we were a little quiet. The fact that a surreal event was about to take place didn't help the awkward situation. As we pulled up to my dad's house, she patted me on the back and said, "Good luck." I smiled and nodded back.

Dad was standing on the doorstep, seeming very anxious. He hugged me and asked, "Are you ready?"

I shrugged and forced a nervous smile. Did I really have a choice at this point?
We entered the house, and I was shocked to see all the people inside. It seemed like an undercover sting was about to happen on a mob boss somewhere. I was curious as to how many of these agents would be "shadowing" me, and where exactly they parked. I didn't notice many cars parked in front of my dad's house. I figured the FBI had so many secret ways they did things—why not covert parking, as well?

After meeting with Agent Gallagher and being introduced to several of the other agents, I was led upstairs by the same female agent I met a few days prior who would be strapping the recording device to my body. Her name was Michelle, and she was nice, but firm in how she handled me.

"You wore a good shirt for this," she commented. I had worn the loosest fitting shirt I had. Something bulky would have worked as well, but I couldn't have worn a sweatshirt or anything too heavy, as it would have seemed odd in the warm California weather.

"I have to pull it tight, so it won't come off," she said, as she pulled the Velcro strap around my waist to hold to recording box to my back. "I know it feels weird, but you only have to wear it for a little while." She re-adjusted the Velcro pieces, and the box, to make sure they would not come loose.

She showed me a small button on the side of the device and instructed me, "This is the button you push to start the recording." She paused to make sure I understood her, "Only push it when you are at the house. Right before you go inside. Okay?" I nodded.

"After you talk to your step-dad, we will come and pick you up when you leave the house again." I nodded. I remembered all of this from my previous meetings. She softened her demeanor and stepped out of the "FBI Agent" role for a second.

"Don't worry." She put her hand on my shoulder. "You are going to do great, and we will be watching you the whole time. I promise." She squeezed my shoulder, then reverted back to Agent mode. "Okay, let's go."

We headed downstairs, and Agent Gallagher once again went over the plan of action for that afternoon. I was feeling so familiar with the timeline that I could have recited it word for word. However, I was still becoming increasingly nervous.

The time came for us to head out. I went with my aunt, and we started our drive back to my house. As we passed the front of my dad's house, I saw two agents leave together and head down the street. Once we were farther up the block, I saw a few more agents leave and walk the opposite direction down the street. I watched them in my aunt's side mirror but lost them and was unable to see what vehicles they entered. I was actually hoping to identify all the cars that would be used, so I would plainly see that I was not alone on this mission.

Now, I would just have to trust what I had been told.

Once my aunt and I were within a few blocks of my house, she motioned toward the back seat. "There are some clothes in the bag. I got a few things I thought you would wear. If you don't like them, I can return them later."

As we pulled into the driveway, I opened the bag and saw some shirts from a department store. "Thank you," I said. I had never spent that much time with my aunt, but I was touched that she went to such lengths to help me during this time. I sighed and said, "I guess I'll see you later."

My aunt also sighed and answered, "I guess so."

We smiled at each other, as I put one hand under my shirt and pressed the button that would start my hidden recording device. I was now "on." I walked into the house and took a deep breath. Mom greeted me, and I had a brief conversation with her about dinner, then I headed upstairs to put the bag away. I saw Tom and asked if he wanted to go for a walk. Since he had been dropping hints for weeks that he wanted to spend more time with me, he immediately agreed.

As we began our walk around the neighborhood, we made small talk about nothing in particular. The warm August weather was making me sweat slightly, and I wondered if the recorder was sweatproof or if it was possible for it to short circuit and electrocute me. I tried not to think about that possibility and focus on what I needed to talk to Tom about. I struggled to find just the right time to start the line of questions I had been prepped on. I finally decided to just get it over with.

I began by acting as if I were confiding in Tom that I was having these really bad dreams about Alex. I explained that in my dream, someone comes across Alex's remains and the case is reopened. Then, the police arrest my mom and Tom, and another trial ensues. Tom, quick to try and relieve my fears, talked with me in great detail about why that would not happen.

As we rounded the last corner of the large rectangle we had followed around our neighborhood, we finished up with more small talk. We even talked about doing this kind of thing again. I agreed with genuine happiness—although it was only because I was so glad this whole taped conversation was over. I hoped I had done everything the way I was supposed to. Hopefully, the recording device recorded everything. Hopefully, I asked the right questions and received the right answers. Hopefully, the recorder picked up the conversation clearly. There was really no way for me to know.

When we re-entered the house, I quickly ran upstairs and grabbed some blank music tapes. I ran back down the stairs and yelled out that I would be walking up the street to Sam's house to give her some tapes I recorded for her. Mom yelled back to make it quick, because she was starting dinner. I left the house and quickly rounded the block.

I frantically looked up and down the street for vehicles that fit my idea of an undercover car. I had no idea what I was looking for. As I walked around the back corner of my block, I wondered if the agents lost track of me or didn't know when they were supposed to pick me up. I whispered, "I'm done," hoping the recorder would somehow relay that message to the agents. I was getting more and more anxious every second I walked down the street alone.

Suddenly, a dark car with slightly tinted windows pulled into the driveway in front of me, and the back passenger door popped open before it completely stopped. It all happened so fast, my first reaction was, "Oh no—I'm being kidnapped!" Then, I saw Michelle, the FBI Agent who fit the device on me holding the door open.

She waved me in quickly, and I slid into the back seat as fast as I could. The car then immediately reversed and headed up the road so quickly, I actually slid across the seat a little. Michelle stopped my slide with her body and put one finger up to her mouth to signal for me to be quiet. She retrieved the recorder from my body and recited some information into it, before pressing the same button I pressed earlier to start the recording. We then drove quickly to the K-mart up the street to use the bathroom. Michelle took all the Velcro and straps off of my torso, and we walked back out to the car. The swiftness with which everything was done made it so no one in the store noticed us slip in and out.

Once in the car, I asked how everything went. I really didn't know how much they could tell me. Michelle seemed somewhat preoccupied with putting the recording device away, so one of the agents up front answered. "We won't really know until they go over the recording in Virginia. I'm sure Agent Gallagher will be in touch with your dad as soon as we know something. Okay?" I nodded sheepishly. I don't know why

I thought it would all happen so quickly. This would take time, and I would have to be patient.

I was disappointed but tried to look happy as we pulled back onto the street where they picked me up. Michelle warned me that I would need to leave the vehicle quickly, so they could leave the area as fast as possible. I nodded, again.

I must have looked upset, because the passenger seat agent who talked to me earlier said, "Nyssa, I'm sure you did great." He smiled at me through the space between the two front seats, and I smiled back. That small act of encouragement made a big difference as I quickly jumped out of the car and watched it speed off down the street.

I walked home with a smile on my face. I scanned the street for unfamiliar cars, to see if any agents were still nearby. Nothing looked out of the ordinary, and I felt foolish knowing that I probably walked right by one of the cars on my walk with Tom and hadn't even noticed. The street was quiet, and I saw no neighbors outside their homes to witness a speeding car pick me up and drop me off. The birds chirped, and it was as if the events of the day had never really happened. I was just a teenage girl on a walk in her neighborhood on a quiet day. Unreal.

I finished the day eating dinner with my mom and family. We talked about the move to Australia and how nice it was that Tom and I took our walk together. I smiled during the whole conversation. My mom seemed to be in a really good mood, to see me so happy at all her new information on our move. She obviously thought I was the obedient, brainwashed daughter. She probably thought that I was so happy about moving away and trying to bond with her spineless husband.

I fully realized that, at that moment, for the first time in my life, I had more control over our situation and future than she did. That realization filled me with confidence, but also a terrifying realty; if my mom knew any of the details about what I was doing with my dad, she would stop at nothing to get rid of me. I had to not only watch my step but think five steps ahead. I couldn't slip even once, or my mom would be right on top of me.

Over the next few days, I kept busy and to myself. I didn't want to say or do anything around my mom that would accidentally mess up all the hard work that had been done and was still being done. I also feared the lengths my mom would go to in order to avoid jail. So, I stayed late at school. I went over to Sam's house. I went to the library, by myself.

I no longer wanted to talk to Dawn about what was happening, for her own protection. The less she knew now, the less likely she would accidentally say something. I had not talked to her since that night we almost got caught talking after bedtime. So, she was unaware that I had worn a wire. I wanted to tell her but figured we were so close to all this being over, it could wait.

When it was time for my dad and I to have our weekly visit, I couldn't even wait until we were out of the driveway before I asked, "So, what is going on?"

Dad knew I wanted to know all about the recording I made with Tom. "Well," he sounded like he would be giving me a lot of information. "They have taken the recording back to Virginia, and they are analyzing it. Agent Lewzader said they are putting a rush on it, because they know your mom and Tom want to leave the country. As soon as they are done with the recording, they will get arrests warrants and come to get them."

I furrowed my eyebrows at him, and he answered my unspoken question. "They don't have a date that this will all be done." I was crushed. I put my head in my hands and cried. Dad pulled over in a parking lot and hugged me. "I'm sorry, Nyssa. I know it seems so close now, but it still isn't ending." I nodded with my head in his chest and continued to cry.

"But if anyone can do this, it's you. You have been through so much with your mom. Please, don't give up now. I promise the end is near." I wiped my tears and sat straight in my seat.

He was right. This is where it would really count, and I couldn't fall apart now.

We met Jay at the Carl's Jr. near their home, which was fast becoming our regular spot to eat. The three of us sat to await our food at our table. I sipped my drink quietly, not knowing what to say; so much had happened over the last few weeks.

Jay asked, "Are you okay?"

I knew that I probably still looked like I had been crying, so there was no sense in playing anything off. "Yeah," I answered, "I'm just nervous and a little worried."

Jay nodded, "Well, I'd be shocked if you weren't. I mean, after all you've been through—it must be so hard waiting to hear back about what is going to happen." She shook her head slowly. "Just not knowing..." She trailed off and drank some of her Coke.

I was so surprised that she so clearly understood my feelings that I didn't answer her. A brief, awkward silence followed, until the food came and we all started eating. As I began eating my cheeseburger, I wondered many things about my step-mom. How much had her previous drug addiction affected her, her moods, and our relationship? Would the fact that she was no longer using drugs mean we could have a functional connection to each other? How much of her previous self was, in fact, a manifestation of the illegal drugs that pumped through her body? I continued to glance at Jay as we ate.

Apparently, I was more obvious than I meant to be, because she finally said, "Nyssa, I know we have had some problems in the past. But now we are both different. That means we can have a different kind of relationship than the one we had before." She smiled and looked at me intently, awaiting my answer.

"Yeah," I said, "I was just thinking that." We both smiled.

Dad laughed, "That's so awesome!" he blurted with hamburger stuffed in his mouth. He finished chewing and swallowed. "Hey, can we talk about the living situation once this all happens." Jay and I knew what event he was talking about. He was referring to the final arrest of my mom and Tom. At least, what the three of us hoped would be the last arrest.

We talked about what room I would stay in at their home. We talked about where we thought Dawn and Novi should stay. Since they had previously stayed with my Uncle Sokie and his wife Linda, it seemed reasonable that it would be best if they went to their home. Although my uncle was the brother of my mom, he was somewhat of the "black sheep" of the family. The fact that he was retired LAPD also trumped the family tree he shared with my mom. We could trust him. He was the only one on that side of the family we could trust.

Speaking freely about our future plans put my nerves at ease. It may take longer than expected, or longer than I wanted, but the arrest was inevitable. I only hoped I had provided the FBI with what they needed on that recording they were analyzing so far away.

Several months later, on September 3, 1993, as I was finishing my homework and getting ready to change into some pajamas—it happened.

From the upstairs bathroom, I heard a knock at the front door. The bathroom was at the top of the stairs, and when I opened the door, I had a clear view of the front door being opened by my grandmother. I heard a person ask for my mom and Tom by name, and saw my grandmother clutch her chest and take a step back.
Several men and a woman, all wearing vests and with badges hanging around their necks, entered the house. The next few minutes were over quickly, but seemed to happen in slow motion for me:

~~ My mom and Tom coming down the stairs...

~~ Novi being passed to my grandmother, and then to the female officer...

~~ An officer advising Dawn and I to pack quick bags to leave...

~~ My mom and Tom being handcuffed...

~~ Mom looking at me and saying, "It's okay. You know what to do," before being led away to a police car outside.

It all seemed unreal as I sat in the Torrance Police Department, awaiting my dad. I played the scene over and over again in my head. Especially the part where my mom looked at me and spoke with such assurance. She really had no idea that I was the one who had set this whole thing in motion. When would she finally learn? Were they telling her at this moment? While I was sitting in a back room of the police station, was she in another room being told I snitched on her? I was in a state of disbelief, until I saw my dad.

"Hey," he hugged me tight and said, "They finally got them."

That was it. They finally got them. The good guys finally won. My upside-down view of the world was finally righted, and the rest of this journey would be all downhill compared to what I had been through.

MAKING THINGS RIGHT

A time of great readjustment followed the arrest of my mom and Tom. Although my sisters had spent some time with my Uncle Sokie and his wife Linda (who I was really beginning to like, the more I got to know her), they still needed some time to become comfortable in their new home. After a few days, Dawn and Novi seemed more at ease with my uncle's family and began to flourish in his home. Dawn seemed more relaxed and confident every day that passed in her new home. Even Novi seemed happier to be able to run around and play. I hadn't realized how much time she had spent plopped in front of the TV at my grandma's house.

At my new home with my dad, there were more positive changes being made. I had to learn to feel comfortable speaking openly with my both my dad and Jay. They didn't want me to say what I thought they wanted to hear; they wanted me to speak honestly. I had to learn that, even if we didn't agree, no one needed to explode in rage or have a total meltdown. Wow.

Altogether, my sisters and I had a peace and happiness, in a safe home environment, which we had never experienced for more than a few weeks at a time. But instead of it being contingent on the constant mood swings of my mom, it was actually concrete.

While we flourished and grew in our new homes, Dawn and I also knew that we would be facing our parents one last time. Every time we visited, our conversation would return to this inevitable fact.

"I'm scared." Dawn looked down at her feet, reverting to her old insecure self.

"I know." I struggled to think of a new way to reassure her. "But this will be the last time we ever have to see them. I promise." I didn't actually know if that was true, but I wanted so badly to put her mind at ease. She should be enjoying her new home, not obsessing about seeing our parents again.

"But," Dawn looked at me with wide eyes, "what if they get out again, and we have to go back and live with them?" I knew she was thinking about the previous trial, and the possibility of them being acquitted.

I shook my head, "No, the case against them is much stronger this time. I mean, they have that recording of me talking to your dad. No, they will be found guilty. I know it." This conversation or variations of it, continued for months. It continued up until the trial itself. And then Dawn seemed to totally shut down.

The trial took place in the summer, which was a relief to many people involved. Dawn and I would not miss school, so we were a little less stressed. Less stress for us meant less stress for our families at home, which made the whole situation a little easier to swallow. Although we had no idea how long the trial would take, we packed a week's worth of clothes and had been told that they would find a place for us to do laundry, if we needed it.

"They" were the state prosecutor and his wife, Mr. and Mrs. Jeff England. Both had been talking to my dad (for our home) and my aunt (for Dawn and Novi's home) to keep us up to date on what was going on with the case. Their personalities embodied what I had always imagined was "southern hospitality." From the moment we stepped off the plane and were checked into our hotel, the Englands were taking care of us.

"Here, sweetie—let me see what you have to wear..." Mrs. England looked through my suitcase and shook her head. "Oh, I'll bet you could fit into most of my clothes." She gave me a hug and looked toward her husband.

"We should head back to the house, so Nyssa can look through my closet. She would look so cute in one of my pant suits!" It was as if I was a long-lost niece of theirs.

Mr. England nodded his head. "Okay but make it quick. We don't want to overwhelm her. After all, she did just fly halfway across the country, dear." He looked at me and half hid his mouth with one hand, "She's very easily excitable," he whispered to me, but loud enough for her to hear.

She lightly punched him in the arm, and the two of them playfully bantered some more. A few hours later, I was standing in front of her closet. She had more clothes than I had ever seen in my life. She began pulling clothes out for me to try on.

"Now, you want to look mature," she made a face and put one of the shirts back in the closet, "but not like an old lady." She seemed happy at the pile that lay on her bed. "You go ahead and try these on. Any you like, you are welcome to take." She began to walk out the door, when she turned and said, "If you aren't sure about one, come out and let us see. We can tell you." She smiled warmly and shut the door.

I stared at the pile of blouses, long skirts, and slacks. I felt like I was playing "dress up," as I would have never worn such sophisticated clothing in my normal life. I heard my aunt and Mrs. England laughing and talking loudly in the next room and figured I better start trying on clothes if I wanted to get back to the hotel room before bedtime. I was already tired from the flight, and just thinking about the upcoming events made me exhausted.

About an hour later, the three of us had picked out four outfits for me to wear. Through the course of deciding what to wear, Mrs. England had suggested that we pick at least four, in case my testimony went for four days. I fought to put that bit of information away and not react too much in front of my aunt and her.

It wasn't until I was back in the hotel room and sat in the oversized armchair in the corner that I let it fully sink in. I could be testifying for four days? I remembered how terrible it felt to have everyone staring at me and scrutinizing every word I said during the last trial and even at the grand jury. I might have to do that for four whole days?

I was more scared at that moment than I had been since my mom and Tom were arrested. I briefly wondered if it was too late for me to back out. Maybe they didn't need me to testify at all, since they had the recording. Maybe I would actually hurt the case by saying something stupid ... Maybe...

Dawn entered the room from the adjoining door to her room that she shared with my aunt and uncle. Since my dad had run down to the lobby to look for pamphlets on attractions or something, it was just the two of us in the room. She sat on the bed next to the outfits I had brought back from the Englands' home. She moved around some of the clothes, and half-heartedly looked at them. I could tell she wasn't really interested in these "grown-up" clothes I brought back.

"How do you like your room?" I figured this was a good way to start small talk with her.

She shrugged and went back to staring at the clothes. "Are you sharing a bed with Aunt Linda?" I asked.

She shook her head.

"Oh, so you get your own bed?"

She nodded.

I sighed and slid down into my lounge chair. I was at a loss how I could reach her. I was stressed out myself, so I didn't think I could be much help to her. We sat in the room together, not saying a word. Dawn finished looking at the clothes and lay flat on the bed, next to the pile. I flopped my legs over one side of the chair and lay my head on the other side. We were both in an altered, stressed-out reality that neither of us knew how to handle. We had adjusted to the madness of our previous home over a period of years. Having to go up against the very people who raised us in that madness seemed impossible.

The hotel room door opened. "Is it beddy-by time?" my dad asked the both of us.

Dawn smiled and quietly walked back to her room.

Dad looked at me questioningly. "What's up with her? Is this whole thing just hitting her now?" Dad was sympathetic but blunt in his question.

I nodded, "Yeah." Then I sighed and added, "She's not the only one."

Dad came and sat on my bed, where Dawn had been. He took a couple deep breaths, and I could tell he was searching for the right words. Finally, he said, "I know you guys will do fine. After all you have been through, this is going to be cake. And then, you won't have to worry about your mom and Tom again." He came over and gave me a hug.

"Thanks, Dad." It was such a simple thing he said, but I did feel better. We would do fine—we had been through a lot—it would be over soon. End of story.

Just then, there was a knock at the shared door. My dad said, "Come in," and my aunt and uncle walked into our room. After my aunt showed my uncle my clothes, and my uncle rolled his eyes (he made no effort to enjoy girly things), they finally brought up what they had really come over for: Dawn's attitude since arriving in Kentucky. They knew this trip would be hard, but they had not expected Dawn to totally shut down and become unresponsive. They confided that she had even refused to testify.

My aunt seemed puzzled. "Why wouldn't she want to send them away for good, after what they did?"

My uncle seemed irritated. "Nyssa is going to be grilled more than her, and she needs to get over it."

My dad was trying to be objective. "Maybe she's afraid to see them or something."

I stood up, "Do you want me to talk to her?" There were immediate nods all around. "Okay."

I walked through the adjoining door and found Dawn laying on her bed, staring up at nothing. I decided to lie down next to her. I remembered this technique from the class I took about relating to others.

I positioned myself on the bed, just like she was. I looked up at the ceiling, just like she was. Then, I waited a few minutes before I quietly asked, "So does this trip suck or what?"

Dawn made a small laugh sound, then quietly answered, "Yeah, it sucks."

I waited another couple of minutes and asked, "Are you really not going to testify?"

"I dunno," she answered.

I wanted to wait before the next question but couldn't hold back. "Dawn, I need you to back me up. I need you to tell them that what I'm saying is true. That my mom and your dad are not okay, that Alex suffered, and that they deserve to be in jail. I can't be the only one saying that. Please," I pleaded with her.

She rolled over with her back to me and began to cry. "I dunno," she murmured between sobs.

I decided to return to the other room, before I became too harsh with her. Part of me knew the emotional and physical abuse she suffered was to blame for her mortal fear of our parents. I also had sympathy for the fact that she was even younger than me.

However, I felt that she was letting me down when I needed her the most. This was a hard fact to face.

"What happened?" my uncle asked me.

I gave them a summary of our short conversation and shrugged. I didn't know if she would testify. My aunt and uncle went back into their room with her, to discuss the matter some more. My dad and I got ready for bed. Once the lights had been turned out, and we were quietly awaiting some much-needed sleep, my dad informed me he would only be able to stay with me in Kentucky for a few days.

"Why?" I held back my tears, as I waited for his reply. I didn't want to be there without him.

"Jay needs my help, Babe. She's got a lot going on with the girls and work and stuff." After a long silence, he asked, "Okay?"

I mumbled, "Okay." I was so angry at him, for leaving after only a few days and not telling me sooner. He had to have known he wasn't going to stay the whole time—didn't he? I was sad that I was missing my sister to back me up and would soon be missing my dad.

I was scared to be facing my parents and dealing with all this by myself. At that moment, I truly hated my life. I lay in my bed, feeling numb. I didn't care anymore. Why should I? I was tired of feeling like I was always on my own. Was there no one who would help me and not desert me when I needed them the most? Then, I remembered my nightly prayers, and I began to pray.

Dear God—please, help me. Please, show me who down here will help me. Please, show me I can do this. Please show me you are with me. Please, God. Please.

Just the act of praying calmed me, as it usually did. Soon, I was thinking of the people who supported me there in Kentucky. Some of the very people who spent their time searching for my sister, only to find out they had been lied to the whole time, were the same people who offered their support to me. The forgiveness they showed me, and their desire to see justice done for Alex, was proof to me that I would not be alone.

Mrs. England offered me her own clothes; her husband wanted to do all he could to make sure my parents got what they deserved; complete strangers offered Dawn and me their support. In the very area where I witnessed the very worst in human nature, I was also seeing the very best. I knew I had people to support me, but I still needed a reason to continue.

As I thought this, my head was immediately flooded with pictures of Alex. If I didn't go through with my testimony, justice for little Alex might not happen. She deserved better. I had to do it, for her.

Feeling relief, my body began to relax, and I was able to slowly drift off to sleep. Just before I was completely gone, I felt one last notion forming in my mind: I was never truly on my own. I had never really, truly been by myself. I had always turned to someone for help, no matter what had been going on in my life. My nightly prayers were proof there was one who would always back me up, calm me down, and offer me guidance. I just had to trust Him.

The next day was the first day we would be preparing for court. The prosecutor warned me that this first day would be mostly the lawyers questioning possible jury candidates and trying to come to an agreement on who would be allowed to sit on the jury. He also warned that this could continue into the second day, then both sides would talk to the judge about "lawyer" things. This would be followed by opening statements made by both the prosecutor and the defense attorneys, if the trial even started that second day.

We, however, would need to be dressed and ready to go, every day from day one, in case we needed to talk to the judge or start our testimony. So, all of us got our nice clothes on, and talked about what we could do to pass the time. We began to discuss what movies were playing in town, but decided against this, since the trial was receiving so much media coverage, someone might recognize and approach us. I wasn't sure what they would say to us, but the adults felt it wouldn't be wise, so we decided against it.

My uncle pulled out a pack of cards and offered to teach my sister and I to play poker. Dawn actually smiled, and the two of us shrugged and sat at the table next to him. As he was passing out the cards, the phone rang. My dad had a brief conversation with someone, then hung up.

"The Englands would like us to head to their office," my dad explained. "They think the judge might want to talk to the girls, and they want to show Nyssa something."

We all wondered what it was they wanted to show me, but none of us had any ideas. Well, any good ideas.

"Maybe they found the world's biggest gopher behind their office." My dad grinned at his own joke. I laughed.

"Ah, come on, Ben," my uncle answered. "I bet it's really Bigfoot. Jeff probably ran it over on the way to his office." All of us laughed as we piled into the car.

"What's so great about a big foot? I got two of them!" Dad blurted, and we all laughed hysterically in the car. Even Dawn was laughing. For a moment, the stress of the week was non-existent. It returned once we got to the prosecutor's office.

When we entered the building, Mrs. England pulled my dad to the side and said something to him. He nodded and the two of them came toward me.

"Nyssa, I have something Jeff wants you to see." Mrs. England led my dad and me to a back room with a table, two chairs and a small TV on a rolling media stand. It reminded me of an interrogation room that you would see on a cop show. No pictures, windows, or anything other than those few items.

My dad and I sat down in the chairs facing the T.V., while Mrs. England stood next to the set and explained, "Jeff wants you to see this interview that your mom did with a news program out here. He wants you to know ... well, he just thinks you should see." She was clearly struggling to explain why I should see this interview. She finally said, "Here..." and clicked on the T.V.

Once the recording began, a news reporter appeared on the screen. This reporter explained that their news agency had done an exclusive interview with my mom, while she was awaiting the trial. It then showed my mom speaking to this reporter. I was so shocked by her appearance, I really forgot to listen to what she was saying.

She was seriously skinny, and the sight of her in an orange prison jumpsuit was strange. When I finally re-focused on her words, I realized she was pleading her innocence. Of course, she would do that. Why did Mr. England think this was so important? Then, the reporter asked her why she thought I was claiming she killed Alex, and if there was anything she wanted to say to me.

She answered, "I don't know why she's doing this to me."

Then slowly, almost as if it were rehearsed, my mom looked into the camera. She made an awful face, like she was trying to cry. Then she cried out, "Why, Nyssa? Why?" Her eyes squinted with pain, and she stared so intently into the camera that I felt she was staring straight at me. "After all I did for you? Why?" She finished by dropping her face into her hands and making crying sounds. I felt sick to my stomach. Would she be able to manipulate the public to believe her? Would she be able to manipulate the judge or jury?

Mrs. England had remained in the back of the room until the interview finished. She came around and turned off the T.V. My dad then stood up, so she could sit next to me. He leaned against the wall and sighed. I wondered if he had the same concerns I did.

Mrs. England put her hand on my shoulder and asked, "Are you okay?"

I nodded. Then, I asked her, "Do people know she is lying?"

She smiled, "Of course, they do. Jeff just wanted you to see this interview, so you know how your mom is trying to trick everyone. He wanted you to know she is trying to blame you, so it doesn't come as a shock." Then, she smiled again. "But, no, Nyssa. People don't believe her. She may think she's a good actress—but she's not." She gave me a big hug. Then, someone came to the door and told her that the phone was for her. She left and my dad sat back down next to me.

"So, are you really okay?" he asked.

I nodded. "My mom is so fake," I blurted. Dad laughed, "Oh, believe me. I know."

"Did you see how she looked into the camera? And she didn't even cry any tears!" I smiled, feeling more confident that people would see through her over-the-top acting.

Dad hugged me, "You are going to do great, sweetie." He kissed me on the cheek.

Mrs. England came back in the room and informed us that we needed to go to the courthouse, because the judge wanted to meet with me. She assured me that I was not going to testify, once she saw my obvious nervousness.

"This is just a meeting," she explained. "I'm sure he wants to go over a few things with you."

I relaxed, and we went to the courthouse. The courthouse in Elizabethtown (better known as E-town) was situated in the middle of a town square that was the definition of "quaint." It instantly transported me to a historical time that brought visions of horse-drawn carriages and women in Victorian- style dresses. It was beautiful. I thought it was a shame I was not just sight-seeing.

A sheriff escorted us across the street, into the very middle of the square, where the courthouse stood. Once inside, another officer showed us the way to the judge's chamber. We went through several doors, until we came to the office that belonged to the judge. The judge sat at his desk. He smiled at me and asked me to sit down. I took a seat across from him. I saw Mr. England and several other people also in the room.

"Well, Nyssa." He smiled when he talked, and I thought he wasn't like I thought he would be. He seemed really nice. "I wanted to let you know, you do not have to be afraid about what you are doing here. I want you to be comfortable and feel safe in my courtroom." He seemed protective of his courtroom and what would happen there. I liked that.

"Okay," I answered. I didn't know what else to say.

"Now, Mr. England has asked, on your behalf, if you could turn the witness chair slightly so you wouldn't have to face your mom and step-father. Is this true?" His eyes narrowed a little, and I wasn't sure if he was disapproving of my request or just curious.

I figured the worst he could do was say, "No," so I nodded and said, "Yes, sir."

The judge smiled again. "Well, that's alright with me. As long as you look at the lawyers asking you questions and face me if I ask you something, then I have no problem with you turning a little. Okay?"

I was so relieved, I wanted to cry. "Thank you," I said, meekly.

That was the end of my meeting with the judge, and I was escorted out. My dad waited in the hall, and I told him what happened. He squeezed my neck and said, "See, sweetie? It's all going to work out." I was beginning to feel that way more and more each day.

Several days passed before the trial officially started. The first day was jury selection. Apparently both sides (or in this case, all three sides—prosecutor, Mom's attorney, and Tom's attorney) had to agree on every juror selected. The second day was more jury selection and motions by the defense attorneys. I learned that in one of these motions, the judge ruled that we could not bring up any prior child abuse that happened in California.

I was very upset by this, since I knew this would make our case much stronger, if the jury could see how badly my mom always treated Alex. I figured the judge knew what he was talking about when he agreed, so I accepted this ruling and prayed that the recording I made with Tom would be enough.

Finally, on the third day, Mr. England called the first witnesses. He started with the officers who first responded to Alex being missing. Then, he called two of the detectives who worked the case. Finally, it ended with Agent Lewzader testifying. My uncle was there all day and was able to sit in the courtroom because he was not testifying in the case. At the end of the day, he would give us a summary over dinner. That night, dinner was subs and chips.

During the testimony from Agent Lewzader, he mentioned the recording I made with Tom. So, now the jury knew that this recording existed and would hear more about it when I gave my testimony. Now that there was testimony leading up to my testimony,

I was so nervous I would mess something up. I kept telling myself that all I had to do was tell the truth. Before, I had to remember a very specific lie to protect my parents, but now I just needed to tell the truth. I could do this.

The fourth day was a continuation of Agent Lewzader's testimony. There were a few other witnesses called who were involved in some way with the recording that would be played when I took the stand. Several FBI agents who were with me when I made the recording, as well as some specialist who worked with the recording to make it clearer for everyone to hear. I waited at the prosecutor's office, ready to testify after him.

Finally, I testified. I answered questions about the abuse Alex received in Kentucky, the way that she died and the ensuing cover-up, and when I came to my dad for help. It was the end of the day, and the judge decided that the jury could hear the tape on the next trial day. Since it was a Friday when we ended that day, the jury would not hear the tapes until Monday. It also meant I still had to go back on the witness stand after the weekend.

I relished the break from all the awful things I had to share with everyone in the courtroom, but I also wanted everything over. Having to wait for several more days seemed awful.

Once the judge dismissed me and my testimony was finished, I was escorted back to the waiting room. My uncle left the courtroom and met me there. Since my dad left earlier that day, I would be returning to the hotel with him.

"You did great, kiddo." My uncle hugged me and patted me on the back. "Are you ready to get out of here? Cuz, I'm hungry." My uncle smiled at me and led me outside to where he parked.

Since my aunt stayed at the hotel with Dawn, it was just the two of us on the way back to the hotel. He let me pick what kind of food we ate, and once again, told me what a good job he thought I had done. This was a huge deal, since my rough-and-tough uncle didn't believe in too much praise. He felt it made people weak.

Once we were inside and the four of us were eating our food, it was my aunt's turn to say some encouraging and nice things to me.

"You really did good, Nyssa. We are very proud of you." Then, she lowered her voice and said, "I know it was hard to have your dad leave. But you still did the right thing by hanging in there." She nodded at me, and my uncle looked over and winked. I almost began to cry but took a deep breath and stopped myself. They had actually known I would struggle with added stress and had been watching over me. I was so grateful I didn't know what to say.

"Fanks," I said with a mouth full of food.

My uncle shook his head, "Really? A smart girl like you doesn't know we don't want to see your already chewed food?"

I laughed and apologized, once I swallowed my food.

My uncle wagged his finger at me, "Just watch yourself young lady, or we'll have to sell you to the zoo or something."

We all laughed, as the sensitive and moving moment had passed. The rest of the evening was spent relaxing at the hotel. Dawn and I watched cartoons in my hotel room, with the adjoining door propped open to the other room. We laughed at the antics of the cartoon characters we watched, and we seemed like any other siblings watching television together. The night ended on a good note.

We spent the weekend inside our hotel rooms. The four of us rotated between playing cards, watching cartoons, and reading. Dawn spent a lot of time in my hotel room, which was quiet, with my dad gone. By Sunday night she seemed to be feeling better about testifying.

"It really wasn't as bad as I thought," I reassured her. We laid on our stomachs, on opposite beds and talked about the next day. "You know Mr. England won't let the other lawyers bully you."

Dawn nodded. "I know. I'm still nervous, though," she softly said.

I struggled with the right words to say to her. "You know." I realized something. "We always had to be careful about what we said, or they would get into trouble. Even you."

Dawn squinted at me.

"Yeah," I explained, "Even you couldn't tell anyone about what your dad and my mom did to Alex. But, now you can."

She didn't seem to get it. "So?" she asked.

"So," I opened my eyes bigger, "you can just be honest. You don't have to be nervous, because you don't have to be careful anymore. You can tell them everything that happened. It's like such a relief to be able to do that."

"Really?"

"Yes, really." I turned over in my bed and looked up at the ceiling. "Plus, they are going to get what they deserve. You know that."

I waited through the silence. Waited for Dawn's reply. Just as I was about to turn over and make sure she hadn't slipped out of the room, she answered, "Yeah, you're right." She was finally ready.

Monday was the fifth day of the trial and my second day of testimony. It started with the entire taped recording being played for the jury. I answered a few more questions from the prosecutor, then was cross-examined, then the prosecutor asked a few follow-up questions.

When it was finally over, I felt like I had run a marathon. I was exhausted but felt an incredible amount of accomplishment. I had seen this through and done my part. That was it for me. It was Dawn's turn.

Dawn's testimony went fairly smooth. It did not last as long as mine but covered all the main points that the prosecutor wanted to stress to the jury. During a break in Dawn's testimony, the judge told the attorneys in his chambers that he had received an anonymous letter about one of the jurors. It caused a bit of a problem but was resolved without incident. Dawn finished her testimony, and four other witnesses were called that day. They included Tom's former Commanding Officer, a U.S. Marshal that overheard a conversation between my mom and Tom, and a former cell mate of my mom's. Then, the prosecutor rested his case.
Apparently, this caused a bit of a problem for the Defense Attorneys, who were not ready to present their case yet. My mom's attorney explained to the judge that he did not expect the Commonwealth to rest their case so quickly, and none of his witnesses were ready. The judge was pretty upset with both defense attorneys, and after Tom's attorney did a quick opening statement, dismissed everyone until Wednesday, giving the defense an extra day to gather their witnesses and an extra day for us to hide in our hotel rooms and wait for the trial to end. My uncle was sure to stress to us that the judge was very irritated that my mom and Tom's attorneys were not prepared.

Wednesday morning, I needed to be up at a reasonable time and prepared to return to court, if anything out of the ordinary happened and they wanted me back. This also meant we would need to "hang out" until the trial was over. Although I was hugely relieved not to be testifying anymore, I was disappointed to be stuck in a hotel all day, instead of back with my friends in California.

Dawn and I tried to make the best of it. We played cards, watched TV, drew pictures, and read books. We couldn't flip through the channels on T.V., since coverage of the trial was everywhere and we were told it was better if we did not watch it. We couldn't go out too much, since someone might recognize us and ask too many questions about the trial. So, we were basically confined to the two connecting hotel rooms that were our new domain.

At the end of each day, my uncle would come back to the room and give us a vague, brief summary of who had been called to testify that day and what they said. Since it was just the defense calling its witnesses, it was mostly a few people who claimed to have seen Alex after the day she was reported missing.

Witness after witness gave their version of where they thought they saw Alex: At a park, at Walmart, waving to them in the back of car ... this was supposed to make people think Alex was still out there somewhere and people had seen her. I felt bad for these witnesses, since I was sure they really did think they had seen Alex and were only trying to help. None of these witnesses concerned the prosecutor, since none of what they said could be enough to reconcile what Tom had admitted to me on the recording.

My mother testified and lied about everything, just like we all knew she would. She tried to say I was an angry teenager who just wanted approval from my father and was willing to make up any lies to get that approval. Again, didn't compete with the taped confession.

Then, my grandmother and uncle from Virginia were called to testify. My uncle mentioned they had testified, then abruptly changed the subject to what we would order for dinner.

"Wait," I had to know what they said. "Did Grandma admit I had told her about what they did to Alex?" I thought she would surely tell them, if asked such a question under oath.

Uncle Sokie shook his head, "No, Nyssa." He took a deep breath and sat on the edge of the bed. "That lady said all kinds of bad things about you. You wouldn't believe the dramatic show she put on for the court. It was embarrassing." He shook his head as he spoke, extremely disgusted by what he had witnessed that day.

I fought back tears, "And Uncle Eddie?" I whispered.

My uncle half-laughed and half-sighed, "Oh, 'The Peacock'?" He leaned back on the bed, "His testimony was absolutely useless and only fed the lies of your mom and Tom." He patted me on the back. "Kiddo, trust me. You can't put too much hope or trust in people like them ... even if they are your family. I learned that a long time ago." My uncle stood up and went to browse through the phone book with my aunt, leaving me to absorb and accept what he told me.

After I agreed with them on a dinner, I quietly left their room and returned to my own. Dawn was lying on my bed, watching cartoons. I sat in the corner chair and pretended to read the book my aunt bought me a few days before. While I stared blankly at the pages, I wondered why it shocked me so much that my grandma had not told the truth.

I mean, she told me she thought we should keep the awful circumstances of Alex's death a secret. I knew she wanted to protect them, more specifically my mom. But, all through my life, my grandmother had always been there for me. She had taken my mom and I into her home and cared for us after each of my mom's failed relationships. She financially supported me by paying for a private school, paying for legal fees during the custody battle, and giving me money for school clothes. I had come to see her as one of the few people in this world I could count on when I needed something. It was a hard fact to face that she blatantly lied about me to a judge, jury, and courtroom audience. I didn't think I ever wanted to hear the specifics about what she said. It would be too awful to hear.

After a few minutes, I remembered my feelings from the first night we arrived. The feelings of who was really helping me, and knowing it was not anyone on this Earth. I realized I needed to take a deep breath and suck it up. So what, if my dad was not with me? So what, if my grandma said lies about me? So what? I made it this far with help from a source unseen, and I didn't need anyone on this earth to hold my hand anymore.

My aunt and uncle called us for dinner, and I came into the room smiling. We talked and laughed and ate pizza for the third time that week.

THE TRIAL—COURT TRANSCRIPTS

Prosecutor Jeff England States the Case for the Commonwealth

Ladies and Gentlemen, good afternoon. This is the indictment, as it relates to this case: The Commonwealth of Kentucky against Roxanne Suleski / Thomas Suleski. The Grand Juries of the County of Hardin, the name and by the authority of the Commonwealth of Kentucky charge:

Count 1—That on or about the twenty-sixth day of October 1989, in Hardin County, Kentucky, the above-named defendants, Roxanne Suleski and Thomas Suleski, acting alone or in complicity with each other, committed the offense of murder by intentionally or under circumstances manifesting extreme indifference to human life, wantonly caused the death of Alexandria Christine Suleski. Capital offense.

Count 2—That on or about the twenty-sixth day of October 1989, in Hardin County, Kentucky, the above-named defendants, Roxanne Suleski and Thomas Suleski, acting alone or in complicity with each other, committed the offense of kidnapping when they unlawfully restrained Alexandria Christine Suleski against her will, with the intention to accomplish or advance the commission of a felony, inflict bodily injury, or terrorize her, and she died as a result, thereof. Capital offense.

Count 3—That in or about 1991, in Hardin County, Kentucky, the above-named defendants, Roxanne Suleski and Thomas Suleski, acting alone or in complicity with each other, committed the offense of tampering with physical evidence when, believing that an official preceding may be pending or instituted against them, they destroyed, mutilated, concealed, removed, or altered physical evidence, which they believed was about to be produced or used in such official preceding, with the intent to impair its verity or availability in the official preceding.

Count 4—That between October tenth 1989, through October twenty-sixth 1989, in Hardin County, Kentucky, the above- named defendants, Roxanne Suleski and Thomas Suleski, acting alone or in complicity with each other, committed the offense of criminal abuse in the first degree, by intentionally abusing Alexandria Christine Suleski, a child twelve years of age or less, or by permitting Alexandria Christine Suleski, of whom they had actual custody, to be abused, and thereby she was placed in a situation which caused or may have caused her serious physical injury, torture, cruel confinement, or cruel punishment.

Count 5—That between October twenty-sixth 1989, through 1990, in Hardin County, Kentucky, the above-named defendants, Roxanne Suleski and Thomas Suleski, acting alone or in complicity with each other, committed the offense of second degree unlawful transaction with a minor, by inducing or causing NRB, a minor, to engage in criminal activity which would constitute a felony.

Ladies and Gentlemen, this is the opening statement, and it has been likened much like a road map or a table of contents to a book. It is presented to you for the purpose of allowing you to understand how the evidence is going to fit together. Now, it is going to be my belief of what the evidence will be, as is going to be presented to this trial, and I will present it to you in that fashion.

On October twenty-fifth, 1989, the Suleski family lived at 1255 South Wilson Road, that's Duvall Mobile Home Park, in lot number 39, here in Hardin County, Kentucky. Living in the house, there were two adults by the names of Thomas and Roxanne Suleski. The Suleskis had come from California, and both had been previously married. They also had living in the household on that date, three children, three minor children. The oldest, named Nyssa Bruno.

Nyssa, as the evidence will show, was the daughter of Roxanne Suleski, and Ben Bruno, from a previous marriage. She was twelve years old, and she was enrolled in the seventh grade at Radcliffe Middle School. You will also hear that there were two other children living in the house, by the name of Dawn Suleski and Alex Suleski.

Dawn, at the time, was nine years old. She was enrolled in the fourth grade. Alex was five years old, and she was due to be enrolled in the first grade, however, she had not made it into the first grade, here in Kentucky. These two children were Tom's children from a previous marriage, when he was married to a woman by the name of Young Suleski.

The Suleskis had moved to Kentucky, in the early time in October of 1989. Previously, they had lived in California, where they had some family. Roxanne specifically had some family out there, and Tom Suleski had been living out there. He had been teaching at school by the name of ITT. It was a technical school, and that is where they met. The testimony will be that the family moved to Kentucky due to the fact that Mr. Suleski had recently re-enlisted in the army and was retaking a training course at Fort Knox.

Normally, from the testimony that you will hear, Mr. Suleski would have been required to stay on post during this training period. He would not have been allowed to live off base. But you will hear that he presented to his commanding officers that he was having problems with his family. His wife was pregnant. He had three young children at home. He also told them that his wife was not to be left alone with those two children, unsupervised. That being, Dawn and Alex Suleski.

(Objection by the Defense. Resolved)

After having told this information to his commanding officers, it will be told that Mr. Suleski was allowed to reside in his trailer, at which time he did. He resided at that trailer in Duvall Mobile Home Park. You will hear testimony from Nyssa Bruno, of Roxanne Suleski, and she will testify to you that during that time period, Roxanne was having a lot of trouble with Dawn and Alex.

Specifically, she was very aggressive, very—I believe the word will be used—she [was] abusive to them. She will testify that during this time period, that – and most of the testimony here will be directed toward Alex—that Roxanne was very, very [abusive] with Alex. She would punish her quite regularly. You will hear testimony that this punishment exceeded normal punishment, what you would expect. The testimony will be that Alex was in trouble for everything.

(Objection by the Defense. Resolved)

When they were in Radcliffe, testimony will be offered to you that Alex didn't really go outside and play. She stayed in the trailer. Alex Suleski was scheduled to be enrolled in school, in the first grade. Testimony will be, however, that although the other two children went, Alex did not go. Alex had not been in school, yet. That she was being held out for problems. In fact, you'll hear testimony that when the child was taken to school to be enrolled, Mrs. Suleski requested that an extra strict teacher be given to Alex Suleski. During this time period...

(Objection by the Defense. Resolved)

... you will be told that during this time period, Alex had a problem. Alex is a five-year-old, and Alex had a problem. A bladder control problem. She would wet on herself, and that infuriated Roxanne. That she could not understand the problem.

The punishment? You will hear of an incident, in which Alex was required to stand in a cardboard box that was lined with a plastic bag, with her hands outstretched—and stand there, and stay there, while she watched the family eat dinner.

(Objection by the Defense. Resolved)

You will hear testimony that she was regularly required to stand with her hands outstretched. To just stand there as punishment.

The sleeping arrangements in the mobile home that were made—it was a two bedroom—Tom and Roxanne slept in one bedroom. Nyssa, the oldest, and Dawn slept in the other bedroom. Alex would sleep on the floor, in the bedroom of Tom and Roxanne.

Alex was told, while she was standing there, being yelled at about her problem of wetting herself, and while she was being lectured on it, you will hear that she did have an accident, and that this infuriated Roxanne.

You will hear testimony that Tom was aware of these disciplining procedures. You will hear that he came home every night. That he would observe that this was going on, that he received regular reports on what happened. In particular, one afternoon, late afternoon – it was after school, apparently—Alex was sick. She threw up in the hallway, at which time she was taken into the bathroom. Roxanne [was] angry, and Alex's head was shoved into the toilet. That she hit her head, that she was held in the toilet.

On October twenty-fifth of 1989, at the residence there at Duvall Mobile Home Park, the testimony will be that Roxanne got so upset that she put Alex into a black trash bag. That when she had been putting her in there, the bag was sealed up over the head of Alex, and that she was required to stand in the bedroom of Tom and Roxanne in the black plastic bag.

Later, Nyssa was in that bedroom, and she was talking with her mother, Roxanne. The testimony will be that during that conversation, Roxanne started wondering about a particular smell that she noticed, at which time she went over to the bag and opened it up. Apparently, Alex had also defecated in the bag. Roxanne couldn't stand that smell and so she put her back in that bag and sealed that bag up, and to make sure that smell didn't emanate any further, she put her in another plastic bag.

You'll hear testimony that though she didn't pick her up when she did it, she had her lay down and she rolled her into the other bag, and left her in that bedroom. You will hear testimony that Alex was heard gasping for breath in that bag that smelled so bad.

Nyssa will testify that she didn't see Alex that morning, the following morning on the twenty-sixth, and she didn't really have any contact and doesn't remember anything until later that afternoon, after she got home from school. At which time, she will state that Roxanne came out to her and stated that she needed to call her husband, because Alex wasn't breathing. You will hear testimony from officers at Fort Knox who were present, who talked to Tom Suleski.

They will state that Mr. Suleski indicated that he received a call from his wife that his child had fallen in the bathtub and was having problems with that. Tom Suleski came home from work. When he arrived, Nyssa Bruno was there. Dawn, who was also home, was outside playing. She wasn't around and didn't know what was going on.

The testimony will be that when he came in, they went back to the bedroom. Nyssa did not go back with them to the bedroom, but she will testify that she heard them taking something into the bathroom—the water came on, in the shower. Tom went outside, and he got, what she will describe to you, as a vacuum cleaner box, about the size of a—that a vacuum cleaner is bought in. That she could tell when it was brought in, that it was empty by the way it was being carried. But when it was being taken out, it wasn't the same. It had something in it.

She will tell you that her mother came out and talked to her and told her they would have to say that Alex was missing, that if they didn't, they'd break up the family, that the kids would be put in foster homes. Tom was there during this conversation— break up the family.

The Suleskis, as they were driving out, saw Dawn out playing and told Dawn that Alex was missing and to go search, and Dawn started looking. Apparently, she talked to some of the neighbors, who also began searching. Stan Heslip, who was with the Radcliffe Police Department at the time, was on patrol, and he came into contact with an individual who was apparently looking for the young child, Alex Suleski, the five- year-old.

Officer Heslip will testify that because of the allegation that there was a missing child, he began to investigate. He started looking around, became concerned. They tried to find out where the child lived. And they—Mr. Heslip and Lieutenant Bailey—will testify to you that they had to locate where this residence was located. No report was ever made that the child was missing.

Testimony will be, after they did make contact with the Suleskis, that they said, 'Yes,' the child was missing. At which time, a massive search was undertaken. You will hear testimony that troops from Fort Knox were called in. Civilians from Radcliffe all walked the neighborhoods. They looked everywhere. They looked in sinkholes; they brought in K-9 units, hoping to follow a scent—nothing.

The testimony will be that as this case progressed, the Radcliffe Police Department began exhausting all the possibilities that they thought were available to them—that they needed help, at which time they called the F.B.I and asked, 'Can you help?' Agent Phil Lewzader was the resident agent at the Elizabethtown office of the F.B.I. At which time, he agreed that they would assist.

He will testify that they began looking at the case, began investigating the case, and you'll have to know that during this whole time period, everything was being done assuming that the child was actually lost, actually had wandered off. The testimony will be that actions were continued, trying to find the child, trying to find this reported missing child. You'll hear testimony that flyers were put out. That pleas were made for this child to be returned. You'll hear testimony that there were reported sightings of Alex from all over. Everyone was trying to help. You'll hear testimony of the investigation into these sightings. What was done in order to try to confirm or do whatever they could to find the child, but it was to no avail. You'll hear testimony that the focus really began to change from the investigation, that they were looking more at Tom and Roxanne, based on their experience.

Finally, one day, you will hear that Nyssa Bruno called and talked to the F.B.I., that she talked to Phil Lewzader from the F.B.I., and related the facts regarding this event. She further related that her mother had told her, that after they left, they took the remains of Alex to Otter Creek Park. She also further related that, in talking to her daughter, Nyssa, that she was always fearful as long as she knew those remains at Otter Creek Park. She was always fearful of being caught, and that she wouldn't feel safe, until they were moved.

(Objection by Defense. Resolved)

Roxanne told Nyssa that they were going to go to Otter Creek Park and remove the remains from the park. Based on the conversation that Agent Lewzader had with Nyssa Bruno, they decided that they wanted to get some additional information, and Nyssa talked with her [step] father, Tom— the conversation that was recorded— regarding this. And during that conversation, which you will be able to hear, you will also hear Tom admit that the remains were at Otter Creek Park. That they went there, and they got them. That they took those remains, that they crushed them into little pieces, that they were removed.

You will also hear from Dawn, who will be telling you about the abuse that was occurring in this case, who will be telling you about the problems that they were having in Radcliffe, about the way that Alex was being disciplined and punished. She will tell you how Alex felt during that time period.

Ladies and Gentlemen, that's the evidence, as the Commonwealth believes it to be presented in this case. Thank you.

Defense Attorneys Opening Statements

Ladies and gentlemen of the jury, you are going to hear evidence in this case of some terrible tragedies. You'll hear evidence first of a tragedy of a young girl wandering away from her home in Radcliffe, from the Duvall Mobile Home park. To this day, she hasn't been found. You will hear the story of a tragedy of Mr. and Mrs. Suleski being accused of murder. You are going to hear of the tragedy of a police investigation that all-too-soon changed its focus from looking for a missing little girl to trying to find some way to charge Mr. and Mrs. Suleski of a crime. Finally, you're going to hear evidence of a tragedy of a teenage girl turning on her mother and making horrific allegations that are not true.

October twenty-sixth, 1989. Alex Suleski went out to play. Mrs. Suleski was sitting in her home at the trailer park, and she was writing a letter. She saw Alex, a little bit playing and kept on writing the letter. The evidence is going to show that Dawn Suleski, Tom's older daughter, came home, did some homework, went out to play.

Nyssa Bruno, who, as you have heard, is Roxanne Suleski's daughter, came home, did some homework and [began] to cook dinner. At that point in time, Mrs. Suleski realized that Alex—[she] had not seen her in a while. She went outside to look, as best she could at the time.

She was eight months pregnant. She had been in premature labor before they moved from California, and she was on medication and was able to get around very well. So, she came back in, asked Nyssa to go outside and look, and then called her husband. Now, Alex had wandered off on other occasions, and they had always been able to find her at a neighbor's house or at a friend's house playing.

So, she called her husband and told him that one of his daughters was sick, thinking that, that would get the most immediate [attention] for Mr. Suleski, and that he would come home. Which he did, found out that Alex was missing, and they immediately went out in their van and started driving the roads, looking for young children.

Now, Dawn was also missing, at the time. She had gone to play at a friend's house, without telling Mrs. Suleski. They found her and told her to go look for Alex, and her and some friends took their bikes around the mobile home park and didn't find anything, and went home, where they waited for their parents and Alex to come back. Their parents came back on several occasions to check to see if Alex had shown up. She had not.

The police arrived around eight o'clock. They had been notified by one of the many neighbors that were out searching for Alex Suleski. There were many sightings of Alex, many credible sightings. Alex was seen in an adjacent mobile home park by a lady on the afternoon of October twenty-sixth, 1989—had some French fries, played with her children, and then wandered off through a hole in the fence. This individual was interviewed by Detective Georgette Kruslik, who was the lead investigator on this case, and gave Detective Kruslik information that she did not even have, at that point in time. Gave an exact description of Alex Suleski and the way she was dressed. Detective had to go back, ask the Suleskis how she was dressed, and they gave the exact description.

You're going to hear of many other leads that the Radcliffe Police Department got. Some of them, they ignored. Some of them, they reacted to slowly. Some of them, they made a cursory investigation of. But, on almost every single one of these leads that could have led to finding this little girl, they didn't do what they needed to do.

Mr. Suleski's ex-wife, Young Suleski, is a Korean National. There was some indication to the police that Young Suleski may have kidnapped Alex, taken her away because she was interested in having Alex live with her. Didn't want Dawn, you will hear, but wanted Alex. She had connections in Georgia, and these leads were not followed up on. Cursory phone calls were made, but no investigation was made, there was no attempt to get local authorities to check those out.

After a short period of time, [the] police department changed their focus. Instead of looking for the little girl, as they should have done, they were trying to charge Mr. and Mrs. Suleski, to put them away. Now, during this time, numerous statements were taken, not only by the F.B.I., Radcliffe Police Department—which Nyssa Bruno stated that Alex wandered off. No mention of this story that we've heard today, in Mr. England's opening statement to you.

He also gave—[Nyssa] was keeping a diary at the time, keeping a calendar, in her private papers, in which she indicated that Alex was missing, she wandered off, she was still missing, she was losing hope. She didn't know if she was ever going to see her again. These writings were made at the time all this was going on. The statements were made within days after Alex was missing. These statements were made when Nyssa and Dawn were at school. The parents weren't around. It was just the little girl and the police officer.

But they kept talking to Nyssa, and eventually, she did change her story and came up with what you'll be hearing. This is at a time when she's seventeen years old; she was twelve at the time her stepsister disappeared. She's gone through many problems with her family. Her parents are divorced; there was a custody battle in which custody was given to Mrs. Suleski. Ben Bruno, Nyssa Bruno's father, was not awarded custody. The evidence will show that he had alcohol and drug problems, that he went through rehabilitation.

Up to that point in time, he had shown very little interest in his daughter and that was something that Nyssa deeply wanted. Love and affection from her father. After the rehabilitation, things began going better with Nyssa's father, and she began living with them on occasion. Nyssa's stepmother was also—Mr. Bruno's remarried, married a lady by the name, I believe Jay DeShear, now Jay Bruno—and there had been some problems between Jay Bruno and Nyssa.

She had also gone through rehabilitation and apparently these problems were worked out. We'll hear that these statements, at the time they were changed, were made at a vulnerable time in Nyssa's life, when she was trying desperately to get the love of her father back.

Now, ladies and gentlemen, it will be your job to assess the credibility of each one of these witnesses, in determining who's telling the truth. We hope after you've heard all the evidence in this case, we know that you will come up with a just decision in this case. I thank you very much for your attention.

Excerpts from the Testimony of Stanley Heslip

England: Mr. Heslip, in October of 1989, who were you employed by?

Heslip: Radcliff Police Department.

England: What were your duties with the police department?

Heslip: I was a police officer and dispatcher.

England: Specifically, on October twenty-sixth of 1989—Were you working on that occasion?

Heslip: Yes, sir. I was. I was on patrol.

England: Do you remember an incident relating to an alleged missing child that happened on that date?

Heslip: Yes, sir. I remember.

England: Could you give us what you remember about that particular incident?

Heslip: I was on patrol in the south part of Radcliff, and a person that I know through the ball parks flagged me down.

England: You talked to this particular individual? And what did you do after you talked to him?

Heslip: As a result of the conversation with the citizen, I called Officer Bailey, who was the Patrol Sergeant at that time, and asked him if he had any knowledge of a missing child in the city. He told me that he did not.

England: Tell us what you did next.

Heslip: I contacted the dispatch to see if dispatch had any knowledge of a missing child in the city.

England: And after you contacted dispatch, what was the next thing that you did?

Heslip: We—when I say 'we', I mean the police department— started a preliminary search for a description of a vehicle with a White male and a White female—a description that had been given to me by the citizen. We also began searching for a small Asian female, a description also given to me by the citizen.

England: What was the description of the female that you were looking for?

Heslip: Approximately five years in age, Asian female, short black hair, approximately two to two and half feet tall, and that answered to the name of 'Alex.'

England: Was the clothing described to you?

Heslip: At that point in time, I don't believe I had a clothing description.

England: You were given these descriptions, and you began looking for the small child. Tell us what you did. Specifically, where did you go and what did you do?

Heslip: In addition to myself, I don't remember the exact number of patrol officers, but we tried to cover the entire south part of the city. Other information that we received, was a possible home address in Duvall Mobile Home. Also, a phone number had been given.

England: What did you do with that information? **Heslip:** I had the dispatcher call that number. **England:** Did you go to that address?

Heslip: Sergeant Bailey did.

England: Did you ultimately go to that address?

Heslip: Yes, sir. I did.

England: When was that?

Heslip: It was after eight o'clock when I personally went to the residence. That's when contact had been made with the Suleskis.

England: When was it that you received the initial report?

Heslip: The initial information about a missing person came to me at about seven o'clock.

England: When you went to the address, what did you observe?

Heslip: The description of the vehicle that we had been looking for was sitting in the driveway. Sergeant Bailey was already there.

England: Can you describe for us who else was at the scene?

Heslip: As I went to the trailer, the Suleskis, Roxanne and Tom, were in the trailer. Also, a small oriental child, about eight or nine years old—identified to me as 'Dawn.' I spoke with her and the Suleskis.

England: Anybody else that you remember at that scene?

Heslip: That I personally talked to right then? No.

England: Now, you said you saw two people identified as the Suleskis. What were their names? Their full names?

Heslip: Roxanne and Tom. I don't remember full names, sir.

England: Are they in the courtroom?

Heslip: Yes, sir. They are.

England: Can you identify them for us, please?

Heslip: Roxanne is the lady that is seated at the end of the table that I just pointed at, with the red hair. Tom is the gentlemen with the glasses and the beard, at the opposite end of the table.

England: Did you talk to them about the report that you received about a young girl missing?

Heslip: Yes, sir. We did. Sergeant Bailey and myself both talked to them.

England: What did they say to you about what was going on?

Heslip: Basically, they told us that the child had wandered off, and Roxanne had said something to the effect of—that she had called, and had Tom come home from Fort Knox to assist her in looking for the child, and that they had left to go look for the child, and my question was, 'Why did you not call the police so that we could assist you?' To the best that I can remember, part of the story or answer was—the child had wandered off in prior times in California, and the police would not ever help them search for the child.

England: How were they acting?

Heslip: To be very honest with you, I didn't think that either one of them was as concerned as I would have been, had it been my child.

(Objection by Schaffer. Sustained by Judge.)

Judge: The jury will disregard that.

England: Just tell us how they were acting.

Heslip: They were fairly calm, sir.

England: Did they seem to be excited or upset?

Heslip: No, sir. They didn't seem excited or upset to me.

England: Did they tell you what time Alex had wandered off?

Heslip: Two o'clock was a time given to me, the best that I recollect. That was the last time that Alex had been seen, by Roxanne.

England: What time was it that you were talking to them?

Heslip: This was after eight o'clock, sir. In the evening.

England: Did they further identify the child for you or provide you with any photographs or anything of that nature?

Heslip: We asked for photographs and immediately [they] couldn't find one. The best I remember, they had just moved here, and a lot of things were still packed up. I know it was sometime the next day when, we were finally provided a picture.

England: How long were you at that particular location?

Heslip: I was at the trailer for a few minutes to start with. I was concerned that the child may be in the area. Having made contact with the family, I asked Dawn, the sister, who was at the trailer, to go with me—outside, in the area, and show me any places that the children had played. Dawn went with me, and we did that. She and I made a search, and we walked the area of the trailer park.

England: Did you return to the trailer?

Heslip: Yes, sir.

England: And how long did you stay at the trailer, this time?

Heslip: I can't really give you a time frame of how long we were there. But, if I remember, Sergeant Bailey had called the dispatch office and had talked with supervisors. They were preparing to start a search for the child. There were a lot of things going on at that time.

England: Okay, what's the next thing that you remember you did?

Heslip: In conversations with Tom Suleski, we were concerned that with his wife living in California that maybe she had come here to pick the child up. Anything is possible, when you have a missing child, and we wanted to cover as many bases as we could. He provided a phone number, and I used the phone, there in the bedroom to try and contact his ex-wife in California. I received no answer. I later continued calls to that phone number, and also enlisted the help of the Los Angeles Police Department, in personally making a visit to that home, to talk to that mother.

England: What else did you do, that evening?

Heslip: We searched the city a lot, sir.

England: Okay, and were you personally involved with that?

Heslip: As a Patrol Officer, yes, I was.

England: Did you do any further action relating to this complaint of a missing child?

Heslip: We turned the complaint over later that evening or approximately the early morning hours the next morning to the detective section. I personally did not have any more investigative work into the case. As my duty as a Dispatcher, from time to time, we had calls that came in on sightings and things like that, that we made records of, that went to the detective section for follow-up information.

England: Do you have any idea of how many of those you would have gotten?

Heslip: Personally, sir, I believe I got four or five. But I would have to go back to the records to tell you exactly.

England: No further questions.

Cross-Examination by Roxanne Suleski's Attorney

Schaffer: Is it your testimony that they couldn't locate a picture that night because their belongings were...?

Heslip: They had told us that they had just moved here from California, recently. They still had things packed up and hadn't unpacked. That's what I remember, sir.

Schaffer: I'm going to show you a document. Can you identify that particular document?

Heslip: Yes, sir. This is a copy of a Kentucky Missing Person Report.

Schaffer: And, on what date was that filled out?

Heslip: On the twenty-sixth of October 1989, sir. Schaffer: And who is the missing person report on? Heslip: It's on Alexandria Christine Suleski.

Schaffer: And does your signature appear on that report?

Heslip: Yes, sir. It does.

Schaffer: I'd like to have this document introduced as Defense Exhibit 1.

Schaffer: Thank you very much. That's all the questions I have.

Excerpts from the Testimony of Lt. Steve Bailey

England: Who are you employed by?

Bailey: The City of Radcliff, more specifically, the Radcliff Police Department.

England: What are your duties with the police department?

Bailey: I am a Lieutenant in charge of Patrol Division of the 06 to 1400 shift.

England: In October of 1989, what were your duties?

Bailey: At that time, I was a Sergeant. My duties were basically the same. Only, I was in charge, at that time of the —we call it the 1800 to 04 shift.

England: More specifically, on October twenty-sixth of 1989. Were you working on that night?

Bailey: Yes, sir. I was.

England: Did you receive or get information regarding a missing child on that evening?

Bailey: Yes, I did.

England: When was the first time you became involved in that particular investigation?

Bailey: Shortly after seven p.m., I was notified by the police radio, by Officer Stan Heslip. He inquired from me if I knew anything about a missing child. At that time, I told him I had no knowledge or information at all. According to Officer Heslip, he had observed several people in the South Woodland/Wilma Avenue area, which is adjacent to North Hardin High School, that were going door to door on a search, allegedly for five-year-old missing girl. Officer Heslip provided me with a name of a local resident, who had provided him with a telephone number. I then proceeded to take that phone number and have my dispatcher through the radio, call that number.

At the time, we got an answer. The caller, being identified as being a resident of lot 39, Duvall Mobile Home Park. That's where I proceeded then, to Duvall Mobile Home Park.

England: Tell us what you saw and what you observed, as you went to that residence.

Bailey: I arrived there at about eighteen minutes past seven that evening. I was met at the door by a young juvenile, I would guess to be approximately eleven to twelve years of age. At that time, I asked the young lady, if there was a family member that was missing.

England: After making contact with her, what did you do?

Bailey: At that particular point, she confirmed that her sister —who she identified as 'Alex,' was missing. And, that her parents were presently out in the neighborhood, looking for the child. I proceeded to give her my name, my telephone number, and told her that the minute the parents came home, to immediately call the police department, so we could conduct an investigation.

England: What did you do next?

Bailey: I notified my immediate supervisor, who at the time was Don Harris. I informed him of the possibility of a missing juvenile. At that particular time, my main concern was over the hours of daylight versus darkness. If we had a missing juvenile, and it was getting, at that time, almost dusk, I was concerned that our chances and probability of having a successful search depended on the hours of daylight. I immediately notified him, and his instructions to me, were that once we could confirm and establish the fact, through the parents, that the child was indeed missing, to re-notify him, and we would immediately call people in and enact the manpower to help us in the search.

England: Then, what did you do?

Bailey: At about five minutes after eight, I had yet to hear from the family. So, I proceeded to go back to lot 39, Duvall. There was a van in front of me, and the van proceeded to pull into the driveway of lot 39. I later learned that it was Mr. and Mrs. Suleski that were returning home.

England: Did you go directly to the residence at that time?

Bailey: Yes, I did. A conversation was initiated with Mr. Suleski. He confirmed that their five-year-old daughter, Alex, was missing, and that he and his wife had been out in the neighborhood looking. I proceeded to inquire as to why—you know, my first reaction is 'Why didn't you notify the police?' We were looking at the hours of darkness. You know, I was just curious as to why they did not notify police. His response to that was that in the other areas where they lived, Alex had run away two to three times, and she would always return home about dark, and that the police would not help them in those searches. Immediately after talking with him and in confirming that we did have a missing child, I notified Officer Stan Heslip, who in turn, I had initiate the report, and I immediately proceeded again to notify my supervising commander, Lieutenant Harris, at the time, who then called out the manpower search.

England: What did you personally do, involving this missing person case, after that?

Bailey: Later that evening, after my shift was over, we had called a canine unit in, which was a bloodhound from Jefferson County, and one of their units was down. Being unfamiliar with Radcliff, I was assigned to assist him in possibly looking for the child. We proceeded to the residence, and at that time, through our conversations with the Suleskis—the officer that was there wanted some kind of clothing that would have a scent, that perhaps only the child had touched. Mrs. Suleski then directed me back into the hallway, where there was a blanket that was folded in the hallway. She stated at that time, that the child slept on the blanket the night before, and my concern was—well, who folded up the blanket? She informed me that the child, herself, had folded up the blanket. The officer thought that perhaps that blanket could have been touched by someone else, and he was looking more in the way of personal clothing. So, I directed that question to Mrs. Suleski. I was directed out to the van. When they went into the van, and they pulled out, what I would describe as the largest Zip-loc bag I have ever seen in my life. Inside of it, it had personal clothing. Like under clothing, maybe a little gown, and I inquired—who's clothing is this? And she informed me that it was Alex's. It had not been touched by anyone else. This was one of the things I thought was very strange, because that clothing was completely separated from any other family clothing, and it was in the bag. We then took that clothing and through utilizing it, we began to start the dog on the search. Basically, the search lasted a couple hours. After that, it pretty much concluded my portion of involvement with the Suleskis.

England: Can you visually identify the individuals that you talked to?

Bailey: Yes, I can.

England: Are they in the courtroom?

Bailey: They are sitting at both ends of this table right here. Mr. and Mrs. Suleski.

England: No further questions.

Cross-Examination by Roxanne Suleski's Attorney

Schaffer: You were told that Alex had run away in the past?

Bailey: Yes. Two to three times. That's what I was told.

Schaffer: Did you notice the condition of Roxanne that evening? Was she pregnant?

Bailey: She had a rather large stomach. I assumed she was pregnant, yes.

Schaffer: Okay. How was she getting around? Were you able to notice that?

Bailey: She seemed fine. The only thing that I did note was— very little emotion.

Schaffer: I ask that be stricken as unresponsive, Your Honor.

(Brief sidebar)

Schaffer: Now, was this clean clothing that was in the Zip-loc bag?

Bailey: No, Sir. It was clothing that she had allegedly worn, because that was the question—if it had any scent of the child, Alex. She assured me that the child had worn this clothing.

Schaffer: Now, this bloodhound. Did you go with the officer from Jefferson?

Bailey: I was with him. I did not. He was doing his thing with the dog, and I basically held back. I was just there to assist him, as far as his efforts to find the mobile home park and for me to make initial contact with the family, because I had previous contact with the family, and so forth. So, I was only with him a small portion of the time that he was actually conducting his search.

Schaffer: Okay, thank you, Officer.

Excerpts from the Testimony of Detective Jack Gruber

England: In October of 1989, who were you employed by?

Gruber: Radcliff Police Department.

England: Are you presently employed by them?

Gruber: I'm retired.

England: When did you retire?

Gruber: Last Sunday.

(Laughter in the courtroom)

England: After how many years?

Gruber: Twenty-nine.

England: When you retired, what were your duties?

Gruber: I was a Lieutenant. I transferred from Detective Section to Patrol and later to Training and Evidence.

England: In October of 1989, what were your duties, then?

Gruber: I was the Detective Section Supervisor, with a rank of Sergeant.

England: And how long had you been the Supervisor of the Detective Section?

Gruber: About four years.

England: How long have you been in the Detective Section?

Gruber: I was in the Detective Section a total of about nine years.

England: At that time?

Gruber: No, not at that time.

England: In October, more specifically, in late October or about October twenty-sixth, did you become involved in an investigation into an alleged missing child, by the name of Alex?

Gruber: Yes, I did.

England: Tell us how you became involved in that.

Gruber: The original report being taken by the Patrol Division of the police department was later turned over, after a period of time to the Detective Section, because Patrol Officers do not have time to work the leads, and so on and so forth. I became involved on that particular evening. I was notified by then Chief of Police, Roger Fahver, and I directed and conducted searches according to his wishes, as he directed us to do.

England: About what time was it when you were contacted? Do you remember?

Gruber: Somewhere in the neighborhood of about 8:30 or 8:45.

England: And what did you personally do at that time?

Gruber: I went out. I was called to the station, and Chief Fahver met with me and told me what was going on, and so on and so forth, and we proceeded together to do some searching of the area. I had different individuals and different officers assigned to go to all the trailers in Duvall Mobile Home Park , and in the course of the starting of the missing person, and several days thereafter, we conducted all types of different kinds of searches.

England: Who all became involved in these searches?

Gruber: There were several agencies involved. My agency, of course, Radcliff Police Department; we had Military Police from Fort Knox; we had gotten some of Jefferson County Police, with their equipment and so on and so forth, and basically the entire community. A lot of volunteers.

England: Were there a lot of people searching on that night of October twenty-sixth of 1989?

Gruber: Yes, there were several people searching, and there was a lot of people searches those next few days afterwards, also.

England: On that night, would you have any idea at how many people were involved in the search?

Gruber: Not right off hand, Mr. England. I couldn't tell you. There was a lot of people, but I didn't get an opportunity to count them.

England: Did you look around the area or go talk to anybody else?

Gruber: Basically, I didn't talk to a whole lot of people. I designated those responsibilities to other people and broke down some of those teams. I did do some searching with Chief Fahver at a particular sinkhole, which was located across from Duvall Mobile Home Park on South Wilson Road. That lasted way into the night. The reason I remember that so well is because a lot of people in the community had brought coffee and fried chicken and everything to all the searchers, and that was sort of a meeting place.

England: Did you talk to either Thomas or Roxanne Suleski that evening?

Gruber: Myself and Chief Fahver talked with Thomas Suleski, in Chief Fahver's office, that evening. If I recall correctly, Mrs. Suleski also came up that evening. She came in after we talked to Tom.

England: What was your conversation with Mr. Suleski about?

Gruber: Basically, about Alex and her habits, and if he had any idea where she would be or if there were any marks scars or tattoos that were on her that were identifiable. Just things of that general nature.

England: What was his demeanor like?

Gruber: He was calm. He talked to us sensibly.

England: What was the geographical area that you were looking at for the search?

Gruber: We conducted searches, of course, within Duvall Mobile Home Park.

England: How big is the mobile home park?

Gruber: Duvall Mobile Home Park consists of about ninety trailers. It's divided into the older section, and then there's a new section, which would be south, but it's all connected. You have two different roadways to get in and two different sides to the mobile home park. That mobile home park, of course, and all of Masdon Mobile Home Park, which is adjacent to Duvall Mobile Home Park, located in a southerly direction. The subdivision located directly behind Duvall Ball Park, which is directly connected to Duvall Mobile Home Park. The only thing separating that is a chain link fence. Areas were searched across the street, around Radcliff Middle School, which backs up to Radcliff Concrete, where the sinkhole was. Those are specific areas that I do know that night, were searched.

England: Did the search area expand at any time?

Gruber: Yes, it did. We broke down officers in teams, to do a door-to-door canvas in a half- mile radius of Duvall Mobile Home Park. Those Officers took notebooks with them and talked to people at various residences, and put their names down and their phone numbers, if they had seen anything.

England: Did any outside agencies assist you in this search?

Gruber: Yes, we had Fort Knox. I don't know if they were there that night. I believe they were. If I'm not mistaken, we had a heat-seeking helicopter out of Jefferson County, which did a lot of work down at the south end of town, because there is a lot of wooded area on that side of Blackjack Road.

England: What would you say was the size of the area that was being searched?

Gruber: Well, that particular night, I would say probably a good two to three-mile radius from Duvall Mobile Home Park. The days following that, there were searches that were extended beyond that.

England: How long did you work that night?

Gruber: All night.

England: After that night?

Gruber: The search continued for the next two or three days after that, because Fort Knox had provided us with military personnel in large groups to actually walk fields and roadways and things abreast of each other, looking on the ground, underneath things, and so on and so forth. That continued for two or three days after the disappearance.

England: After that time period, after those days that you continued those searches, did you have any further contact with Tom or Roxanne Suleski at that time?

Gruber: I don't recall having any contact with Tom Suleski. I did talk to Roxanne one time, on the telephone. She called me on Halloween evening, and I was at the police department, in my office. It was around five o'clock in the evening. I believe, at that time, Tom was with Detective Kirby, and she was wanting to know when Tom was going to be home. At that point in time, I didn't know. I couldn't tell her anything. I did advise her, though, that I would call and find out when Tom would be home.

England: What was her response?

Gruber: She said, 'Thank you. I wish you would find out for me, because I do have other children that I need to take trick or treating.'

England: At this point, you would say that the searches had about ended?

Gruber: Well, we didn't have any results from the searches. The case was ultimately turned over to the Detective Section. Basically, what we did was try to follow up those leads that we could follow up on, that had enough information, where we could do something with them. I don't recall all the leads and all the names that we did get, in that period of time. Of course, as time went by, leads began to come in fewer and fewer.

England: You said 'leads'. What are you talking about when you say 'leads'?

Gruber: We're talking about people calling in and saying they saw Alex in a car in Louisville. That's the type of lead we would get. Of course, there's no way you can follow a lead like that, unless you get a license plate number or something of that nature – which we did get some, and we followed those up.

England: Were there leads you were able to follow up on?

Gruber: Yes.

England: During that time period, what kind of hours were you putting into this particular case?

Gruber: I don't even remember how many hours we put in.

England: Was it in excess of your normal work hours?

Gruber: Yes. Absolutely.

England: How long would you say that your section continued to investigate this matter?

Gruber: This case has been open since 1989. It's never been closed.

England: After that initial search period, did you ever enlist any other agencies to assist you?

Gruber: Federal Bureau of Investigation. Military Police at Fort Knox. Jefferson County Police. Any other agency that might have come in contact with following up a lead. Out-of- state agencies that we used to follow up on leads from out of state.

England: So, no matter where you got a lead from, that you would follow up on it?

Gruber: If we had enough information. If we got a license plate number or something of that nature, we would get a hold of the agencies within that jurisdiction and have them go to houses and check people and talk to people, and so on and so forth.

England: That's all the questions I have for this witness.

Cross-Examination by Roxanne Suleski's Attorney

Schaffer: Did you send information to the National Center for Missing and Exploited Children, in reference to this case?

Gruber: Alexandria Suleski was entered into the National NCIC Computer on the evening of her disappearance.

Schaffer: Was this kidnapping case on Alex Suleski, was it ever placed on an inactive or dormant stage?

Gruber: This case we're working now—that we're here on now?

Schaffer: Yes.

Gruber: No, it's never been closed.

Schaffer: Do you consider yourself to have a hard time examining the details of a case, on occasion?

Gruber: I don't know what you mean.

Schaffer: Have you ever overlooked details in a case?

Gruber: Absolutely.

Schaffer: As a matter of fact, that is one of the problems that you had in the police department, back in 1984. Is that correct?

Gruber: You'll have to refresh my memory.

Schaffer: I'm going to show you a document and have you take a look at it. I ask if you recognize that document.

Gruber: Yes, I recognize this document. It's an evaluation report from August the second, 1984.

Schaffer: And does it not state on the last page, that 'Detective Gruber needs to slow down, so as not to overlook details that may aid in solving a case'?

Gruber: The writing on the back of this page—'As the supervisor of this officer...'

Schaffer: I'm asking you if you can read...

Judge: He can read the whole statement, if he wants.

Gruber: 'As the supervisor of this officer, describe his or her attitude towards work and co-workers. Jack's attitude is very positive. He likes his position as Detective, because of the challenge it offers. Occasionally, like most of us, he gets down when things are not going his way, but it is short-lived and he rebounds well. Basically, there are no performance problems. He complies well, both with procedure—I can't read that word—he is hasty on some investigations, but this is due to the fact of having so many cases stacked up. It's Jack nature to be in high gear, perhaps he should slow down to ensure that he is getting complete attention and not overlook some details that may aid in solving a case. Jack is a cop's cop. He knows his business and does it well. He has a tendency to be sarcastic at times, but that's the nature of the beast. He's a damn good cop."

(Hushed laughter)

Schaffer: Thank you.

Gruber: You're welcome.

Schaffer: Did you overlook any details in this case?

Gruber: I may have.

Schaffer: Thank you, sir.

Gruber: You're welcome.

Excerpts from the Testimony of Detective Tony Kirby

England: Who are you employed by?

Kirby: The City of Radcliff. The Police Department.

England: What are your duties with the police department?

Kirby: I am Patrol Supervisor.

England: Your rank is Sergeant?

Kirby: That's correct.

England: How long have you been in that capacity?

Kirby: About three years.

England: In October of 1989—were you still then employed by the Radcliff Police Department?

Kirby: That's correct. I was in the Detective Section, at that time.

England: How long have you been with the police department, now?

Kirby: Almost fifteen years.

England: What were your duties at that time?

Kirby: Investigate cases.

England: Did you become familiar with a report of a missing child on October twenty-sixth of 1989?

Kirby: Yes.

England: Tell us what your contact with that was and how you became aware of it.

Kirby: We were notified of the missing person, and it was called to practically everyone in the police department and community, to search for Alex. I was assigned specific duties to take people to different places and to search different places.

England: Where did you come from?

Kirby: I believe I was at home at the time. I got a call from the dispatcher.

England: Your normal duty hours are what?

Kirby: Nine to five, at that time.

England: You received a call and you came out. Where did you go to?

Kirby: I don't remember if I went to the Detective Section first, or straight to the scene. I probably came to Post first, to pick up equipment—radios and stuff—and then went to Duvall's Mobile Home Park.

England: When you went to Duvall Mobile Home Park, what did you observe?

Kirby: There were a lot of people there. Just being assigned duties, not anything in particular.

England: What duties were you assigned to that evening?

Kirby: I believe I was given the duties to go and search under the trailers and just canvas the neighborhood and look for the child. Find any witnesses that could be rounded up. That type of thing.

England: And is that what you did?

Kirby: Yes.

England: Did you talk to Tom or Roxanne Suleski that evening?

Kirby: Nothing that I made note of. I don't remember talking to them. I didn't do an interview or anything like that. I may have spoken to them, in general. I remember that they were there.

England: How long were you involved in that search that evening?

Kirby: I don't remember the time we ceased, but it was late in the evening.

England: Did it carry over into the next day?

Kirby: Oh, yes. From that point on, there was always something to do. The next day, we organized again.

England: What did you do the next day?

Kirby: I don't remember specifically what we searched.

England: What was your procedure in the days following that?

Kirby: We took a map down—when I say 'we', I mean the Detective Section—and we lined up all the houses within a mile radius, and we started assigning ourselves, along with Patrolmen to go door to door, to canvas. We beat the bushes, to recover what we did the night before, between the trailers and out in the ballpark. Just the entire area around there.

England: Were there any other agencies assisting in this search?

Kirby: At one time or another, yes, practically everyone. We had the volunteer Fire Department come out and, of course, everyone in the Police Department. The Army – Colonel Schueler gave his troops from the Army. We had Jefferson County use their helicopters and their dogs. There was a bloodhound association, I don't remember the name—they came out and assisted. All kinds of citizens showed up, doing different things—searching and just assisting us any way that they could.

England: In the days following, what were the types of searches that you were engaging in?

Kirby: Well, other than the door-to-door canvas, we were assigned different troops, and we moved out into an area where there was a sighting. On the other side of the trailer part, on the other side of 31-W, and we walked in line and checked all that area, within shoulder distance of one another. We moved in that area to clear that area. We pumped out a sump hole that one of the dogs had indicated that she might have gone in that direction. So, we pumped all the water out of there and went inside of there, down at the concrete plant.

England: What was involved in doing that?

Kirby: Well, we brought out a pumper, and they pumped out all the water, and we sent a guy down into the hole to see what was in there, after all the water was out.

England: Was it a diver that was sent down in there?

Kirby: Yes. Two, in fact. Two went down in there.

England: What else, in that two or three-day period, after?

Kirby: There were just masses, everywhere. We just looked everywhere. People were sent everywhere, but specifically— the hole, I was there for that. The inline searches outside of the trailer park, on the other side of 31-W, coming from Fort Knox.

England: Did you have any contact with Tom or Roxanne Suleski, during that time period?

Kirby: Not in those next couple of days. My first real, lengthy involvement came on the thirty-first of October.

England: And who was your contact with?

Kirby: It was with Tom.

England: What was that contact?

Kirby: I was transporting [him] up to the City of Louisville, for an interview.

England: Did you have a conversation with him, on that date?

Kirby: Yes. It was about three and a half hours, in length.

England: Do you remember what you talked about with him?

Kirby: Mostly about his history. You know, where he comes from, who he'd been married to, how he got to Fort Knox, where he'd been—that type of thing.

England: What did he tell you about his family situation?

Kirby: Um, where should I start with this?

England: Okay, he told you who his spouse was...

Kirby: Yes, of course. He talked about his first wife, Young. How he met her in Korea, and that situation, there.

England: When he met her, and he was in Korea, what was he in Korea for?

Kirby: He was with the Army, there. I think he said he was with a signal group—a signal outfit in Korea.

England: And from Korea, where did he go?

Kirby: He moved to—I think it was Augusta, Georgia. I think that's Fort Gordon, but I'm not positive of the post there.

England: Did he remain in the Army?

Kirby: No, then he moved to California, with her and the children. That's where he met Roxanne.

England: Did he tell you about his children?

Kirby: He didn't talk much about them. He would answer specific questions. You know, like where they were born and that type of thing. But he didn't mention them much, at all.

England: I presume he got divorced from his first wife?

Kirby: Yes.

England: Did he remarry?

Kirby: Yes, he was teaching in a school out there, and Roxanne was a student. That's how it was related to me and how he come to marry her.

England: Did he indicate when he had come to Kentucky?

Kirby: Yes, he told me when it was, but I don't remember. He had not been here long.

England: He had come to Fort Knox for training?

Kirby: That's correct.

England: Where was his family living?

Kirby: Well, his parents were in New York. His ex-wife was in California, and Roxanne was from California.

England: What was his demeanor like when you were talking to him?

Kirby: He was pretty matter of fact. He talked and engaged in conversation.

England: Did you talk at all about his daughter, Alex?

Kirby: Yes. Just trying to determine where she might be. Who their neighbors were—that kind of thing. Who the child's friends were. Where she had been going to school. Who his friends were. That type of thing. Most of that was negative. She didn't go to school. They didn't have any friends. They didn't go anywhere. He wasn't able to give me any leads, where I might look. That's when he related to me about his first wife, Chung. That she lived out there and the conditions there.

England: How was his demeanor when he was talking to you about his daughter, who had been reported missing?

Kirby: Again, very matter of fact. Not too much emotion. Not emotional, at all. Just 'yes' and 'no' answers. That type of thing.

England: Did you do any other investigation on this case?

Kirby: There were lots and lots of sightings that I investigated. People would—anytime they saw an Amerasian child, about her age—they would give us a call, and we would run all of those down. There was an instance where a man told us she was in Louisville. We went to Louisville and spoke to the people there, and they had an Amerasian child, but it was not Alex. They had birth certificates and adoption papers, that kind of thing.

England: You investigated other sightings?

Kirby: Yes.

England: How many of these particular types of leads do you think you might have investigated?

Kirby: A ballpark figure would be one hundred.

England: Would you have investigated all the leads that came into the Detective Section?

Kirby: Some went to Aaron, some went to Jack. Sometimes, it was the particular Patrolman who took the information. He may be able to investigate it, right on the spot depending on what it was.

Cross Examination by Roxanne Suleski's Attorney

Schaffer: Now, you testified that Tom gave you some information about Young?

Kirby: That's correct.

Schaffer: As a result of this information, did you do any investigation or do anything at all?

Kirby: Yes, that was one of the reasons we got a hold of the F.B.I., was to have them send agents out there. He was saying that possibly, Young came and got her, and that's what we wanted them to do. We contacted the LAPD, also. They checked her residence.

Schaffer: Did you ever receive a report back, in reference to that?

Kirby: Yes. Negative.

Schaffer: Did you ever check Georgia? The Fort Benning area?

Kirby: Yes. I called down and spoke to a detective down there, and he gave me what he knew. He didn't really know too much about them. They'd had a couple run ins, but nothing significant.

Schaffer: Did you ever perform a search of Otter Creek Park, in reference to this case?

Kirby: Well, I'm not sure of that are is actually inside of Otter Creek Park—but, we were up in that area.

Schaffer: Did you find anything?

Kirby: No.

Schaffer: That's fine. Thank you.

Judge: Mr. Maples, any questions?

Maples: No.

Excerpts from the Testimony of FBI Special Agent Phil Lewzader

England: How long have you been with the F.B.I.?

Lewzader: I have been with the F.B.I. a total of twenty-two years. I've been a Special Agent for eighteen.

England: What are your duties as a Special Agent?

Lewzader: I'm a Senior Resident Agent in the Paducah Resident Agency, and my duties are the administration of the Resident Agency. In addition, we investigate violations of federal law and report our findings to the United States Attorney's Office.

England: Prior to being assigned to the Paducah Office, where were you assigned?

Lewzader: The Elizabethtown Resident Agency.

England: How long had you been at that Agency?

Lewzader: I was in Elizabethtown for approximately five or five-and-a-half years.

England: What were your duties at that office?

Lewzader: They were the same.

England: What is the area that the Elizabethtown Resident Agency covers?

Lewzader: The Bureau divides the state into counties for the Resident Agencies. When I was here initially, we had fifteen, then it was thirteen, in addition to the Fort Knox Military Reservation.

England: In October of 1989, would that be accurate?

Lewzader: Yes, it would. Thirteen counties and the Fort Knox Military Reservation.

England: Did you also include Hardin County as one of the counties in which you were responsible?

Lewzader: Yes, Hardin County was assigned to me.

England: In October or November of 1989, were you contacted regarding a missing child by the name of Alex?

Lewzader: Yes, I was.

England: Do you remember what the contact was that you had received?

Lewzader: I was contacted by a member of the Radcliff Police Department. They informed me that the missing child that they were searching for and had been searching for, for approximately four days and nights, had not developed any significant information which would lead them to believe that that child was in the area. Our assistance was requested, and I opened up a kidnapping investigation.

England: Why did you open up that type of investigation?

Lewzader: It was appropriate for the facts known to us.

England: So, tell us what your agency did, what your office did.

Lewzader: We initiated a complete kidnapping investigation. The Louisville Division, which is where all of my supervisors and superiors are and is our headquarters for Kentucky, they dispatched, I believe four or five additional agents to the Elizabethtown Resident Agency. At the time that this occurred, there was myself and two other agents assigned to Elizabethtown. I believe they sent one support person to help us, while we were in the field. We began a kidnapping investigation, which would include, among other things, the review of all previous investigation conducted by the Radcliff Police Department and any other agencies that had conducted investigations.

England: Do you remember when it was that you were initially contacted?

Lewzader: It was either the end of October or the first of November. It would have been October thirty-first or November first.

England: Okay, as soon as you were contacted, you contacted your supervisors, additional people were sent out, and then what did you do?

Lewzader: We then began our kidnapping investigation. That would include a review of all previous investigations done by other agencies, it would include interviews of all family members, all friends, neighbors, schoolmates, and follow any logical investigation that came to our attention. I was ultimately, at the field level, responsible for the investigation. It was assigned to me. I became known as the case agent. The person who the case is assigned to.

England: What did you delegate your agency to do at that time?

Lewzader: As the case agent, I became, in effect, a field coordinator. I would handle the necessary administrative paperwork that went along with the kidnapping investigation, which is considerable. I handled the delegation of duties to other agents that were working on the case.

England: The agents that you were delegating to—in that process—did you talk to Tom and Roxanne Suleski at that time?

Lewzader: Personally, I did not interview them, immediately. Within the first day or two, I spoke to Roxanne Suleski. I visited the trailer and said 'Hello' and introduced myself. Later, I interviewed Thomas Suleski.

England: How much later would that have been?

Lewzader: Approximately one week.

England: Was there anyone else from your agency at that time period that may have interviewed them?

Lewzader: Oh, yes. They were interviewed, on at least one occasion and perhaps more than once, by other agents.

England: And would you, as the case agent have reviewed those interviews?

Lewzader: Yes. I not only reviewed the written interviews, but on a daily basis, at some point in the evening, when we had reached some sort of a stopping point for the day, all of the investigators assembled at the Elizabethtown Resident Agency, at our office, and our findings for the day were reviewed. Our findings were passed on to out superiors and decisions were made on what the next investigative steps would be.

England: Have you had the opportunity, while you have been with the Agency, to have worked cases of this type? A kidnapping case, where you have a missing child?

Lewzader: Yes, sir.

England: In beginning your investigation, what were you looking for?

Lewzader: Initially, a kidnapping investigation, particularly one of this type, starts out rather broad. Your attempt is to focus your investigation, and your ultimate goal is to logically follow and determine what did occur. You sort through things as they happened and look for inconsistencies and look for places that you want to focus.

England: How did this investigation progress that you became involved in?

Lewzader: As it progressed, we began to focus our attention on Tom and Roxanne Suleski.

England: Why did you do that?

Lewzader: There were inconsistencies that we observed after reviewing interviews of Tom Suleski and Roxanne Suleski and the children, in addition to—

(Objection by Schaffer. Overruled by judge.)

Lewzader: In an interview with Roxanne Suleski by other agents, it was determined that she could not recall any events—

(Objection by Schaffer. Sustained by judge.)

England: Okay, you said your investigation started to narrow. What did you do as your investigation started to narrow?

Lewzader: I requested an interview with Tom Suleski. England: Did you, in fact, interview Thomas Suleski? Lewzader: Yes, sir.

England: And what took place in that interview?

Lewzader: I explained to him my position and that I believed there were some inconsistencies, which I thought he could clear up. I asked him for his explanation and cooperation in the interview.

England: And what happened?

Lewzader: He told me that if I allowed him to speak to his wife—

(objection by Schaffer. Overruled by judge.)

England: Please continue.

Lewzader: Tom told me that if I let him talk to his wife, and to his attorney, then he would tell me the truth.

England: And did he subsequently talk to you?

Lewzader: No, sir.

England: Did you have any conversations with Roxanne Suleski?

Lewzader: After that date—no.

England: Before then?

Lewzader: Did I personally have conversations Roxanne Suleski?

England: Yes.

Lewzader: I recall going to the house, early in our investigation—going to the trailer and introducing myself.

England: Did you talk to the children?

Lewzader: Personally, no sir.

England: As your investigation continued, was there anything that happened that caused you to question whether the Suleskis were involved or not.

Lewzader: Yes, sir.

England: What was that?

Lewzader: In August of 1993, I received a telephone call from Ben Bruno.

England: And did you act on that telephone call?

Lewzader: Yes, sir. I returned his call.

England: As a result of that phone call, what took place?

Lewzader: I spoke to Nyssa Bruno.

England: And after speaking to her, what was your action?

Lewzader: I flew to Los Angeles, California.

England: And what did you do while you were there?

Lewzader: I asked Nyssa Bruno, in the presence of her father and stepmother, if she would consent to wear a recording device and record a conversation between herself and her mother.

England: And then what happened?

Lewzader: I returned to Paducah, Kentucky, and investigators in Los Angeles continued the investigation. Special Agents of the Los Angeles division.

England: Did you have any further contact with the investigation, after that?

Lewzader: As a coordinator, I did. But, specifically to conduct interviews, I don't recall doing any subsequent to that.

England: On occasions, when you talked to Roxanne Suleski and Thomas Suleski, what was their demeanor?

Lewzader: They were calm. Unemotional. Relaxed.

England: When you talked to them about their child, and they discussed Alex, how was their demeanor? Which of those did you talk to about Alex?

Lewzader: I spoke to Tom about Alex.

England: Did you talk to Roxanne about Alex?

Lewzader: I may have mentioned Alex's name when I spoke to her at the trailer. I went in there to introduce myself, and it would not surprise me if I didn't express some condolences and tell her that we would make every effort to find her child.

England: How long after the disappearance would that have been?

Lewzader: That would have been November first, November second – within a week or six days, seven days.

England: What was her demeanor?

Lewzader: Calm. Unemotional.

England: When you talked to Tom about Alex, what was his demeanor?

Lewzader: Initially, he was calm and unemotional. Later, when our interview concluded, he appeared nervous.

England: Did either one of the Suleskis thank you for assisting in looking for their child?
Lewzader: No, sir.

England: Nothing further.

Cross Examination by Roxanne Suleski's Attorney

Schaffer: Did you have any conversations with Ben Bruno in 1989?

Lewzader: Yes, sir. I did.

Schaffer: Did you ask him to try and get Nyssa to tell you what you wanted to hear?

Lewzader: No, sir.

Schaffer: Did you ask him to try and get Nyssa to talk to you?

Lewzader: No, I asked him to try and get Nyssa to tell the truth.

Schaffer: The statement that you took from Nyssa on August twenty-first, 1993, was this a taped, recorded statement?

Lewzader: No, sir.

Schaffer: Was it a handwritten statement by Nyssa?

Lewzader: No, sir. I didn't take a statement from her on that day. I interviewed her telephonically on that day.

Schaffer: Was this interview tape recorded?

Lewzader: No, sir. I recorded notes on a piece of paper, while I talked to her. Then, I transcribed them onto what we call a FD302, a report of an interview.

Schaffer: That would be your interpretation as to what she said.

Lewzader: Yes, sir. It is what she said.

Schaffer: The F.B.I. has received some reports of sightings of Alex. Is that correct?

Lewzader: Yes, sir.

Schaffer: Are you the lead investigator on this particular case?

Lewzader: Yes, sir.

Schaffer: Do you have an opportunity to review all information, such as sightings and reports on those sightings, as they come into existence?

Lewzader: I have, I believe, seen every piece of paper that has been generated relevant to this case, and that would include those reports on sightings.

Schaffer: Can you tell me how many sightings the F.B.I. investigated?

Lewzader: I've never counted them. I would say there were several dozen, perhaps a hundred. I've never counted them.

Schaffer: So, somewhere between thirty-six and a hundred?

Lewzader: At least. I've never counted them.

Schaffer: What type of investigation did you perform, in reference to these sightings?

Lewzader: An agent from the F.B.I. would have contacted the person who reported the sighting, if that was possible—if it was not an anonymous caller. If there was enough information where we could contact the person who is reporting it, there would be a face-to-face interview with that person. They would show them a picture of the victim. They would interview them and get whatever information they could from them.

Schaffer: So, are there written interviews on each one of these particular sightings?

Lewzader: There should be written interviews on many of them. Again, it would depend a great deal on whether or not there was a person to interview.

Schaffer: How many were actually investigated?
Lewzader: All would have been investigated, wherein there was something that would allow us to investigate it further.

Schaffer: Do you know how many people were actually interviewed?

Lewzader: The specific number, I do not know. I've never counted them.

Schaffer: In reference to your investigation, did you have an opportunity to canvas the Duvall Mobile Home Park?

Lewzader: Yes, sir. We did.

Schaffer: Did you speak to everyone in the trailer park?

Lewzader: To my knowledge, we did.

Schaffer: And did you receive any information which would have aided in your investigation of the kidnapping of Alex?

Lewzader: Yes, sir. I believe we did. That was another one of those places in the investigation, where I was talking about yesterday, where there were discrepancies. We had been told that Alex was outside playing that day. As a part of our investigation, where—to the best of my knowledge, we interviewed everyone in the trailer park— I'm not sure we ever found anybody who said that they saw Alex on that day.

Schaffer: Did you find anyone that had seen Alex, during the canvas, at any point in time?

Lewzader: We found people—*(witness named)* for one—who believed she had seen Alex. That was later refuted.

Schaffer: I don't believe I have any further questions.

Re-Direct by Prosecutor

England: Agent Lewzader, how many kidnapping cases would you estimate that you have been involved with?

Lewzader: Although those numbers are never kept in the F.B.I.—we don't keep statistics on those. I would say in eighteen years, as a Special Agent, I've probably been involved in, in one way or another, at least one hundred.

England: In your experience in your investigation of these types of cases, would it be normal for the family of a person that has been reported missing not to cooperate with you?

Lewzader: No. That would...

(Objection by Schaffer. Sustained by judge.)

England: When you did this investigation, you talked about the focus narrowing. Mr. Schaffer asked you a bunch of questions about sightings, where Alex was alleged to have been seen. Did you continue to investigate those, even though you had narrowed your focus in the investigation?

Lewzader: Yes, sir. We did.

England: Was there ever a time where your office declined to investigate any of those particular leads that you received?

Lewzader: There was never and has never been a reported sighting that we did not actively investigate.

England: I have nothing further.

Judge: Anything else?

Schaffer: I have one question.

Judge: I didn't mean to pass you over Mr. Maples. Do you wish to ask any questions?

Maples: No, Your Honor.

Schaffer: Do you recall when the last of these sightings was investigated by the F.B.I.?

Lewzader: I don't recall when it was. It would have been the last one we received. I don't know when the last reported sighting was received.

Schaffer: Thank you.

Excerpts of Testimony from Nyssa Bruno

England: I'm going to start with, and I'm going to ask you some questions relating to the time period of October 1989. Where did you live at, at that time?

Nyssa: We lived in Radcliff, Kentucky.

England: Where in Radcliff were you living?

Nyssa: Duvall Trailer Park.

England: Who were you living with?

Nyssa: My two stepsisters, my stepfather, and my mother.

England: Who are your stepsisters?

Nyssa: Dawn and Alex Suleski.

England: Let me back you up a little further. How long had you been living with Tom Suleski and his two children? At the time of October in 1989, was your mother working?

Nyssa: No, sir.

England: What about Tom Suleski. Was he working?

Nyssa: Yes, sir.

England: Do you know what he was doing?

Nyssa: He was in the military.

England: How long had you been in Kentucky in October of 1989?

Nyssa: I think we got there the first week of October.

England: After you got to Kentucky, did you get enrolled in school?

Nyssa: Yes.

England: Do you remember where you went to school at?

Nyssa: Yes, sir.

England: Where was that?

Nyssa: Radcliff Middle School.

England: Was that very far from your residence where you lived?

Nyssa: No, sir.

England: If you would, describe for us the residence that you were living in.

Nyssa: There were two bedrooms, a living room, one bathroom, and a kitchen.

England: Where did everyone stay in the house? Where did everyone sleep?

Nyssa: My parents slept in the back bedroom, me and my sister slept in the other bedroom, and usually Alex would sleep in my parents' bedroom.

England: Where would she sleep at?

Nyssa: On the floor.

England: What would she sleep on?

Nyssa: Sometimes blankets, sometimes on the floor.

England: In October of 1989, what was your relationship like with your mother?

Nyssa: Very close.

England: You were very close with your mother?

Nyssa: Yes.

England: Would you say that you talked to her quite a bit?

Nyssa: Yes, sir.

England: How about Tom, what was your relationship like with him?

Nyssa: I didn't talk to him much because he was usually gone all day, but we got along.

England: Now what about your two stepsisters, Dawn and Alex, how did you get along with them?

Nyssa: We got along well.

England: What was the relationship like that you observed between your mom and Dawn and Alex, at that time?

Nyssa: Um, she had a much shorter temper with them than she had with me. They were always getting into trouble. Most of the time, it was Alex.

England: Do you remember the types of things that she would get into trouble for?

Nyssa: She had a problem with going to the bathroom. Sometimes she couldn't get to the bathroom, and she would go to the bathroom on herself. Um, sometimes she would talk 'baby' talk, because she didn't speak really good English. Mostly it was those two.

England: When those things would happen, how would your mother, Roxanne, react?

Nyssa: She would get really angry. She would yell at Alex a lot. Sometimes she would hit her. She did a lot of different things.

(Crying.)

England: How would she hit her?

Nyssa: Um, she would slap her or hit her in the back.

(Continues to cry.)

England: Okay, take a breath. Okay, if you would, maybe it would be easier for you, can you remember some particular incidents that you can describe for us or particular times when Alex was punished that you can relate to us, during that time period in Radcliff?

Nyssa: Um, one time she threw up on the floor. She got sick. Mom grabbed her and pulled her to the bathroom, and she smacked her head into the toilet, and she was yelling at her.

(Sobbing.)

England: You said she smacked her head into the toilet, did she also hold her head down?

Nyssa: I don't remember. I just remember her pushing her head into the toilet.

England: Do you know if Alex struck her head on the toilet or not?

Nyssa: I heard it.

England: You heard it?

Nyssa: Yeah.

England: Were you in the bathroom when this happened?

Nyssa: I was in the doorway.

England: You said she had a problem wetting on herself. Do you remember any particular incidences regarding that?

Nyssa: I don't remember what she had gotten into trouble for, but she was standing in the living room, and she had her arms straight out in front of her—that was a punishment— and my mom was yelling at her for something...

England: Now, show me how her arms were. Just show me...

Nyssa: She was standing with her arms out, like this...

England: Her arms straight out, with her palms up? Like that?

Nyssa: Yes, sir.

England: Go ahead.

Nyssa: My mom was yelling at her, and she was really angry at her, for whatever she did. I don't remember—and she was yelling at her, and Alex was really scared, and she wet on herself, and that made my mom even more angry. She grabbed Alex and—I don't remember what her punishment was for that.

England: Did she have to stand like that very often?

Nyssa: Sometimes.

England: How often would Roxanne punish Alex, during that time period in Radcliff?

Nyssa: Everyday she would get into trouble for something.

England: How did Alex act when she was being punished?

Nyssa: She was scared.

England: Can you remember any other particular incidences from that week? Or during that time period in Radcliff?

Nyssa: Well, I don't remember what she had done, but she probably wet on herself, because that's what she mostly got into trouble for. My mom put her in a plastic bag.

England: Now, before we get to that—I want to ask you— where did the family eat?

Nyssa: Either in the kitchen or the living room.

England: Would you all eat together, at the same time?

Nyssa: Usually, except Alex.

England: When would Alex eat?

Nyssa: I'm not sure, because I wasn't home during the day. She might have eaten during the day.

England: During the nighttime, when you were there, did you see her have any meals?

Nyssa: I don't remember. I don't remember ever seeing her eat.

England: Now, you were telling us about an incident where she probably wet on herself. Go on, please.

Nyssa: My mom put her in a plastic bag, and she was in their room. She was there—I don't remember how long she was there for...

England: Go ahead and tell what you remember.

Nyssa: I don't remember how long she was in the bag. But I went into my parents' bedroom to talk to my mom about something, and I remember my mom saying that something smelled really bad in the room. She started smelling around, and she got to Alex's bag, and she opened it up. She looked really disgusted, and that's what was smelling. She closed it back up, and she got another plastic bag, and she put the first plastic bag into the second plastic bag, and she sealed that bag up, also.

(Crying)

England: Do you remember how those bags were sealed?

Nyssa: It was something that tied it, shut. I don't remember what.

England: Now, when the first bag was put into the second, how was it done? Did she lift it?

Nyssa: It was rolled in. She had the second bag open, and she rolled Alex in the first bag, into the second.

England: What time of day was this conversation?

Nyssa: It was in the evening or night.

England: Tell us what the next thing you remember specifically regarding this incident is.

Nyssa: I remember my mom was leading me out of the room for something, and I was following her, and the bag was right next to the door. I remember hearing something coming from the bag, and I was listening to try and figure out what it was. And I figured out it was Alex breathing really hard.

England: Was that the same evening?

Nyssa: Yes.

England: What would you have done the next day?

Nyssa: I got up and went to school.

England: What happened after you got home? Did you see Alex?

Nyssa: No. I don't remember what happened until my mom asked me to get dinner started. Dawn was outside playing. She went into the back bedroom, and I was taking things out of the cupboard, and I was getting dinner ready. She came back and she was—not nervous, I guess, scared. She said, 'Alex isn't breathing,' and then she said something else, I don't remember. And then she said that she had to call Tom.

England: What was the next thing that you remember?

Nyssa: I remember Tom coming home and rushing through the living room to the bedroom. I stayed out in the living room, on the couch. Then I remember Tom coming back into the living room from the bedroom, with my mom following him.

He said that we had to call an ambulance, and my mom said, 'No, we can't do that'. She was saying that if we did, the police would come and take them away, and they would take me and Dawn away, and we would never see each other again. I remember my mom coming over and telling me that we couldn't tell anyone, because—the same thing she told Tom. I remember being told that the basic story was supposed to be that Alex went out to play, and we can't find her. They were going to do something with Alex's body. I remember them saying they had to wash her or wash something, and they went to the bedroom. I was still in the living room, on the couch. I looked down the hall and saw Tom bend down to pick something up, and then I looked away. I heard them go into the hallway and I heard the water go on in the bathroom. But I don't know what they were washing or what they were cleaning. Then, Tom went through the living, outside to the van, and he got a big vacuum cleaner box. He came back through the living room and into the bathroom. Then, awhile after that, he came back with the box and went outside. My mom came over to me and said something, and then they left.

England: Could you tell if there was anything in the box when it was brought in?

Nyssa: When he was carrying it out, it looked like something was in it. It looked heavier than it was before, when he was bringing it in.

England: Tell us what happened next. What you did.

Nyssa: I went, and I stood on the outside steps, and Dawn came with a bunch of her friends, and they were all riding bikes. She said that she saw my parents, and they said they couldn't find Alex. I told her that that was right. I asked her if her and her friends could ride around the trailer park and find Alex. A policeman called, and I answered the phone. I told him that Alex was missing, and I gave him a description.

England: What do remember after that?

Nyssa: I remember the next day, there was a huge search for her. A lot of people were coming in and out of our trailer home.

England: Did you talk to anyone about Alex being gone?

Nyssa: Yes, I did.

England: Who did you talk to?

Nyssa: I don't know who it was who questioned me, but it was a Police Officer or F.B.I. Agent.

England: And what did you tell that Police Officer at that time?

Nyssa: That Alex had gone out to play, and we couldn't find her after that.

England: Tell us the next thing that you remember.

Nyssa: It's all the same for a long time after that. A lot of people were looking for Alex. We got questioned by a lot of police officers and F.B.I. Agents. There were a lot of people that helped us to get things, like a Thanksgiving dinner.

England: You said a lot of people were searching. Could you tell us what you knew that they were doing? What you observed people doing.

Nyssa: I remember watching soldiers going through the forests. I remember them draining some swamp or something that was behind my middle school. I remember them passing out flyers.

England: At one point in time, you talked to an Agent Phil Lewzader. Is that correct?

Nyssa: Yes, sir.

England: Did you talked to Agent Lewzader in August of 1993?

Nyssa: Yes, sir.

England: What was your conversation about?

Nyssa: I told him that Alex going out to play was a made-up story, and I told him what really happened.

England: Is that what you told us today?

Nyssa: Yes, sir.

England: As a result of your conversation with Agent Lewzader, what did you do?

Nyssa: I had a recorded conversation with my stepfather.

England: Tell us how they came about.

Nyssa: After talking with Agent Lewzader, I was scared that my word against their word wasn't going to mean much. So, somehow, somebody suggested that a recording...

England: And you consented to this recording?

Nyssa: Yes.

England: Tell us when it happened and what happened during the time of the recording.

Nyssa: It was in August. They put a tape recorder on me, and I went home. I asked my stepfather if we could go out for a walk to talk. We went out for a walk, and I didn't know what to say. I told him that I was having a nightmare that someone had found Alex's body and that the police and the F.B.I. took them away. I wanted reassurance, like, what happened to her body.

England: And he told you?

Nyssa: He told me that there was nothing left of her body.

England: We will play that tape later, so I want to get you passed that for now. When Alex was getting punished, did she ever fight back?

Nyssa: No, sir.

England: Did she ever show any emotion during the punishment?

Nyssa: She cried, sometimes.

England: Judge, that's all the questions I have for her at this time.

Excerpts from the Bruno/Suleski tape

Bruno: It's just ... it's just weird that I would have the same nightmare. I mean...

Suleski: Yes, I understand. Well, and then on top of it ... I haven't really heard a good explanation of just a regular old dream yet.

Bruno: Uh-huh.

Suleski: I've heard people saying well, dreams are your subconscious mind trying to tell stuff to your conscious mind and every person in the dream is not really that person but...

Bruno: Well...well listen, I think maybe it's because I have these fears of like I don't know, like I don't know for sure, cause I don't remember, but was Alex ever on the base? Her body? She never was? *(Responding to a gesture by Suleski).* Was she in a place where there's soldiers or like they trained or something? No?

Suleski: That's just what they're trying to say, but it was never...

Bruno: Never true.

Suleski: Never. And a...

Bruno: Is there...okay. I know this is going to sound weird, I just want to know.

Suleski: No, okay, it's cool.

Bruno: ...because I don't know. Is she like, all destroyed? I mean, like there's nothing left of her?

Suleski: As far as I can tell, yes. And I know that's not very reassuring. Let's put it this way....

Bruno: That's not...I mean, I don't know. Alex...

Suleski: I know exactly what...okay. Let me tell you this. You know, tell you what was going on.

Bruno: Right. I didn't really ask questions at the time, because I really didn't want to hear about how you destroyed Alex's body.

Suleski: Well, I had very little choice on what to do. Remember, that State Park? Otter Creek?

Bruno: Otter Creek?

Suleski: State Park? It was up the road quite a bit.

Bruno: But, that's not where you left her after you destroyed her?

Suleski: Okay, well, I...there was uh ... there was ... couple trees that had fallen down, and they were like making an 'X.' Right?

Bruno: Uh-huh.

Suleski: That's the best thing I could do. I just went over there and covered everything up.

Bruno: That was the first time?

Suleski: That was the first time.

Bruno: Okay.

Suleski: Went back.

Bruno: Uh-huh.

Suleski: I was guided to that spot. I mean I could feel ... the time ... the only time I've ever really felt any kind of psychic thing.

Bruno: Uh-huh.

Suleski: I could feel it right here. I knew where I was at.

Bruno: Like maybe Alex's body was calling to you or...

Suleski: Well ... sort of. Somebody, possibly Alex, possibly... who ... who knows. But in any case, I was guided there.

Bruno: Uh-huh.

Suleski: The only thing I could find was a ... the head, the skull.

Bruno: The skull.

Suleski: Which ... the only thing that ... and I looked.

Bruno: Uh-huh.

Suleski: And that was ... it was, you know, a tricky operation, and I was all camouflaged.

Bruno: Uh-huh.

Suleski: But, I mean ... I ... I went to that spot and said well, this doesn't look right. Even though, I felt it.

Bruno: Right.

Suleski: I walked away. I turned around, got to that spot again, and I had such a tightness in my gut. Alright, this has gotta be it, so I sat there and waited. It was pitch black.

Bruno: Uh-huh.

Suleski: And I waited until a little bit of light started, and then I was looking around, and I couldn't find anything and all of a sudden, I see this rock. It was a big rock, and I said wait a minute, that's too round and smooth to be a rock. And that's all there was.

Bruno: Oh, it was her skull.

Suleski: Okay, that's all that was there.

Bruno: Alright, but what I want to know is, like, you destroyed it and...

Suleski: Yeah, well, then it got totally smashed, and to be honest, there's nothing left of it but powder. Little, little, little particles...

Bruno: Okay.

Suleski: ... and that's totally out of the state of Kentucky.

Bruno: Okay.

Suleski: Alright? So as far as that's concerned, I think that's cool.

MONDAY—DAY FIVE

Day Two of Nyssa Bruno's Testimony

The taped recording made between Nyssa Bruno and Tom Suleski is played for the jury.

England: Okay, Nyssa. I just wanted to touch base with you on a few other things. You mentioned some times in Radcliff, in which Alex was disciplined in certain fashions, and you talked about them in terms of your mother, Roxanne. Where was Tom at, during these time periods?

Nyssa: Sometimes he was home, and sometimes he was at work.

England: Did he ever object to the discipline that was given to Alex?

Nyssa: No, sir.

England: Did he ever talk to Roxanne about what happened to Alex after she left the trailer on October twenty-sixth?

Nyssa: Yes, sir.

England: What did you talk to her about?

Nyssa: She said that Alex's body had been put—I don't remember if she told me it was a park or it was a forest area, but it was somewhere where there were a lot of leaves, and she was under a lot of leaves.

England: Did she ever discuss anything else that she had done regarding the body, after that point? Did Roxanne ever come back to Kentucky?

Nyssa: Yes, sir.

England: And when was that?

Nyssa: I was either in seventh or eighth grade. I don't remember the year.

England: Did she tell you why she came back to Kentucky?

Nyssa: Yes, sir.

England: What did she tell you she came back to Kentucky for?

Nyssa: To destroy Alex's body.

England: I have no further questions. Thank you.

Cross Examination by Tom Suleski's Attorney

Maples: Nyssa, I believe that you had already indicated on Friday, in your testimony, that you had given different statements before, regarding what you said in this courtroom. Is that correct?

(silence)

Before August of 1993, before the day that you say they wired you up with a tape, before that day, you had made different statements. Is that correct? As to what happened on October 26th, 1989.

Nyssa: Yes, sir.

Maples: And you had made statements several times, before that date, which were different, regarding what happened on October 26th, 1989, to FBI Agents, Radcliff policemen, and on two occasions in court. Is that correct?

Nyssa: Yes, sir.

Re-Direct by Prosecutor

England: Nyssa, do you deny that you have given previous statements relating to the disappearance of Alex?

Nyssa: No, sir. I don't.

England: Why did you give those previous statements that she was missing?

Nyssa: Because my parents told me to.

Cross Examination by Roxanne Suleski's Attorney

Schaffer: I have a few questions about your testimony last week, Nyssa. Now, you had stated that your mother had put Alex in a bag. What date was that?

Nyssa: The twenty-fifth, sir.

Schaffer: About what time of the day did that happen?

Nyssa: I don't remember.

Schaffer: Was it the early morning? Was it the afternoon?

Nyssa: I don't remember.

Schaffer: Do you have any idea what time of the day it was?

Nyssa: Not at all, sir.

Schaffer: Can you tell me how the bag was sealed?

Nyssa: It was sealed with something that tied the bag shut. I don't remember...

Schaffer: Was it tightly sealed?

Nyssa: Yes, Sir. It tied the front of the bag, like...

Schaffer: Like in a knot?

Nyssa: No, sir. Like ... it's hard to explain. Um, if you grabbed the bag and sealed the end and tied something around it...

Schaffer: So, it was tied tightly, would you say?

Nyssa: I didn't look that close, sir.

Schaffer: And you have no idea what time of day this happened?

Nyssa: No, sir.

Schaffer: You stated that there was a second bag. Do you know how long after the first bag that the second bag came up?

Nyssa: I don't remember.

Schaffer: You have no idea on the time frames?

Nyssa: No.

Schaffer: Do you know how long Alex was in the second bag?

Nyssa: Overnight, sir.

Schaffer: Then you heard her breathing the next day?

Nyssa: No, sir. That was that night.

Schaffer: How late that night? Do you know?

Nyssa: I don't remember.

Schaffer: Now, you also stated that Alex threw up, but you're not sure what day that was on. Is that correct?

Nyssa: Yes.

Schaffer: So, that wasn't on the same day as this bag incident that you've described. Is that correct?

Nyssa: Um, the first bag ... I don't remember.

Schaffer: Do you remember when your mom and dad separated?

Nyssa: Um, they separated a long time ago.

Schaffer: How did that make you feel?

Nyssa: I was really young. I thought it was normal.

Schaffer: Did you feel like you had to make a choice back then?

Nyssa: No, sir. I went back and forth.

Schaffer: At some point in time, your mom and dad got divorced, and he started seeing a lady named Jay. Is that correct?

Nyssa: Yes, sir.

Schaffer: Do you remember her?

Nyssa: Yes, sir.

Schaffer: How did you get along with her, when your dad first started seeing her?

Nyssa: I didn't like her, sir.

Schaffer: You didn't like her at all, did you?

Nyssa: No.

Schaffer: Did she eventually move in with your father?

Nyssa: Yes, sir.

Schaffer: Did you like that?

Nyssa: I wasn't sure. I don't remember.

Schaffer: At that point in time, did you ever make complaints to your dad or your mom about Jay belittling you?

Nyssa: Tom my mom, sir.

Schaffer: Ever make any complaints to anyone about her hitting you?

Nyssa: Um, yes, sir.

Schaffer: Did you ever tell anyone that Jay used a belt on you?

Nyssa: Yes, sir.

Schaffer: Isn't it true that back in 1987, your dad was pressuring you to come back and live with him?

Nyssa: I don't remember, sir. I don't think so.

Schaffer: Do you recall when your mom and Tom started dating?

Nyssa: A little bit, sir.

Schaffer: Do you know when that was?

Nyssa: Um, I think I was in the fifth grade.

Schaffer: And up to that point in time, you had been living with your mother. Is that correct?

Nyssa: And my grandmother, sir.

Schaffer: Did you do a lot of things with your mom?

Nyssa: Um, not really, sir.

Schaffer: There were no other children around at that point. Is that correct?

Nyssa: Yes, sir.

Schaffer: And when your mom and Tom moved in, Tom brought two children with him. Is that correct?

Nyssa: Yes, sir.

Schaffer: That was Dawn and Alex.

Nyssa: Yes, sir.

Schaffer: Did Dawn start spending some time with your mom, at that point in time?

Nyssa: No, sir.

Schaffer: Did you get along okay with Dawn?

Nyssa: Yes, sir.

Schaffer: Was there any competition between you two?

Nyssa: No, sir.

Schaffer: Did your father have any alcohol or drug problems? When I speak of your father, I mean Ben Bruno.

Nyssa: Yes, sir. He did.

Schaffer: He drank to excess and did some drugs. Is that correct?

Nyssa: Um, yes, sir.

Schaffer: Your father, he went into alcohol rehabilitation in 1992. Is that correct?

Nyssa: I don't remember the year, but yes, he did.

Schaffer: Did things change between you and your father when he came out of the rehabilitation?

Nyssa: A little bit.

Schaffer: Was your father angry about losing custody to your mother?

Nyssa: I don't remember, sir.

Schaffer: Did he blame your mother for his problems?

Nyssa: No, sir.

Schaffer: Did you blame your mother for his problems?

Nyssa: No, sir.

Schaffer: Do you, now?

Nyssa: No, sir.

Schaffer: Did your mom and Tom have enough money during that time period? Were they having any financial problems?

Nyssa: A little.

Schaffer: Did that make things kind of hard on you?

Nyssa: No.

Schaffer: Not being able to buy some of the clothes that you wanted to buy?

Nyssa: My grandmother helped.

Schaffer: Now, after Alex wandered away on October 26th, 1989, you spoke with a lot of police officers. Do remember that?

Nyssa: Yes, sir.

Schaffer: Do you recall testifying before the grand jury in 1990?

Nyssa: Yes, sir.

Schaffer: And at that point in time, you were sworn to tell the truth. Is that correct?

Nyssa: Yes, sir.

Schaffer: And at that point in time, your mom and Tom were not with you. Is that correct?

Nyssa: Yes, Sir.

Schaffer: You told the grand jury that Alex had wandered off. Is that correct?

Nyssa: Yes, sir.

Schaffer: I'm going to show you a document and ask if you can recognize this particular page.

Nyssa: Yes, Sir.

Schaffer: What is that?

Nyssa: This is part of my calendar.

Schaffer: And that is your writing. Is that correct?

Nyssa: Yes, sir.

Schaffer: I ask that this be marked as defense exhibit 3 and entered into evidence.

(Brief sidebar)

Now, on this particular document, which is marked as defense exhibit 3, it says 'on October 25th Alex is missing'. Is that correct?

Nyssa: Yes, sir.

Schaffer: Okay, and you also have marked there that you had started school at Radcliff Middle School on October 26th. Is that correct?

Nyssa: Yes, sir.

Schaffer: Those are not exactly the correct dates. Are they?

Nyssa: No, sir.

Schaffer: Alex actually came up missing on October 26th. Is that correct?

Nyssa: Yes, sir.

Schaffer: I'm going to show you another page from that calendar and ask you if you recognize that.

Nyssa: Yes, sir.

Schaffer: And this is another page from your calendar.

Nyssa: Yes, sir.

Schaffer: I would ask that this be marked as defense exhibit 4.

(brief pause)

And on this particular page, you have noted that on November 9th, Alex was still missing. Is that correct?

Nyssa: Yes, sir.

Schaffer: This next document is dated October 27th, 1989. I ask if recall that particular document.

Nyssa: Yes, sir.

Schaffer: What is that?

Nyssa: It's a page from my diary, sir.

Schaffer: Nyssa, on this particular page, is it correct that you stated that 'Alex is missing, went outside to play with Dawn and never came back, she's been gone for two days now and I'm really worried.' Do you recall writing that?

Nyssa: Yes, sir.

Re-Direct by Prosecutor

England: Nyssa, just a few questions ... Mr. Schaffer asked you about your father's new wife, Jay. I want to ask you a few questions about that. Remember Mr. Schaffer asking you if you had made some statements regarding Jay, that you didn't like her.

Nyssa: Yes, sir.

England: That she beat you.

Nyssa: Yes, sir.

England: Why did you make these statements?

Nyssa: My mom told me to, sir.

England: Why did she tell you to do that?

Nyssa: She didn't like Jay, either, sir.

England: Mr. Schaffer had asked you about your calendar and your diary. When would you make notations in your calendar and your diary?

Nyssa: When I had the time and when I felt like it.

England: How would you decide what to write on your calendar and your diary?

Nyssa: Just what I felt like writing or what I felt was okay for my friends, who read my diary to read.

England: So, other people read your diary?

Nyssa: Yes, sir.

England: Did Roxanne or Tom ever read your diary?

Nyssa: I showed my mom my diary a few times.

England: Nyssa, why did you come forward?

Nyssa: My mom was being really hard on Dawn, my other sister, and it reminded me a lot of what she put Alex through. I didn't want the same thing to happen to Dawn as what happened to Alex.

(crying)

England: Thank you.

Excerpts from the Testimony of Dawn Suleski

England: In October of 1989, do you remember where you were living?

Dawn: Yes, we were living in a trailer park in Radcliff.

England: When you were living in the trailer park, how were things going in the mobile home?

Dawn: At first, it was pretty good, and then a little bit while later, uh, I guess you could say that Alex kinda had some accidents. Like she couldn't get to the bathroom on time, and so Roxanne had put Alex in a plastic bag a couple of times and said that if she had to go the bathroom, she could go in the plastic bag, since she couldn't get to the bathroom on time.

England: You said she had done that a couple times. Could you describe for us what kind of plastic bag it was?

Dawn: It was a trash bag. Like one of those black garbage trash bags.

England: Ok. You said she put her in and how did the garbage bags stay there?

Dawn: Um, for a couple of times I believe Alex would hold it up, so it would stay up on her.

England: Where would Alex be standing when that would happen?

Dawn: Um, sometimes in the living room, by this wall, in a corner wall. And other times she would be in the back bedroom.

England: Now you mentioned that Roxanne would do that. Where would Tom be when this was occurring?

Dawn: Either he was on the base, work, I guess, or he would just let Roxanne do what she thought was best.

England: So, he was able to observe some of these instances?

Dawn: Yes.

England: Did he ever object?

Dawn: No, he didn't.

England: Do you remember the date when Alex was reported to be missing? That's October 26th of 1989?

Dawn: Yes.

England: Do you remember noticing anything about the punishment that Alex had been receiving the day before?

Dawn: Yeah. The day before, Alex had another accident, so Roxanne put her in another trash bag, and I don't know where she put Alex at that time.

England: Do you remember if Tom was home at that time?

Dawn: He was not home at the time that she put her in the bag, but he did come home later that night.

England: Did you ever see Alex that evening?

Dawn: No, I didn't.

England: Do you remember if Tom stayed the night, at the home that night?

Dawn: He normally does come home at night and stay the night, and then wake up in the morning and go back to the base.

England: Do you remember seeing Alex the next morning?

Dawn: No, I don't. I didn't see her all day the next day.

England: You got home *(from school)* at two o'clock. Who was home, when you got home at two o'clock?

Dawn: The only person I saw was Roxanne.

England: Would it be normal for Nyssa to be home when you came home from school?

Dawn: No, she would normally stay at school a little longer.

England: Do you know what time she would get home?

Dawn: No, because most of the time I would be outside playing.

England: Did you play outside a lot?

Dawn: Yes, I did.

England: What about Alex? Did she play outside a lot in Radcliff?

Dawn: No, she always stayed home and played with cards or just watched T.V. or sleep or played with her Legos.

England: Now, Roxanne was the only one home, do you remember what she was doing when you got home?

Dawn: I think she said that she was paying the bills.

England: When was the next time you talked to anybody from your family, after that?

Dawn: Um, I don't remember what time it was, but my dad and Roxanne were coming down the street, and I guess they spotted me and told me that Alex was missing and to gather my friends and go see if we can find her.

England: Which direction were they going? Were they coming in or going out of the trailer park?

Dawn: They were going out of the trailer park. It was somewhere in the early evening.

England: When they told you this. Where were they? Were they in the van?

Dawn: Yes, they were in the van. They just stopped to tell me that.

England: Now tell us about what you remember and about what you did next.

Dawn: Okay. When they told me that Alex was missing, I told my friends that we should go look for her. We all got on our bikes and we rode around the trailer park, looking for her. It was getting pretty dark, and everyone had to go home, so I just went home and waited there. And then Tom and Roxanne came home, and the police were there looking for Alex, and they had got some dogs to go look for her. And that was pretty much it.

England: Did you see Tom and Roxanne at all when you were riding around the trailer park?

Dawn: No, they went out the trailer park, and they didn't come back until a little later.

England: What is the next thing you remember regarding the disappearance of Alex?

Dawn: I guess the candlelight service on her birthday that everyone in the neighborhood, and I guess in Radcliff, gathered around with candles and had a little celebration there to remember her.

England: Do you remember any times when she (Alex) was happy?

Dawn: I guess just when Nyssa or I was just playing with her, like when we were playing with cards or Legos. That was the only time when she was kind of happy.

England: When Alex was being punished, did she ever rebel against that punishment?

Dawn: No, I think she was too scared to.

The Anonymous Letter

Judge: An anonymous letter, with a Louisville postmark and no return address, unsigned and typewritten. It says, "To Whom it May Concern".

(Laughs)

Of course, they did mail it to me. "It may be worthwhile information for you to know that (juror named) has claimed to all who would listen that she would do anything she could to be on the Suleski trial, to make sure they went to the chair. She was in Poor Folk's Restaurant Thursday, August 4th, at twelve o'clock, talking to anyone who would listen. As you surely know, this woman is a very questionable character, as it is—with all the problems with child abuse and ex-lovers."

You cannot conceive of how many anonymous letters a judge gets, but I think obviously I am obliged to tell you that. Now, if you choose, I can have (juror named) come in. I didn't want to do anything, until I showed it to you.

Schaffer: Judge, I would note that this is the second juror that allegedly said something.

Judge: Well, I'm going to bring her in and find out if she said something, and I hope she didn't, but we'll have to figure out what we will do from there. I think we just have to ask and not jump to any conclusions. This could just easily be just someone who is trying to slander her in some way or another. She is divorced, she says, and apparently has custody of a child, because she was in here this morning making a call to a doctor's office because her child is ill and wanted to make an appointment. This very well could be an ex-husband or an ex- paternal grandma or who knows?

(Some time later)

Juror: Did I do something?

(Laughter)

Judge: Well, I don't know. Um—well, this came in my mail this morning. I'm a person who gets a lot of anonymous letters. But this one concerned this trial, so I showed it to the lawyers, and it concerns you, so I want you to give me your reaction to it.

(Juror reads the letter to herself)

Juror: Oh, okay. Well, when I went into Poor Folk's to eat and I was asked if I got chosen, and I told them 'yeah'. And when we were sitting, a lady did come up to me and asked if I was on the jury, just as we were eating, and I said, 'Yeah, I can't talk about it.' But, that's all that it was.

Judge: You were having dinner or lunch at Poor Folk's?

Juror: Yes. With two other jurors, too.

Judge: Oh. Were the two other jurors present when this happened?

Juror: Yes.

Judge: Who were they?

Juror: (Names other two jurors)

Judge: Do you know anyone who would have written a letter like this? And the reason I say that is because some of these things are slanderous remarks.

Juror: Yeah. They seem that way. The child abuse—yeah, I would like to know where that one comes from.

Judge: Didn't you say that you were accused once, because your child fell up the stairs and something—maybe?

Juror: No, that wasn't me.

Judge: Maybe we were thinking of someone else.

Juror: I'm sorry that this...

Judge: Well, it's not your fault.

(Juror leaves the chambers and the two other jurors are called in and questioned. Both give similar accounts, to that of the first juror, of the event stated in the letter.)

Judge: Well, my finding is that this is another 'crackpot' letter.

(Everyone laughs)

Fairly typical of what occurs sometimes in these cases. Unless you all have some other information than what was found out—I find that there were no violations.

Excerpts from the Testimony of Mr. Sutton, Tom's Superior in the Army

England: Mr. Sutton, on the twenty-sixth, you indicated that Mr. Suleski received a phone call. Is that right?

Sutton: Yes, sir.

England: And, after that phone call, did he come and talk to you?

Sutton: Yes, sir. He did.

England: How quickly did he come and talk to you?

Sutton: Immediately. As soon as he hung up the phone, I assume he came down to see me.

England: And what did he tell you?

Sutton: Mr. Suleski told me that his wife had just called him and told him that his daughter was sick and had passed out. That's what he said.

England: Okay. And then what did he do? Did he make a request?

Sutton: Well, he asked for permission to go home. I gave him specific instructions, by saying—go straight home and as soon as you get there, call me and tell me what the situation is and what you are going to do.

England: Do you know approximately what time it was?

Sutton: No, sir. All I can say was early afternoon. I can't remember the time on that.

England: After he left, when was the next time you had any contact with Mr. Suleski?

Sutton: Approximately nine o'clock at night.

England: And what was that contact that you had?

Sutton: I received a phone call from Mr. Suleski informing me his daughter was missing.

England: And what did you do at that time?

Sutton: I went directly to his house, to the trailer.

England: Now, when you arrived there, what did you observe?

Sutton: As soon as I arrived there, I saw Mr. Suleski and asked him to tell me from the moment he arrived what had happened and what he had done, so far.

England: Did Mr. Suleski indicate how long his daughter had been missing?

Sutton: When I asked him to explain to me what he had done once he had arrived there, and what was going on—he had told me that when he had arrived, his daughter had been missing for a couple of hours. And that he had been out searching for her, until this time.

England: Did you notice anything in particular about Mr. Suleski at that time when you were talking to him?

Sutton: The only things that came to mind, immediately for me, was: One—he wasn't in uniform anymore, and two—he was just so calm, to me. As if it was just any normal day and normal conversation for us.

Excerpts from the Testimony of Bill Zurillo, US Marshal

England: Mr. Zurillo, what is your occupation?

Zurillo: Right now, I'm a Chief Deputy for the United States Marshal Service in the District of South Carolina.

England: Were you formerly a U.S. Marshal in Louisville, Kentucky?

Zurillo: Yes, prior to my promotion to South Carolina, I was the United States Marshal for the Western District of Kentucky.

England: On October 18th of 1993, did you have an occasion to come into contact with a Thomas Suleski and a Roxanne Suleski?

Zurillo: Yes, sir. They were being produced in Federal Court.

England: Where did you see them at?

Zurillo: In our cell block, in the courtrooms and then back to the cell block.

England: Describe what the cell block looks like.

Zurillo: The cell block is rectangular. Off to the right of the rectangle four cells, then a gate. The cells are up against the back wall, there is a walkway in front of them, then there's a gateway that separates that area and then outside of the gate area is a square room where there's a sink and a processing area.

England: On October 18th, 1993, were you present when there was a conversation between Thomas and Roxanne Suleski?

Zurillo: Yes, sir.

England: Would you tell us what the conversation was between the two of them?

Zurillo: Yes, sir. Tom Suleski and two male prisoners were in the first cell. Roxanne Suleski and Julie Harvey were in the next adjacent cell. I was doing something in the processing area of the cell block when I heard Tom Suleski call for Roxanne by name. She answered, and Tom said, 'Roxanne, we need to get it together. We have to get together at the jail and get it together, because we're in this together.' At which time, Roxanne replied, 'I know we do. Obviously one of us doesn't know what's going on in there. You're right, we do need to get it together.'

And Tom stated, 'Maybe we can get the Captain to get us together over at the jail, so we can get our stories together, because we're in this together.' At which time, Roxanne replied, 'You're right. You've been lying to me. I don't know what's going on in there. I don't know how much you've told them.' That was the gist of the conversation.

England: And that was the end of the conversation that you heard?

Zurillo: Well, I left.

England: You didn't hear any further conversation between the two?

Zurillo: No, I didn't.

Excerpts from Testimony of Julie Harvey, cellmate of Roxanne Suleski

England: Do you know a woman by the name Roxanne Suleski?

Harvey: Yes, sir.

England: Do you also know a Tom Suleski?

Harvey: Yes, sir.

England: Did you meet them personally?

Harvey: Yes, sir.

England: Where did you meet them at?

Harvey: Clark County Jail.

England: Did you know them prior to this occasion?

Harvey: A little bit.

England: What was the date on that—that you met them?

Harvey: Twenty-fourth of October of '93.

England: Now, when you saw them—where were you at and where were they at?

Harvey: Me and Roxanne was in the same pod and Mr. Suleski—I met him in the Marshal's van, going to the courthouse in Louisville.

England: Were you present during a conversation that they had that day?

Harvey: Yes, sir.

England: Could you tell us where you were, and where they were, when they had that conversation?

Harvey: Mr. Suleski was in one cell, that's Cell One, a holding cell—and then me and Roxanne and another girl was in Cell Two, that's another holding cell for women.

England: Do you remember a conversation that they had?

Harvey: Yes.

England: Could you relate that conversation to us, please?

Harvey: Well, they came back from court, and she told me to sing, because they don't know if it's being bugged and we have cameras on us. Roxanne kept on saying, 'Don't turn me in. Don't turn me in.' And I didn't have no whereabouts, you know understanding...

England: What else did they say?

Harvey: Roxanne said, 'Get your attorney, and I'll get mine and see if we can't talk at the jail, tonight.' And that was it.

England: When was the next time you had a conversation with Roxanne Suleski?

Harvey: It was Tuesday night, when we got locked down.

England: And what was the conversation about?

Harvey: Her daughter.

England: And which daughter was that?

Harvey: Alex.

England: And what did she tell you about her daughter, Alex?

Harvey: She didn't like her.

England: Did she tell you anything else about Alex?

Harvey: She was a problem. She gets in the way.

England: Did she talk to you about Alex's disappearance?

Harvey: Yes.

England: And what did she say about that?

Harvey: She had to, because of the first wife—Tom's first wife.

England: What did she call Alex?

Harvey: B****.

England: Did she relate anything to you about the disappearance itself, of Alex?

Harvey: Where she took her. Fifty feet behind the bathroom at Otter Creek.

England: What?

Harvey: Where the body is.

England: When you were talking to her, you said it was after eleven thirty. How were you all talking?

Harvey: Quiet. She didn't know if the room was bugged or if anybody was listening.

England: Did she tell you anything else about her daughter, Alex?

Harvey: How she killed her.

England: What did she say?

Harvey: She was tired of all the messes and the complaints and phone calls, and she was in the way—and day after day, it would just keep going on...

England: What was the method that she said?

Harvey: Put her in a garbage bag, tied it to her neck and then after she messed the stuff on herself, she put the baby's head in there.

England: When would you talk to Ms. Suleski?

Harvey: It was always when we were locked down.

Cross Examination by Roxanne Suleski's Attorney

Schaffer: Was there anyone else present when this conversation was going on?

Harvey: No.

Schaffer: I mean the first conversation between Tom and Roxanne, where you said you were sitting there singing.

Harvey: There was another lady present, but she went on to another place.

Schaffer: What was her name?

Harvey: Oh, I couldn't tell you because they took us—like, she went before us. She wasn't in our jail; she was from another jail.

Schaffer: And it's your testimony that you sat there and sung, while they had this conversation?

Harvey: Yes, sir.

Schaffer: Did you read all of this in the Courier-Journal?

Harvey: No, sir. We're not allowed newspapers in the jail.

Schaffer: And she said that she was jealous of Mr. Suleski's first wife?

Harvey: Yes, sir.

Schaffer: And Mrs. Suleski told you exactly where this body was in Otter Creek Park?

Harvey: Yes, she did.

Schaffer: Isn't it true that Roxanne took sleeping medication every night, when you were in the jail?

Harvey: I don't know. We're not informed of stuff like that.

Schaffer: You're telling us that there were also conversations about the jail being bugged?

Harvey: That's what she thought.

THE VERDICT

"Oh, I don't think it will take that long," my uncle said. We had spent the car ride talking about the closing arguments and were now in front of the gate to our flight. I was grateful that we didn't have to stick around while the jury deliberated, but I had brought up that it could be days before we knew what the verdict was.

"Well, I've been to a few trials in my life," my uncle said sarcastically, "and I have a feeling it won't take them more than a few hours." I knew my uncle's long employment with the LAPD had given him plenty of experience, but I was scared to get my hopes up.

"Why is it taking so long to board?" My aunt was a heavy smoker and freaking out that it had been a while since her last cigarette and would be another few hours before her next one. Oh, and she was deathly afraid of flying.

My uncle motioned for her to sit down. "They'll be calling us any minute, for Pete's sake, just sit down."

My aunt shook her head. "I will sit down when we are on the plane and I can order a stiff drink." She continued to pace back and forth.

About ten minutes later, we began to board. Once inside the plane, Linda became more anxious, until we were heading out and she was allowed to order a drink. The alcohol didn't cure her of her extreme anxiety, but it did seem to dull it. She relaxed slightly and thumbed through a magazine. My uncle went straight to sleep, and Dawn and I played card games on our tray tables. The time passed quickly, and we were soon landing.

While at the baggage claim, my aunt Linda was greeted by her daughter, who began talking quickly and pulled her to one side. I couldn't hear what they were saying, and I figured it was too early to know what was happening back in Kentucky, anyways. So, I joined my uncle and Dawn in finding all our bags and regrouping toward the far exit doors.

My aunt approached us with a small smile on her face. She stood looking at us for a few seconds, not saying anything. Then her smile got bigger and her eyes began to fill with tears. "The jury found them guilty." She continued to stand still and watch us for a response.

I was the first to respond, "Are you sure?" I needed to know that I heard her right and she heard the prosecutor right and none of this was a dream.

Linda wiped the tears from her face and wrapped her arms around me. "Yes, I'm sure." She whispered to me. "They are going away for a long time."

Linda and I hugged and cried, until Dawn suddenly started to cry, as well. Then, the three of us hugged and cried. My manly uncle hugged us tight once, then whispered, "Maybe we should head out before security thinks I'm beating or robbing you guys."

We all laughed with sighing laughs of relief. It was over.

People in the airport that day had no idea how life had changed for Dawn, Novi and I that day. They knew nothing of the hardships we had endured, the awful secrets we had kept, the reality that meant our parents were locked away for at least twelve to fifteen years. All they saw were two teens and an adult woman, crying and walking away from the baggage claim, being led by a quiet and imposing adult man, trying to hide the tears in his own eyes.

IMAGES FROM OUR STORY

Alex and Dawn when I first met them.

October 27
The search for Alex continues near the Suleski's Duvall Mobile Home Park residence as Tim Cleary, a diver and Elizabethtown police officer, swims a murky sinkhole to no avail. Fort Knox soldiers — 500 in all — join the search.

N-E/Jayme Burde

My mother and Tom walking to the courthouse for the final trial.

N-E/Jayme Bur

Tom Suleski listens to a tape recorded conservation of him and stepdaughter Nyssa Bruno during the fifth day of the Suleskis murde trial Monday.

N-E/Jayme Burder

Nyssa Bruno, 17, outstretches her arms showing a pose her mother, Roxanne Suleski, allegedly made her stepsister, Alex Suleski, assume as punishment.

PART TWO: MY NEW LIFE

My senior year of high school, following the trial, was fairly uneventful. This was mostly because I tried to keep a low profile and not draw attention to myself. I was very fearful that everyone at my school would learn about the trial and its uncomfortable details. I wasn't entirely sure what my teenage peers would do with that kind of information, and I didn't want to find out.

Although I had been approached by several talk shows and news programs for an interview with me, my dad and stepmom would always politely decline on my behalf, while advising them that I might be interested after I graduated. The three of us thought the attention to Alex's case could be a beneficial tool to exposing the problem of child abuse. I was not brave enough, however, to embark on that public journey while I was trying to finish public high school.

So, I filled my time working at the mall, doing schoolwork and attempting to be a "normal" teen.

After graduating from West High School (Torrance, California) in June of 1995, I worked hard as a house cleaner and saved enough money for my first semester of college. I entered El Camino College as a full-time psychology major. I thought I might be able to help others who were hurting from past traumatic experiences. I continued to work hard and study hard, while also having my first interview that would air on T.V.

Primetime Live aired "Dark Secret" in 1997. This episode laid out Alex's horrific story for all their viewers to see. I struggled deeply with exposing very personal things about my life to anyone who turned on that show that night. But I also struggled with the idea if more people had understood what was really happening to Alex, someone could have stepped in and saved her. Maybe her story could make a difference for a child in the future...

I received a lot of positive feedback from the airing of "Dark Secret." Talk shows began calling again. People from all over the country were calling and offering encouragement in my speaking out. Some confided about abuse they experienced or witnessed. The fact that strangers felt comfortable enough to talk to me about such personal experiences gave me some confidence in my choice to give public interviews and to pursue a career in psychology.

Fueled by this positive response to my first interview, I soon agreed to a second on The Montel Williams Show. This also went better than I expected. Montel came back to the Green Room and talked with me before I was led to sit under bright lights, on a stage facing a very large audience.

I remember feeling shocked at how much larger the audience was compared to how it always looked on my television. Had it not been for Montel giving me an idea of what his questions would be like and encouraging me to be strong and just "tell my story," I would have been completely petrified.

Because other talk shows were calling to get an interview with me, as well as television movie producers, we obtained the services of a talent agent who was friends with my dad's boss.

Suzanna Camejo became more than my talent agent over the years I knew her. She always reassured me and loved on me, even though I didn't make her any money. I needed someone like her at this time, because my hopes of continuing my journey to help abused children would soon be derailed.

First, I made the naïve decision to go on a talk show that would diminish my credibility as a real advocate. Not fully understanding the difference between talk shows and trash talk shows, I agreed to go on a show known as the latter and paid for it.

Several movie producers that had previously been "very interested" in making a television movie of my experience, soon had other projects to attend to and were not sure when they would have time for me—but assured me that they would "be in touch."

Suzanna comforted me and tried to explain the fickle nature of Hollywood, but I really didn't listen. I felt so stupid for not thinking ahead and doing my own review of the show before agreeing to be on it. With working and going to school, I hadn't really been watching much daytime television. So, I thought they were all the same. I remember sitting with her and my dad for lunch.

I was clearly disappointed at the sudden drop off interest by previously "motivated" producers. They made me believe that they would bring my sister's story to life and reach many households. How incredible it was going to be to have Alex's sad story bring attention to extreme child abuse and possibly save the lives of other at-risk children.

Then, in an instant ... that hope was gone.

"Nyssa, please don't be discouraged," Suzanna touched my hand from across the table as she smiled. "Don't ever quit what you have been called to do." She paused for a moment and finished. "We all believe in you ... and Alex would, too."

Although her words rang in my head, and I wanted to believe her, I wasn't sure. To add to my confusion during this time, I had decided that I hated the field of psychology and needed to switch my major. There was only so long I could sit and listen to how deranged the human mind was, before I began to lose hope in humanity or the idea that any of us are truly "sane."

So, after a year and a half of devoting full-time studies to psychology, I changed my major to sociology. With no more calls for me to do interviews or meet with movie producers, I fully immersed myself into work and school. Then, after one more year of college, I felt I had made another bad choice in choosing my new major. I had envisioned becoming a social worker and helping children in need. Instead, I had been studying statistics and listening to professors give their opinions on why the world is so messed up. I had hit a low point in my young adult life.

Feeling I wasted almost three years working menial jobs and studying nonsense, I wondered how I could salvage the time I lost. What would I do with my life now? What was my purpose? What did Suzanna mean by "what I was called to do?"

Unaware of how vulnerable I truly was at the time, I let myself get sucked into a group at my school that claimed to be "white witches." At first, the title they gave themselves seemed strange and even a little frightening. Wasn't a witch someone who would cast spells on you? Was that even possible? However, after going out to lunch with them a few times, I felt better about who they claimed to be.

They explained that they were merely nature-loving, peaceful girls who wanted all women to feel confident and free. They all practiced natural healing remedies for sicknesses and well-being. This all sounded good to me. I still didn't understand why they referred to themselves as "white witches," but assumed it had to do with their all-natural healing practices and possibly their appearances. They mostly wore long and flowing skirts or dresses, with their medium-to-long hair down, and little-to-no makeup. They looked like cute hippie girls. After a couple of weeks of hanging out with these girls, I found out there was much more to them than their self-given label.

Lana and Stacy were two of these new friends, and the girls I spent the most time with, within the larger group at the school. While eating our lunches at our usual spot under a large weeping willow tree, these girls invited me to a "gathering" of like-minded women.

"It's so great when they do this," Lana cooed and hugged Stacy tightly. She reached over and pulled me into their hug. All the girls in this group tended to hug and touch each other a lot, so I wasn't sure if Lana was genuinely excited or just touchy like usual.

"Um, I don't know yet ... I mean, we have our first drafts due in English the next day, and I think I have to work later that day..." I trailed off and looked at the ground. I felt bad about not going, but I really didn't have time for socializing. I was trying to get through my classes for the semester before changing my major again for the next. I didn't want to mess up in the last few weeks.

Lana brushed the hair out of my face with one hand and lifted my chin with the other. "Sis, it's okay to do things for you," she whispered. I had to admit that their practice of calling each other "sister" or "sis" had been very appealing to me. It was nice to feel such a close connection with such nice girls.

"Plus, there are some other sisters who are really wanting to meet you," Stacy added, as she placed her hand on my shoulder. Not wanting to let anyone down, I agreed to go to this "gathering."

Squealing and hugging, Lana began revealing more and more details about our big night out. What I understood by the end of lunch was that we would be meeting out in the woods with about twenty to thirty other young women who shared the same lifestyle and beliefs as us. It would be like camping with a bunch of sisters.

Two days later, I was driving the four of us out to the middle of nowhere. The fourth girl was another white witch from our school who I had met before but didn't know that well. Since I was the only one with a car big enough for the four of us and our basic camping supplies, I had offered to drive.

Stacy and Diana were sitting in the backseat, and Lana sat up front with me. I could hear the girls in the back going on and on about how great these little "festivals" were, and soon little details began to pop up. The two girls talked about the bonfire that would be lit and how amazing it was. They talked about the dancing and music that would be there. By the time we were getting close to our destination, they were giddy with excitement.

Driving through a heavily wooded area, I didn't see the masses of cars and people until we were right next to them. There was a lot more than twenty to thirty women. It seemed like a small sea of women scattered through this section of the forest. Long dresses and flowing hair blew in the breezes and wafted through the trees. Smiles and laughter were abundant, and I felt like I had found the best group in the world to be a part of. Females being incredibly kind to other females. This was not something I had ever experienced in my life.

I never would have guessed that several hours later I would be shaking behind the wheel of my car as I sped through the forest, desperately trying to put as much distance as possible between me and that same group. My ideas of who those people really were began to splinter as soon as we walked into the group.

First, I noticed several smaller groups of women chanting together, while other small groups were mixing concoctions and reciting strange poem-like verses over these mixes. It didn't take me long to see that they were actually practicing witches who were either casting spells or invoking some otherworldly power for something they wanted. I didn't even know there were people who really did those things and felt uncomfortable that my friends had left that part out of their description of this event. What else had they left out?

Next, the bonfire started, and the real uncomfortable part began. A band of women drummed as the fire was lit. Several older women chanted something about praising a mother goddess, and everyone screamed. Apparently, this was the sign to lose your mind, because women began stripping off their shirts and jumping over the fire. Other women began touching each other in more than a "sisterly" way.

My friends blended into the chaos of the crowd and I lost sight of them. Alone, in a large group of strangers, doing strange things, I began to back up instinctively. I thought I could disappear into the forest and wait until this whole thing was done. I planned to reappear when it was time to leave, and just get myself and my friends home safely.

As I was cautiously backing up, I bumped into something. Assuming I had bumped into a shrub or tree stump of some kind, I reached back to feel how big it was. I did not want to take my eyes off of the terrifying anarchy that was breaking out before me. The object I felt was clearly human, and I had to turn around to see who I had walked into.

A middle-aged woman, sitting with several girls my age, looked up at me. I removed my hand from her shoulder—and she grabbed it with her own hand. Her grip was uncomfortably strong. "You can sit with us, sweetie," she said with a sneaky grin. She began to pull me down next to her. This was too much. She wasn't letting go. I had to get out of there.

"I think I'm going to throw up!" I blurted out. She quickly let go, and I ran as fast as I could through the woods. I ran away from the group of frenzied witches and doubled back to the parking area in a very large horseshoe. I did not want to accidentally bump into anyone else. Several minutes later, I found my car, made sure none of my friends' belongings were still inside, and sped off in the direction we arrived from.

Shaking from exhaustion and stress, I fought to remember the way back to the highway in the dark. It wasn't until I saw the small familiar gas station by the highway on-ramp that I took a long deep breath and allowed myself to relax a little. The entire ride home, I went over the events of the night. The things my friends told me and the things they left out. Why hadn't they been totally honest?

By the time I finally pulled into the parking space behind my apartment, I knew that Lana and Stacy were not good friends. They had clearly left out important details about who they were and what they did, and that meant I could not trust them. I felt so stupid for trusting people I had not known for very long. I had behaved like a naïve little girl, and a lot worse could have happened to me as a consequence.

Over the next few weeks, I had a blow up with Lana and Stacy, I worked incredibly hard on my final papers and tests for the semester and continued to work part time jobs to cover my living expenses. I felt like I was spinning my wheels and going absolutely nowhere.

Once the semester was over, I returned to my school to take a "professions" test that my counselor recommended. I spent almost an hour answering questions that didn't seem like they applied to anything in particular. At the end, my head was pounding, and I was relieved to hear that my results would be sent to me and I wouldn't need to stay and talk to my counselor that day.

Walking to the parking lot, I saw two girls from the white witch club running away from the parking lot and laughing. One of them saw me and motioned to other. They looked at me and ran as fast as they could in the opposite direction. My heart began to race, and I sprinted towards my car.

"Please don't let my car be totaled," I thought.

When I arrived at my spot, I could see that my car had been egged. About a dozen eggs were cracked, split and oozing all over my car. After walking around the car and making sure nothing was broken or "totaled," I sat down on the parking brick next to my car.

Those girls were my friends, and now they were egging my car and running off like little kids. I slumped over and rested my head on my knees.

"There has to be something better than all of this for me," I whispered to myself. I sighed and looked up at the sky. "What do you want me to do?" I ask half-heartedly. I figured God had bigger issues to deal with, but I was desperate and tired.

Just then, I saw someone get into their car a few yards away, out of the corner of my eye. I didn't look over, out of embarrassment. I saw the car back out of its spot and then continue to back up, until it was right in front of me. I looked up from my parking brick seat and realized that I knew the driver. Her name was Grace, and we had worked together at a bar. She had been an assistant manager and had always been very nice to me. She glanced over at my car and smiled.

"Rough day?" she remarked.

I rolled my eyes. "Yes, Grace. It's not been my best day. Okay?" We had worked enough hours together that I knew I didn't have to sugarcoat things for her. "Is that all?" I asked.

"No." She pulled into the parking space next to my car and motioned for me to get in. I sat down in the passenger seat of her fairly new and eggless Honda. "I know you're kinda in a rough patch right now."

I was taken aback by her bluntness. I had talked to her about changing my major and some of my problems with "friends" at school, while not disclosing some of the more embarrassing details.

I shrugged and said, "I guess so. I just took another aptitude test, so..." I wanted to convince her that I was fine. Maybe even convince myself.
"Haven't you taken like five of those in the last few years?" she asked. I realized that she had actually been listening to me, over the time I had been working with her and venting. I nodded and shrugged again. I didn't know what else to say.

"Well," Grace began, "do you remember how I talked about opening my own bar on Guam?" I nodded, although I had to admit that I hadn't really been listening to her as well as she had been for me. I vaguely remembered her mentioning some foreign sounding place that really didn't interest me at the time.

From that point, Grace began explaining to me about an opportunity that had come up for her. She had found an investor that was going to help her start her bar. She needed people she could count on to go with her—and she wanted to invite me.

"What?" I was shocked. "I don't even know where Guam is." I took a deep breath, "Plus, I have a lease on my apartment and car payments. I will know what to change my major to, once the test results are in..."

"Really?" Grace smiled. "Are you going to keep taking tests and changing the course of your life every year?" She shook her head. "Maybe you need a break."

I was a little peeved that Grace felt like she had me all figured out. I was even more upset at how accurate her analysis was.

I sighed and asked her, "So, what do you want from me?"

She told me that she would pay for my tickets and share her townhouse with me, and in return, I would earn minimum wage and keep any tips I made. She continued to explain where Guam was and what it was like there. I was shocked to learn that it was a part of the U.S., and I had never heard of it. It did sound beautiful and exotic. It also sounded like a temporary escape from my confusion. Maybe Grace was right, and I needed a break.

Several weeks later, I was on a plane to Guam. I had used my tuition money for the next semester to pay my bills for the few months I would be gone. I had also made arrangements for my car and apartment to be cared for. Once I had made the decision to go, I felt strangely free and not anxious about anything at all. Sitting on the plane, preparing for the longest flight of my life, I marveled at the lack of stress I felt. After reading through a few chapters of the book that Grace gave me about Guam, I fell asleep.

GUAM

The island of Guam was more beautiful and striking than I imagined. Growing up in Southern California, I was very familiar with coastal beaches. But I had never experienced beaches like the ones I found on this tropical paradise. The sand was so soft and fine. The water was so unbelievably warm and shallow out for yards. The wildlife from the nearby reef was so abundant. It was like visiting a hands-on aquarium every day. The beauty of the island made my transition to my temporary home go more smoothly than I expected.

After a month of adjusting to the humid tropical weather and my consistent "night owl" schedule, I was feeling very much at home on this little island in the middle of the Pacific Ocean. Even so, I reminded myself every chance I could that I had a life back in California that I needed to get back to. I had responsibilities and people who were expecting me to return in a few months. To encourage this "extended vacation" mentality, I decided (at the advice of Grace) not to put myself in a position where I would meet someone and become attached. This meant, to the disappointment of my new co-workers and friends, that I would not go out to the clubs or bars with them on our nights off.

Since Guam was a heavily military island, there were many clubs and bars that catered to the many airmen, sailors and other military people who filtered through the region. Again, I reminded myself that becoming involved with a military person would be the absolute worst thing I could do at that point, if I really wanted to return home to California as planned. In fact, the only way I would agree to go to any of the beaches during the day was if my friends agreed to help me "repel" any guys who showed any interest in talking to me. This became a hilarious game for myself and a few of my more courageous friends.

When approached by interested males, we could choose from the following: Speaking to each other in a made-up language, acting like we had boyfriends in the mob, or imitating the voices of Beavis and Butthead. Eventually, I became so comfortable with this approach for staying single that I finally agreed to go out with a few of them to a bar, on our off day.

Temple was a club known for having great live music. That night, a band called John's Bad Wheel was performing alternative music from popular artists of that time. The lead vocalist sounded so much like Eddie Vedder from Pearl Jam that it was like being at their actual concert. I was having a great time with my friends, and when they suggested that we move on to another bar when the band was done playing, I agreed. After all, my friends had continued to honor their promise of "group-repelling" any guys who came on to me, and it had been working.

As we were leaving Temple, we ran into a group of guys who knew one of my friends, Sandra. She stopped and talked to the four guys for a few minutes and then rejoined our group.

"Hey," Sandra asked coyly, "do you think we can drive over to Hard Rock with Mike and his friends?" She knew we had collectively agreed to stay away from guys for the night, so she added, "Mike is totally cool, and his friends won't hit on us. He said they wouldn't." She looked very serious, and I felt pressured to give in, since I had the rental car we were using. Sandra had been a pretty loyal and trusted friend for the four weeks we had worked together, and I had no reason to doubt what she said.

After we all agreed to meet at the next club together, our group of eight walked down the concrete steps to the parking area behind the club. My friend Tara and I got into my car. I sat in the driver's seat, and she scooted into the passenger side. I started the car and heard the two back doors open behind me. The weight of the car shifted dramatically. I knew my two small girlfriends had not climbed into the back seat. I turned around and saw two unknown males sitting in my vehicle. Sandra tapped on my window, and I lowered it.

"Is it okay if they ride with you? We're going in Tom's car." A male called out something to her from a few cars away, "Oh, I mean Todd's car." She giggled at her mistake and then said, "Okay! See you guys there!" before running off and jumping into the other vehicle with our fourth friend Debbie and two other guys. I sat there for a moment with my mouth partially open to answer her question that she had obviously not really needed an answer to. This sudden turn of events made me nervous, but I tried to play it off and began to drive us to our new destination.

Tara made small talk with the two guys in our car. It turned out that Sandra's friend Mike was actually sitting directly in back of Tara. I thought it was strange that he didn't go with Sandra, since she said that they were friends. The guy sitting behind me was named Aaron or something like that.

I couldn't really concentrate on what my passengers were all chit-chatting about, because I was focusing on weaving through the crowds of drunks and party goers who were wandering through the main strip of the island, known as "Hotel Row."

It wasn't until I was about to miss my turn into the new parking area, that the guy in back of me said, "Oh, it's right here."

I cautiously moved into the center lane and waited for a group of oblivious Japanese tourists to walk out of my way. I looked up at my rearview mirror and said, "Thanks."

Before I could turn back to view my upcoming entrance again, a pair of sparkling blue eyes stared back at me. The same voice that helped me, answered, "No problem."

I made my turn and looked for an empty space, all the time thinking, "Okay, so he's got nice eyes. So what? He's a stranger in my car and I'm sure I know what his final goal is. It's not just to be my new friend."

In fact, Mike was already working whatever magic he had on my friend Tara. By the time we found a parking spot and were ready to leave the car, Tara was amazed that Mike had lived in Washington state, where she was from. Imagine that! She seemed so amazed by the coincidence that she had forgotten I was even around.

She hopped out of the car, and she and Mike walked side by side toward the club, laughing and talking. I slowly pulled myself out of the driver's seat and turned to see who had off- set the weight distribution of my car. I was fairly shocked. The guy with the piercing blue eyes was blond, tan, and built like a body builder. His tight wetsuit-like shirt showed how defined he was.

Okay, I had obviously not paid any attention to Mike's group back at Temple to have missed this guy.

"Are we going?" Big Blond asked me.

"Yeah, I guess," I shrugged indifferently before walking by him and heading in the direction I last saw Tara and Mike going.

He walked next to me, but not too close. I didn't look at him but focused on trying to figure out the way to the club's entrance. I looked down a row of cars and didn't see any doors. I walked quickly to the next aisle and glanced down. Again, I saw nothing. I began walking fast towards the next row, when Blue Eyes said, "Um, I think the entrance is this way."

I turned around and saw that I left him standing at the last aisle of cars. He stood with his finger pointing in the opposite direction of where I had been looking. I smiled sheepishly, "Oh. Thanks."
I slowly walked back to where he was standing and felt like I should apologize or something. I mean, he wasn't trying to put moves on me or anything. Yet, it looked like I was trying to escape him. I was about to smile and make a joke about getting lost in a parking lot, when voices coming from the direction that we needed to go caught our attention. We both looked over and saw a group of loud and drunk military guys walking into the parking structure. Without my group of friends with me, I felt very vulnerable and a little scared.

"Stay on this side." Tan and Blond stepped over to my left side and motioned for me to walk with him. I nodded and we walked toward the entrance.

As we neared the group, they quieted their loud behavior and seemed to be whispering and gesturing to each other. I looked up and one of the guys locked eyes with me. He opened his mouth to speak to me, when suddenly my bodyguard positioned his body between us and murmured something to the guy. I vaguely heard the other guy say, "Sorry," before we were passed the group and around the corner.

Quickly, my new friend opened the door for me, and we were inside. He saw the missing couple from our car, and I followed him to the table they were sitting at.

Then Mike and he left to get drinks, Tara squished up next to me. "What happened to you guys?" Wanting to get that mischievous look off her face, I explained what happened in the parking garage.

"Yeah, Mike said that Allen was a really good guy," she nodded and added, "and not bad to look at, either." She smiled and snuck a peek at him and Mike at the bar.

I rolled my eyes. "You know I am NOT interested," I said in my most serious tone.

Tara rolled hers "Okay. We'll see."

Her disbelief that I could control myself made me even more determined to prove her wrong. So what, if he was good looking? So what, if he had instinctively protected me and had not used that time to inappropriately touch me in any way? So what, if he had actually opened the door for me? And really, so what if his name was even Allen?

"Mike said you guys drink Miller Light," Allen said as he placed the two beers in front of Tara and me. "I hope that's okay," he looked at me, waiting for an answer.

"Yes. Thank you." I politely answered. Just then, the rest of the group arrived at the club and joined our table. They explained some complicated story about missing the turn and not finding a place to turn around or something. I was trying to listen, so I could get my mind off the fact that Allen's eyes had turned from blue to bright green.

The rest of the night, and even the next few weeks was just an extension of those first few hours that Allen and I met. I knew I was interested in him but continued to try and convince myself why it would be insane for me to act on that interest. His friends, and eventually my friends continued to tell me what a great guy he was and that I should give him a chance. It just didn't seem that easy.

The more I got to know Allen, the more questions I had about who he really was. He seemed very responsible in his position as a Naval Police Officer and not at all like the other sailors I met on Guam. However, he had also dated mostly strippers on the island, which made me think he really wasn't looking for a meaningful or serious relationship.

Also, I was shocked when he had told me he had already been married twice before and had two children, one with each ex-spouse. I was struggling to reconcile the genuinely nice guy I was getting to know in our newly formed group with the information I was compiling about him. So, I decided to shut everyone up and go on ONE date with him. I figured that after that one date, we would both see that we had nothing in common, and he could move on to some other girl, and I could go back to being the "unavailable" girl of the group. I was sure the date would be dead from the start. After all, I already knew that he was from North Carolina and had grown up a military brat. What could the two of us even have to talk about?

Two hours into that first date, I realized I had made a huge mistake. I had unjustly prejudged Allen and almost missed out on the most genuine fun I'd had since arriving on the island. The surprises started from the very beginning when we both said that we wanted to eat sushi for dinner. I had not met many non-Asians who really like sushi like I did. Over our sashimi appetizer, the similarities continued to come; we both wanted to live in Alaska, we both loved log cabins, we both liked hiking and fishing, we had both even lived in Germany during the same time period (his dad had been stationed there).

After dinner, we were so excited about our common interests that we decided to go on a small hike off one of the beaches. Nothing too intense, since I was wearing sandals. Allen didn't want me to "twist my ankle, fall down, and break my butt." I laughed so hard at that. It was also dusk, and we didn't want to accidentally trip on a local oddity called a coconut crab. These were hermit crabs that were so big, they would eat coconuts and small rodents.

As we walked through an area where the beach met the jungle, we scanned the cliff line for caves and talked about how we could come back the next day and hike up to any caves that we saw that evening. We were so caught up in talking about the places we wanted to explore on the island, we hadn't noticed how dark it had suddenly become.

Allen stopped and said, "Did you hear that?" I could barely make out his eyes squinting in the moonlight.

I held my breath and listened. I heard a strange rustling sound. "Yeah," I whispered, "I hear something."

Allen held my hand with one hand and pulled his flashlight he had brought from his car out with his other hand. He turned on the flashlight and pointed it down in front of us. We both gasped.

Directly in front of us was the most amount of coconut carbs that I had ever seen. As Allen moved his flashlight in a zigzag pattern in front of us, we could see they were all over the beach.

Allen said, "Maybe we should turn back for now."

I agreed, quickly. With just a narrow beam of the flashlight lighting our way through unfamiliar terrain, I was acutely aware of the fact that I was wearing open-toed sandals. I could just imagine one of those giant crabs biting off one of my toes. We walked quickly back the way we came and saw more crabs crawling over the rocks and falling onto the beach. One landed right next to my foot, and I screamed!

"Do you want me to carry you?" Allen asked.

I shook my head "no." I was determined to show that I was a brave young lady and make up for the girlish squeal I let out.

"Okay. Then, I think we should go a little faster," he suggested.

We were both looking at the little avalanche of crabs falling over the rocks and moving over the sand. I agreed with him, and we started jogging toward the car. One crab came out of nowhere and touched the side of my foot. I screamed again, and we both started sprinting!

Once we were at the car, I began laughing uncontrollably!

Allen smiled and asked, "Was this still fun for you?"

"Are you kidding?" I asked as I calmed myself. "That was hilarious! I can't wait to tell my parents I was chased by giant crabs!" I wiped the tears from my eyes and took a deep breath. "That was so cool," I said.

"Yeah, that was pretty cool," he sat on the hood of his car. "So ... can we do this again?"

"Yes," I answered, before realizing that I had spontaneously agreed to another date. It was not like me to impulsively answer what I thought was a fairly important question. But I decided to go with my instinct and stick with my answer. I experienced the most fun date with Allen. Maybe the next time would be even better.

The next date, and many more after that, were also "so cool."

We explored many places on the island that most tourists wouldn't take the time to see. We went to beaches that visitors to the island never got to see, because they were time consuming to get to. We went snorkeling and cave exploring and took the time to learn the rich cultural heritage and tumultuous history (including many WWII sites) of the island. Things between us developed so quickly after our first date, it was only a matter of time before we had "the talk."

I was approaching the deadline I had set for my return to life in California. Allen and I were sitting on the balcony of his condo in the village of Tamuning. Even though it was ten o'clock at night, it was still warm enough to be out in our t-shirts and shorts.

We were relaxing and enjoying the stars and beauty of the tropics at night. We talked about the hike we had done earlier that day. I mentioned another site I heard about and how I really wanted to see it.

"You mean before you leave?" he asked.

I had tried not to think about my upcoming trip back to the States and the hard decisions I would need to make.

When I didn't answer right away, Allen sighed and asked, "Are you planning on coming back?"

Again, I tried not to think about having to make this kind of choice. I recognized what a life-changing choice it would be. I had a life in California. Although I had moved around a lot in my childhood, I had spent most of it in California. It was the only home I had ever known, except for the brief time in Kentucky.

I looked at Allen, who was patiently awaiting my answer. I had made a bond with him that was unlike anything I had ever made with anyone in my life. I felt completely comfortable to be myself with him. I trusted him. But something was still nagging me. It was this feeling that a major life decision should take a long time to make.

This is why I couldn't commit to a major in school. I mean, what if I spent all that time studying for a field, then discovered that I hated it after I already graduated? Maybe Allen and I were just having fun, but after a while, we might find that we had grown in two different directions. It would be just wasted time for the both of us.

Allen seemed to sense my inner debate and leaned forward. "Look," he began, "I know this all happened pretty quickly, and it wasn't what you were expecting when you came out here. But I want you to know that I really care about you, and I really enjoy our time together every day." He took a deep breath and seemed to be choosing his words very carefully. "I guess what I wanted to say was ... I don't want to go to clubs and hang out with people who are just looking for a good time out in town. I want to settle down and do the things we've been doing." He took another deep breath, and finished with, "and I want to keep doing them with you."

I looked at him and saw that he was very serious, and that he was again waiting for my response. I still didn't know how to respond and quickly asked myself, "What is wrong with me?"

Even though, I already knew what was wrong. My whole life I had watched my mother make big, life-altering choices without giving much thought to consequences or how those choices might affect others. I was desperately trying not to be like her.

Still not receiving an answer from me, Allen said, "I want you to be honest with me, either way. Just please don't waste my time, if you are not planning on coming back." He sat back in his chair, looking frustrated.

I watched him look out at the view of the bay and realized something that altered the way I saw my dilemma. Allen was in no way like any of the guys my mother had been in relationships with. He was strong and honest in his beliefs and views. He didn't need or want me to be a mother figure to him. He was fully capable of thinking for himself. Also, the very fact that I was painstakingly analyzing this decision about my life showed that I was in no way like my mom. This was my decision, and I needed to choose for myself what I wanted. I wasn't going to continue to overanalyze or see my mom anywhere in this situation—because she wasn't there.

"Allen, I'm sorry." I leaned forward and touched his hand. "I didn't mean to be quiet for so long. I'm just a little scared, and this is kind of a big deal..." He looked confused by my inconclusive rambling. "What I mean is—I do want to come back. I will come back. I just need to know that you meant what you said."

"You mean about not hanging out with our group of friends and bar hopping?"

"Yes."

Allen smiled. "Yeah. I'm serious." He leaned forward and kissed me. "Are you?"

I smiled back. "Yes. I am."

He let out a whew sound and said, "The next time you are debating things in your head, could you just say it all out loud so I don't go crazy imagining what you're thinking?"

I laughed, "Sure. I'll try."

TIME TO GROW UP

When it was time for me to fly back to California, I did so with a very different intent than I would have before I met Allen. I was going back to tie up loose ends and close that part of my life. I was flying back to Guam as soon as I could and starting a new chapter of my life—with Allen.

Once I was back in my home state, I had a heart-to-heart with my dad and stepmom about my plans to return to the little island in the Pacific. My stepmom was very worried and didn't think it was a good idea. I felt like most of her concern came from not knowing Allen and wondering how some guy could have convinced me to leave my family and friends and return to him. I understood her worry about the situation and tried to relieve some of her stress by telling her all I could about him. My dad was a different story. He seemed to understand that I needed to make my own life.

"I am really going to miss you, sweetie." My dad hugged me and gently patted me on the back. "But I know that you need to find what is right for you. I guess that might not be here in Southern California," he smiled as he said, "maybe it's in Guatemala."

"Oh, Dad..." We both knew he was making a joke to lighten the mood.

After I talked to my parents, I found someone to take over the lease on my apartment so I could take my name off of the contract with no penalties. My step-grandparents paid off the remaining balance on my car, and I signed the title over to them. I gave away all my furniture and said my goodbyes to all my friends and co-workers. When I was finally ready to fly back to Guam, almost one month had passed.

During this time, Allen and I talked on the phone every night, with very few exceptions. I had kept him up to date on the progress I was making, and he was filing me in on the new friends he had made on base. They sounded more mature and less like the party crowd we had both come from.

He also found a stray puppy that was most likely left by a "booney" dog. This was the name for the mellow, nomad dogs that wandered throughout the island. Allen brought the puppy home, named it Humpy (because that was all he wanted to do, according to Allen), and he was now "our dog." I was feeling more and more like I had a "home" waiting for me—and I missed it.

It was also during this time that Allen and I had a lot of time to talk. We agreed that if we were really going to make lasting changes in our lifestyles, not only would we need to make new friends, but I would also need to find a new job. Working at a bar wouldn't exactly help us in our quest to mature and move on. I began to reach out to some friends that I made at the bar. Most of them owned or worked for various businesses around the island.

After many phone calls and reimbursing my parents for all the long-distance phone charges, I was able to find someone who put in a good word for me at the FedEx station on the island. Allen and I were so excited! A real job, with real benefits, with a really good company, that would pay a real consistent paycheck—and no alcohol was involved! I flew back the next week and had my interview two days later. I was hired!

My new life on Guam was a huge adjustment. Working for FedEx was both physically and mentally demanding. It was also the most rewarding work I had ever done. Allen also had a new work schedule, since he had been put on a task force that worked with the Military Police. This group was known as "Spec Ops" and consisted of a group of four guys who were basically Game Wardens for all of the area considered naval property. He loved his new job and would normally have an exciting account of chasing poachers through the jungle with his team and arresting people he would occasionally recognize or be familiar with their families (it was a small island, after all). His new job also meant that he sometimes worked odd hours, and we had a hard time connecting as often as we wanted to.

But we made the most of our time together and enjoyed our new domestic situation. Then, I became very sick. At first, I thought I had a flu of some kind. When it continued for more than a week, I thought that my body might be having a hard time getting used to my new rigorous schedule. Finally, after a month of feeling "under the weather," Allen and I had a pretty good idea of what my "sickness" was. I had missed my period by about two weeks. I took a pregnancy test, and it came back positive. I had only been back on Guam for three months, and now I was pregnant!

This was not what Allen and I had planned for. I made an appointment with an OB/GYN I found in the phone book and continued pushing through my long schedule, feeling incredibly sick and anxious.

The day before my appointment, I was home on my day off.

Allen was working and I was keeping myself busy by cleaning the linoleum floors that stretched through half of the three- bedroom condo we lived in. Suddenly, I felt a sharp pain in my lower abdomen. It was unlike anything I had ever experienced before. I doubled over and felt a wetness in between my legs and spread down my sweatpants. I ran to the bathroom to find blood all over the inside of my legs and pants. I sat on the toilet and began to clean myself off. I tried to remain calm and assess the situation.

Another cramp came and I doubled over in pain. I knew the situation was getting serious when I saw more blood coming from my body. I was feeling that familiar light-headed and spinning feeling I had right before passing out. I immediately leaned over and smushed my face against the cold tile wall. I breathed slowly and kept my eyes closed.

Just as I was getting ready to drag myself to the phone and call for help, I realized that the cramps had stopped. I was also feeling much better and clear-headed. I slowly got up and began cleaning myself off, while trying to determine if I had some crazy "catch up" of my period. Was that even possible? I thought about driving myself to the Urgent Care at one of the clinics, when I noticed something in the toilet. It seemed like the biggest blood clot I had ever seen. But, when I looked closer it seemed to have something else attached to it... suddenly, the room started spinning again. I began to understand what had most likely happened.

When Allen got home, I explained what I had experienced, and he felt terrible for me. "Do you think you miscarried?" he asked with concern.

I shrugged. I really didn't know, and I really didn't want to think too much about it. I didn't know if that meant I couldn't have children and my body was rejecting any new life I would try to carry. I didn't know if I had caused it to happen by working such a physical job. I was sad, confused—and just numb.

The next day at my appointment, the doctor ran a few tests. He confirmed that I was not pregnant anymore. He wanted me to get a blood test to show more conclusively and make another appointment to see him in a couple of weeks. He warned me that, in the meantime, my body might take a while to readjust to not being pregnant anymore. My hormones might be "out of whack," and I might not menstruate right away. But he assured me, "It will just take some time."

Back home, I told Allen all about the appointment and the hormonal surprises that might follow. Although neither one of us were ready to start a family together, the thought of a baby that did not make it was a sad one. We didn't talk much about the incident after that day, for the next few months.

During those next months, we both continued to work and look for ways to further our educations. Allen began taking a long-distance course in Wildlife Conservation to go along with his own job experience. I began picking out a few classes at the junior college on the island, Guam Community College. I also continued to struggle with "hormonal issues," as the doctor said I would. I still felt tired and sick most days but struggled to push through it so I wouldn't lose my job. I had also developed some extra weight in my stomach area. I dieted, but only lost weight from other areas of my body. My doctor didn't seem concerned and continued to attribute everything to "struggling hormones after a miscarriage."

Then, one day, Allen and I were setting up for a day of relaxing indoors on our day off. We had rented some movies and video games for our PlayStation. Allen was getting our drinks and snacks for the first movie, and I was sitting in our papa-san chair. As I leaned over to adjust the pillows for two people to sit comfortably, I felt a "flick" in my lower stomach area. I had never in my life felt something so odd and stopped immediately where I was. Allen came over with the drinks and snacks and looked at me strangely.

"What are you doing?" he asked.

I sat upright and moved over to allow him space to sit. I opened my mouth to answer, when—flick. There was another little bubble popping feeling in my stomach. My face must have looked concerned, because Allen sat down immediately and asked, "Are you okay?"

I tried to explain to him what I was feeling, and he decided to put his hand on my stomach. Not feeling anything, I pushed his hand down into my stomach and said, "It was more right here..." There was a strong flick, and we both looked at each other.

"You felt that?" I asked.

Allen nodded. I called my doctor immediately and made an appointment for the next day.

By the time I walked in for my appointment, I was fairly worked up. I was angry and frustrated that the doctor had brushed off all my symptoms, and now I could have something seriously wrong with me. The night before, Allen and I had come up with twenty different things that could have been wrong with me. I was not going to leave the doctor's office without an explanation.

After peeing in a cup and giving blood, I sat in the examining room and steamed. I was going to sue this doctor if I had some serious condition that he could have solved early on. Finally, the doctor entered the room with a small electronic device that looked like an old cassette player with a microphone attached to it.

"Miss Bruno, it looks like you are pregnant and most likely have been for the last five to six months," he spoke calmly and glanced over at his nurse, who smiled continuously at me. The information he was giving me didn't make any sense, so I stared blankly at the both of them.

"The only explanation I have, is that you were actually pregnant with twins and miscarried only one of them. Your blood tests could have been affected by your hormones fluctuating from this miscarriage or by your pregnancy being further along than what we thought." He held up the small machine he brought in with him. "I would like to see if I can pick up the baby's heartbeat. If that's okay with you."

I slowly nodded and laid down on the exam bed. I reran the information the doctor had given me over again in my mind. I still did not fully understand what he had told me. I jerked suddenly when the coldness of the microphone object covered with lubricant jelly touched the surface of my stomach. I watched the doctor move the wand-like piece around on my skin, until he seemed to hear something and stopped.

I didn't know what to expect at that point but knew in an instant what we were listening to. A pitter-patter of a heartbeat way too fast to be my own, could be heard from the speaker the doctor held in his other hand. What? I felt like reality punched me in the face. I laid my head back onto the paper-covered pillow that crunched loudly and covered my eyes with my bent arm. I tried to calm myself but couldn't stop the pouring of tears and pathetic sobs that emitted in front of two strangers.

I stayed at the doctor's office for what seemed like a very long time. The doctor and his nurse calmed me down and tried to help me process what had happened over the last few months. They talked about what my options were at that point. The focus seemed to switch from my health, to the health of the baby that had been quietly growing inside me.

When it was all laid out, the three of us realized that I had done almost everything you are NOT supposed to do when you are pregnant. I had taken antibiotics for several different things during that time that were not recommended as safe to use during a pregnancy. I had also smoked occasionally during the pregnancy and drank alcohol every day that I had off from work. But, our biggest concern? The fact that every morning I worked, I was clearing packages through customs which required me to push boxes through the oldest X-ray machine on the planet. It hummed loudly and had large orange stickers that warned pregnant women not to be near it. The FedEx loading dock was even right next to the area where hazardous waste was kept. I literally could have reached over and touched a drum of toxic chemicals while sorting my route packages for the day. Even my diet was not sufficient for someone who was trying to grow another person.

The doctor finally braced me that there was a good chance that I had a baby with serious developmental or physical impairments. After breaking down again, the nurse gave me the contact information for the only doctor on the island who did abortions. I wandered out of the office and somehow made it over to the doctor's office. I didn't think he would be able to see me then, but I just felt like I needed more answers, and I didn't want to go home to an empty condo.

I was explaining my situation to the receptionist, when a tall, elderly man came out from an open office behind her desk and listened to the rest of my story. The two of them shook their heads and looked at each other in disbelief.

"The quality of healthcare around here never ceases to amaze me," the man said. He talked to the secretary about having some time to see me then, and I realized that he was the doctor of the clinic. He waved me into his office and introduced himself as Dr. Brandt. He gave me some patient forms to fill out, while he did some end-of-day paperwork. Apparently, he was finishing up for the day when I had walked in. If I had shown up fifteen minutes later, they would have been closed.

When we were both done writing, the doctor looked over my forms and went through my backstory once more. He seemed concerned that I wasn't entirely sure about ending a pregnancy that I had only found out about a few hours earlier.

"Well," he began, "if you are looking to terminate the pregnancy because you think there is some kind of deformity or abnormality, then our first step would be to do an ultrasound. I can get a look at how the baby is developing and about how old it is."

I agreed, not fully understanding what an ultrasound would be like.

The secretary was also his nurse, and she came in and sat next to me while Dr. Brandt put the second gooey electronic object of the day on my belly. His nurse pointed up at the small black-and-white screen and told me that the baby would show on it. I squinted at the swirls of grey that enlarged and went away as the doctor moved the large wand over my stomach. He stopped at different times to press buttons and mumble to himself. The nurse smiled and watched him. I never saw anything on the screen that looked like a baby. Once the doctor was done, the two of us went back to his desk, while his nurse continued to close down the office.

"Well, I will tell you that I didn't notice any obvious abnormalities," he explained, "and I'm not sure that your pregnancy is under the five-month cut-off for this procedure." He took out a pad of what looked like oversized prescription sheets and jotted something on the first one. "If you take this to Guam Memorial Hospital, they can do another ultrasound and get a much better look than I can. My machine is not as good as theirs." He took a deep breath and made more serious eye contact with me. He then explained the specifics of the procedure that would end my pregnancy. When he was done, he said, "Okay, so give me a call tomorrow, and we can decide what to do from there."

I nodded and took the paper from him. My hand was shaking a little, and I moved so quickly to leave the office, I almost tripped on the secretary's chair. I was actually glad to have another place to go to. Allen would still not be home yet, and I just wanted to keep moving, so I would not have to think about what was really happening.

As I drove to the only civilian hospital on the island, I thought about my strange visit with the abortion doctor. I had actually driven two friends to abortion clinics around Los Angeles and remembered how crowded and impersonal they were. At both clinics, my friends had gone through the procedure and had a small amount of time to rest before being told that they had to leave to make room for another patient. It seemed like a fast food version of surgery for unwanted pregnancies.

I felt sad for the girls in the waiting rooms and the girls being "helped" out the door after their abortions. The whole thing seemed unemotional and wrong. But this doctor was different. He seemed to want me to be sure of my decision.

Sitting in my third waiting room of the day, I fought to not think about the procedure that Dr. Brandt explained to me. I could not believe all the girls at those clinics I had been to had gone through such a nightmare. He told me in a calm and matter-of-fact way, that he would inject something into my uterus that would kill my baby. Then, he would give me something to force my body into labor and I would give birth to a dead child. If the baby was stuck or would not come out, they would vacuum it out of me. I felt like a zombie sitting and thinking about all the information that bounced around in my head.

When I was finally called by the technician, I followed him into the exam room and immediately laid down on the table. He laughed and said, "Okay, I guess you're eager to see your baby." He smiled, but I didn't smile back. He cleared his throat uncomfortably and began to set up for the ultrasound. I looked around the room and found a chart with information about the hazards of smoking. I began to read it to myself, as the tech began rolling the now familiar jellied metal over my belly. I continued to read the chart and tried to focus on absorbing the beneficial information on cigarettes. I just wanted a few moments not to have to acknowledge my current situation.

"Oh, here we go," the tech's utterance made me look over at what he was seeing. "That's a really good shot for you," he said. I knew the second I saw the giant screen on the wall that I was looking at a little person's profile. I could see the nose and eyes. I could see the ears and neck. Little hands looked like they were in a praying position near a little pointed chin. I gasped and tears rolled down my face.

The tech stared at me for a moment, then asked, "Is this your first time seeing your baby?"

I nodded, unable to speak.

"But," he looked up at the screen and then back at me, "this baby is almost six months old," he said in disbelief.

I nodded again. "I just found out today that I'm pregnant," I whispered.

"Wow! That's a lot to take in," the young man shook his head. "Do you want to see more?" He seemed unsure of what to do.

Without thinking, I answered, "Yes."

The tech showed me all the parts of the body that they check to measure healthy growth. The head and face looked good. The spine was good. The legs and arms all matched up with the age of the baby and stage of development they were supposed to be in.

Then, he said, "Oh, it's a boy."

I held my breath. A boy?

"Oh, I'm sorry. Is it okay that I told you?" I realized that I had not really looked at this tech. He was not much older than I was. Maybe mid-twenties?

I smiled for the first time, since arriving, "Yeah, it's okay."

The tech smiled and let out a relieved sigh. As he found more shots of the baby for me to see, I filled him in on my crazy day. By the time we were done, it seemed like we were friends visiting each other. His name was Joe, and he seemed to have been sucked into the drama of my last four hours.

Joe sat in the exam room with me and asked, "What are you going to do?"

"I don't know," I said.

When I finally arrived home, I curled up on the bed and waited for Allen to get home. When he walked through the door, he knew something was wrong. I cried as I walked him through every step of my journey that day; finding out I was pregnant, the concern for the baby's health, the abortion doctor, the ultrasound at the hospital, the fact that he was a healthy baby boy ... By the time I was done, he was tearing, too.

"We can't do that to him," he whispered, as he shook his head. I knew he was still thinking about the gruesome details of the abortion, as I was. We clung to each other and were quiet for a long time, trying to acclimate in our ways to the new set of circumstances now flung upon us.

That night we talked for hours about what we needed to do to prepare for this new life. We only had about three months to get our home ready for a baby! Life was going to move quickly during this time.

Every day off from work seemed to go to preparing for the arrival of our son. We found another home for our dog, knowing that we needed to minimize the stress in our chaotic situation. We bought all the baby items we thought we would need for the first few weeks of our baby's life. We bought several books on pregnancy and early childhood parenting, and I read all of them. I gave Allen the summaries of each, as I read them. I even started my maternity leave early, so we would have more time to be ready. During this entire time, Allen and I worked on feeding me and the baby as much food as possible, to make up for my lack of weight gain previously.

It was during this time that I found out that my grandpa, Tata, had passed away. I was so sad and angry that I had not been allowed to visit him during the last few years of his life. Because my grandmother had "disowned" me from the family after the trial, I was not able to see him. I had heard from my Uncle Sokie that she told Tata that I lied and had my mom and Tom put in jail. She told my grandpa that I had done this so I could live with my dad and "run around with boys." This is what my beloved Tata thought of me, in his last few years of life. I hated my grandmother for this but had to find a way to let it go. I had a child that was due to arrive any day, and that was what I needed to focus on.

OUR BABY

My due date came and went with no new baby. I went to see my Obstetrician on my due date and was told that it was probably better for the development of my unborn son if I went a little over the expected date. This would ensure that the baby would be a healthy weight (considering the strained pregnancy), and it would give Allen and me a little more time to prepare.

Then, the second week came and went, with no new baby. When my third week past my due date was behind us, Allen and I were growing concerned. I had gained fifteen pounds in those last few weeks and was having a hard time getting around. I had never been so big in my whole life! By the time I went in for my last appointment, I had packed 175 pounds of motherhood onto my 5'2" frame. The doctor could see I had reached my limit.

Several hours later, Allen and I were at the same hospital that I had seen our son on an ultrasound for the first time. I was induced at Guam Memorial Hospital on the evening of June 2, 1999. After about thirty minutes of contractions, I passed out and both my heart rate and the heart rate of our unborn son began to drop drastically.

One minute, Allen was listening to me describe the feeling of the contractions, and the next thing he noticed was that I suddenly became very quiet. Just as he was getting out of his chair in the corner of the room to check on me, a group of nurses quietly, but urgently, entered the room and surrounded my bed. They immediately began giving each other information on vital signs for both me and the baby.

When I opened my eyes, I saw each of the three nurses at different places in my hospital room. Allen was at the foot of my bed with a look of concern on his face. Once I had all my faculties about me again, my doctor explained what happened and what would happen. Apparently, letting a woman go past her due date was not an exact science. The placenta that houses the growing baby has a "shelf life" of some kind and begins to break down after that time has expired. If a woman goes too far passed her due date, it's like food going passed its expiration date. It might be okay for a while, or it might not.

I was in the latter group. My doctor told me I needed to be prepped for a C-section immediately. A nurse took Allen to get changed for the operating room, and I began quick preparations for the surgery. I really didn't have time to be scared. Before I knew it, I was lying flat on the operating table, and Allen was standing next to my head, dressed in scrubs. He peered over the sheet that separated the upper and lower half of my body, and I asked him what he saw.

"They're cutting you," he paused, and I wondered if he would be passing out like the new dads I had seen on America's Funniest Videos. But he seemed unphased and continued, "There's black stuff." He smiled at me. "I see him..." he trailed off, as the sound of our son screaming echoed through the room.

Our son, Robert Tyler Corbin, was born perfectly healthy that night. He would pass down the family name of Robert Corbin, which had been given to one son each generation in Allen's family (his full name was Robert Allen Corbin). Then, we picked out the name Tyler for no particular reason, other than we both really liked it. Had I known that Tyler had been born on my paternal grandfather's birthday, we might have named him Tommy, after my dad's dad. But, nothing of the last few months or even hours had really been planned very well, so we were just glad that Tyler was okay.

In fact, Tyler was better than okay. He was what I would recognize now as an "easy baby." He only cried when he was hungry or something was wrong. He never got sick or fussy for no reason. He slept through the night at three months old and smiled at everyone. I really thought that most parents were wimps, because taking care of a child was so incredibly easy. It was really just that taking care of Tyler was so easy.

Allen and I took our son everywhere. He went on his first jungle hike with us when he was five months old. We took him to all the beaches that we liked. We hiked all the historical sites again. One of the first things we had purchased for our new baby was a special heavy-duty hiking baby carrier. It was worn as a backpack, with the baby sitting high and able to see around or over the adult's head. It was reinforced with steel beams that folded in when being carried.

Tyler would sit in this carrier for as long as we were walking, just looking around and cooing. He would drink from our camelback like he was a fellow hiker. He solidified the relationship that Allen and I had started and made us a "family."

By the time Tyler was six months old, we had enough money to fly the three of us out to see our families for the first time. We were both incredibly nervous. Allen's family had already seen him through two wives, and I was very worried that they might think I was just another one who may or may not stick around. Allen was also uneasy about meeting my family for the first time. He felt like they might not approve of his past marriages, and they may judge us for having a baby so soon. Thankfully, any ill feelings or prejudgments were either non-existent or immediately forgotten once everyone met Tyler.

My dad's side of the family welcomed the first grandchild. My sisters and brothers were thrilled to be aunts and uncles. My brothers, Charlie and Tony, loved the idea of having a little nephew. My sisters, Novi, Dawn, Gloria, and Monica, all thought Tyler was adorable. My dad and stepmom doted on their first grandson and also welcomed Allen into the family. Although they asked us when we planned on getting married, they didn't pressure us too much.

They had lived together for several years before getting married and didn't feel they could rightly judge us. Overall, Allen was less nervous after finally meeting my family, and I was relieved there was no "grilling" of Allen by my dad or stepmom.

The second leg of our trip was out to the east coast, to visit Allen's family. Things went better than I expected. I met Allen's daughter, Cassie, and tried very hard to make a good impression. Having been through divorce as a child, and having stepparents myself, I was determined to make her feel as comfortable as possible with me.

We took her with us to Virginia to see Allen's extended family, and I was able to spend some time with her. Cassie seemed happy enough with me, but I felt self-conscious because of my own childhood experience and worried that I would somehow negatively affect her, just by being around.

The highlight of that part of our trip was meeting Allen's grandmother on his mom's side. Granny Jenkins, as everyone called her, made me feel more like part of the family than anyone. She loved on me from the moment I met her, and we spent most of our visit getting to know each other.

When Allen and I returned to Guam, we were relieved to have our initial family visit behind us and anxious to move on to the next phase of our life together. Allen made a rather serious career decision and decided he wanted to leave the military when his time on Guam was up.

"This job with Spec Ops has been the best position I've had in the Navy," he explained, "I will never have another job I enjoy this much, if I stay in."

I knew he enjoyed his job. The flexibility of his schedule and the thrill of chasing illegal poachers, while also growing very close to his team made his explanation reasonable. I tried to understand his reasoning and support his decision. I wanted him to be happy in his profession but being in the Navy had given me a sense of job stability that would suddenly be gone once he was discharged.

We began working on resumes for him that we sent out to agencies all over the country. I continued to work at FedEx and even looked up some jobs that were open Stateside, in case Allen didn't find another job right away, or had to take a cut in pay. It was during this uncertain time that I received devastating news.

Allen, Tyler, our good friend Frank and I, had just spent the evening at Chamorro Village. This was an outdoor shopping area known for its local artists and food. The four of us had a wonderful time, trying to enjoy our last few weeks on the island. Frank had been Allen's friend from a ship they were both on, the USS Frank Cable. He had supported us through our surprise pregnancy, and was even our first babysitter. We had become so close, we referred to him as Uncle

Frank to Tyler. The day had been so fun, I never would have expected it to end the way it did.

The phone rang within a few minutes of us entering our condo. Frank had just left us to walk over to his own condo in the adjacent building. Allen was carrying Tyler, who was in a deep sleep from a long day spent in the sun. Allen took Tyler to his bedroom to change him and lay him in his bed. I kicked off my shoes and was looking through the bags of local items we had bought. When the phone rang, I thought it was Frank calling to tell us something he forgot.

"Sweetie?" My dad's voice seemed different and farther away than usual.

"What's wrong?" I instinctively asked.

"Sweetie." He sounded out of breath or something that I couldn't quite put my finger on. "Tony's been shot..." He trailed off as I rolled those words over in my head and tried to understand what they meant. "Someone came into the shop and shot him in the face..."

When he trailed off again, I realized my dad was crying. I had only seen my dad cry once in my entire life.

"Daddy? Is he going to be okay?" My voice unintentionally squeaked out of me, as I thought of the pain my brother would be going through.

There was an incredibly long pause, before he finally said, "No, sweetie. He didn't make it."

Those words fell on me like a ton of bricks. Time stopped for me, and reality seemed warped and confused. I didn't realize I was sobbing into the phone, until my dad said, "Sweetie, I know you need some time with this. So, do we. I'll call you again tomorrow. Okay?"

I guess I answered him, because he hung up. Allen came into the living room and found me sobbing on the couch and still clutching the receiver of the phone. I told him through the choking sobs that my brother was dead.

That night seemed to never end. Just as I would start the process of calming down, I would imagine the horrifying events of Tony's last few minutes of life and lose control of myself again.

When my father called the next day, he was able to give more details of the circumstances surrounding my brother's murder. The man who shot Tony had been one of the many people that my brother had tried to help. He had let this man stay at his home, because he had nowhere to stay. He got this man a job at the watch store that he worked at, so he could "get back on his feet again." He had done everything he could to help this man. In return, this man walked into the watch shop, shot my brother and the owner in their faces, and then took what little cash he could find in the shop, before leaving.

This man had looked my brother directly in the face, then raised his gun and shot him. I was numb with disbelief. Tony's boss had survived his gunshot but would need his jaw wired shut.

More bad news would follow. Because Allen and I were preparing for his discharge in the next few weeks and our move back to the States, I would not be able to attend my brother's funeral. Plane tickets were almost a thousand dollars each, and we had already bought our final tickets a few weeks earlier.

While everyone was working through Tony's death, I was preparing for the next few weeks. Those weeks were a hectic time of year anyway. With Christmas just weeks away, having to pack for the move, preparing for our trip back—it was extra busy. Allen also didn't have any solid leads for a new job, so I was more urgently looking up any openings in FedEx using the online network for current employees at my work.

I was keeping myself very busy.

As the time for us to leave Guam finally arrived, it was met with an incredible mix of emotions. We were sad to leave our beautiful island home. We were excited and scared to face the uncertain future that lay before us. We were still in shock about the sudden and violent death of my brother. Allen and I figuratively and literally clung to each other, as we got on the plane with Tyler and flew away from Guam for the last time.

STATESIDE

The first month of 2001 was an emotional time for our little family, as well as our extended family. We spent almost two weeks with my family, with me trying to work through my brother's death and Allen having several interviews for jobs in the area. I felt disconnected from my family, since they had already reached a different stage in the grieving process.

They had the funeral for Tony and made their uncomfortable but necessary peace with what happened. I was still in a state of disbelief and confusion. I expected that my brother would show up at any moment to greet us. I was feeling very distant from my dad and family. This was only aggravated by other changes being made in the house, with my parents and sisters attending church regularly for the first time.

Suddenly, certain television shows were no longer okay to watch in the house. A large amount of time was being devoted to church functions and Bible studies. And everything was related to the Bible.

Although I believed in God, I found all these sudden changes another hard adjustment to understand. Why was watching The Simpsons such a bad thing? Why wasn't my family spending what little time we had there with us, instead of always at church? Why were they always talking about the Bible?

Although Allen had job opportunities in the area, I actually hoped something else would open up for him somewhere that allowed us to be on our own again.

We also went to visit Allen's family again, while he continued to do phone interviews and send out resumes online. The pressure from a few family members to relocate back in North Carolina was strong. Even using Allen's daughter as a reason for us to stay in Allen's hometown, with absolutely no job offers in the area. It ate at the both of us.

Allen should be near his daughter, but how would we support ourselves? Not to mention pay child support for that very child that these family members were using to make Allen feel guilty about having to leave again? These experiences from both sides of our families made the two of us draw even closer to one another. We had to look at the big picture and do what we thought was best.

It wasn't until we were packing up to head back to California and reluctantly have Allen accept a job just an hour away from my parents, that he got a call from a VA hospital in Sacramento.

Although Sacramento was in California, I knew it was at least a whole day's drive from where my family was. Allen had a phone interview with someone from the

Sacramento VA Medical Center, as we were settling back into my parent's home. Both Allen and I kept our fingers crossed that this job would come through, but we also didn't want to waste time by sitting around. Allen continued to send out more resumes and do interviews, even with jobs that offered barely livable pay. We wanted to move on and be able to have our own space. Allen even picked up an application for the LAPD (at the suggestion of my Uncle Sokie), although neither one of us were thrilled with this idea. Halfway through the application packet, the VA hospital called us and offered Allen a job as a police officer. It was such a relief for both of us.

By the beginning of February 2001, the three of us were packed into a rented SUV with all our luggage that had been brought on our trip and headed north for an almost eight hour drive.

While I was sad to be leaving my family and grateful for them letting us stay for several weeks, I was relieved to be with just Allen and Tyler again. Allen understood and agreed with my feelings about loving our families but wanting space to live our own lives.

While this was not Allen's ideal job, we were so grateful that he had found something to help us get on a path to where we wanted to be—on our own.

The Sacramento area was surprisingly beautiful. We were both pleasantly surprised to find many outdoor activities, wildlife and mild weather, especially coming from an island with year-round, high humidity. Once again, we could take out our hiking backpack for Tyler and explore the outdoors together. While the terrain was vastly different from our previous island home, it was beautiful in its own way. One of our favorite places to hike was along the American River. The river was surrounded by forested area that was home to deer, wild turkey, amazing birds and snakes. All of which we would see almost every single time we went on a hike. This was how we spent most of our spring.

While Allen worked hard to adjust to his new work schedule and environment. I had decided to take a couple summer classes at the community college in the area, American River Community College. We put Tyler into a part-time preschool program, just as he turned two years old. We figured this would help him adjust to going to school in a couple of years. With these new things added to our schedule, the summer passed quickly.

Sacramento was quickly growing on us and we even looked at buying a home, instead of continuing to rent. We imagined staying in the area for at least a few more years. But just as I was getting ready to start full-time classes and we were exploring our options for a long-term stay, September 11 happened.

I awoke to the home phone ringing. Startled, I looked up and saw that it was almost nine o'clock. Why was I still sleeping? My little human alarm clock had not gone off like normal. Tyler always woke up at 6:30 to 7, then woke me up. The phone rang again, and I wondered why anyone would be calling me at that time. Allen had already left for work late the night before and would be almost done with his shift. I was confused when I answered the phone.

"Hello?"

"Are you still sleeping?" I recognized Allen's voice. Initially, I was irritated he would give me a hard time about oversleeping. Tyler never let me sleep in, so this should actually be a treat. Instead, I was being made to feel guilty?

"Yea, I guess Tyler is still sleeping. But..."

"Do you know what's going on right now?" Allen seemed stressed and upset.

"What do you mean?" I wondered if we were having some kind of disastrous weather. Maybe I had slept through an earthquake or something.

"You need to turn on the television. I have to go. I'll call you in a few minutes." Allen hung up before I could answer.

I jumped out of bed and ran down the hall to our living room.

I turned on the T.V. and stood in front of it. Whatever Allen was talking about, I hoped I could find some information on it quickly and easily. As soon as the screen lit up, an image of a smoking building filled my view. Between reading the captions and listening to the newscaster, I understood that a plane had crashed into one of the World Trade Center towers.

I was shocked as I thought of the people in the burning building, who at that very moment were either dead or fighting for their lives. How could this have happened? I turned up the volume so I could hear more easily, but not loud enough to wake up Tyler. It seemed that the news anchor didn't know much more than what I could see playing live on the television. I switched from the local channel I was on to a cable news station. Still, there was mostly speculation being aired about how a plane had crashed into one of the towers.

I squinted my eyes to try and make out the smaller details on my screen. Just then an explosion of some kind seemed to come from the other tower. My eyes instinctively opened wide, and I struggled to understand what was happening to our buildings in New York. Over the next few minutes, the commentators were able to replay the footage, and it was becoming clear that planes were purposely being flown into buildings! The air felt like it had been punched out of my body and I quickly sat straight down on the couch. Why was this happening? Who would want to do this?

The phone rang, and I quickly grabbed it from the coffee table next to me. It was Allen. I looked over at the clock and saw that less than ten minutes had passed since he woke me. How could all of this have happened in such a short amount of time?

"Have you seen?" he asked.

"Yeah," my answer was breathless and weak. "There was a second plane..."

"I know." I heard him take a deep breath. "We all know."

He began to explain how they were passing information around and something about leaving an hour after his normal shift. I was only half-listening. I squinted my eyes again to focus on the details I tried to see earlier. I walked over slowly toward my television. The debris from the buildings ... something seemed off about the way it moved. The camera panned closer, and the newscaster stopped talking. It seemed he realized the same thing I did, at that same moment. "Dear God, those are people jumping from the building!" His words resonated from my T.V. and sank deep in my stomach.

"Did you hear me?" Allen had been talking.

I didn't know what to say. I pushed out, "People are jumping from the buildings..." I didn't know how to finish, so I just stopped.

"Sh**." Allen took another deep breath. "Okay. Listen to me. Are you listening?"

I made myself look away from the television and focused on what he was saying, "Yes," I answered, "I'm listening."

"Stay inside the apartment. Do not go outside or open the door for anyone. I will be home as soon as I can. Got it?" I could hear him pant slightly as he moved around quickly and talked at the same time.

"Yes, I got it." We told each other that we loved one another and hung up.

As the morning progressed, the news became worse and worse. While Tyler ate his Cheerios, I watched the second tower that was hit crumble to the ground. I could only tell my two-year-old that Mommy was crying because the news was very sad. He told me to change the channel, but like so many Americans and people all over the world, I couldn't. I had to know what was happening to my country and why so many innocent people were dying right before our eyes.

I set Tyler up with some Play-Doh at the kitchen counter, just as the first tower that was hit also crumbled to the ground. All the people who worked in those buildings, all the people on those planes, all the first responders who went in to help...

When Allen came home, we held onto each other and continued to watch as the rest of the day's events unfolded. We didn't leave the apartment once. By the time we were tucking Tyler into bed, a lifetime of events had transpired in less than twelve hours.

The Pentagon had been hit by a third plane. Still another plane had crashed in Pennsylvania, and it was being speculated that the passengers fought their hijackers and saved a fourth target from being hit. They had sacrificed themselves to save more innocent people from more death and destruction. People all over the world were mourning, dumbstruck, or even cheering for the devastation done that day. And we were all hearing the name of our heartless enemies, many for the first time.

Allen and I hadn't talked much all day. Mostly we watched the news and tried to keep Tyler busy. It wasn't until that night that we had a chance to talk about how this might affect us.

"You know there is a good chance that I will be recalled."

Allen looked at the floor and rubbed the back of his neck. I knew he was feeling emotionally tired, just like me.

"What do you mean?" I hadn't considered that Allen would be recalled. He had only signed back on as a Naval Reservist a few weeks earlier. He hadn't even been to his first weekend duty yet. Could they really recall him?

It turned out that they could, and they did. Many reservists with law enforcement in their background were being called to secure our bases all over the world. Within two weeks of September 11, Allen was in San Diego getting processed back into the military and finding out where his duty station would be. For twenty-four hours after Allen flew out, I prayed almost continuously. I just wanted Allen within driving distance, even if it was a long drive. My prayers were answered.

"They're sending me to Fallon, Nevada," Allen informed me.

"Yes!" I had no idea where Fallon was, but I knew Nevada was right next to California, and that was good enough for me!

The next few weeks was a difficult time of adjustment for all three of us. Allen was going through the process of arriving to his new base. He had meetings and paperwork and training that filled most of his time. I had classes that started and a schedule to keep, as well as taking care of Tyler on my own. This was made more difficult when our usually easy- going young son began to act out ferociously.

It began with Tyler losing his temper and throwing toys at me. I tried to use the redirection approach I was learning in my Early Childhood Education classes. This seemed to make him angrier. He soon started to come at me with his toys, clutching them tightly in his fist and using them as weapons.

I tried to hold him still by both arms and talk to him soothingly (also recommended by my new classes), but he would spit at me and scream what sounded like made-up toddler profanity.

Allen finally convinced me that I would have to do what I was trying to avoid. I would need to spank Tyler. Confused by the disagreement between the new information I was learning on why spanking was wrong and the advice of the man I trusted and loved the most, I decided to call my dad.

"Sweetie, I know you don't want to spank Tyler," my dad spoke as softly as a baritone could, "because you saw that kind of thing go too far as a child. It sounds like you're taking in a lot of new information in these classes you've got." He paused and I knew he would have been hugging me just then, if we had been talking in person. "Some kids need to be spanked as a consequence. It's up to you to know if Tyler needs that."

After a minute, I agreed. What he said made sense.

"Oh, and be careful what you read, even in school. Just because a professional says something, doesn't mean he knows everything." That made sense, too.

The next time Tyler came at me with his toy, I held him by both arms and tried to talk to him. When he spit at me, I turned him over, took a deep breath and spanked him on the butt. He instantly flipped himself over and grabbed his action figure that was laying on the floor next to him. He held it over his head and screamed incoherently as he came toward me chopping the toy like an axe! I jumped up and ran down the hall, my two-year-old running after me.

I ran into his room and around his bed. He was smarter and jumped onto his bed and landed at my heels! I screamed and jumped towards the door! While I passed the doorframe, I grabbed the outside of his bedroom door and pulled it closed behind me. I caught a glimpse of Tyler's crazed eyes coming at me, as the door slammed! He pounded on his side of the door, screaming his made-up bad words at me. I gripped the door handle tightly and begged him to calm down.

The next few minutes continued with this stand-off situation, until finally there was no more screaming on the other side.

"Tyler?" I called through the door.

"Yes, Mommy." The familiar little voice sounded nothing like the screaming child from just several minutes earlier.

"Are you okay?" I wondered if he had hurt himself while he was banging on the door. The force had been so hard, I thought he might have been throwing his whole body against it.

"Yes, Mommy." He sighed a tired little sigh and said, "I'm done now, Mommy."

A wave of relief washed over me. This was done! He had worked it out of his system and now it was done! I turned the handle, ready to gather my child up into my arms and hug him. I pushed the door open slowly and saw he was sitting on his bed. I smiled and started to speak, when Tyler's eyes turned angry again and he lifted the familiar army-man- turned-weapon over his head. He ran toward the door, screaming his warrior cry, just as I shut it again.

"Tyler! You lied to me!" I cried as I returned to my position, kneeling by the door, grasping the door handle to keep Tyler from opening it and reigning his terror upon me.

I stayed in that position for almost two hours. I cried and tried to reason with my toddler. I listened to him pause his screaming fits to play by himself in his room, only to resume his yelling and banging without any notice at all.

During a calm time, I ran silently to my backpack and retrieved my child psychology book. I returned to my child's door and desperately searched through the large textbook for a cause and a cure for his behavior. After more time passed, I realized that I was nodding off. Allen was due to make his nightly call, and Tyler had been quiet for some time. I opened the door slowly and found him lying under his bed, asleep. I walked over to him and gently began lifting him up to place him on top of his bed. He halfway opened his eyes and my heart raced! I saw my vision blurring from the tears that immediately began forming at the thought of starting this ordeal all over again.

"Mommy, I have to pee," he mumbled.

Worried that anything might set him off, I decided not to talk, but just to carry him silently to the bathroom. Once there, I helped him go and carried him back to his room.

"Jammies?" he asked, as he rubbed his tired eyes.

Again, I silently picked out his favorite pajamas and helped him change. He climbed into bed.

"Bert?" He reached out his little hand for his stuffed toy that he slept with. I frantically scanned Tyler's room for Bert from Sesame Street and found him next to a Lego pile. I quickly grabbed the mean-looking toy and placed it in Tyler's outstretched hand. He snuggled it close and instantly fell asleep.

Exhausted and desperately needing another adult to talk to, I slumped into the living room couch and stared at the phone, until Allen called. After explaining the events of the last few hours to him, he sighed and was quiet for a long time. Finally, he whispered, "I'm sorry."

We both sat silently on the phone, taking in the new challenges of our current situations. When we were finally able to talk and strategize a plan to deal with these new trials, I became less stressed and exhausted and more hopeful and determined.

Between the two of us, we had surmised that Tyler was acting out because Allen had been suddenly removed from his life, and he didn't understand why. To try and remedy this, I was going to talk to Tyler more about why his Daddy was gone. Also, Allen was going to try and call before Tyler went to sleep, so they could talk.

Finally, Allen had been paired up with a roommate that also lived in Northern California, and he had been nice enough to offer to drop Allen off and pick him back up on his way to his own home and back to the base on their days off. This would happen about every other weekend. Then, Allen had some interesting news to share with me.

"The government is doing a mass hiring for positions in Homeland Security. I think I should put in for one of the positions."

He continued to explain that he didn't know when his time on Fallon would be done. There was even a chance that he could be sent to another base that was farther away. The only way the military would let him out of his Reserve obligation was for a better job in the government.

"You know, I also don't know how much good I'm really doing out here—guarding warehouses and counting tumbleweeds. I would like to make more of a difference somehow," he finished.

"Then you should definitely put in for the job," I answered. I didn't know what this new job would be like, but it had to be more fulfilling for Allen and better for our family.

By the time we got off the phone, I felt even closer to my future husband, despite the physical distance between us. We had worked together as a team to solve our problems, and this would be more important over the course of the next year than either one of us could have imagined.

THE END OF 2001

As our country went through many changes following September 11, so did our little family. Allen and I did the best we could in our own circumstances. Allen worked hours away from us in Fallon, Nevada, and did everything he could to visit us as often as possible, as well as call us every day. I studied hard in my classes and got a part-time job at a gym near our house in Fair Oaks, a suburb of Sacramento. The gym membership and on-site childcare were bonus to an already enjoyable job.

California Family Fitness was a newer chain of gyms that was spreading across Northern California. I was impressed with their philosophy of family fitness versus what most gyms offered as childcare.

CalFit (as we called it) offered classes and structured activities for children while their parents worked out. I had always stayed away from gyms because the one-room childcare that was usually offered always seemed overcrowded and barely supervised.

Working in CalFit's Children Department let me practice what I was learning in my Early Childhood education classes in an applicable environment. I was able to plan activities for the kids. I was becoming more and more comfortable teaching and relating to kids.

Tyler loved coming to the gym with me, and I was even finally making some friends with a few of my coworkers. I was slowly feeling more at home in Sacramento. I just needed Allen to come back.

By December, Allen still had no idea when he would be released from active duty and be able to return to his job and family. So, I registered for the next semester of classes, this time continuing with my same major. I was finally confident that teaching young children was where I belonged.

Things were going relatively well, considering I was without Allen, family or close friends, until I needed help with something big. Although I was making friends in the area, I still didn't know anyone well enough to call when I was in trouble. When our Bronco broke down, Allen called one of his coworkers from that area to drive out and help me. It was awkward, since I didn't really know him, but Robert proved to be a true good Samaritan who helped me and Tyler when we didn't have anyone else to be there for us. Having been in the military himself, he understood the concept of helping family members when loved ones were deployed. Still, I wished I knew some people in our area a little better, so I didn't have to just rely on Robert, Allen's coworker.

"Why don't you try a church?" Allen had made this suggestion a few times. His reasoning made sense. Christians were always looking for ways to help others. Right? I mean, I was like a single parent (for lack of a better term). I had no friends or family in the area. I was working and going to school. A church did seem like a good place for me to find honest people who would help me through this turbulent time. I decided to give up my one day to sleep in and make the effort to go to church.

The first Sunday morning, I decided to drive up the street to a church whose members had knocked on my door a couple of times since we moved into that neighborhood. The two ladies who greeted me both times when I opened my door seemed nice and didn't push the information about their church on me. They smiled and were incredibly polite, even after I brushed them off abruptly both times. In fact, the second time I opened the door to them, Tyler had been throwing one of his violent tantrums and upon hearing the exorcist way my child was screaming in the background, they had simply asked if they could pray for me.

I shrugged and mumbled, "Sure," before closing the door on them. After going and making sure that Tyler's door was closed, I returned to peek out the window next to the front door. One of the ladies was speaking quietly and after a few seconds, they both lifted their heads and continued to the neighbor's house. They had prayed for me.

Remembering the name of their church, I drove over to the building that first Sunday morning. The parking lot was full. I drove up and down the street, still finding no legal place to park. Frustrated, I drove home. I explained later that day to both my dad and Allen why I hadn't tried the church that morning. Both had the same advice, "Try a different church." Fine.

The next Sunday, I got Tyler and myself up again. Tyler wanted to know if we were going inside of the church this time. "I hope so," I told him.

This second church had been one that I picked out of the phone book. It was only about ten minutes up the road and had a cute logo next to their name. As we drove up, I could see that there were plenty of parking spaces. I parked and noticed several families with small children entering the main door of the building. I smiled as I thought about the friends that Tyler might make there.
When we entered the main hall, an older man reached out his hand and introduced himself. He was an elder at the church and obviously knew all the regulars, because he knew that Tyler and I were new. He welcomed us to the church and showed me where the kids' church was held. Tyler ran off into the room, and I was happy to see him excited to be there.

The elder, Todd, informed me that this church had hired a new pastor and was in the process of starting some new programs and groups within the church. He seemed fairly excited about the innovative things happening in the church and with the chance to share them with someone new. His joy seemed contagious, and by the time we walked back up to the main auditorium, I was excited for this church, too!

The service was better than what I expected. The music was very modern, and the pastor was not very much older than Allen and me. He had a pretty wife and a young son, about Tyler's age. His sermon was on being tested and staying strong. It was so meaningful for me and what my small family had been going through. By the end of the service, I felt a connection to this church. When Todd the Elder invited me to the Bible study group that he and his wife led at their house, I agreed. When the main teacher at the children's church found out I was studying to be a preschool teacher, she asked if I would like to help in the kids' area. I agreed. I had found a church and friends.

Over the course of the next few weeks, as I served in the children's church and gave out more information about myself, the attitude toward me seemed to change. My fellow teachers seemed shocked that Allen and I were not married yet. When I tried to follow up on the invitation I received to the Elder's Bible study group, his wife suddenly grabbed him and whisked him away. All the while looking at me like I should not have been talking to her husband.

By the end of the month, I could see that I was no longer wanted in the church. Even my last attempt to call the Elder's wife myself and talk to her ended in disappointment. She said she didn't have time to talk and their Bible Study group did not have childcare, so she didn't think it would be a good fit for me. Hanging up the phone, I felt incredibly rejected.

I knew Allen and I didn't have the ideal situation. With everything that happened the last few years, getting married hadn't been a priority. But it wasn't like I was hitting on the men in the church. Why would I do that? No, it was they who had done the wrong thing. No longer feeling rejected and sad for myself, I transitioned to feeling irritated that these people claimed to be followers of Jesus. I decided to go back to my own personal relationship with God. If the Christians in churches were like that, then I definitely didn't want any part of it.

That year was coming to an end, with me coming full circle. I continued right back where I had been for the last few months. Tyler and I spent most of our time together, just the two of us. Allen visited four to five days out of the month. My busy schedule kept me from focusing too much on how hard life was.

Then, some good news. Allen had been called for an interview for the Homeland Security position he had applied for when he first arrived at Fallon. The federal government wanted to fly him out for a medical assessment and an interview. Although this would take away one of our weekend visits, it was an incredible opportunity that couldn't be passed up.

A CHANCE FOR SOMETHING BETTER

The start of the New Year brought exciting new information!

Allen had been hired for one of the new positions that were needed in our post-9/11 world. He would not start training until June, and in the meantime, there would be a very in- depth background investigation done on him. If, for some reason he did not pass the background check, the job offer could be revoked. Until June, Allen would continue to be stationed in Fallon and work his Naval Police job.

The next few months did get better for the three of us. Not easier, but better.

Because of the extra money I was making by working at the gym, we could afford gas to drive out to see Allen on the weekends when he could not get a ride to come and see us. This meant that we were able to see each other every weekend! Although it usually amounted to just shy of two days a week, it was consistent and more than we had for three months. The drive itself was long (almost four hours), but the scenic drive through Lake Tahoe made it less stressful. Tyler was also a perfect little traveler, so the drive didn't seem to bother him. His behavior had altogether improved with the time he was able to spend with his dad.

The first time we had driven out, I was very confused about how or why there would be a navy base in the middle of the desert.

Allen informed me that it was actually a Naval Air Station and that the famous *Top Gun* pilots trained there. I watched the movie *Top Gun* in middle school and was pretty excited to see these elite pilots in action. Unfortunately, the base was not as interesting as I had thought.

Fallon was really out in the middle of the desert. No mountains or forest or water in sight. Besides the buildings that made up the Air Station and the tumbleweeds blowing through, there was nothing but sand and rocks. Of all the times we stayed out there, we only saw the jets fly by three or four times. But it wasn't about the base anyway. It was about spending time as a family. Allen's roommate, Rueben, would give us plenty of room when we came, and we would try to make the most of our short weekends together.

One weekend, we drove out to a Mastiff breeder that Allen found in Nevada and picked up the biggest puppy I had ever seen in my life. She was a fawn, which meant that she was a light cream color with a black face. She had a really impressive pedigree and had used up most of our Christmas funds to purchase. Her grandfather had been the dog in the movie Sandlot, and she was like a miniature version of him, complete with the extra slobbering.

Allen kept the dog, named Lania (after the term used on Guam for "Oh, my goodness") with him on the base. It seemed good for him to have Lania to take care of during the week, when Tyler and I were gone. He trained her well, and she was incredibly smart, with a unique personality. I often thought she acted more like a cat, with her cool indifference and ability to sense a person's demeanor. Being a naturally protective breed, Lania was the perfect family dog for us.

Once June arrived, we were all ready to move along to something new, Lania included. While Allen went away for his three weeks of training, I finished my classes for the semester and packed our belongings for our move. I regretfully sold our Bronco, and we bought a new minivan. Before Allen left for training, we sat down and did the math. What we spent on repairs in the last six months on the Bronco had been as much as car payments on a new car.

Also, Allen wanted us to have a reliable car for our drive to wherever we would be moving next.

Where we were going would not be disclosed until Allen's second week of training. When he called me and told me that we would be moving to Illinois, so he could work out of an office near Chicago, it really didn't matter to me. I would have moved to China, if it meant that we could all be back together as a family.

Once Allen's training was done, he flew back to Sacramento, then we had exactly one week to get our family and all our belongings out to the Chicago area. Allen had to report to his new job seven days later. So, the three of us packed up a U-Haul as fast as we could and began our cross-country journey to our new home. Tyler, Lania and I rode in the van, while Allen drove the U-Haul. We stayed in contact with walkie-talkies, since we only had one cell phone.

As we drove through six states and over 2,000 miles that separated Northern California and Illinois, a mix of emotions ran through me. I was excited and happy to be a complete family again. I was nervous about having enough time to get us to Chicago and get Allen to work. I was also feeling a slight déjà vu from our cross-country trip.

The last time I had taken a trip similar to this, I had been going to Kentucky with my dysfunctional family. We had also drove through many terrains. We stayed in cheaper motels, to save money, just as we had done on that ill-fated trip. I pushed the comparison out of my mind, as I glanced into the back seat at my son who was quietly working on stringing beads from his box of "car ride fun" that I put together for him. He squinted his eyes and bit the side of his lip as he concentrated on stringing the beads. Our extremely large puppy stood in the trunk area of the minivan and panted at the cars that passed by. Just then, a crackle came over the walkie-talkie.

"What was that?" I asked into the smaller mic. "I said..." Allen was clear this time, "I love you." "I love you, too," I answered.

This trip was nothing like the one from my childhood. This was *my* life and *my* family.

CHICAGO

Woodstock, Illinois, was a charming family community with a cobblestone-paved "square" located centrally in the town, and only one main road that runs through the length of it. Their claim to fame was the fact that the 1993 movie *Groundhog Day* was filmed there. It is considered a "far northwest suburb" of Chicago, because it is commutable by some standards (if you are willing to drive an hour and a half). This is also where Allen and I found our first home.

Although we had a place together on Guam, and a rental house in Sacramento, this would be our first home that was truly "ours." Allen used his VA loan to purchase our first house together.

It had three bedrooms and one bathroom, with an unattached two car garage. It had a back yard that was big enough for a small vegetable garden (I had been experimenting with planting since our place on Guam) and still had room for both Lania and Tyler to run around. It was just over 1,200 square feet of living space that seemed plenty for our small family, even with our large dog.

Once settled into our new house, Allen and I sat down and looked at our new budget. Buying a new van, a new house, and the cost of moving out to Illinois had meant that our monthly bills were more than they had ever been. Allen's new job was paying him more than the one in California, but we both knew that I would need to go back to work as soon as possible if we were going to pay for our new life with more ease.

I began printing off resumes and dropping them off at any businesses that had route drivers. Within days Culligan Water in the neighboring town of Crystal Lake called me.

They had an opening for a bottled water delivery person and scheduled me to come in for an interview. Although the physical aspect of the position seemed more difficult than what I had hoped for, the pay and benefits were good, so when I was offered the job, I gladly accepted.

Our family settled into the Midwest life easier than we anticipated. Despite being warned that "everyone ditches during their first Chicago winter" (this is where newbies overestimate the traction on their car and slide into a ditch), neither Allen nor I experienced sliding off the road. The winter was cold, and the wind was bitter, but we were so busy with our new work schedules that it seemed we didn't have the time to complain.
Our workdays were hectic, with his always changing and never set, while mine started at six a.m. every weekday morning. Poor Tyler would get woken up at five a.m. every morning and be the first kid at his preschool. Rubbing his little eyes, he would walk straight over to the breakfast table and sit down in a trance,

awaiting his morning meal from the friendly cafeteria lady. It was hard, but at least we were all together. Then, several months into our new schedule, the problems started.

While I had been determined to prove to myself and my fellow male coworkers that I could handle fifty-pound bottles of water all day long, my body was telling me that I, in fact, could not. It started with a shooting pain up the side of my forearm. Then, it was a consistent pain in my lower back. Finally, my right knee began to make a disturbing clicking sound and hurt when I bent it more than 90 degrees. I was constantly taking the maximum amount of Ibuprofen just to do my job every day.

Next, Tyler's preschool had become a place where I was reluctant to drop him. Every day I went to pick him up, the teacher seemed like she really didn't like her job. She was agitated or irritated with the children in her care. Since I was the first one to pick up my child in her class, I wondered if I was the only one to witness her bad attitude. Maybe by the time school actually ended (which seemed like the time most parents picked up their children), there was such chaos with the children gathering their things and the parents gathering their children, that no one noticed the mean teacher glaring at the students. Allen noticed the teacher's sourness, as well.

"Maybe we should talk to the owner of the school," he suggested. But I was not willing to chance that she would retaliate against us by being mean to Tyler. I reasoned that any person who would take a job with children and then act like a witch would not hesitate to sink to such a level.

During this time, I returned to a constant time of prayer and reflection. I desperately needed guidance in how to deal with these two pressing problems and knew that God could point me in the right direction. My experience with the church in Sacramento had not affected the way I viewed my Heavenly Father. So, I prayed every chance I could and looked desperately around me for some sign that He was hearing my pleas for help.

After about two weeks of praying and stressing, just as I felt my body would break apart from my daily routine and I would flip out and punch Tyler's teacher right in her face—it happened. I received a phone call from a school where I had left an application when he had first arrived in Illinois. It was a private preschool and daycare attached to a large corporation's building. They needed someone for their infant room who could also "float" to other rooms as needed.

I drove out to the school the next day for an interview. After the interview, I spent an hour in the "infant room" where I would be working, if I got the job. I loved it! I couldn't believe that I would be able to play and take care of babies all day, and get paid for it! The other teacher in the room seemed very nice and wanted so badly for the open position to be mine.

The two days I waited for the other interviews to be done and the decision to be made seemed like forever. I prayed continually that God had not shown me the perfect way out, only to dangle it in front of me like an unattainable solution. Finally, the school called me and offered me the job. After accepting graciously, I hung up the phone and cried. Who was I that God would answer my prayers so perfectly? What could I ever really do to show I was worthy of how He had come to my aide, time and time again?

Working at my new job with Bright Horizons was an incredible experience. Caring for the babies in my room was a joy! I grew so close to my "little people," I really felt a love for them. I became friends with the other teacher in the room, Carol, and never had any problems or issues with her.

Also, I enjoyed "floating" to other rooms when teachers took time off or were sick. I became familiar with the different stages of growth in each room and was able to adjust accordingly. The "Two room" was a great room, because the two-year-olds were so open to instruction. As long as you didn't mind giving constant direction, the Twos were always ready to learn. The Three room was very fun and creative. The three-year-olds seemed just able to convey their ideas and thoughts, and you never knew what hilarious things they would say. The Preschool room was so interesting because I could really practice my teaching there. Everything and anything we did in that room could turn into a lesson for the children.

While I was truly enjoying my new work environment, I began to struggle with what could only be described as a "cookie cutter" approach to teaching children. I noticed some children who were otherwise extremely intelligent having difficulties in following the instructions that worked for other children. When I asked the main Preschool teacher, (Tyler's teacher, Tammy) about this new realization I had, she agreed.

"Unfortunately, that is a sad reality of mass education," she nodded and looked around at her students. "I've been a teacher for over twelve years, and I can't tell you how many of my kids have slipped through the cracks because they couldn't grasp the way we have to teach things." She bent over to help a student tie their shoe.

The gentle way she helped the little girl and the time she took to kneel down and be eye level with her, told me that she didn't want to see any of her students struggle with learning. She really cared about them. Once the little girl had run back to her friends to play, Tammy continued, "I guess you can only hope that their parents are willing to spend the time needed to bridge the gap and help them."

I thought about the students in Tammy's room. I knew from working with her that the majority of parents had their children in preschool from eight or nine in the morning until five or six at night.

Then, many of them had a long drive home. Then, they would be eating dinner, maybe getting a bath and finally, bedtime. When would these parents have the time to help their kids? I also knew that there were several boys in the class who were on medication for ADHD. I wondered if it was just a coincidence that those same boys were also at the preschool for the longest amount of time and had parents that seemed very distant or uninterested in what was happening with their children. These same few boys seemed very

intelligent, but also bored with most of the lessons that were taught. I knew that ADHD was a very real learning disorder, but was it possible that some of these children actually needed parenting instead of medication? Maybe a personalized learning approach, instead of the same boxed one that was handed to every child? I had no idea that this would be an issue I would have to deal with, personally.

At the end of every quarter, the teachers would have meetings with every parent to discuss the growth and development of their child, as well as address any concerns either side had. These "Wellness Sessions" were one of the things that set Bright Horizons apart from many other private daycares or preschools. I thought it was funny that I would be "meeting" with my friend and coworker Tammy, to discuss the things I could see for myself every day at work with Tyler.

I knew he had a lot of energy and had a hard time sitting still, but he was only three. The only reason they had put him in the preschool room was because his birthday was only a few months away. I thought he was doing quite well for being one of the younger kids in the class. And at first, Tammy echoed my opinion.

"I have to tell you, Becky. I know you work with him at home, because he really knows his letters and numbers!" We both laughed, since she already knew that I witnessed Tyler helping kids older than him to learn these basic preschool skills.

"Thanks, Tammy. I think he has a great teacher, though," I meant what I said to her. Tammy really enjoyed her job and I had a tremendous amount of respect for her.

After thanking me, she opened Tyler's folder and shared with me all the milestones she had marked him off on. Then, she closed the folder and looked seriously at me. "Becky, do you remember that conversation we had about some children slipping through the cracks?"

I nodded.

Tammy took off her glasses and rubbed her eyes. I sat back in my chair, halfway understanding what she wanted to tell me.

"Tyler has an extremely hard time sitting still during lessons. I know that he can learn the lessons, it just requires a different technique than most of the other kids. You know that most teachers won't have the time or resources to..." She trailed off, and I could tell she was getting upset.

"Tammy," I reached out and touched her hand, "It's okay."

She nodded and took a deep breath. "I wish we had more teachers and more say in our curriculum..."

"I know, Tammy," I really did know what she meant because I had been witnessing it for myself. The "one size fits all" approach to teaching was the only way to get a lesson done without using up half the day. It wasn't Tammy's fault. It wasn't my fault. It definitely wasn't Tyler's fault.

Later that night, after Tyler went to bed, I told Allen what Tammy said to me. I tried to explain to him the Cliff Notes version of the different learning styles that I studied in college. I explained the concerns I had about some children not being taught in a way that would best benefit them. I was also concerned about some teachers branding Tyler as ADHD because of his different learning style. My last concern resonated strongly for the both of us. At Tyler's last preschool, his grumpy teacher had actually said, "Your boy won't stop moving. You should get him checked for being hyperactive or something." Thankfully, Tammy had not formed that opinion of him—but what about his next teacher?

After spending most of the night brainstorming different ideas on how to deal with our new issue, we finally agreed on a solution. I was going to open an in-home daycare. This way I could stay home with Tyler, continue to care for children, and still bring in some extra income. Although it broke my heart to leave what I felt were my "day babies," and all the other children I had bonded with, I knew this would be best for my family.

Before leaving, I made sure to thank Tammy for being so honest with me. I also tried to encourage her, knowing that most parents who came to pick up their children had no idea how hard she worked to be a positive influence for them and how much she really cared.

FAMILY

Having an in-home daycare was the most fun I ever had while being paid to do a job. I had four kids during the day (two sets of siblings), besides Tyler. Some evenings, I had a toddler whose mother worked as a waitress for a restaurant in town. My days were full, but also fulfilling. I was able to put together curriculums for the kids during the summer, when they were in my care for the majority of the day. We spent a week learning about a specific country. First, it was Mexico, then Egypt, then Japan ... and so on. I let the kids pick the countries that they were curious about. We did crafts that revolved around each country (for Mexico we made Dia de los Muertos masks) and had a different national dish for lunch each day. Tyler and I bonded with the kids I cared for, and they became like family to us.

"What country are we on now?" Allen asked Ashley, the younger of two sisters who came every day. Allen had the day off and also looked forward to our exotic studies and the delicious food that went along with each one.

Ashley smiled at Mr. Allen and answered, "England." She laughed afterward, knowing that the food had not been as enjoyable for this week as it had been for other countries.

Allen looked at both Ashley and her sister Brooke and made a gagging sound. Brooke was confined to a wheelchair, so she rolled her chair over next to Allen and whispered to him, "English food is the worst!" Then she also laughed, at the sight of Allen's contorted face.

And so, the rest of the year passed pleasantly enough. I really enjoyed having the flexibility of using different methods of teaching, and the ability to do so. The kids all seemed to have fun and looked forward to whatever new subject we would be covering for that week. Once the schoolyear started, I still cared for them after school until their parents got off from work. I helped them with their homework and was shocked at how much they had! I didn't remember having so much homework when I was in elementary or middle school. I was also confused by some of the new way to teaching old ideas. Some of the new ways seemed more confusing to both the kids and myself. But, I reasoned, there must be a reason that it was changed. Right?

Partway through the school year, I decided to put Tyler in the preschool program that was offered through the city. One of my kids, Tommy, who was a boy that was Tyler's age, also went to this preschool, and he seemed to really enjoy it. When I would pick him up after class, he would be smiling and wanting to know, "Why is Tyler not going to my school with me?" I really didn't have a good answer for him. So, I finally decided to put Tyler in the program.

Allen and I both had mixed feelings about sending Tyler to another preschool. This was made worse over the course of the next few months, as we witnessed a change in our son's behavior and the familiar, irritated attitude given off by the assistant teacher in his class.

"Tyler just said a cuss word," Allen informed me one day. "Also, he said our minivan is dumb because kids at school said so."

Allen was clearly agitated. We both knew that Tyler had not learned swear words in our home. Both of us were very careful not to let curse words slip out around him. And since our minivan was our sole source of transportation, stating that it was dumb seemed to sting more. I was getting ready to address his statements, when he continued with, "And that assistant teacher reminds me of that mean lady from his other school."

I sat down on the couch and let out a slow breath. I was also concerned with these same items, but really didn't know what to tell him. Allen sat on the couch next to me. "Maybe we should send him to a private school." Allen wanted to find an alternative to the issues we had seen in Tyler's three schools. "Maybe we can get him a private teacher or something."

I spoke with some frustration in my voice, "Honey, I don't think we could afford a private teacher. Besides, I'm a teacher. I would just teach him myself......" Allen and I both looked at each other. A sudden realization hit both of us, but with totally different reactions.

"That's a great idea!" Allen smiled, and his blue eyes shone bright.

"No, that's not what I meant..." I never imagined myself as a stay-at-home teacher. Or "homeschooler," as I knew they were called.

"But, didn't you say that there were some homeschool families that came to the gym you worked at?" Allen was remembering the small stories I would share about the two families who homeschooled, back in Sacramento. They were the only kids who came during the day for the kids' program at CalFit, while other children were in public school.

"Well, yes. I did, but..." At that moment, I regretted sharing stories about them.

"Didn't you say that all the kids were really well behaved for their ages?" Allen's eyes narrowed as he zeroed in on me.

"I guess I did. But..."

"And didn't you tell me that the family seemed to work together better than most families you see nowadays?" Allen was inching toward me on the couch.

"Maybe..." I knew that I had, in fact, said those things. I just hated that I was now having to face the consequences.

Allen held my hand in his, "Why don't you just try it over the summer? I mean, if you see that it is not benefitting Tyler, then we will send him to kindergarten in the fall."

I shook my head slowly. "I don't know..."

Allen smiled. "Isn't that kind of what you've been doing already?"

I thought about the lessons I put together for my daycare kids. Like a fast-moving PowerPoint presentation in my mind, I went through all the different countries, character building lessons, and history we had been over in the last year. It was pretty amazing how much the kids could learn in a small group setting.

"I don't know about you," Allen stretched back on the sofa, "but I can't think of very many five-year-olds who know all the American presidents and so much about so many countries in the world. And I think that's because of you."

I was grateful that Allen had so much confidence in me. I wondered why I didn't have confidence in myself. Maybe it wasn't a confidence issue, but more of the idea of keeping Tyler home with me all day. I remembered how easily brainwashed I was by own mother and reasoned it probably wasn't good for kids to be under one adult's supervision with little outside influence. It would create a problem with his ability to socialize correctly. Right?

I reluctantly agreed to Allen's homeschool experiment, only because I knew I had an alternative course of action if it didn't work out: I could send him back to school.

With Easter only a week away, Allen also shared with me his hope that we would go to a church together and celebrate the holiday. I tried to talk him out of this idea, as well. But, in the end, I agreed on the same type of condition: if we found the churches in Illinois to be as judgmental and fake as the one I had previously experienced, then we wouldn't go to churches for a while. Deal.

Woodstock Christian Church was a church we literally picked out of the phone book at random. We put on our nice "church clothes" and headed out to what I felt would be our last trip to visit a bunch of hypocrites. Allen had an even lower tolerance for fake people than me, and I began to worry that a bad experience at this church could even affect his belief in Christianity itself. He had not been in a church in a long time, and what he remembered might not be accurate anymore.

Two hours later, we were sitting in our minivan smiling and recanting the various conversations we had with members of this church. A couple had invited us over for dinner and offered to show us around town. An elder had talked to Allen for a long time, and although it was brought up that we were not married, he did not seem affected by this information. Instead, he just asked if and when we had plans to wed, and then moved the conversation along.

Finally, we had met a very nice family that had been homeschooling for years, and they offered to assist me in any way they could. Allen and I actually wanted to come back the next Sunday.

"I like that place," Tyler's little voice stated from the backseat. "They were really nice."

Allen and I smiled and agreed.

This church would become our home church, and the members there would become our "church family." Whenever I needed something and Allen was gone, I had reliable people I could call in my time of need. When Allen and I needed advice, we had trustworthy people we could go to. Although people aren't perfect, the friends we made at this church seemed that they were trying their best to love one another. And that's what I had always thought a church should be.

Thanks to the help of the Garcia family at our new church, I did not give up on homeschooling. By the end of the summer, Tyler had learned how to read and add basic numbers. He had learned a whole year's worth of curriculum in three months. It had only taken about two hours a day. With the rest of the day free, Tyler would help me around the house. He would help me run errands, plant in the garden, and take field trips. With the majority of people at work and kids at school, we found that the museums were always empty during the week. The zoo was so easy to navigate through without crowds of people. The apple orchard felt like our own private plantation. I was enjoying being a homeschooler more than I ever thought I would.

Over the next fifteen years, our life grew steadily outward from that point.

We stayed with that first church for over twelve years (and through three major splits). It wasn't easy to remain in the chaos of beloved fellow church members leaving because of major decisions made that they didn't agree with. And it was VERY hard for us to finally make the same decision to leave. However, many of the friends I made at that church are still people I love like family.

Many of the skills I learned by leading small groups, teaching the preschool class, and starting a family ministry have helped me in my growth as a person and in my faith. The pain our entire family went through when we left our church took several years to recover from, but thankfully, it did not shake our faith in God.

I still homeschool. Although now, Allen and I have a larger student body; Sophia (born 2004), Emily (born 2008), and Benny (born 2011). In 2006, Allen's daughter Cassie came to live with us, and I was able to homeschool her as well, until she graduated high school, five years later. I enjoy helping others who are interested in homeschooling through workshops, video, social media and meeting in person. My family and I love talking to others about the benefits of homeschooling and encouraging open dialogue about concerns or myths surrounding this growing way to educate your children.

Another one of our family passions is training Brazilian Jiu Jitsu. It started with my husband training for exercise and additional self-defense to use in his job, then my kids began classes. As soon as my youngest child, Benny, could play quietly with his siblings, I began classes. To have all of us training in this incredibly useful style of self-defense together has bonded us even more solidly as a family. We also enjoy talking to others about the usefulness of BJJ and breaking stereotypes of the types of people who train this martial art.

In 2004, I did attempt to reconnect with my mother and find a way to forgive her for all she had done. I visited her twice at the Correctional Institution for Women in Kentucky, and we had awkward conversations just to fill the allotted time we had to visit.

We then had a cordial postal relationship, which consisted mostly of birthday cards with short letters written inside them with some pictures. Finally, it became apparent through her letters and one collect call she made to me from the jail, that she wanted me to recant my testimony against her. I refused. The cards stopped. I have had no contact with her since then.

Allen and I have worked very hard to make our home loving, encouraging, respectful and safe. We both are working against family cycles that make it harder to do. We didn't have it as an example in our lives, so we look to others, we read books, we do Bible studies and look to the Bible itself. We hold each other accountable and have hard and uncomfortable conversations when we see that either of us are slipping into the dark patterns that are engrained in the deep memories of our childhood. We refuse to give up.

Sometimes, in the middle of homeschooling, training and whatever else pops up in the day to day, I forget my childhood and the criminally insane woman that I share a bloodline with. But in those quiet moments when it all comes rushing back, I always find comfort in this:

"Be strong and courageous. Do not fear or be in dread of them, for it is the Lord your God who goes with you. He will not leave you or forsake you."

Deuteronomy 31:6

IMAGES FROM OUR NEW LIVES

Novi, Dawn and me—after the trial.

Dawn, Novi, Tyler and me—2001.

Tony, me and Charlie. The last visit with my brother.

EPILOGUE

Life is never easy after a traumatic experience, but, as my husband says, "Life isn't really easy at all, and the sooner you accept that—the better off you are". I guess it depends on how you let that traumatic event affect you, shape you, or influence you. I can't say it's been easy, but in my adulthood, I have tried to let my faith guide what I do with my past.

I have learned to let go of the anger, pain and sadness—in order to love my life and those around me as I should.

I have learned to forgive—in order to move forward in a positive and hopeful way.

I have learned to let my past strengthen me—in order to be a stronger wife, mother and friend.

I have learned that I can trust God in every aspect of my life, even when I don't understand where this road is leading me.

And if all else fails—I think, "What would my mom do in this situation?" Then, I do the exact opposite.

Tom and Roxanne Suleski both received life sentences without the possibility of parole.

All three sisters —Novi, Dawn and Nyssa have since moved on with their lives in positive ways.

Nyssa—still known as Rebecca—is currently living in the Midwest with her husband and four children. She homeschools and is active in the homeschool community, as well as reaching out to those who are interested in homeschooling their children. She, her husband, and all four children train Martial Arts together and enjoy traveling and cosplaying at comic conventions.

Dawn is also intently involved with her church and lives in Southern California. She has written and speaks on the importance of sexual abstinence before marriage.

Novi, having little memory of the events in this book, was raised by Uncle Sokie and Aunt Linda in a loving and safe home. She was told about the history of her biological parents as a teenager. She also lives Southern California.

A memorial to Alex can be seen in Radcliffe, Kentucky—the community that cared so much for a lost little girl.

UPDATE

June 13, 2018, I found out that my mother's parole hearing had been moved up two months from what was put on her online inmate profile. The Parole Board sent me a letter to inform me, but it was misplaced or accidentally thrown away by the occupants of the last known address they had for me. I was informed when I called to check on her hearing date, that not only was it in less than a week—but if I wanted to speak to the Parole Board, I would need to fax paperwork in by the end of the next business day. I sent the paperwork back within a few hours of talking to them.

What could have been a terrible missed opportunity for me to make sure my mother never was released into society, thankfully came together just in time. Allen was able to drive me down Sunday night (the seventeenth), so I could speak the next morning to the Parole Board. I was the only person who showed up to speak for the victim, Alex.

Members of the Victim Services for the Kentucky Parole Board helped me to understand what would happen that day. They also explained that my mother had requested a "serve out." She wanted to just stay in prison and serve out her life sentence. I was shocked! I still do not understand why she did this or what her reasoning was behind her request. However, I still spoke to the board and relived the events of Alex's last night alive for them. I wanted them to understand the depravity and cruelty that lives inside this woman, in case she rescinded her request to serve out.

Again, thankfully, she never rescinded, and the board unanimously agreed to have her remain behind bars for the rest of her life! I cannot begin to explain the relief I have now, knowing she will not be released—ever! My children and family are safe from her. I am safe.

Several weeks later, Tom had his chance to meet with the Parole Board. Both my sister Novi and I wrote letters to the board expressing our concerns. We both wrote that while Tom was never violent on his own, he was easily used as a tool for violence by our mother. We left the decision to the Parole Board, who had been extremely fair and felt would make the best decision regarding him.

The Parole Board voted to deny his parole and extend his next parole hearing for ten years. He will not see them again until 2028! I am so grateful to the Kentucky Parole Board for their wise and just decisions, and to the Victim Services ladies who took care of me while I was an emotional wreck during this time.

I am so grateful to all my friends and some family who encouraged me, reached out to me and prayed for me

during this time. Hard times show you who really cares. Now I know. Thank you.

I am so grateful to my awesome husband for racing me down to Kentucky in the "nick of time." For comforting me during the sudden turmoil and always being right there for me.

I am so grateful.

ACKNOWLEDGEMENTS

In the twenty-one years it took me to write and complete this book, many people have come along who have encouraged, helped or otherwise deserve a place for appreciation in this book.

First, I would like to thank my Lord and Savior Jesus Christ for giving me an unconditional love and forgiveness that no earthly person could ever do. And to my Heavenly Father who watches over the lost and awaits them to choose Him over the empty promises and selfishness of this world.

In order to properly thank my husband, Allen, I would need an entire chapter. But I will try to give a condensed version: Thank you for always believing in me, for always supporting me, and for being my life partner. Thank you for continuing to grow with me and always pushing me onward and upward.

Thanks to my kids—Tyler, Sophia, Emma and Benny. You have been more encouraging and thoughtful about this whole book process than I ever could have imagined. You all have made me a better person, and I love you so much!

To my dad and step-mom, Jay: Thank you for coming in the nick of time. I can't imagine how different my life would have been, if both of you had not made the changes needed in your lives, so I could make the ones that were needed in mine.

Thank you so much to Carol Butler from Butler Books in Louisville, Kentucky. Your guidance was generous and extremely valuable. Thank you to Michelle Embry. The time you took to help me polish my dearest project will not be forgotten. Also, a huge

Thank You to Cortni Merritt at SRD Editing Services for polishing my story while truly respecting its content.

Thanks to my Uncle Sokie and Aunt Linda, who stood bravely with me, even at the cost of losing family ties. You stood for what was right, and my sisters and I could never repay you properly for that.

Which brings me to my sisters, Dawn and Novi: Although times and circumstances may change, the bond that was forged through traumatic events will always be strong. No matter where we are in our lives, don't ever forget that good will triumph over evil.

All that is needed are good people who aren't afraid to do what is right and faith that you are never alone in that fight.

Lastly, thank you to the people of Radcliffe, Elizabethtown and the surrounding Kentucky area. You all cared for Alex more than anyone ever did in her short life.

Thank you.

Made in the USA
Columbia, SC
26 December 2024

50616703R00278